LIVERPOOL'S

ROYAL COURT

A BRAVE VENTURE

1826 TO 2018

ROS MERKIN

First published 2019 by
Liverpool University Press
4 Cambridge Street
Liverpool
L69 7ZU

British Library Cataloguing-in-Publication data
A British Library CIP record is available

ISBN 978-1-78694-223-4

Typeset by Carnegie Book Production, Lancaster
Printed and bound by Gomer Press, Llandysul, Wales

Contents

To Roger,
Thank you for being part of our journey so far. We are extremely grateful for all your support and advice throughout our first years as an NPO. We have made a friend for life and you will always be most welcome at the Royal Court!
All best wishes
Gillian & all at the RC.

Foreword

My first job when I came out of drama school was to play Ophelia at the Old Vic and before we opened a season we did one week somewhere else – for me to warm up I think – and it was at the Royal Court in Liverpool and I have such great memories about it. Barbara Lee Hunt and Adrienne Hill and Juliet Cooke and I went up on the train. I'll never forget it and we had a glorious week there. I do congratulate you on eighty years and I'm very glad to have been a part of it. Congratulations.

Dame Judi Dench

Every time I've either performed or been to a show at the Royal Court it's always been fabulous. I performed there quite a few times with my old band Slade, and it was the very last UK venue that we ever played together with the original band; and as usual the atmosphere was fantastic. The sound was great and the show and the audience really took off. I love it there.
Keep on rockin' the Royal Court.

Noddy Holder

Acknowledgements

Thanks go to Gillian Miller, Kevin Fearon, Iain Christie and all the staff at the Royal Court; Roger Hull and Helena Smart and all the staff at Liverpool Record Office, Liverpool Libraries; Emily Parsons and all the staff at LJMU Archives and Special Collections; Matthew Lloyd, Arthur Lloyd.co.uk: The Music Hall and Theatre History Site.

And a special thanks to Jane for her research and proofreading services.

Note: Dates following shows indicate when they were performed at the Royal Court, not the date of the first performance.

Auditorium, 2018

It is a brave venture in the times through which we are passing, to embark upon a scheme of this kind.

Demolition of the old Royal Court building, *Daily Post*, 6 February 1937 (Liverpool Record Office)

1 A New Beginning: 1938

> It is a brave venture in the times through which we are passing, to embark upon a scheme of this kind.[1]

When Robert Arthur surveyed the ashes of the old Royal Court in 1933, vowing to rebuild it, he little thought that it would take him five years. Nor did he have any idea that by the time he was looking to reopen on 17 October 1938, the circumstances were far from promising for a new theatre. The city was still struggling with unemployment, which had been double the national average throughout the decade. The world had (just) breathed a sigh of relief with Chamberlain's declaration of 'Peace for our time' on 30 September. And, with the opening fast approaching, the building was not ready. When Cecily Courtneidge and Jack Hulton, the comic husband and wife team who were to star in the new

Royal Court's first show, arrived at the theatre, they found the builders were still busy.

> There were no proper passages down from the dressing-rooms to the stage, men were nailing down carpets, and windows were being fitted. Jack was determined to get on with the job whatever the conditions. He called the Company together and spoke as follows:
>
> 'They may not finish building this place by the time we open but that is not going to affect us. Just ignore everything that is going on and concentrate on the show and your part and you'll have nothing to worry about.'
>
> My! How that man can kid himself.
>
> This meant that in addition to our own musical score, we had to rehearse against what I call 'The Builders Song', which, as you know, consists mainly

Exterior, 1938

Entrance hall, 1938

> of hammering, sawing, shouting, and an infinite variety of bangs ... Jack shouted his instructions over the building noises. The lights were the worst trouble. They were operated by remote control instead of direct from stage. But there was no remote control. He could not telephone his instructions to the electrician in his box up in the gallery, so he had to come forward and shout ... And this was not all. The actors could not hear each other and so could not take up their cues. This went on without a break from Saturday midday, when we arrived in the theatre, until Sunday morning at 9.30 a.m., when Jack gave us three hours off, to get our breakfast and a night's sleep. We returned at one o'clock and went on working throughout the afternoon and evening, well into the night and through until Monday morning.[2]

The building being hurriedly completed was to be a thoroughly modern affair, a statement for a brighter and more confident future for the city. Designed by J. B. Hutchins of Liverpool, the brochure produced for the occasion declared it to be 'a fine example of the school of architecture now setting up its own standards in a healthy independent spirit that breaks away from slavery to the style of the past'.[3] It was, it continued, 'set to take its place among the city's most noteworthy structures of progressive recent years'. With frontages to Roe Street, Rose Street and Great Charlotte Street, the theatre presented a confident redbrick and cream stone front to the world. In the public areas, no expense had been spared. Aberdeen granite, San Stefano marble floors bordered with black Issorie marble, figured walnut floors and restrained gilding all gave a sense of luxury and style to complement the modernity of the building. In the entrance hall, an unusual feature was the fireplace 'for electric heat, with its handsome moulding in Vert Antico and Sienna Brocatelle marbles, and surround of mirrors engraved and brilliant-cut with bands of contrasting coloured glass'. A magnificent marble staircase of an 'unusual and striking design' boasted a marble balustrade that curved gently upward about a central marble column, 'like the whorl of a seashell round its columelia', inviting the audience into the theatre. Below the auditorium was the main social centre, a lounge and bar complete with a fireplace and armchairs, which offered to be 'of special convenience for business people who cannot spare time for tea at home before attending a play'.[4]

Inside the auditorium, which seated 1,612, the

> two prime requisites – that the public should be able to see without obstruction and to hear without straining – have been achieved in a quite triumphant manner. There are no pillars and not only does every seat command an unimpeded view of the stage but the curve of the Grand Circle and Balcony is so shallow that sitters at the sides enjoy as complete a prospect as those in the centre.[5]

From the imposing proscenium arch, the curved ceiling and walls encouraged 'every sound to pass unhindered to the listeners in all parts'. The new theatre was proud also of the artistic effect of the relief decorations and cornicing, the walnut woodwork of doorways and barriers, and more restrained gilding, which was 'introduced with telling effect'. The stage had been designed to provide every possible facility and, at only five feet shallower than the old stage, offered an 'elaborate system of counterweights' enabling no fewer than 87 sets of scenery to be handled. The stage lighting was impressive and promised 'more complete and flexible' equipment than any other theatre in the country with the exception of London's Covent Garden. There was also a 34-foot revolving stage. But the greatest praise was offered for the use of electricity, the heating and the ventilation. The former, carried by 25,000 feet of heavy steel conduits, allowed for floodlighting of the exterior as well as energy for the plethora of new technical equipment from projectors and spot lanterns to electric clocks and internal telephones and sound amplification from the stage. The heating and ventilation had been 'dealt with on the most modern scientific principles', incorporating air-conditioning

> by which air entering the building is brought in from above the roof, drawn over a heated battery, thence through a water-mist chamber for washing,

and so over scrubbing plates that intercept dust particles. After this the air is then re-heated to the temperature requisite for the auditorium, which it reaches from the front and sides of the proscenium, thence passing in an imperceptible current across the audience.

> The vitiated atmosphere is withdrawn from the ceiling level of the theatre and of its balconies by high powered fans. It is removed at about 85 per cent of the volume introduced, thus keeping the theatre under a pressure of 15 per cent, with the result that when the door is opened the inside pressure minimises draughts. These conditions prevail also in the basement bar and lounge…[6]

The whole was designed to feel totally up to date, a new modern theatre that 'the city can be proud of'.[7]

Cloakroom, 1938

Staircase, 1938

Auditorium, 1938

Cecily Courtneidge and Jack Hulbert, who reopened the theatre in Vivien Ellis's musical comedy *Under Your Hat* (*Theatre World*)

The opening show was also new, although its two stars had first visited the Court in 1914 with *The Cinema Star*. But the occasion was one for celebration, as the husband and wife team had not appeared together on stage for seven years, having been busy making films; hence their reappearance, according to *Punch*, was front-page news.[8] Described by *Theatre World* as 'brilliant, sparkling, lavish, witty, fool-proof entertainment', *Under Your Hat* seemed like the perfect show to celebrate the new theatre.[9] It was a musical comedy, in which Courtneidge and Hulbert played married film stars, Jack and Kay. They were pitted against a foreign spy ring determined to steal a secret aeroplane carburettor. At the request of the government, Jack agrees to follow Carol Markoff, believed to be in possession of the device, to the South of France. As it is top secret, he cannot tell his wife what he is up to and, inevitably, since Carol is attractive and has flirted with Jack, Kay is jealous and follows him. The fun comes from the chase and the disguises adopted en route, as Cicely Courtneidge changes from a French maid to a mechanic to Mrs Sheepshanks of Poona, 'an Anglo-Indian lady of formidable girth and forbidding mien'.[10] Together they manage to outwit Boris Vladimir, the mastermind behind the spy ring, and return the carburettor safely to England, with their marriage intact. The show enabled 'Jack Hulbert to indulge to the full his flair for light comedy, nimble dancing and debonair charm and Cecily Courtneidge to prove with a variety of burlesques'.[11] The local press reported that the theatre was 'crowded to capacity', the audience appreciating 'the beautiful brand-newness of everything'. The official opening had taken place with a reception the previous day; this first night ended with a speech from the stars, who apologised that the production of the show had been slowed down by a week of international crisis.[12]

This first night seemed a promising start for the new theatre, but it was a long way from being the first performance at a theatre on the site. The Royal Court had actually begun its journey in 1826 as the New Olympic Circus, and today, eighty years after the opening of the new building, it is the oldest theatre still operating in Liverpool. Its history has, at times, been chaotic, and it has faced not just fire but also floods and financial crises. It has seen two world wars and has survived in a city that has been through some tough times. It has also enjoyed years when the stage was filled with the stars of the day, and when it was seen as the jewel in Liverpool's theatrical crown. This book traces the theatre's history, a history that started with a burst sewer, and explores how over time it has evolved and reshaped itself to keep pace with the times and to reinvent its place in the city. In the process, there have been many occasions when those struggling to keep it going must have felt as though they too were heading a brave venture in tough times.

Notes

1 From the brochure for the reopening of the Royal Court, 1938.

2 Cicely Courtneidge, *Cicely* (London: Hutchinson, 1953), 127.

3 This and the other descriptions in this paragraph are from the brochure for the reopening of the Royal Court, 1938.

4 *Daily Post*, 23 September 1938.

5 From the brochure for the reopening of the Royal Court, 1938.

6 Ibid.

7 *Daily Post*, 18 October 1938.

8 *Punch*, 7 December 1938, 636.

9 *Theatre World*, January 1939, 168.

10 *The Times*, 25 November 1928, 12.

11 *Theatre World*, January 1939, 168.

12 *Liverpool Evening Express*, 18 October 1938.

A place of recreation, calculated for people of any rank and respectability

North-west view of Royal Amphitheatre by J. Harwood (engraved by Rogers), 1830 (Liverpool Record Office)

2 The Royal Amphitheatre, 1826–1881

Arriving at the Olympic Circus on Christian Street in November 1825, where he had been holding his winter equestrian seasons since 1821, John Cooke discovered a problem.[1] It was not the first time he had encountered difficulties. In the years during which he had leased the theatre from Banks and Lewis, 'a succession of petty, contemptible vexations' had confronted him, including a demand for a considerable advance in rent, but he had persevered with his venture.[2] This time, however, the obstacle was insurmountable. Sewers in the surrounding streets and one that ran directly under the circus ring itself had burst. As a consequence water was sapping the foundations, and the lower part of the circus, under the stage, was filled with mud. Fearing it was unfit for purpose, Cooke hired surveyors who confirmed his worst fears: it was too dangerous to use. However, coming from a large circus dynasty Cooke was no stranger to entrepreneurship and risk taking. His response to the problem was to make it public on the pages of the local newspaper, publishing the surveyor's report condemning the building and seeking permission from the mayor to erect a new theatre, which he proposed to open in direct competition with the Olympic.

The land Cooke found for his new venture was on the corner of Great Charlotte Street and Roe Street, the site of the city's ancient Fall-well, which had been in use until 1790. With money raised through subscriptions from shareholders, the first stone of the new building was laid on 27 November 1825, with Cooke declaring that he would be open for business by Christmas. In the event, bad weather delayed the opening of the (confusingly named) New Olympic Circus until 27 February 1826 but, even in these circumstances, the *Liverpool Mercury* was impressed by 'the rapid erection' of the theatre, which 'has astonished everyone'. Although only partially decorated and 'altogether in a very unfinished state', the paper could still see that 'it will be a credit to the town and a lasting monument to Mr Cooke's persevering industry' and it was convinced that it would ultimately rank 'amongst the most elegant theatres in the kingdom'.[3] Above all, the paper was impressed by the theatre's spaciousness and its ability to accommodate an audience of some 3,000–4,000

St John's market in Great Charlotte Street by G. and C. Pyne, 1831 (Liverpool Record Office)

people. This disparity in numbers came about from the collision of the theatre's design with the existence of half-price admission. The theatre incorporated not just a stage and seats in boxes and the circle, but also a circus ring. The evening's performance was generally broken into three sections: a drama on the stage, then events in the ring, followed by an afterpiece, possibly a ballet or a farce back on the stage. Audiences could arrive late and pay half-price, missing some or all of the first section, being accommodated on the stage to watch the action in the ring and then moving to the ring to watch the final stage performance. What is most significant about the estimated size of the audience is not simply that, as the paper noted, it was larger than Liverpool's Theatre Royal but that it was also larger than Astley's Theatre in London, seen as the home and birthplace of circus (which in its third reincarnation of 1815 could hold 2,000–2,500 people).[4] This was a real statement of intent.[5]

Cooke kept his promise to the town to complete the theatre and in the summer of 1826 extensive refurbishments were undertaken so that at the opening of the season on 26 December 1826, the *Liverpool Mercury* could let its readers know that

> [t]he interior of this beautiful Building has been re-embellished, the avenues and approaches widened, and altogether rendered more commodious, the respective entrances being now all situated in Great Charlotte Street. The boxes are refurbished, the Pit and the Gallery have been remodelled for the better convenience of visitors ... and the utmost care has been taken ... to render the whole perfectly warm and comfortable.[6]

The new decorations suggested ambitions to class and style, drawing on classical proportions and aspirations. A new proscenium, complete with a 'splendid Thryaus' and a tablet representing the Olympic Games, had been erected, and the ceiling was decorated with maritime panels. A prevailing feature had been made of the Arms of Liverpool and a moveable gas chandelier had pride of place in the centre of the building.

Such expense and aspirational decoration suggest that Cooke expected a profitable future. Indeed, the situation of the town at the time would have encouraged him. Liverpool's population had grown from 60,000 in 1792 to nearly 165,000.[7] Expanding overseas markets and the growth of transportation also meant increasing wealth, and the opening of the Adelphi Hotel in 1826 suggests a growth in visitors and business. On the same street chosen by Cooke, St John's market, one of the first and largest fully enclosed markets, had opened in 1822, in a building described by the American painter and naturalist James Audubon as 'an object worth the attention of all traveller strangers'.[8] At nearly two acres in size, it was an impressive building; on entering, the author of *The Stranger in Liverpool*, an early Liverpool guidebook, was convinced that the spectator would be 'amazed at the immense size of the structure, its loftiness, lightness and airiness' going on to assert that compared to it 'the celebrated Fleet-market is a miserable shed, and Westminster-hall a moderate-sized room'.[9] Discussions were also underway about the need to improve transport into the centre of the city; the existing terminus of the Manchester railway at Edge Hill was too far from the centre and by 1833 construction of the tunnel to allow for the building of Lime Street station, just up the road from Cooke's site, had begun, which was to open ten years after his theatre. At the same time, the 'philistinism' and 'barbarism' of eighteenth-century Liverpool identified by Muir seemed to be changing.[10] At that time, the town could only boast one theatre, the Theatre Royal on Williamson Square, which opened in 1772, and one circus. The latter, described by Muir as 'never very successful', was the Olympic which, after the problems with its sewers, was improved and strengthened, reopening in December 1825 as the Royal Olympic Circus.[11] By the time Cooke opened his new venture, two other theatres were also in existence. The Pantheon, later the Liver, opened in 1824 on Church Street and, in 1825, the Sans Pareil chose the same street as Cooke for its home. Great Charlotte Street was also home to Wombwell's Royal Menagerie, housed in part of the new market, and one of several travelling attractions to visit the city on a seasonal basis. It would seem that Cooke had good reason to be optimistic.

Yet scarcely had the season begun when Cooke seemed to be in trouble. Although still advertising a production on 'a scale of unprecedented magnitude' with a succession of magnificent scenes got up at enormous expense, by April Cooke was also 'respectfully' informing his friends that as some of the original subscribers had forfeited their shares, there were some still to be sold.[12] The original subscriptions had been for £100 each, on which Cooke promised to pay 5 per cent and a 'silver ticket' enabling free entry to the theatre. Shareholders were required to pay £10 straight away with the balance following as needed. However, as the *Liverpool Mercury* noted later in the year, the scheme of building by subscription, 'like many others that have recently exploded, has proved an unfortunate business … the subscribers foreseeing, perhaps, no ultimate benefit to themselves, neglected to pay up their quotas…'[13]

By May a small advert hidden at the bottom of a notice about an upcoming production asked anyone who had 'demands against Mr Cooke' to send their statements to a solicitor's office and to attend a meeting of creditors the following week.[14] In June *Gore's* carried a notice of sale for the theatre, which included Cooke's celebrated stud of horses and all the machinery, costumes and trappings, alongside an excellent and complete circus in Hull.[15] In September 1826 Cooke found himself, alongside shareholders Samuel Orme and Owen Jones, taken to court by the brickmakers who had supplied him with £366 worth of bricks but who had not been paid. Cooke tried to argue that the building superintendent, James Longworth, was responsible as he had ordered the bricks. Longworth argued that the trustees had not been forthcoming with any money. The court found in favour of the brickmakers.[16]

Despite these problems, Cooke continued as the lessee for the 1827–28 season, after which the theatre was taken by Andrew Ducrow, who leased it for the winter months until 1832. After this time, until the arrival of William Copeland in 1843, the theatre changed its managers as often as it changed its name. Until the mid-1830s when the Royal Amphitheatre was finally settled upon, it appeared variously as the New Olympic Circus, Cooke's Olympic Circus, Cooke's Royal Circus, Ducrow's Royal Amphitheatre and the Royal Amphitheatre of the Arts. The addition of the term Royal was nothing more than a label to add an air of legitimacy and respectability to the venture and certainly did not mean that the theatre had been given royal assent. After Ducrow's departure (although his company did return to perform on a number of subsequent occasions), the theatre was run variously by George Bolwell Davidge (1832–33), who also ran the Coburg Theatre in London, and William Batty (1834–35). By 1840 Ducrow's name was once again added to the theatre's title, but by the end of that year it was being run by a Mr Egerton (at times with the help of Ducrow's company), who was also the lessee of the Queen's Theatre in Manchester. In 1842 the lease was taken by Messrs Sloan and LeClerq, whose names are also mentioned in conjunction with Alice Stebbing, the owner of the Royal Amphitheatre Tavern on Roe Street. Owners are harder to trace than managers (or lessees). Cooke had originally purchased the land for 4,000 guineas and in March 1827 sold it to Mr Armistead, a straw hat manufacturer, who paid 12,000 guineas for the land, the circus and the gas chandelier.[17] Like Cooke, he faced financial problems and in 1834 found himself in bankruptcy court, given two years to pay off his debts. As a consequence, the theatre was once more up for auction. This time it included four shops and billiard rooms on the south side of Roe Street adjoining the theatre and a notice that the property was held under lease to the corporation of Liverpool for 'three good lives and twenty-one years' at the usual ground rent of £6,000 a year.[18] Unsold on this occasion, it was up for auction again in 1836 but no purchaser is noted.[19] At some point after this the theatre was bought by Alice Stebbing, who in December 1850 received a letter threatening to burn down the Amphitheatre (she still also had an interest in the Royal Amphitheatre Tavern) in an attempt to extort money from her. For this, William Greg received seven years transportation.[20]

With each change of name and each change of manager the theatre was also redecorated and embellished. Despite the newness of the theatre when he acquired the lease, Ducrow ended his first season by boasting that he had already spent £7,000 (which included a new frontage and refurbishment of the theatre's interior) and had set aside a further sum for the completion of the theatre.[21] By 1830,

> [t]he front of the three tiers of boxes and galleries presents to the eye a prevailing mass of crimson ground enriched with burnished gold mouldings and ornaments. A large and splendid moveable gas chandelier suspended from the ceiling and numerous subsidiary ones ranged the front of the boxes, serve to shed over the whole of the place, the glow and radiance of an Oriental palace. During one part of the evening's performance, while the various plays of horsemanship were exhibited in the circle, the whole opening of the proscenium is occupied by an admirably executed representation of the Death of Nelson, on the deck of the "Victory" painted as a large picture in a gigantic gilt frame, richly ornamented with emblematical devices. The passages and entrances are judiciously contrived, and the avenue leading to the boxes is adorned with busts, paintings and other appropriate ornaments. The extensive stabling required for the accommodation of the large stud of horses is ingeniously formed under the side wings of the stage.[22]

Davidge then totally re-embellished the theatre four years later in a style 'that challenges competition with any theatre in Europe' and redecorated the proscenium with a representation of Neptune rescuing the *Navigation* of Liverpool from a storm off the Black Rock. He also boasted a new act drop representing a general view of the town and port of the city as seen from the river.[23] In 1837 the view of Liverpool was changed to a representation of the Battle of Waterloo 'at a critical moment', portrayed on a new 900-foot backdrop (the largest ever produced). At the same time the theatre underwent further refurbishment and repair, with improved ventilation, the addition of private rooms to the boxes to accommodate ladies and children, and the addition of the Queen's Arms to the proscenium.[24] With the arrival of Egerton, the theatre took on a Moorish style and the new act drop depicted a view of the Court of Lions in the Alhambra, designed to show 'the extent of knowledge in the arts possessed by that extraordinary and renowned people the Moors of Spain'.[25]

The levels of spending suggested that each new manager thought the theatre a worthwhile investment, striving to give it a sense of class, style, spectacle and (sometimes) novelty. The pages of the press indeed attest to its popularity. Usually advertising it just under the Theatre Royal listing (a sign of prestige), the papers were full of praise, describing it variously as 'this favourite place of public amusement'

Part of a playbill for the Amphitheatre, n.d. (Liverpool Record Office)

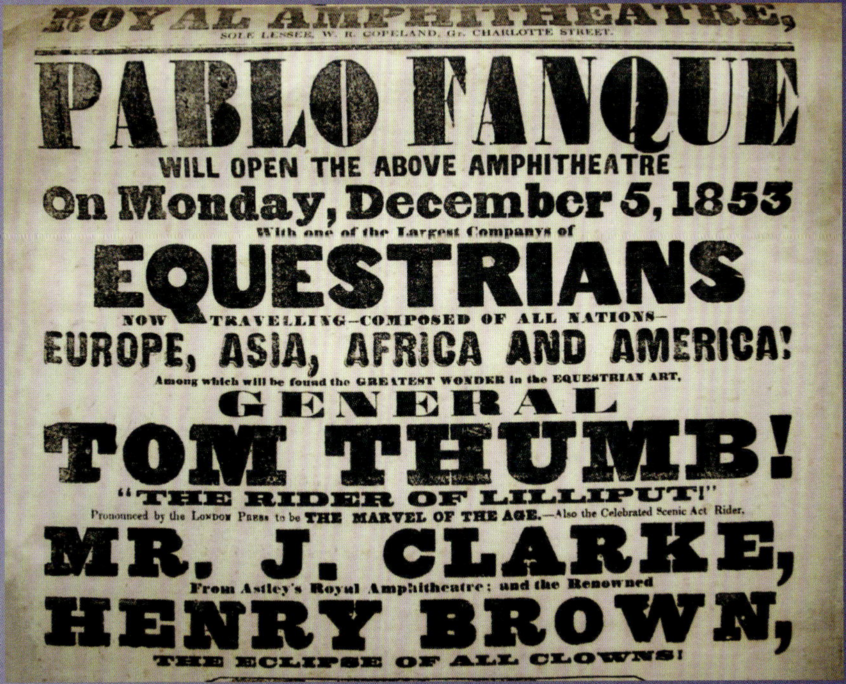

Playbill for Pablo Fanque's Christmas visit to the Amphitheatre, 1853–54. Fanque (born William Darby) was an English equestrian performer and circus owner, the first recorded non-white circus proprietor in Britain. (Liverpool Record Office)

and 'the most extensive and superb Amphitheatre in the country'.[26] The theatre's popularity was helped by improved accessibility; the additional steamboats from Woodside and Tranmere that returned after the performance advertised in 1827 were replaced in 1836 by the opening of Lime Street station, allowing *Gore's* to suggest that the situation of the theatre 'is one of the most central in Liverpool' and that with the opening of the new rail tunnel, Roe Street would become 'one of the greatest through-fares in the Town'.[27] By 1840 the *Liverpool Mail* could point out that the town was 'so nearly connected by railway, water and other conveyances with other large and populous places, from which myriads visit the town daily, on business or in search of pleasure', that people from throughout the north were able to flock from far and wide to attend performances.[28] The people who did come were from all classes of society. As A. H. Saxon points out (in relation to Astley's), it would be erroneous to assume that the appeal of minor theatres was restricted to any particular social class, and Marius Kwint (also in relation to Astley's) argues that because the performances were based on the 'common appreciation of the horse', the shows transcended 'the normal differences of class and cultural outlook', enjoying the 'custom of prosperous working classes and aristocracy alike'.[29] The limited number of theatres in Liverpool and the fact that they were sited in the city centre, a stone's throw away from each other, and that they all operated a tiered pricing system and separate entrances suggests that the Amphitheatre attracted people from all strata of society. The audiences are often referred to as fashionable, especially on those occasions when performances were patronised by the Earl of Sefton or Lord Sandon, but at other times it was noted that 'the circus' was 'a place of recreation, calculated for people of any rank and respectability', a theatre guaranteed to 'afford gratification and amusement to all classes of the community'.[30]

The most popular of the managers, in a period described as 'an age ... of sparkling dramatic celebrity', was undoubtedly Andrew Ducrow, whose 'spirited and popular management' made the theatre 'the resort of all resorters' and whose name 'is a guarantee that lovers of picturesque and splendid spectacles of daring and easy horsemanship, of wonderful feats and of all kinds of lawful fire and frolic' would have their expectations met.[31] When he returned to Liverpool in 1840, for the first time since giving up his lease in 1832, the crowds were so great that the ferries had to schedule extra runs to accommodate spectators living across the river, and on his death in 1842, when he was on the point of joining the company performing at the Amphitheatre, the Liverpool press mourned the loss of 'a zealous caterer for the amusement of the audience'.[32] However, the consistent change of managers also suggests a lack of stability, consistency and potentially poor returns in what could prove to be a risky business. Cooke was not the only manager to face financial difficulties, and there were moments during this period when the Amphitheatre was described as 'steadily … sinking under a succession of less expert managers'.[33]

On Stage at the Amphi

Cooke's opening programme was a model of the pattern of performance that dominated the theatre until the mid-1840s. Banned by the Licensing Act of 1737 from performing 'legitimate' (spoken) drama, which was the prerogative of the Theatre Royals, 'minor' theatres like the Amphitheatre had to rely on other forms of entertainment. These might include burlettas, melodramas, ballet and extravaganzas, but the Amphitheatre was best known for its horses, performing in the ring or involved in performances on the stage in hippodramas (usually melodramas or extravaganzas that included horses in the action). This kind of circus performance had started with Philip Astley who, having fought in a cavalry regiment, took to performing feats of horsemanship on his return to England. Developing displays of daring horsemanship already popular in the pleasure gardens of the capital, he started exhibiting his skills in a field in Lambeth in 1768, building a more permanent theatre a few years later. Along with his rivals at London's Royal Circus, which opened in 1782, the riding tricks gradually became increasingly complex, introducing aspects of the drama. Astley visited Liverpool for the first time in 1773, performing in a large field near Mr Roscoe's bowling green in Mount Pleasant, and made a number of return visits including performances at the Olympic Circus in 1805.

In the ring, dancing on horses, often known as scenes or acts in the circle, was common and could stretch from a solo performance to the Cossack Hourra performed by twelve equestrians or a grand waltz and gallopade performed by the whole company.[34] One of the most famous and celebrated equestrian dancers was Miss Woolford of Ducrow's company, later his second wife, who also worked on the tightrope. On the horse, she was renowned for a shawl dance and the 'jeux des drapeaux', an act involving the manoeuvring of two flags while making circuits of the ring.[35] She performed with Ducrow in a number of acts including one in which they acted out a rustic courtship while dressed as a Swiss milkmaid and a Tyrolean peasant. Reviews describe her as graceful and elegant, words often used in relation to female equestrians. Acrobatic feats on horses also abounded, from jumping over ribbons or through hoops to the Brazilian youth Carlo Paddingtoni's celebrated feat of standing on his head on a quart pot with the horse at full speed.[36] Clowns were a consistent feature, often portraying drunken characters struggling to control their horses, and infant riders, using dwarf ponies, were admired. Young equestrians,

Andrew Ducrow as The Yorkshire Sportsman or British Foxhunter by William Heath, c. 1830 (© Victoria and Albert, London)

including Le Petit Ducrow and Master and Miss Ginnett, appeared in scenes that reflected their stature, from 'Jack the Giant Killer; or the Castle of Little Thumb' to 'The Lilliputian Bonaparte and His War Horse'.

The displays might include shows of skill in managing a number of horses, as when Mr Batty demonstrated 'his unrivalled act never attempted by any other person' in which, accompanied by a fox, he rode four horses simultaneously while leaping over a five-bar gate.[37] Not to be outdone, Ducrow later presented an act in which he entered the ring on two horses, during which anything from three to seven horses galloped between the original two with Ducrow gathering up their reins as they passed beneath him until he could be in charge of up to nine horses. Increasingly, these shows of skill were performed in costume, and the previous act was presented as 'The Courier of St Petersburg'. Ducrow's popular 'The Vicissitudes of the Tar' represented the story of a sailor, from taking leave of his friends for a voyage to returning home, all performed on horseback. This would include imitating 'the motion of a vessel going gaily along', smoking a pipe and dancing a naval hornpipe. As the ship returns home it is caught in a storm, and

> [i]t is astonishing with what effect Ducrow contrives to represent this conflict of the sailor with the elements. He doffs his jacket, pulls up his sleeves, hauls the ropes, mounts the shrouds, displaying all the bustle and anxiety of a seaman amid the perils of the storm. The ship is lost, and he is then seen swimming amid the stormy waves. The position necessary to convey this idea is most perilous, one foot only being on the horse, which is at full speed, while the body is thrown forward in a very daring manner.[38]

Other equestrians boasted acts in which they changed character a number of times without leaving the horse, as in Mr G. Woolford's 'Septem in Uno' in which he portrayed seven characters or Mr A. Cooke's portrayal of several characters from *Pickwick Papers*.[39]

Horses also played a key part in the spectacular action of the stage dramas. Monk Lewis's *Timour the Tartar* included a daring rescue by a son as his mother leaps into the sea to try to escape from the tyrant Timour:

> She is seen struggling with the waves of the cataract, and her child plunges in on horseback to save her. After rising from wave to wave, the Princess and her son gain the land and ascend the cascade on horseback.[40]

At the top they are met by the Georgian forces besieging Timour. The castle is attacked. The walls are beaten down by a battering ram and the cavalry rushes through the breach at a gallop. The play also contained a large equestrian procession and a subplot in which two Tartar chieftains, Kerim and Sanballat, fight over a slave girl. Their differences are settled in a tournament, the stage directions for which, as Saxon notes, leave no doubt as to who was the true star of this episode. The two men enter on horseback:

> They charge with lances – at length Kerim's horse takes part in the combat, seizes Sanballat, and drags him to the ground – Sanballat rises, and attributes the victory solely to the horse – Kerim proposes to renew the combat on

> foot – the horses are led away, and the fight begins – Kerim falls and loses his sword – His rival rushes to dispatch him, when Kerim's horse leaps the barrier, prevents Sanballat from advancing, picks up the sword, and carries it to his master – Sanballat, in fury, stabs the Horse, who falls and expires ... Kerim's desire to avenge the faithful animal increases his strength – he disarms his rival, drags him to the horse, and sacrifices him on the body, during which all descend [from the balconies to the lists].[41]

The scene ends with Kerim strewing his horse with flowers and falling on him, weeping.

In *Mazeppa; or The Wild Horse of the Ukraine,* a hippodrama performed several times at the Amphitheatre (including once in 1865 with Adah Isaacs Menken as Mazeppa), Mazeppa is punished for having an affair with a married Countess. Tied to the back of a wild horse desperately trying to get back to its home, he is carried along precipitous pathways and up mountain ridges. In the final scene Polish troops and the Tartar cavalry meet in full battle. In *Turpin's Ride to York and the Death of Black Bess,* the second act follows Dick Turpin's adventures while escaping from London, including a leap over a closed tollgate and an encounter with the York mail coach. Bess manages to get Dick to York but dies as they arrive, allowing for a touching scene between master and horse. The whole ends with Turpin standing over the body of Bess fighting off his pursuers as lawlessness triumphs 'over the forces of order, and the barn, set afire for some reason or other, lights up the final tableau'.[42] *The Secret Mine,* performed in 1827, offered a 'most extensive display of Oriental Scenery' and concluded 'with a desperate attack of Persians and Hindoos, Horse and Foot and Destruction of the Mine of Rubies'.[43]

Other hippodramas drew on military spectacle. *The Battle of Waterloo,* 'with its clashing armies of supernumeraries, heroic charges and counter charges by foot and horse, exploding ammunition wagons and crackling musketry', was presented by Cooke as faithfully depicting 'The Glories of England in 1815'.[44] Similar verisimilitude was praised in the case of Ducrow's 'Historic and Magnificent Tournament', presented for the first time in Liverpool in 1840 and boasting strict attention to the correctness of armour, costume and general effect. *The Life and Death of Napoleon* included the march of the grand army over the Russian mountains where the horses traversed raised mounds at the rear of the stage, followed by upwards of 80 well-disciplined soldiers and, in the last act, the field of battle where the audience saw 'a terrific melee of horse and foot and Shaw, the Life Guardsman, fighting with six Frenchmen at the same time'.[45] The scale of these productions demanded large casts of humans and horses; Ducrow's company of 1842 numbered over 150 and his tournament featured a stud of 58 horses.[46]

Not all of the plays on the stage made use of horses, and many relied on staging and settings to create the spectacle. Cooke's early production of *Cherry and Fair State; or The Children of Cyprus* offered a succession of magnificent scenery,

> among the most prominent of which will appear the Grove of Enchantment, with the descent of Airicanna. The Fairy Queen, in a magnificent Cloud Car – A Sea beach, Morning After a Storm, with part of the Wreck of a Greek vessel – Villa and Grounds of Hassanbad, with the Magic Aloe – Pier and Port of Cyprus, with the Arrival of the Grand Fairy Present, the Golden Galley, which was built expressly for this piece, at an enormous expense – the Valley and Lake by Moonlight, with the Town of Cyprus in the Distance – The Fiery Forest and Dancing Waters, which change to the Frozen Mountains of the Caucasus, concluding with the Grand Palace of Cyprus.[47]

The Queen of Cyprus, advertised as a new aquatic spectacle, included one scene where the stage was converted into 'an immense moat of real water in which a number of hair-breadth escapes ... transpire'.[48] Fires were often key features as in *The Life and Death of Napoleon,* in which Moscow was seen to burn in twenty different places simultaneously.[49]

Nor were all items in the ring reliant on horses. Acts of strength, balancing and juggling, along with clowns, slack-rope dancing and the *corde volante* (a length of rope attached to the ceiling of the theatre to form a swing) were all popular. In 1842 the American Circus promised 'summerset-throwing, stile vaulting, slack-rope dancing, polandering, gymnastic grouping' alongside graceful horse riding.[50] Managers worked hard to find novelties. Freeman, the American Giant, attracted large houses when he performed in 1844, as did the Patagonian Strongman in 1835. The Russian Horn Band made an appearance with 25 musicians playing 55 horns of various lengths, the longest being 8 feet long, although the *Liverpool Mercury* complained that the sawdust dampened the sound.[51] Exoticism was also popular, encompassing everything from parades of the Chief of the Chippeway Nation accompanied by his wife, sister and three warriors in 1834 to Mr Sweeney 'with his banjo and Nigger songs', who arrived with Mr Sands' American troop in 1842 and became a firm Liverpool favourite.[52] Saxon notes that a number of black performers flourished during the nineteenth century in circus performance and several rose to prominent artistic and managerial positions, including Pablo Fanque, whose circus appeared at the Amphitheatre in the late 1840s. Reviewers and spectators considered their presence natural enough, and much of the time no comment was passed on their colour.[53] Often exoticism was created by performers dressing up, and Saxon observes that Ducrow was fond of making up in blackface and created several acts for his infant pupils in which they appeared as negroes.[54] The Amphitheatre played host to a number of these 'performances of the exotic' across the decades. In the 1820s Mr Avery offered a novel Asiatic act in the character of a youthful Turk, and Mr Adams appeared riding two horses without bridle or saddle in an act called 'The Wild Indian'. In 1835 it was the turn of a Turkish cavalcade. In 1840 a Chinese flag fete in which 'the peculiar movements of the Chinese cavalry' was exhibited was a striking addition to the show. Alexandra Appleton argues that such exoticism was a real physical reminder of the 'distant and continuously expanding trading outposts, whose goods and merchandise came through the port's bustling docks on a daily basis'.[55] Accompanying the weekly reports in the *Liverpool Mercury* that listed the current imports arriving at the docks, the productions 'acted as a reminder of the global importance of the town's maritime economy' as well as reinforcing 'a proud notion of its imperial superiority'.[56]

Horses were not the only animals to perform. The popularity of travelling menageries such as Wombwell's, which was a regular Liverpool visitor, and the opening of Liverpool's zoological gardens in 1833 showed a growing Victorian fascination for encounters with wild animals. At the Amphitheatre, bears, zebras and camels were on show and Mademoiselle Jack, the famous elephant, allowed 'as many of the spectators as can find sitting room and are disposed to such elevation' to get upon her back, to be 'dislodged by her in a very ingenious and ludicrous manner', an event which 'elicited shouts of laughter and approbation'.[57] *Hyder Ali; or the Lions of Mysore* included a stupendous elephant, several monkeys, two boa constrictors and a llama, but most popular of all was Mr Carter, the fearless lion king, and his forest of wild animals. While the *Liverpool Mercury* declared the dramatic narrative of Carter's shows as 'contemptible in plot and dialogue', it was captivated by the lions.

> We could not have believed it possible had we not seen it, that man could render the savage monarchs of the desert so docile and obedient to his will … In the first act he is discovered reposing on one of them, and they afterwards sport about him with all the playfulness of young kittens; and in the last he is thrown into the den of the lion, with which he enters into combat, apparently so real as to make the spectators tremble for the consequences.[58]

The reviewer is full of admiration for Carter's skill and also alert to the real sense of danger in one 'false reading' or 'mistake as to his cue'. In 1840 Egerton engaged Carter again in a melodramatic sketch set in Algiers in which

> [t]he animals, consisting of a splendid tiger, a noble lion and lioness, two leopards and a puma are presented in a cage which Mr Carter enters, and in the course of nearly ten minutes performance sufficiently shows the power which

Mr Carter, the fearless lion king, wrestling a tiger, undated newspaper cutting

> he had obtained over these members of the brute creation. He exchanged all sorts of caresses with them and makes them serve the purpose of beds, sofas, stools and other articles of domestic use.[59]

To add to the excitement, the audience were invited after the Monday performance to a public feeding of 'Mr Carter's splendid collection of carnivores' when 'the ferocious attributes and amazing muscular power of these Forest Monarchs' were on display.[60] As with the audience's appreciation of the horse-riding skills on display, here they were being asked to admire the 'apparently miraculous "taming" on stage' as proof of 'the power of nurture over nature', alongside the frisson of very real, potential danger.[61] Both the fear and the admiration of the skills of the trainer are apparent in an incident from 1840 described in *The Era* when, at the end of his performance, Carter left the stage accompanied, as usual, by one of his leopards,

> [w]hen a lion and tiger commenced a terrific fight. The scene was most extraordinary; the whole of the company assembled on the stage prepared to take flight, and the audience were in a great excitement. Mr Carter rushed on the stage and in an instant was in the cage and threw himself between the combatants, felling the lion on one side and hurling the tiger to the other. A wild burst of applause rewarded this daring feat and was loudly continued,

> when the excited animals were seen to cower in to the corners of the den in the most abject state of subserviency ... In a cage, hardly ten feet square, stood a man, unarmed and alone, so perfectly a master of the wildest and most savage creatures of the forest that they forgot their animosity to each other and actually trembled with fear at his presence.[62]

Although performances were varied, there was a sense of unity in their overall appeal. All relied for their success on spectacle, sensation, novelty and skill, appealing to the emotions of the audience.

Throughout this period, evenings were long. Shows started at 6.30 or 7 o'clock and ended at about 11 o'clock, although there were many occasions when they overran. The circus season was short. They were only allowed to run for three months (from late December) so as not to compete with the Theatre Royal, which closed during the winter months. Most of the lessees ran summer theatres in other cities, often London, and used the Amphitheatre when these were closed. This meant that, as the largest public space available in Liverpool until the building of St George's Hall in 1854, the Amphitheatre was a popular venue for other events. Italian opera occasionally appeared, as in 1831 when Signore de Begnes performed six grand operas. In 1837 Madame Pasta was making her farewell appearance in a grand evening concert and Paganini made three visits in the early 1830s.[63] There were also concerts as part of the Liverpool Grand Musical Festival, which for a while was an annual affair, taking over many of the town's venues. Commemorative or anniversary dinners, concerts, amateur dramatics and above all political meetings filled the theatre (often noisily and acrimoniously) in the summer months and connected the space more closely to the people of the town, creating what Maria Barrett describes as a sense of 'shared revelry' and of 'collective participation'.[64] This also worked in reverse at times during the season when the managers held benefits for local causes, from the distressed weavers in 1826 and the Night Asylum for the Homeless Poor in 1831 to 'the suffering poor' in 1838 and the wives and relatives of the crew of the *President* in 1840.

Troublesome Neighbours

An argument between Ducrow and the Theatre Royal about an elephant illustrates some of the competitive tensions that existed between the Theatre Royal and the Amphitheatre until the Theatres Act of 1843 changed the state of affairs. In an 1830 letter to the *Liverpool Albion*, 'An Amateur of the Drama' accused Ducrow of infringing the patent rights of the Theatre Royal in an 'ostentatious and unwarrantable manner' by, among other things, announcing a performing elephant.

Writing in response, Ducrow pointed out that he had delayed opening that season for a month beyond his intended start date so as not to interfere with the interests of the Theatre Royal. This had damaged his finances and those of the tradespeople of the town who received a 'considerable portion' of his £400 a week expenses when the theatre was open. He went on to say that in announcing the appearance of the elephant at the same time as the managers of the theatre, he was merely acting on the defensive and had been preparing the spectacle in which the elephant was to appear for three weeks previously.[65] A slightly different version of the story is told by Ducrow's stage machinist who was despatched to Liverpool to prepare for the opening of the season on Boxing Night in 1829. On his arrival, he found

> [t]he dead walls of the city covered with posters announcing the forthcoming appearance of a then fashionable "star", no other than the celebrated trained elephant of Siam, "Mdlle Dejeek" ... This ponderous performer had been introduced to the London public by Yates at the Adelphi, and it was now announced that she would make her first bow to a Liverpool audience on Easter Monday evening, in a piece prepared for her.[66]

As he was about to write and inform Ducrow, the stage machinist realised that Wombwell was in town with his menagerie, which included a performing elephant. As Wombwell was struggling financially, he agreed to let them have every animal they needed and Ducrow despatched the machinist to London to organise the props and scenery and publicity. All of this suggests that no preparations had been made previously, but they did manage to produce a grand Eastern Spectacle, *The Elephant of Siam*, in February 1830, several months ahead of their competitors who, despite advertising the forthcoming attraction at the start of the year, did not manage to stage their version until June. The whole episode captured the town's imagination and led to the *Liverpool Mercury* printing a poem or 'Lines on seeing the Elephant at Mr Ducrow's Amphitheatre remove the Crown from the Head of the Usurper Korassan and place it on that of Almanzor, the rightful Heir'.

> The Elephant, beyond dispute,
> Is, as we're told, a reasoning brute,
> And those that doubt that he is so,
> Need but to Ducrow's Circus go;
> There will they see the noble beast,
> Though born in the despotic East,
> Strip a usurper of his crown,
> And trample despotism down.
> Oh! That Ducrow to Miguel's Court

This noble creature would transport,
And to the bigot's vassals show
The way to lay a tyrant low.[67]

The stage machinist was convinced that the Theatre Royal had 'made up their minds to hurt our business, if possible', but it was Ducrow who, in jokingly chastising the Theatre Royal for announcing on the same bill performances by Miss Fanny Kemble and an elephant, seemed aware of the bigger problem. In this he was right. This was not the first nor the last time that the patent theatre looked to illegitimate forms to boost its box office, encroaching on the terrain that the minor theatres felt was their right. In subsequent years, Ducrow himself was to perform there, and in 1839 and in 1841 Van Amburgh was engaged with 'the whole of his matchless collection of LIONS, LEOPARDS and TIGERS', on which occasion the *Liverpool Mail* was moved to regret that they had not left the lions to the Amphitheatre.[68] While there are some counter-examples of the Amphitheatre rather boldly challenging its competitor, including Horton's assertion that Mr Gore, the scenery painter, sold tickets for the Amphitheatre from his hat-making premises in Williamson Square, most attempts to stop performances came from the protectionist Theatre Royal, convinced that the minors were infringing on its territory. As Barrett argues, the entry of the Amphitheatre into the field would certainly have been a threat to the Theatre Royal, especially with its cheaper prices. The Theatre Royal had been updated in 1822, raising its prices to pay for the work, and this may have made it particularly sensitive to the advent of a rival establishment.[69] In the Amphitheatre's first season, the Theatre Royal prosecuted Cooke for performing *Rob Roy* and prohibited the theatre from performing a burletta for the famous actor Ellar's benefit, seeing both as an infringement of its rights and privileges.[70]

These early warning shots soon died away, only to gather momentum in 1841 in a fight that brought all the minor theatres together in conflict with 'the spirit of monopoly infested' against them.[71] The main force of the Theatre Royal was used not against the Amphitheatre but against the Liver, which was prosecuted a number of times in the late 1830s. By 1841 it was fed up with this state of affairs and raised a petition, with 11,000 signatures, for a second patent for the city. This nearly achieved its aim and was only foiled at the very last hurdle. News of the petition for a second patent (submitted in July 1841) seems to have infuriated the Theatre Royal, which in February sent notification to the managers of the Liver and the Amphitheatre (and other 'minor' places of amusement), directing them to close their establishments by 15 February, the date the Theatre Royal was due to open. This alarmed Egerton, who immediately announced that the Amphitheatre would close early and that he would return to open his Manchester theatre, the Queen's. This withdrawal earned him the wrath of the *Liverpool Mail*, which regretted that he 'had not the courage to resist this most oppressive proceeding and try the question whether in reality any patent right to the exclusive performance of dramatic productions does exist in Liverpool'. The paper was more than a little scathing about the fact that he was not staying to aid Mr Raymond, the manager of the Liver, instead of 'sounding a retreat at the first blast of the bugle from their adversary'. It was also keen to point out to him that the Queen's would also be under threat, as the Theatre Royal in Manchester had the same lessees as the one in Liverpool – which proved to be the case the following year, when they did force the early closure of his theatre in Manchester. There was some resilience from the actor, Mr Hammond, who on his benefit night prior to the closure made a speech outlining the real heart of the argument. Having lamented the fact that they were being driven away 'from a scene of profitable pleasure' (and that the closure would have a serious impact on the wages of those employed by the theatre), he continued,

> [w]e must endeavour to amend the law that gives an unjust and useless monopoly to one theatre ... We must petition parliament, not for another patent – Oh no! That is a small kind of liberality admitting only another party to share in injustices, in a part and portion of the spoil. We must have a free trade in drama.[72]

The following year, after further arguments, another and more impassioned speech was made from the Amphitheatre stage, this time by Mr Emery, one of the company. By now the theatre was tired of being dictated to by the Theatre Royal, and he invoked the anger of the people of Liverpool who were being told that 'this is the only theatre you must attend, you *shall* support us; and if you want twenty theatres you shall have none but ours!' Continuing in a manner that must have been familiar to those who had attended the rumbustious political meetings at the theatre in the previous decades, he declared, 'The cry should be – an unpolluted free stage – no monopolies', encouraging Liverpool 'to be the first to strike the blow of abolition to this famous patent right'. Winding up his audience further, he finished by declaring, '[l]et it be destroyed as one of the last of the old abuses of imbecile government and this town will possess the repute of having been the first to throw open the theatrical gates of information to the people...'[73] He left the stage to hearty and prolonged applause.

Throughout 1842 and into 1843 actors from both theatres found themselves summoned to appear before magistrates charged with acting, representing and performing for gain and reward without lawful authority. The fine for this offence was £50, but in most cases the magistrates decided that nothing could be proved. By April 1843 the magistrates were clearly becoming irritated by these prosecutions, which the *Liverpool Mail* noted had become a constant occurrence in Liverpool, and fining the Amphitheatre a nominal 20 shillings for performing the spectacle *The Horse of the Rialto*, they suggested that the theatres come to some arrangement among themselves.[74] In the end, the matter was taken out of their hands with the passing of the Theatres Act of 1843, and by the start of the new season there was a free trade in drama.

1843–1881: Managing the Move to Legitimacy

Following a number of years of constant changes in management, in 1843 the Amphitheatre moved into a much more settled period with the start of William Robert Copeland's 'memorable reign' of twenty-three years.[75] In 1850 Copeland also took on the management of the Theatre Royal, at last uniting the old adversaries and allowing him to move actors between the two theatres. In 1853 Copeland ensured greater stability by purchasing a 75-year lease for just over £16,000.[76] In keeping with previous managers, Copeland stamped his mark on the Amphitheatre, this time removing 'a general and well-founded complaint of the impossibility of obtaining a complete sight of the Equestrian Performance from the back of the Boxes and Gallery'. He also added a new practical stage, which could be removed after the initial drama to give increased space for the circle performances. Above all else, his improvements had an eye to the comfort of the audience and the respectability of the theatre; boxes were carpeted, some having additional anterooms for families, and the pit looked 'infinitely more sociable than formerly', leading the *Liverpool Mail* to hope that 'the disgraceful scenes which were of the yore enacted there' would be prevented by 'rigid police surveillance'.[77]

On Copeland's retirement in 1866, the popular and prolific playwright H. J. Byron, also co-lessee with Miss Wilton of the Prince of Wales in London, took over. He acquired the lease of the Theatre Royal as well and went one step further by taking on the Alexandra Theatre, opened in 1866 as the New Prince of Wales Theatre. The latter may well have been his downfall, as R. J. Broadbent points out:

> Byron's managerial reign here was as artistically brilliant as it was regretfully brief ... the Alexandra Theatre, which had proved unfortunate to Mr Henderson, had been a disastrous speculation to Mr Byron. The actor-dramatist got the newest and best pieces, and put them on stage in the most complete style; but the nett result of his managerial enterprise was the loss of some £5000 or so.[78]

By February 1868 rumours were flying that Byron was about to give up theatre management in Liverpool, and in April he was appearing in bankruptcy court, attributing his situation to the depressed state of trade. In the meantime the actors from both the Amphitheatre and the Alexandra met together to express their profound sympathies at his 'present anxieties', and offer an appreciation of his 'past unvarying kindness and liberality in the face of the many and perplexing difficulties' with which he had been beset, suggesting that although his reign was brief it was appreciated by those who worked for him. This was further emphasised in the speech made at one of the two benefits organised by the actors during which Mr Eldred proclaimed:

> I come now to the name of one,
> The much loved captain of our ship was he,
> He launched his barque on angry waves,
> He's wrecked upon a troubled sea,
> He tried his best to steer alright,
> But winds will blow and billows roar;
> Let's man a boat this very night,
> And land him safely upon the shore; (*Prolonged cheers*)
> And start him in the world again.
> His honour stainless, as is bright his fame.
> Good steadfast friends I see around me here,
> For Byron's cause I now have naught to fear. (*Continued applause*)[79]

The theatre was then taken over by Miss Elizabeth Copeland and the estate for her father, who had died in 1867, and was managed for them by Henry Leslie. This suggests that Copeland's estate still had responsibility for the mortgage, and there were two attempts to auction the theatre in 1871. At the first, the only bid of £20,000 from Leslie did not meet the reserve, and at the second, the bidding was even lower and the theatre was withdrawn, despite the fact that potential buyers were being guaranteed £6,000 by the council, which wanted to purchase the four shops attached to the theatre as part of an improvement scheme for Roe Street. Eventually, at the end of 1871, the council bought the whole lot for £19,000, reckoning that with fifty-seven years left on the lease and with a potential income of £2,000 a year it was a good investment.[80] Henry Leslie duly leased the theatre from the council and was joined by Lindo Courtenay in 1873, who then became sole lessee in 1879, until the theatre was auctioned in May 1880 to David Radcliffe for £20,000 as part of a wider sale of council property. During this latter period, the theatre went through a difficult time as the council argued among themselves about the best use of the

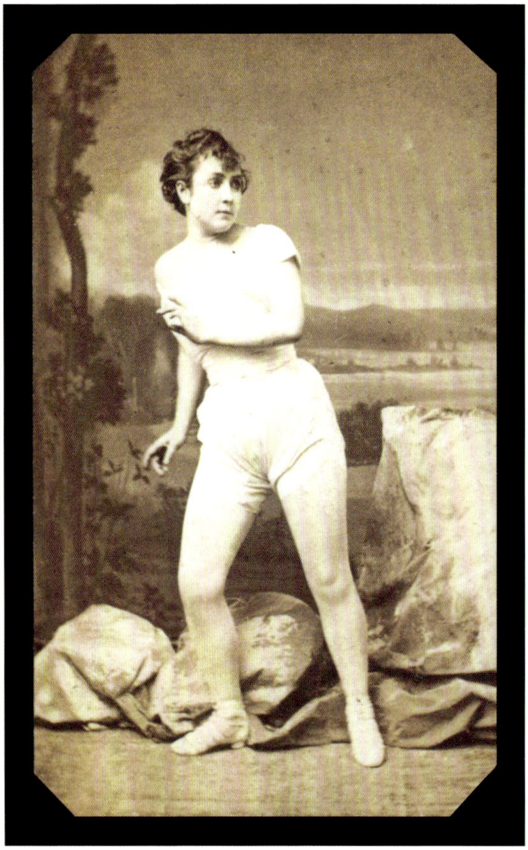

Ada Isaacs Menken in her costume for *Mazeppa* by Jean Laurent, 1864 (© Victoria and Albert, London)

space. Some vociferous voices maintained that a wholesale fish market would be of more value to the city. Others thought it needed to be pulled down to help with street improvements. In the end neither happened, but the rumours flying around were enough to undermine the security and stability of the Amphitheatre in its last years.

Staging Legitimacy

The theatrical landscape had transformed since Cooke's time, and with the change in the law as Copeland arrived things were about to alter again. While the Theatres Act of 1843 enabled Copeland to perform spoken drama at the Amphitheatre, it also meant that he could no longer sell alcohol in the auditorium. This prohibition led to the formation of music hall, as the public houses, unaffected by the legislation, began to offer free musical entertainment alongside their food and drink. By the 1850s Broadbent notes the existence of several of what he terms 'concert halls' in the Lime

Street area alone, including the 'Hop' (a Temperance Free and Easy), the Albany Concert Hall and the Garibaldi Concert Hall.[81] On Great Charlotte Street itself, the Parthenon Music Hall had opened in 1845 as the Royal Parthenon Assembly Rooms, showing variously Iowa Indians and Bianchi's waxworks. By 1846 it was announcing 'an unrivalled company of dancing and vocal talent'.[82] In Williamson Square the Star, from 1847, was advertising free entrance to its concert room alongside first-class chops, steaks and wine, and at the York Hotel (on the corner of Williamson Square and Tarleton Street) harmonic evenings were being held. These were clearly popular and lucrative enough to enable the original venues to be pulled down to make way for purpose-built music halls; this was the case at the Star which in less than twenty years was rebuilt as the New Star Music Hall (later becoming Liverpool Playhouse), and the Garibaldi was replaced in 1859 by the Theatre Varieté, the precursor of the Tivoli Palace of Varieties. At the other end of the scale, new and luxurious theatres were being built. The Prince of Wales in Clayton Square, a 'very cosy comfortable little house', opened in 1861, but the biggest competition was to

Prince of Wales Theatre, c. 1866, *Illustrated London News* (© Victoria and Albert, London)

come in the shape of the Alexandra Theatre, opened in 1866 as the New Prince of Wales Theatre (becoming in 1896 the Empire).[83] Its imposing frontage, with five arches and a carriage drive leading to the main parts of the house, included statues of the heads of Shakespeare, Schiller, Molière, Beethoven and Rossini and suggested that this was a competitor to be reckoned with. The interior, described by the *Illustrated London News*, increased the competitive stakes:

> The interior is most conveniently arranged. As parties alight from the carriages they enter a roomy apartment, warmed by a stove, and handsomely furnished and decorated, which is intended for a waiting and conversation room. From this room a wide stair-case, 10 ft. wide, covered with a costly carpet, leads to a superb ante-room to the dress-circle. The decorations of this fine room are particularly rich. Ladies' rooms open from it, and by two large folding doors the circle is entered ... from it a short flight of stairs on each side leads to that part of the house commonly known as the pit, but which here is to be entirely occupied by commodious arm-chairs, called stalls ... The fronts of the upper circle and gallery are panelled in blue satin tufted with gold stars, the panels separated by artistically-modelled female figures holding festoons.[84]

At the same time Liverpool was changing from the town it had been in 1826. In the campaign for the abolition of the slave trade it found itself on the wrong side of the argument and 'stood condemned for barbarism, philistinism and lack of civilised culture'.[85] In an attempt to redress its tarnished image, John Belchem argues that the city underwent its first rebranding, putting itself at the forefront of the campaign against slavery and at the same time trying to distance itself from the image of a city only interested in 'the getting of money'.[86] At the forefront of this were men such as William Roscoe, who, in looking for appropriate models for a civilised city, alighted on Florence, which as well as being a great commercial city was also the home of poets, scholars and artists. There he found 'at once refreshment from the brutal materialism of his native town and inspiration for the attempt to breathe into it new spirit'.[87] While Roscoe's attempt to turn Liverpool into the Florence of the North was not entirely successful, the middle of the nineteenth century did see a growth in clubs, reading rooms and societies promoting literature and the arts. Alongside this was an explosion in civic pride, from the Philharmonic Hall (1849), Central Library (1852) and St George's Hall (1854) to the Walker Art Gallery (1877), the Picton Reading Room (1879) and finally, in 1880, the granting of city status. Many of these were more than statements of civic pride; they were also statements of the importance of being seen as a cultured city. This was an idea underlined by Philip Rathbone in a lecture of 1875 when he maintained that

> [i]t is for us, with our vast population, our enormous wealth (as a town), but without either politics or philosophy that the world will care to preserve, to decide whether we will take advantage of our almost unequalled opportunities for the cultivation of Art, or whether we shall be content to rot away, as Carthage, Antioch and Tyre have rotted away, leaving not a trace to show here a population of more than half a million souls once lived, loved, felt and thought. Surely the home of Roscoe is worthy of a better fate?[88]

Caught in the midst of all this change, Copeland plumped for making the Amphitheatre more respectable, and his vision was the one that dominated the last forty years of the Amphitheatre. While the last plays under the regime of Sloan and Leclerg were the melodrama *Jack Sheppard of France* and *Esmerelda*, a grand spectacle based on Victor Hugo's novel *The Hunchback of Notre Dame*, once Copeland had made it through the Christmas season, the playbills of 1844 read like a Shakespeare festival. Starting with an advertisement for the 'novel and effective arrangements' of 'the legitimate drama by a new and talented company', the Amphitheatre produced *Henry IV*, *The Merchant of Venice*, *Coriolanus* and *Richard III* (June 1844), followed by *Othello*, *The Merchant of Venice*, *King John*, *Romeo and Juliet* and *King Lear* (October 1844). In between, Copeland offered Massinger's *A New Way to Pay Old Debts*, and in October 1844 the *Liverpool Mail* noted that the Amphitheatre 'maintains its reputation for a close adherence to the legitimate drama'.[89] In the following season, *Antigone* was advertised as 'the greatest triumph ever achieved in Liverpool' and having had its first British performance at Covent Garden in January, it arrived on the Liverpool stage in June. But Shakespeare was undoubtedly the most performed playwright from the time Copeland took the reins; between 1843 and 1881 there were 91 performances of *Hamlet*, 88 performances of *Macbeth*, nearly 80 of *Othello* and over 50 each of *The Merchant of Venice* and *Romeo and Juliet*. By the 1850s 'ballets were given nightly'.[90] Music too became a regular feature. In 1848 Monsieur Julien, the celebrated tenor from La Scala, made his first appearance attracting 'many respectable persons'.[91] Touring opera companies were a regular feature, from the Pyne and Harrison Opera Company in 1852 and the English Opera Company in 1855 to the Blanche Cole Opera Company in 1877 and the Frederick Archer Opera Company in 1880. The Carl Rosa Opera Company made its first appearance in 1874 in what was to become a long association with the theatre.

To enhance the stock company, Copeland (and ensuing managers) attracted many of the leading performers of the day, including the Vanderhoffs, Charles

Matthews, Helen Faucett, Madame Celeste and Charles Wyndham (who had been born in the city). One of the most popular was Barry Sullivan, once a member of the stock company and described by Broadbent as 'an immense local favourite', who appeared regularly at the theatre from 1850.[92] On his return in 1868, *The Play* suggested that no engagement 'could more auspiciously open' the new regime at the 'People's Theatre', for he was well known in Liverpool before his talent was recognised in London, and it noted that the theatre was crowded nightly with 'an audience whose enthusiasm was almost too demonstrative'.[93] In 1872 he was still playing to overflowing houses and while he was offering no new roles, 'his numerous admirers in Liverpool seem well content to see him over and over again in those characters which are now inseparably associated with his name'.[94] Indeed, Copeland had worked so hard to encourage a familiarity between actors and audiences that on his retirement he was criticised for placing the same faces constantly before the audience. To this he had a robust response, convinced, as an actor-manager himself, that the role of actors was not just to 'appear and to be shifted like the tinsel scenes of a pantomime transformation tableaux'. Instead, he believed they needed time to learn and study and this was best achieved by appearing before a familiar and appreciative audience.[95]

Famous performers were also attracted to offer benefit performances. Jenny Lind performed a morning dress concert in aid of the Southern and Toxteth Hospital, and in 1848 Charles Dickens was involved in a performance of *The Merry Wives of Windsor* to raise money for the endowment of the perpetual curatorship of Shakespeare's house.[96] On this occasion, Dickens took on the part of Justice Shallow (although at a disadvantage as there was 'manifestly not sufficient scope for his histrionic qualifications') and played Flexible in the farce *Love, Law and Physic*.[97] The move to legitimate drama and increasing respectability was clearly successful, and in 1849 the *Liverpool Mercury* could declare that the Amphitheatre was 'at present deservedly one of the most popular places of resort in the town' with the 'acknowledged best dramatic company in the provinces' and that Copeland had ensured a 'high tone and exalted character'.[98]

The Challenge of Maintaining Respectability

Yet despite attempts to make the Amphitheatre more respectable, some things conspired against the managers. By 1862 the area around the theatre was less inviting and the nearness to the market, rather than being the attraction it may have been in the 1820s, meant that, according to *The Porcupine*, on approaching, 'every sense is offended' by the 'stenches from market refuse and close dank stinking streets are even dangerous to health'.[99] The article continued by suggesting that 'the sights and sounds are so offensive that hundreds of ladies are denied the pleasures of theatrical entertainments in consequence of the certainty of having their eyes and ears polluted in a manner which will be well understood by mere allusion'. And it was not just the streets that were proving off-putting. The theatre entrance was 'narrow, dirty and badly lighted. There is no proper provision for the care of external articles of clothing – no decent *foyer, or refreshment saloon*; nothing in fact, but narrow, cheerless, ill-lit lobbies, paltry rooms, and draughty staircases.' Seating and ventilation were another cause for concern; human ingenuity could 'not invent anything more miserably deficient in every quality than the dress and side-boxes' and '[i]n summer the ardent playgoer is parboiled ... while in winter, the gusts of

View of Roe Street showing Royal Amphitheatre, 1867 (Liverpool Record Office)

Barry Sullivan as Hamlet by W. & D. Downey, 1860 (© Victoria and Albert, London)

icy air from both stage and lobbies is enough to freeze even a Polar bear'. Behind the scenes things were even worse with 'useless, antiquated machinery', dressing rooms that were 'the veriest dog-holes' and the whole place, 'dangerous from absence of light', pervaded by 'noisome smells'.

The Porcupine was not the only one complaining, and letters to the local papers bemoaned the state of the theatre, in particular the long passageways leading to the pit and gallery entrances.[100] The papers also carried reports of petty crime associated with the theatre and encouraged by the crowded entrances, such as the occasion when Mr Lichfield's watch was stolen in the great swarm of people around the door on the occasion of a benefit for Barry Sullivan.[101] And on occasions those working in the theatre were discovered to be flouting the law, as when Margaret Farrell found herself in the police courts for sending out for alcohol to sell inside the auditorium.[102]

Prostitution was also an ongoing problem. In 1829 *Gore's* could celebrate the fact that things had been improved and that, at least, 'no indecorous characters' could 'gain access to that part of the house allotted to the respectable portions of the community'.[103] In the early 1860s the problem had expanded again, despite the fact that Copeland had found himself in court, in 1858, for permitting prostitutes to enter the theatre. *The Porcupine* complained that for several years the promenade had been 'the common-sewer of the town's profligacy'. In the course of the evening, the audience was gradually surrounded by a thickening assembly of 'gay women' (albeit 'the most select of their class') and when respectable women came to collect their bonnets in the refreshment room at the end of the performance they found themselves in a room full of these 'gay women' being treated by their 'fops'. The presence of prostitutes in the theatre then started to attract the 'wrong audience' and to prevent others from attending. The theatre, grumbled the paper, was 'resorted to ... regularly by men who either wished to patronise prostitution, or, what is more frequent, to enjoy looking at and speculating upon those who practice it, and to participate to that safe extent in the glorious sport of seeing life', and it was not at all surprised that parents were prohibiting their sons from attending.[104]

All of these problems militated against the management's attempts to ensure that the Amphitheatre was the home of respectable drama and a respectable audience, and the problem rumbled on when Byron took over the management, with the papers hoping that he would 'put down the crying evil' which had done 'so much to prejudice respectable playgoers against the Amphitheatre'.[105] One letter to the *Daily Post* in 1869 suggests something about the general atmosphere in the theatre. A frequent visitor wrote to complain that for the previous nine months he had been much annoyed by the frightful howling of a dog, which seemed to choose the quietest times in the play to make the most noise. On the previous Monday, 'when Mr Brade was playing *Hamlet*', the noise was, he wrote, louder than ever and he was now finally forced to write and complain in an appeal to the manager to do something, as the problem had been totally ignored.[106] James Picton's assessment that, by 1875, the 'building and its arrangements' were 'rough, uncouth and slovenly' seems to have ring of truth to it.[107]

But We Have Still Got Horses

Despite firm attempts to ensure that the theatre was the home of legitimate drama, not all other forms of performance were neglected and, maybe with one eye on the rise of the music halls, Copeland and his successors did not by any means abandon the more popular entertainment. The theatre continued to hold an equestrian season at Christmas, playing host to companies including Monsieur Tournaire's French equestrians from the Cirque Royal de Paris, Batty, Franconi and Signor Quaglieni's Sardinian Equestrian Company. In 1849 Pablo Fanque's circus advertised its arrival by Mr Emidy driving twenty horses in hand through the streets, and as late as 1871 the theatre was promising a Grand Mammoth Procession introducing Aztec warriors, Nubian chiefs, snake charmers, elephants, camels, alligators and the Indian cavalry mounted on ostriches, all completed by the triumphal car of King Wangdoodle.[108] Shakespeare performances too did not eschew novelty – or horses. The February production of *Richard III* in 1844 included a highly trained stud of horses, and in November, the role was performed by the 8-year-old Miss Heron, 'the Infant Power', eliciting great approval from the audience.[109]

Nor were more popular plays ignored, and melodramas continued to grace the stage. Most performed was Boucicault's *The Poor of Liverpool*, a potboiler of a play described by Dickens as 'the most depressing instance, without exception, of an utterly degrading and debasing theatrical taste'.[110] A complicated plot involving an evil financier, a stolen fortune, parted lovers and the spectacle of a burning tenement building contained some simple emotional appeal. At the start, the old sea captain, soon to be cheated out of his money and to die as a result, tells the financier Bloodgood not to talk of his family, for

> [t]ears of joy come into my eyes whenever I think of those children – and my dear wife, the patient, devoted companion of the old sailor, whose loving voice murmurs each evening a prayer for those who are at sea; and my children, sir, two little angels; one a fair little thing … all red and white like a little bundle of flowers; and my eldest – my son Paul – we named him after Paul Jones – a sailor's whim; well, sir, when the ship is creaking and groaning under my feet, when the squall drives the hail and sleet across my face, amidst the thunder, I only hear three voices – through the gloom, I can see only three faces, pressed together like three angels waiting for me in heaven, and that heaven is my home.[111]

The conclusion, once fortunes are restored to the family and the happy couple reunited, asks the audience to look outside the theatre, as Mrs Fairweather, the Captain's wife, who the audience have witnessed live through the trials of poverty, suggests,

> when you leave this place, as you return to your homes, should you see some poor creatures, extend your hand to them, and the blessings that will follow you on your way will be the most grateful tribute you can pay THE POOR OF NEW YORK.[112]

An appeal to a real world familiar to the audience was also apparent in the settings, with references to a coffee stall on the Goree, Prince's Park, the Theatre Royal and a view across the river to Liverpool. The scene set in front of the Adelphi Hotel caused such great applause that 'the performance was interrupted for some minutes until Mr Dawson, the artist, was induced to come on to the stage'.[113] An appeal to the local is also apparent in another melodrama popular at the Amphitheatre. H. J. Byron's *The Lass of Lancashire; or Tempted, Tried and True*, a play with another complicated plot, was particularly praised in the press for its scene with the Egremont ferry:

> Remarkable to say, the stage carpenter has precisely followed the construction of the ferry; while the artist has produced with unusual vividness a night view of Liverpool with a fidelity truly charming. Then we have several craft on the river, which make way for the night steamer from Liverpool. It comes alongside puffing and splashing as Egremont steamers do puff and splash.[114]

Given the move to respectability and more serious drama, the newspapers were at times critical both of these plays and their production. The plot of *The Lass of Lancashire* was thought to be 'utter confusion', the spectator needing 'a memory like that possessed by Alexander the Great to form a consecutive story of the scenes'.[115] Adah Isaacs Menken's appearance in *Mazeppa* drew some ire from the *Liverpool Mail* which, despite the applause from the crowded pit and gallery, thought 'an increase in attire' would have added to 'the decency' without detracting from the effect of her performance.[116] And, as in the rest of the country, there was an air of 'moral panic' over the mania for the *Jack Sheppard* plays concerning the life of a 'notorious thief, highwayman, and jail escape artist'.[117] When a version of the play made an appearance in 1848, the *Liverpool Mail* felt moved to reiterate its previous disapproval on the grounds of its 'immoral tendencies and bad morals'.[118] For Copeland and the managers who followed, 1843 had allowed them to present legitimate drama, but they also found themselves walking a tightrope between legitimacy and popularity and discovered that sometimes it could be a difficult balancing act.

The Last Night of the Old Amphi

On 28 February 1881 the last performance at the theatre was a benefit night for Lindo Courtenay. The evening included Frank Harvey's *John Jasper's Wife*, a celebrated comedy drama in which Courtenay appeared, succeeded by a musical melange and concluding with the first act of *Robert Macaire*. Actors from local theatres including the Alexandra and the Prince of Wales offered their services for the evening. Courtenay's address, thanking the audience, suggested that he had been given first refusal for maintaining the lease and also indicated that both he and the audience were unaware that this really was the last night of the old Amphi. As far as he was concerned, the theatre would reopen in the middle of September following improvements, and he reassured people that 'there was no danger of the Old Amphitheatre disappearing'.[119] In a tradition in keeping with the spirit of the theatre, the audience was lively, 'the gods and the pittites especially so':

> [t]here was a continuous fusillade of popping ginger-beer corks and veritable showers of nut shells from the gallery. A gentleman who was in the house ... was nearly blinded by a hat. Which was repeatedly tossed from pit to gallery and gallery to pit, always hitting someone and finally reaching its owner in a hopelessly battered condition.[120]

However, without being aware of it, they were marking the end of the 'dear old Amphi', a fine house for the legitimate theatre where 'any actor who dried up in his part soon had the lines given him by the gods'.[121]

Notes

1 The first permanent building, known as the Christian Street Circus, had opened in 1789, becoming known as the Olympic Circus in 1805 when it was rebuilt.

2 R. J. Broadbent, *Annals of the Liverpool Stage* (Liverpool: Edward Howell, 1908), 188.

3 *Liverpool Mercury*, 3 March 1826, 6. Cooke had suggested as early as November 1825 that his intention was to partly erect the building 'in a temporary, but commodious manner' for the first season, and to finish the work 'with substantial brickwork and every desirable embellishment' the following summer. See *Gore's Liverpool General Advertiser*, 2 March 1826, 3.

4 A. H. Saxon, *Enter Foot and Horse: A History of Hippodrama in England and France* (New Haven, CT: Yale University Press, 1968), 15.

5 Saxon, *Enter Foot and Horse*, 13, also notes that the proscenium opening was 40 feet, whereas Cooke's measured 42 feet.

6 *Liverpool Mercury*, 15 December 1826, 1.

7 Ramsay Muir, *A History of Liverpool* (Liverpool: Liverpool University Press, 1907), 243. Muir gives the figure of 165,000 for 1831, adding that if the newly populous suburbs of Everton, West Derby and Toxteth were included in the old city limits an extra 40,000 could be added.

8 National Museums Liverpool, *St John's Market, Liverpool, 1827*, by Samuel Austin, http://www.liverpoolmuseums.org.uk/picture-of-month/displaypicture.aspx?id=92 (accessed 27 November 2018).

9 *The Stranger in Liverpool*, 10th edn (Liverpool: Thomas Kaye, 1833), 194.

10 Muir, *A History of Liverpool*, 284.

11 Ibid., 283.

12 *Gore's Liverpool General Advertiser*, 6 April 1826, 1.

13 *Liverpool Mercury*, 8 September 1826, 2.

14 *Liverpool Mercury*, 5 May 1826, 1.

15 *Gore's Liverpool General Advertiser*, 22 June 1826, 1.

16 *Liverpool Mercury*, 8 September 1826, 2.

17 *Liverpool Mercury*, 6 September 1881, 7.

18 *Gore's Liverpool General Advertiser*, 24 April 1834, 4.

19 *Gore's Liverpool General Advertiser*, 12 May 1836, 1.

20 *Liverpool Mail*, 14 December 1850, 6.

21 *Gore's Liverpool General Advertiser*, 16 April 1829, 3.

22 Broadbent, *Annals*, 224. This account quoted by Broadbent is taken from a manuscript by J. G. Underhill.

23 *Liverpool Mercury*, 2 November 1832, 1.

24 *Gore's Liverpool General Advertiser*, 23 November 1837, 1.

25 *Gore's Liverpool General Advertiser*, 19 November 1840, 3.

26 *Liverpool Mercury*, 10 July 1829, 8; 19 January 1827, 3.

27 *Liverpool Mercury*, 23 February 1827, 1; *Liverpool General Advertiser*, 12 May 1836, 1.

28 *Liverpool Mail*, 18 January 1840, 3.

29 A. H. Saxon, *The Life and Art of Andrew Ducrow and the Romantic Age of the English Circus* (Hamden, CT: Archon Books, 1978), 212; Marius Kwint, 'The Circus and Nature in Late Georgian England', in Peta Tait and Katie Lavers (eds), *The Routledge Circus Studies Reader* (Abingdon: Routledge, 2016), 332.

30 *Gore's Liverpool General Advertiser*, 25 December 1828, 1; *Liverpool Mail*, 28 December 1841, 2.

31 Jane Moody, 'The Theatrical Revolution, 1776–1843', in Joseph Donohue (ed.), *The Cambridge History of British Theatre. Volume 2: 1660–1895* (Cambridge: Cambridge University Press, 2004), 199; *Liverpool Mail*, 2 January 1840, 3.

32 Saxon, *Life and Art of Andrew Ducrow*, 335; *Liverpool Mercury*, 17 February 1832, 4.

33 Saxon, *Life and Art of Andrew Ducrow*, 335.

34 *Liverpool Mercury*, 30 March 1832, 1; 5 April 1848, 2.

35 Saxon, *Life and Art of Andrew Ducrow*, 156.

36 *Liverpool Mercury*, 17 March 1826, 1.
37 *Liverpool Mercury*, 9 January 1835, 1.
38 *Evening Courant*, 15 December 1827, quoted in Saxon, *Life and Art of Andrew Ducrow*, 203–4.
39 *Liverpool Mercury*, 21 January 1831, 1; 29 December 1840, 2.
40 *The Times*, 30 April 1811, quoted in Saxon, *Enter Foot and Horse*, 88.
41 Saxon, *Enter Foot and Horse*, 89.
42 Ibid., 70–1.
43 *Liverpool Mercury*, 9 February 1827, 1.
44 *Liverpool Mercury*, 23 February 1827, 1.
45 *Liverpool Mercury*, 29 December 1840, 2.
46 *Liverpool Mail*, 18 January 1842, 3; 15 February 1842, 3.
47 *Liverpool Mercury*, 24 March 1826, 1.
48 *Liverpool Mail*, 26 February 1842, 2.
49 *Liverpool Mercury*, 29 December 1840, 2.
50 *Liverpool Mercury*, 5 April 1842, 2. Slack-ropes were a variety of tightropes. Polandering was a balancing act using a break-away ladder. The performer struck attitudes on top of the single upright after the rest of the ladder had fallen away.
51 *Liverpool Mercury*, 6 January 1832, 5.
52 *Liverpool Mercury*, 12 December 1834, 1; *Liverpool Mail*, 26 March 1842, 2.
53 Saxon, *Life and Art of Andrew Ducrow*, 331–2.
54 Ibid., 332.
55 Alexandra Appleton, 'In Search of an Identity: The Changing Fortunes of Liverpool's Theatre Royal, 1772–1855', PhD thesis, Royal Holloway, University of London, 2015, 246.
56 Ibid., 247.
57 *Liverpool Mercury*, 6 January 1832, 6.
58 *Liverpool Mercury*, 17 February 1832, 6.
59 *Liverpool Mail*, 1 December 1840, 2.
60 *Liverpool Mail*, 5 December 1840, 2.
61 Kwint, 'Circus and Nature in Late Georgian England', 336.
62 *The Era*, 20 December 1840, 2. It is possible that the tiger was actually a jaguar, as in the early nineteenth century there was a tendency to refer to all large cats that were not lions as tigers, and some shows proudly advertised 'Brazilian Tigers'. There was also a lack of concern about verisimilitude in the use of animals, and Thomas Frost noted seeing a production of *Mazeppa* in which a zebra appeared in the Cossack camp; Thomas Frost, *Circus Life and Circus Celebrities* (London: Chatto and Windus, 1881), 90, 121.
63 *Liverpool Mercury*, 29 September 1837, 1; Broadbent, *Annals*, 255.
64 Maria Barrett, 'Fish out of Water: Habitus, Cultural Capital and the Working Class Experience of Theatre', PhD thesis, University of Warwick, 2017, 62.
65 *The Kaleidoscope; or Literary and Scientific Mirror*, 26 January 1830, 10.
66 Broadbent, *Annals*, 222.
67 *Liverpool Mercury*, 19 February 1830, 8.
68 *Liverpool Mail*, 16 February 1841, 2.
69 Barrett, 'Fish out of Water', 70.
70 Broadbent, *Annals*, 221.
71 *Liverpool Mail*, 22 April 1841, 2.
72 *Liverpool Mail*, 13 February 1841, 2. Ironically, Hammond found himself on the other side of the argument, and much lambasted, when in January 1842 he became a manager for the Theatre Royal.
73 *Liverpool Mail*, 21 May 1842, 3.
74 *Liverpool Mail*, 29 April 1843, 3.
75 Broadbent, *Annals*, 227.
76 In 1851 Copeland also took over management of the Strand Theatre in London, rechristening it Punch's Playhouse, but his metropolitan adventure only lasted two years.
77 *Liverpool Mail*, 9 December 1843, 2.
78 Broadbent, *Annals*, 241.
79 *Liverpool Post*, 27 March 1868, 4.
80 *The Era*, 15 January 1871, 13; *Liverpool Mail*, 15 July 1871, 9; 4 November 1871, 10.
81 Broadbent, *Annals*, 341.
82 Ibid., 346.
83 Ibid., 342.
84 *Illustrated London News*, 17 November 1866; quoted by Matthew Lloyd, Arthur Lloyd: The Music Hall and Theatre History Site, http://www.arthurlloyd.co.uk/index.

html (accessed 27 November 2018).

85 John Belchem, 'The New Livercool: History, Culture and Identity of Merseyside', in Christoph Ehlnd (ed.), *Thinking Northern: Textures of Identity in the North of England* (Amsterdam: Rodopi, 2007), 220.

86 Muir, *A History of Liverpool*, 270.

87 Ibid., 293.

88 Quoted in John Belchem, 'Celebrating Liverpool', in John Belchem (ed.), *Liverpool 800: Culture, Character and History* (Liverpool: Liverpool University Press, 2006), 18.

89 *Liverpool Mail*, 26 October 1844, 6.

90 Broadbent, *Annals*, 228.

91 *Liverpool Mail*, 15 April 1848, 3.

92 Broadbent, *Annals*, 228.

93 *The Play*, 28 April 1868, 4.

94 *Liverpool Mercury*, 13 April 1872, 16.

95 *Liverpool Daily Post*, 15 October 1866, 9. The role of provincial theatres in offering training and experience was emphasised by Henry Irving, who, in relation to his own experience under Wyndham at the Theatre Royal in Edinburgh, argued 'In a country where there is no Academy the only professors of acting are the actors and the only true school of acting is a well-conducted playhouse.' (*The Nineteenth Century*, vol. 27 (1890), 1040–58; quoted in Paul Iles, 'Issues in Theatrical Management: Howard and Wyndham and the Evolution of the British Touring Circuit', MPhil thesis, University of Glasgow, 1997, 21). All of the managers at the Amphitheatre from 1843 were actor-managers and performed there on numerous occasions.

96 *Liverpool Mail*, 6 January 1849, 4; 10 June 1848, 3.

97 Dickens was involved with a second benefit in 1860 for the widow and children of Robert R. Brough, the founder of the comic periodical the *Liverpool Lion*. This was organised by the London Savage Club (both Dickens and Brough were members), but on this occasion Dickens was not performing. See *Liverpool Mercury*, 13 August 1860, 1.

98 *Liverpool Mercury*, 20 January 1849, 3; 3 February 1849, 2.

99 *The Porcupine*, 1 November 1862, 3.

100 *Liverpool Mercury*, 19 January 1859, 4.

101 *Liverpool Daily Post*, 11 December 1860, 3.

102 *Liverpool Mercury*, 3 April 1847, 2.

103 *Gore's Liverpool General Advertiser*, 15 January 1828, 3.

104 *The Porcupine*, 17 August 1861; 11 June 1864; *Liverpool Mercury*, 20 March 1858, 3.

105 *Liverpool Mail*, 13 October 1866, 2.

106 *Daily Post*, 14 May 1869, 9.

107 James Picton, *Memorials of Liverpool. Volume II: Topographical* (Liverpool: Edward Howell, 1907), 174.

108 *Liverpool Mail*, 17 November 1849, 3; *Liverpool Mercury*, 17 January 1871, 1.

109 *Liverpool Mail*, 17 February 1844, 2; 5 November 1844, 3.

110 Robert Hogan, *Dion Boucicault* (New York: Twayne, 1969), 67.

111 Dion Boucicault, *The Poor of New York* (New York: Samuel French, 1857), 5.

112 Ibid., 45. The play had nearly as many names as the Amphitheatre, adapting its location to wherever the text was being performed and appearing variously as *The Poor of New York* (or Liverpool or Manchester or Leeds) and *The Streets of London* (or Dublin or Islington).

113 *Daily Post*, 11 February 1864, 5.

114 *Daily Post*, 29 October 1867, 5.

115 *Daily Post*, 29 October 1867, 5.

116 *Liverpool Mail*, 23 December 1865, 5.

117 Moody, 'Theatrical Revolution', 110.

118 *Liverpool Mail*, 8 July 1848, 5.

119 *Liverpool Mercury*, 2 March 1881, 7.

120 Broadbent, *Annals*, 248.

121 *The Stage*, 9 September 1881, 7.

South side of Roe Street showing Royal Amphitheatre, 1862 (Liverpool Record Office)

Christmas at the Amphitheatre

> In which cheap omnibuses, cheap tea, cheap malt, cheap postage, cheap newspapers and all the other popular topics of the day will be the subject of satire... (*Liverpool Mail*, 26 December 1846, 5)

In 1857 William Cooke brought the last equestrian company to perform for the Christmas season. The Amphitheatre then embarked on a new festive venture and, after a season of opera, from 1859 to 1873 pantomime finally arrived. By 1873 the theatre was advertising itself on its bills as 'The Drury Lane for Pantomime'. Pantomimes followed the traditions of the day, starting with an increasingly elaborate and increasingly lengthy opening after which, following a spectacular grand transformation scene, came a Harlequinade. The pantomime was always preceded by a drama, making it a very long evening; in 1869 the pantomime did not start until 10 o'clock and it was after midnight when the transformation scene began (*Daily Post*, 27 December 1869, 8). Occasional morning performances reversed the order so that children did not have to sit through the drama.

1859 *Davy Jones's Locker; or Harlequin and the Lucky Lass of Liverpool* by William Dorrington

> The Royal Amphitheatre is filled to excess every evening by delighted audiences ... The scenery in the opening story is full of beauties and the wonderful scene of the wreck is one of the most extraordinary and ingenious contrivances we have ever witnessed on any stage. The comic business that follows is full of 'hits' at the follies of the day, and the tricks are numerous and good. (*Daily Post*, 7 January 1860, 3)

1860 *Little Bo Peep; Or the Girl That Lost Her Sheep* by Mr Buckstone

> The story is an old one ... Bopeep was hardly ever wide awake, for her great fault was a propensity to fall asleep when she ought, like a good shepherdess, to have been looking after her flock. Some neighbouring wolves, having a taste for mutton, took advantage of her dozing, and carried off her sheep and cut off their tails. She had, however, that most desirable of relatives – a fairy godmother – and a lover named Colin ... the sheep were recovered and re-tailed. The scene is set in Arcadia, a rural spot closely resembling Hale. (*Daily Post*, 22 December 1860, 3)

Detail from 1848 map, Ordnance Survey Liverpool (Dale Street) 1848–64

1861 *The Old Woman Who Lived in a Shoe; or Harlequin Child of Childwall and the Choice Spirits of Dingle Dell* by William Crompton

> The scenery and 'sites' are all local. The first scene represents Nursey Lane, Walton, Walton Church and Spellow Mill (destroyed). The old lady in the shoe inhabits hereabouts … the scene changes to the toffee shop, Everton and is succeeded by a series of old views of Liverpool, after Mr W Herdman. A picture of Dingle Dell is followed by an antique court of justice at Cabbage Hall. (*Daily Post,* 24 December 1861, 8)

1862 *Harlequin and Tim Bobbin; or The Lancashire Witches*

> [T]here has not been so brilliant a transformation scene at this theatre in many previous year. It is designed and painted by Mr G. Dawson, and does the highest credit to his invention as a draughtsman, his ingenuity as a mechanician, and his fancy as a colourist. The scene is very intricate,

occupies the whole expanse of the stage, and develops itself gradually after the fashion prevalent in all the great transformation scenes of recent years. The arrangement of palm trees in the scene, as first disclosed, is charmingly graceful; and when the leaves unfold and the fairy denizens of the 'retreat' are disclosed, the ensemble is really a great triumph of scenic art. (*Daily Post*, 25 December 1862, 5)

1863 *Harlequin and the Child of Hale; or the King of the Red Nose and the Liver Queen* by J. R. Buckstone

> Once upon a time there was a King whose palace was beneath the rocks of the Red Noses, and which are still extant on ye Cheshire side of ye Mersey. He was called Kooky ye Great, King of ye Redde Noses and was enamoured of Prosperine, ye Liver Queen, whose domain ye town of Liverpool now standeth upon; and whose name of Prosperine foretold ye prosperity in after time of this now great and prosperous seaport. Ye Queen did reject this King's suit, whereas in his rage, he was replaced to have revenge. Ye Queen having promised Ye Dame of Hale to be godmother to her Little Sonne, in return for a kindness done to Ye Queen by Ye Dame. Kooky did contrive with help of demons to make Ye childe grow up a monster; within four and twenty hours after his birth, even to Ye height of nine feet three inches, and to Ye great discomfiture of Ye mother and Ye Queen; but Ye latter in order to frustrate Ye King's malice, did cause Ye childe to appear as a godlike man and became enamoured of the beauties of Speke Hall. Therefore instead of Ye uglie monster, Ye childe was made ye spite of Ye King. Ye power of love did cause him to be a fine and collie person as is now represented in his effigie at Ye Village of Hale. It is believed after many chances and changes, he was united with the Ladye of his Love and appeared at Court. (*Daily Post*, 31 December 1863, 1)

1864 *Jack the Giant Killer and Ye Knights of Ye Round Table*, a burlesque pantomime by H. J. Byron

> Mrs J: (*calls*) Jack! Thou'rt an idle varlet and a drowsy;
> 'Tis eight o'clock – come, Jacky darling, rouse ye!
> He's fast asleep – fast – rise for goodness sake!
> But that's no wonder, for he's fast awake.
> He smokes cigars, prefers pale ale to tea,
> Calls me 'old girl' and talks of a latch key.

Old-fashioned children, parents' prides and joys,
Are bygone quite – we've now no girls and boys –
The boys are youths – young men; and then the girls
Are nought but lumps of crinolines and curls.
When I was young – oh retrospect delightful!
I was, as all remarked, completely –
Jack: (*entering*) Frightful! (*Daily Post*, 24 December 1864, 4)

1865 *The Yellow Dwarf; or Harlequin King of the Golden Mines and the Beautiful Mermaid with the Golden Hair*, founded on the Olympic burlesque of J. R. Planché

The Cavern of Despair in the land of 'Oh We Never Mention It' including the first appearance on this or any other stage of the real original Pharaoh's Serpent of Old Nile
The Grand Fan and Flower Ballet
The Illuminated Garden of Delights
The Grand Reception of the Royal Suitors
The Desert Drear
The Cottage of the Yellow Dwarf
The Palace
The Steel Castle and enchanted dungeon of the Yellow Dwarf
Stalactite Cavern in the Mermaid's Haunt
Beneath the Deep, Deep Sea
The Desert Drear (with a difference)
Transformation scene: The Garden of Paradise, or the Peri's Home
The Harlequinade
A Final Scene, which is hoped may equal, though not excel, the
Transformation scene: The Opal Throne of the Amazonian Fairy Amidst the Golden Glories of Fingal's Cave. (*Liverpool Mail*, 30 December 1865, 4)

1866 Harlequin Blue Beard, the Bad Bashaw and his Beautiful Bride; or Selim Shacabac, Sister Ann and the Secret Chamber

The rhyming dialogue is very brilliant and full of good and bad jokes and local 'hits.' At the Royal, Mr Byron was evidently somewhat reticent of his humour and wit – a shade too genteel in fact – but on the congenial boards of the old 'Amphi' he has given the rein to his fondness for hearty fun. (*Liverpool Mercury*, 29 December 1866, 6)[1]

1867 *The Fool's Revenge*

With *Gulliver and the Lilliputians* at the Theatre Royal and *Robinson Crusoe* at the Alexandra, Byron decided to avoid a pantomime at the Amphitheatre.

1868 *Jack Sprat; or The Three Blind Mice*

> In a minute the vast scene changes into the 'Abode of Amusement' ... [and] we were told in a very novel manner how the hours, the weeks and the months of the year passed. For the hours, we had children very diminutive...; for the fifty-two weeks, we had almost as many children, larger in stature, and older in years; and for the months we had young ladies dressed too gorgeously to escape recognition ... When they had all been arranged on the stage, an admirable idea of converting the Abstract into the Objective had become a theatrical success. But this was not all. In danced Spring, typified by nine ballet ladies dressed in light and airy costumes. Next came Summer ... Then followed Autumn...; and lastly, dressed in blue came the fays whose task was to assume Winter... (*Daily Post*, 28 December 1868, 10)

1869 *Columbus; or Harlequin Bold Explorer, Yankee Doodle and the Bright Spirit of Adventure* by Mr C. Millward

> The sober history of America-discovering Christopher has of course been pooh-poohed, and the story of his adventures has been told in a manner in which most extravaganzical writers delight to indulge. The pantomime opens ... with a picture of what is called 'Shadow of Dreamland'. Here the discoverer's future career is pretty freely canvassed, first by Mischief and his attendant imps ... and then by the Spirit of Adventure and her attendant nymphs. War to the knife is declared, and the real business of the pantomime begins in good earnest. (*Liverpool Mercury*, 27 December 1869, 8)

1870 *Sinbad the Sailor. Or the Pet of the Peris, the Old Man and the Sea and the Dwarfs of the Diamond Valley*

> The antics of King Wangdoodle's retinue, the frolic love-making of that sable monarch himself, and the touching connubialities of his Queen, were all greeted with appreciative laughter, and the parody of the Christy Minstrel's called forth the customary demand for an *encore*. The clown's dogs and the velocipedes afforded fresh occasion for merriment that only ceased in order to be renewed. (*Liverpool Daily Post*, 17 January 1871, 5)

1871 ***Dick Whittington*** with a burlesque opening by Mr L. M. Morrison

The first scene is set in the crypt of the Guildhall where the mayor and his aldermen are discovered smoking, drinking and singing a most un-municipal chorus. Called to order by the mayor, he declares that their business is to spend money:

> Bouncer Just for a lark, I vote we have another Sefton Park.
> Stumpy And when we've got it, let it for a song;
> Then won't the papers pitch into us strong.
> Thumper I move for fun we fill up all the docks.
> Mayor 'Twould play the deuce with Mersey Dock Board Stocks;
> Remember too our annual Dock Board spree.
> Rowdy Which ain't the only time that we're at sea.
> Bouncer Can't we build something new or raze some old street?
> A happy thought. Suppose we pull down Bold-street.
> Thumper Let's raze the Bedpost Palace, then rebuild it.
> Bouncer Raise it twice over! Stuff. Suppose we gild it?
> Small Beer Suppose we purchase Compton House on spec? (*Daily Post*, 23 December 1871, 5)

1872 ***Harlequin, Prince Blue Cap; or The Enchanted Rose of the Coral Isle***

> At the Amphitheatre, the pantomime is Prince Bluecap, and in this … great pains appear to have been taken by the management to make it worthy of the past reputation of the theatre, while there are some novelties introduced which will render it specially attractive. (*Liverpool Mail*, 28 December 1872, 10)

1873 ***Twinkle, Twinkle; or Harlequin Hearty Tom Tucker and the Funny Old Woman Who Lived in the Shoe***

In a scene where the Queen Bee praises the industry of her followers, she tells the lazy drones:

> My tiny fairy masons now at hand
> Before your eyes shall build a structure grand;
> To raise a building here, I shall not wait,
> Nor tax one townsman with another rate.
> As they would tax who did the project start,
> To build a local gallery of art,
> That scheme once mooted, generous men were found
> Who promised to it each a thousand pounds
> But he who occupies the civic chair

Came first with generosity most rare,
And, giving twenty thousand, places his name
Imperishable on the scroll of fame.
He didn't draw it mild then, you'll allow
The name of Walker[2] should be honoured now.
Crouch there, and work; let silent wonder seize
Your souls the while you watch my busy bees
By magic art construct, to townsmen dear,
A thriving temple of the drama here.
(*Liverpool Mail*, 25 December 1873, 6)

From 1874 the theatre ceased performing pantomimes, turning instead to plays and opera, and the last Amphi Christmas season saw the Carl Rosa Opera Company, soon to make the theatre a more permanent home.

Notes

1 The Theatre Royal pantomime was *Dick Whittington and his Cat*.

2 Andrew Barclay Walker was a Liverpool brewer and alderman who offered to make a gift of a home for the city's art collection to mark his time as mayor. Not known as a patron of the arts, some thought his offer was made to give alcohol and brewing a better name at a time when the Temperance movement was popular.

A transformation more wonderful than any pantomime change

3 A New Theatre, 1881: Cosy, Commodious and Convenient

Shortly after midnight on 1 March 1881, as Lindo Courtenay left the building, the demolition of the Old Amphi began under the supervision of local architect Henry Sumners. By the opening of the new theatre on 11 September that year nothing remained of the original theatre apart from four walls. Its new name, the Royal Court, marked a real break with the past. *The Era* celebrated the change from the sombre character of the 'old Amphi', revelling in a 'transformation more wonderful than any pantomime change'.[1] *The Stage* was in more reflective mood, suggesting that no one with an interest in dramatic affairs

> could have entered the Royal Court Theatre ... without some slight feeling of regret. The thought that the old Amphi was numbered with the past must have brought to mind the once familiar dingy interior, with the largest stage and, perhaps, the best acoustics in the kingdom. Who does not remember the benches that constituted the seats in that wilderness of a pit ... the shabby-genteel dress-circle, and the stalls and private boxes, which with the help of

The new Royal Court, 1881, from *The Playgoer*, 1901 (Iain Wotherspoon/Matthew Lloyd)

anti-macassars and curtains at any rate tried to look worth the money paid for them?[2]

What now greeted the audience was a comfortable, attractive and cosy theatre where the gallery and dress circle had been brought closer to the stage but that could still seat 3,000. The comfort of the audience, from the pit to the 'celestials', had been a chief concern, and Sumners had ensured that there was 'not a single seat in it from which the spectator has not a most comprehensive view of the stage'. Even those loitering by the back wall behind the now-polished pine seats of the pit, thanks to the newly inclined floor, could see 'a great height up the back wall of the stage', and it was hoped that 'the rush usually made to obtain a good seat in the popular parts of the Theatre' would no longer be necessary.[3] Convenience and elegance were the watchwords for the public areas; for the circle, a foyer, cloakrooms and a refreshment

Detail from 1890 map, Ordnance Survey Central Liverpool 1890

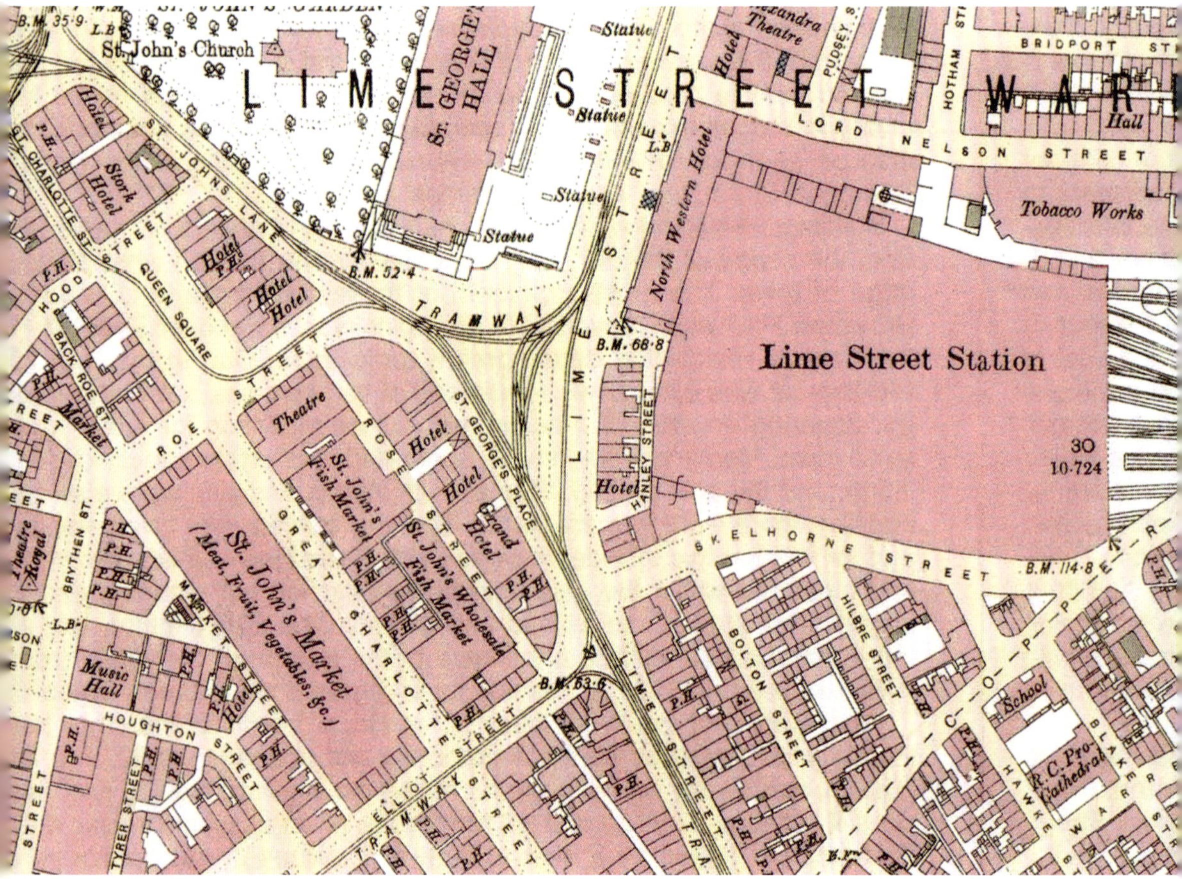

buffet were now on the same level, and all other areas of the theatre were provided with their own refreshment rooms. The cosiness of the theatre was added to by the crimson velvet curtain, and the act drop of Thespis reading to assembled villagers against a background of a sun setting in the mountains cocooned the audience in the warmth of a summer's evening. It was a theatre, remarked *The Era*, that would prove to be 'one of the most comfortable and convenient Theatres in the provinces'.[4]

On stage, the emphasis was on modernisation. Having removed 27 feet of rock from under the stage and raised the grid-iron to 72 feet above the stage, it was now possible for scenery to be changed in a few seconds. Newly installed gas lighting was deemed novel and 'bewildering' in the effects it could create. The exterior of the theatre had also undergone a metamorphosis. The Queen Square frontage, with entrances serving the boxes, dress circle and stalls (with the convenience of plenty of space for carriages) was decorated with five heads including Shakespeare and Handel. It was much admired for its simplicity. Entrances for the pit and gallery were found on Great Charlotte Street and the theatre accommodated seven shops at ground floor level, a valuable source of additional revenue.

The First Season

The Royal Court was David Radcliffe's first theatrical adventure in the city. He put the management in the hands of Duffield and Bainbridge, who were also running the Theatre Royal in Manchester, uniting 'Cottonopolis and the Metropolis of shipping' in a manner 'likely to be advantageous to the play-going public of both cities'.[5] They announced their intention to open with a six-week season of English opera, of which four would be new to the Liverpool audience. It seemed a strange decision in the light of Picton's argument that all attempts to naturalise opera in the city had uniformly been a failure, the Liverpool audience not 'being excited by any stimulus to respond to the great outlay which the opera necessarily involves'.[6] But it was not an arbitrary decision, since it allowed Duffield and Bainbridge to return to shows they had previously performed in Manchester. The opening night performance of R. T. Gunton's *The Lancashire Witches* had premiered at the Theatre Royal, where the composer, Frederick Stanislaus, was musical director. It was followed first by John Crook's opera *The King's Dragoons* and then by Alfred Cellier's *The Sultan of Mocha*. Both Crook and Cellier had also been musical directors in Manchester theatres. In contrast to the modernised staging capabilities of the new theatre, the chosen operas all had an old-fashioned aura. *The Lancashire Witches* did have some sense of local appeal, boasting scenery based on the actual places depicted in William Harrison Ainsworth's novel on which the opera was based. Set in 1612, at the time of the Lancashire witch trials, it involved King James disguising himself so he could witness what the witches were up to. The 'strong and simple plot' gave 'opportunity for plenty of traditional comedy' and much of the fun came from the indignities suffered by the disguised king, played with a thick Scottish accent, when he is mistakenly arrested by the witchfinder.[7] *The King's Dragoons* was set in 1702, and like *The Lancashire Witches,* included much rustic revelry and 'an old-fashioned story'.[8] John Barnett's *The Mountain Sylph,* performed with Cellier's work, offered an 'old fashioned romance' and the *Liverpool Mercury* suggested that people 'whose ears have become accustomed to the modern school of "thought" ... may assert that the vocal and instrumental numbers are somewhat out of date' but that they should not overlook the good quality of the opera.[9]

Having affirmed the new identity of the theatre with six old-fashioned operas, the new managers had a partial change of heart. Continuing with a conservative programme, opera was replaced with comedies and dramas, none of them new to the stage and none of them new to the city. These included Miss Wallis in *Ninon,* one of several popular dramas about the French Revolution, and a return of the T. W. Robertson and H. Bruce Company with the 'ever-acceptable' *Caste,* which 'drew the largest houses Mr Bainbridge has had since he opened his new theatre'.[10] T. W. Robertson's plays (performances that week also included *School* and *Ours*) had been touring the country since the late 1860s, sometimes with five or six different companies on the road at the same time. The week's performance at the Royal Court was announced as the last. The plays were being withdrawn for five years to prevent them 'lagging superfluous on the stage'.[11]

Managing the New Theatre: Carl Rosa

Duffield and Bainbridge continued to run the theatre in a similar vein with a penchant for popular plays (particularly melodramas) until March 1884 when the theatre's lease was sold to the Carl Rosa Opera Company. Established in 1875, the Carl Rosa Company was the leading provincial opera company. Their work was all sung in English and they looked for the development of 'a national lyric school', the resurgence of a native school of opera.[12] The company was committed to presenting opera to all classes of people, offering tickets at affordable prices, as Paul Rodmell notes of their 1875 London debut season, which was 'socially less exalted and aimed at a more middle class audience than those of the Italian companies'.[13] This was also reflected by their choice of playing six nights a week, instead of the traditional four. They were also distinctive in the opera world by operating an ensemble company rather than relying on star performers, and by their choice, in 1884, of a

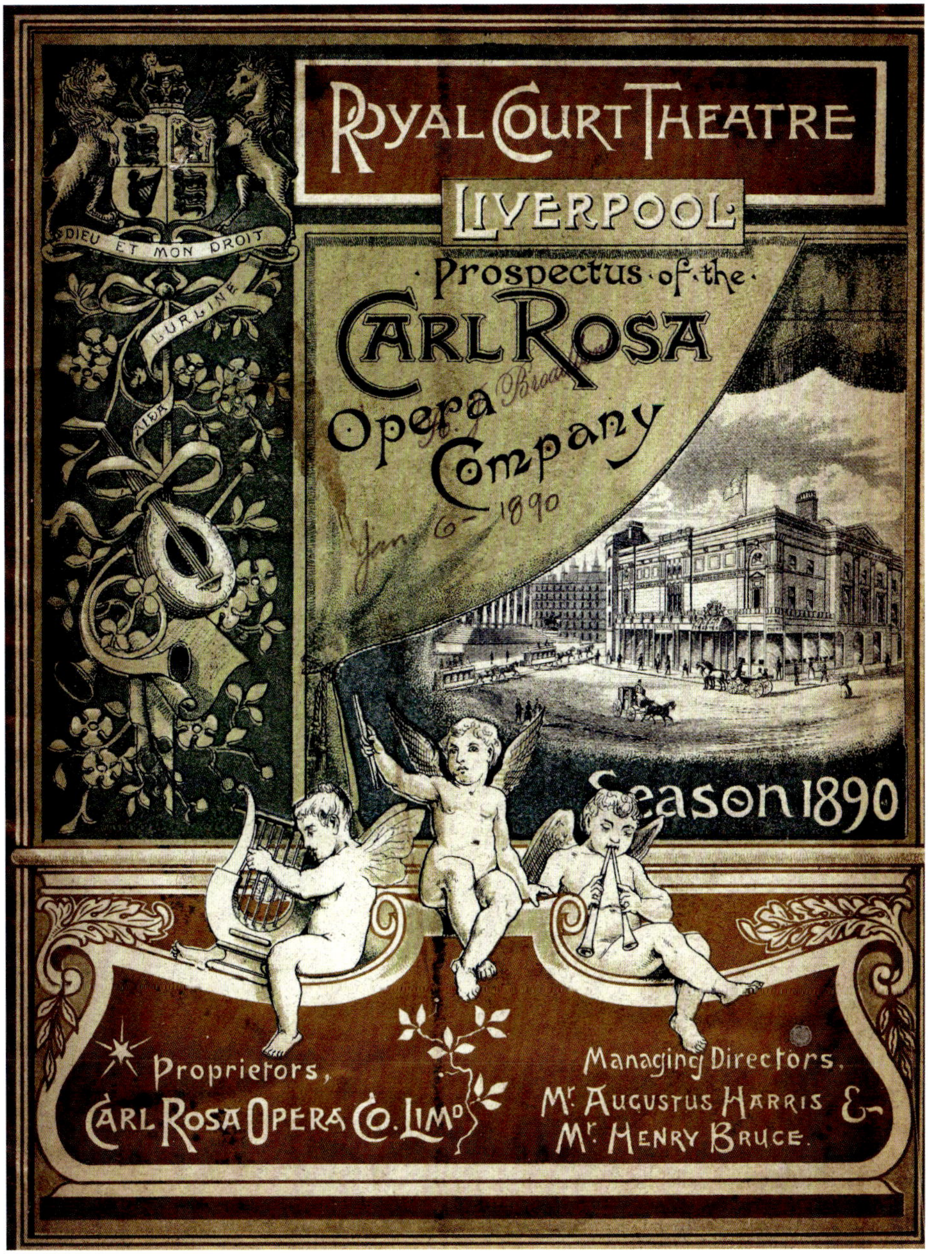

Carl Rosa prospectus for 1890 season

provincial base. Carl Rosa was not unfamiliar with the theatre, having toured to the old Amphi and returned to the new Royal Court for two January seasons in 1882 and 1884. For the company, it would provide a permanent base to prepare and perform new productions and, with its good railway connections, would allow for easy travel to other northern cities, while the port made Ireland readily accessible. It was, in the words of the local paper, to become a 'safe haven' where he felt 'he was appreciated at his full value'.[14] The company established a pattern of working which included a month's season in the city, starting with what was to become a traditional Christmas Day concert of sacred music, followed by a programme of touring the country including, where possible, a London season, as this 'was essential for Rosa's reputation as a producer of superior opera'.[15] At the Court, the rest of the year was given over, primarily, to melodrama, popular drama and a little other touring opera.

In keeping with all previous managers, Carl Rosa stamped his mark by redecorating. This time the theatre took on an exotic and elaborate character, the ceiling boasting an arabesque design with 'a centre sunlight which has a glow that spreads over the whole ceiling'. The walls were papered with Japanese embossed paper and the chosen colours, predominantly olive green with touches of turquoise, blue and crimson, were declared to be much deeper in tone than those usually associated with the theatre.[16] Rosa also tried to subtly alter the name of the theatre, and periodically it was advertised as the Royal Court Theatre and Opera House. In terms of work, Carl Rosa seasons offered the city a mixed repertoire of revivals and new work. There were well-known operas such as *Carmen*, *Lohengrin* and *Faust*. There were lesser-known European operas, seen as novelties, such as Millocker's *The Beggar Student*, performed for the first time in Liverpool in January 1885, and Boito's *Mefistofele*, the British premiere of which the company had given in Dublin in 1884. There was also new British work, some specially commissioned, including Goring Thomas's *Esmeralda* and *The Golden Web* and Charles Villiers Stanford's *The Canterbury Pilgrims*. A popular choice was the Irish composer Balfe's *The Bohemian Girl*. Rosa's tenure at the Royal Court saw a number of first nights including a world premiere in January 1887 of Corder's *Nordisa*, and the first UK performances in English of Meyerbeer's *The Star of the North*, Gounod's *Romeo and Juliet* and Mascagni's *Cavalleria Rusticana*. Most notable though was the British premiere of Massenet's *Manon* in January 1885, just a year after its opening in Paris, which attracted national attention. In a short time Carl Rosa had not only led a campaign to create a national opera and taken opera out of the capital, but had also gone a long way to proving wrong Picton's assertion about opera being a failure in the city. As the *Liverpool Mercury* noted, his purchase of the Court 'proved an important turning point in the artistic history of our city'.[17] A sense of his popularity both nationally and locally came with his sudden death in 1889, which the *Liverpool Mercury* described as removing 'the head and front of the English operatic enterprise'.[18]

Carl Rosa's death was, however, far from being the end of the company's tenure at the Royal Court. The company was taken on for a number of years by Augustus Harris, who had become a shareholder when the company became a limited liability company in 1887. Their repertoire increasingly focused on grand opera, including the formation of a special Carl Rosa *Carmen* company to meet demand for the popularity of this work. This was joined by a third company, the Marjorie Company, which specialised in the performance of light opera. First performances almost dried up and throughout the 1890s finances were increasingly uncertain. This may have been what prompted the company to take its leave of the theatre in 1896. A year later, following heavy losses at a Covent Garden season, the shareholders voted to liquidate the company. This was not the end of the Carl Rosa Company, however, which survived until 1960. Its years at the Court left a lasting connection with Liverpool and it continued to give regular performances until its demise.

Managing the New Theatre: Robert Arthur

The lease and management were now taken over by Robert Arthur. He was one of a new breed of theatre managers who owned or leased more than one theatre. While not on the same scale as some of the larger companies when he took on the Royal Court, Arthur already ran the Theatre Royal in Newcastle, the Theatre Royal in Nottingham, Her Majesty's in Aberdeen and Her Majesty's in Dundee. In keeping with previous managers, Arthur wanted to mark the theatre's new chapter by redecorating. Still being seen as 'the premier theatre in the second city' as well as 'second to none in internal beauty and comfort either in London or the provinces', he looked to enhance its status. He focused on improving the interior, and *The Era* was full of admiration for the 'fairy-like aspect' of the new interior with its colour scheme of creamy white and crimson complete with a new front to the dress circle with cupids and festoons of flowers. In the public spaces, plaster in heavy relief was accompanied by a deep frieze of panels designed for the Imperial Institute. The walls were hung with embossed leather, and palm trees were 'dispersed everywhere'. Floors were covered in crimson Axminster carpets, adding a sense of luxury and richness. In the pit, the seats were upholstered, space was added between the rows and the floor was covered in a cork carpet so that all movements became 'perfectly noiseless'. The most significant alteration was the addition of electric light, *The Era* noting the replacement of 'the old sun-burner' by 'an enormous brass electrolier which in itself would have been sufficient to light the house'.[19] On his first night,

Images of the Royal Court theatre from the *Arthurian Annual* of 1904 (Shirley Cowdrill/Matthew Lloyd)

despite opening with an old-fashioned play in the shape of Charles Reade and Tom Taylor's *Masks and Faces* (first performed in 1852), the out-going manager, Henry Bruce, who had run the theatre for much of the Carl Rosa tenure, welcomed Robert Arthur as 'one of those up-to-date managers'. There may have been some hope that the Royal Court would enter the twentieth century with a more forward-looking outlook.

Unfortunately for Arthur, on the night of 8 January 1897 a fire broke out, starting in a rubbish bin in the gallery. There had been a small fire in 1882 which, although 'alarming at first', had proved not to be too serious, destroying some scenery and a valuable tapestry carpet but doing little damage to the fabric of the building.[20] The fire of 1897 was a different matter and, with strong winds blowing, it looked for some time as though the whole building was doomed and crowds gathered to watch. In the event, part of the roof was burned out and the gallery destroyed. Much of the rest of the building and some adjoining businesses suffered water damage and four hundred costumes were destroyed along with 'The Fairy Bower' scene, 'one of the most magnificent in the pantomime'.[21] The fact that the fire had happened during the pantomime season, the most profitable time of year, made it potentially even

Arthur Lawrence became the theatre manager in 1898 and is credited with popularising the theatre as a home for pantomime. (Shirley Cowdrill/Matthew Lloyd)

more disastrous. With extraordinary speed the theatre was patched up, the costumes remade (many by Bon Marché, one of Liverpool's stylish department stores), the scenery rebuilt and the theatre was open again for business on 14 January, just six days after the fire. The speed of the reopening alarmed some people, and Robert Arthur was forced to write to the local paper to quell rumours that the theatre was

Programme from 1910

Roe Street, 1921 (Liverpool Record Office)

still damp and might prove a health hazard to the audience, assuring everyone that it was perfectly dry and that some thirty stoves had been kept burning day and night for two weeks.[22] During the scheduled summer break, repairs to the theatre were finished; the temporary roof was replaced with an iron one and the new ceiling allowed for the acoustics to be perfected. At the same time, Arthur took the opportunity to upgrade the heating and ventilation and to excavate more rock beneath the theatre, adding a carpenter's shop, a band room and an extra green room. The theatre was redecorated (again) in the style of Louis XV, leaving 'a sense of refinement and repose', and the whole was finished with the Royal Arms above the proscenium, marking both the name of the theatre but also the fact that the restoration had taken place in the year of the Queen's Diamond Jubilee.[23] Despite a plasterers' strike, the whole was completed within six weeks.

At the same time, Arthur was rearranging his business affairs, launching himself as Robert Arthur Theatres Ltd. In the prospectus for the new company, he listed a scenery warehouse as part of his Liverpool property held on a 75-year lease from the council at a 'peppercorn' ground rent. He was estimating a profit in excess of £2,416 a year – suggesting a figure more like £4,000. However, Arthur's business did not go smoothly and his estimates of profits were somewhat optimistic. He made what Paul Iles suggests was a significant error by trying to move into London. After taking short leases on the Prince of Wales and Princess's Theatre in the West End, he then decided, in 1898, to build his own theatre, the Princess of Wales, in Kennington, completing what was known as the 'Arthurian Round Table' of six theatres. The idea was to provide suitable shows for all the theatres from the London base and to rotate the pantomimes around his circuit. A year later another fire broke out, this time at the Theatre Royal Newcastle. Arthur was not insured and was responsible for £20,000 worth of damage that was sustained.[24] To add to his outgoings, he took on the lease of Liverpool's Shakespeare Theatre in 1902. While he managed to continue, his profits over the next few years were very depleted and the last payout to shareholders was in 1907–08.

In an attempt to keep going, in 1912 Robert Arthur entered into an agreement with Howard and Wyndham, a management organisation with five theatres based in Scotland with whom he already had links. Initially, this covered the booking and management of his Newcastle venture, but in 1913 his entire company was taken over and Arthur was forced to resign from the board. One pressing motive for the merger may well have come from the fact that he found himself facing bankruptcy in January of that year, with liabilities of over £46,000 against assets of £935. For the time being Howard and Wyndham and Robert Arthur Theatres Ltd were run as two separate but connected organisations. Each maintained their own profits and responsibility for their losses, but Howard and Wyndham provided part of the working capital. The day-to-day management was taken over by Howard and Wyndham, with Fred Wyndham as managing director. So, although the Royal Court was managed in name by Robert Arthur Theatres Ltd until 1941, when Howard and Wyndham finally dissolved that company, in reality those in charge were from a much bigger, much more competitive corporation which now ran ten theatres.[25]

Notes

1 *The Era*, 17 September 1881, 7.
2 *The Stage*, 16 September 1881, 10.
3 *The Era*, 10 September 1881, 7.
4 Ibid., 7.
5 *The Era*, 9 April 1881, 8.
6 Picton, *Memorials of Liverpool. Volume II*, 251.
7 Kurt Ganzl, *The British Musical Theatre: Volume 1. 1865–1914* (Basingstoke: Macmillan, 1986), 148.
8 Ibid., 165.
9 *Liverpool Mercury*, 22 October 1881, 5.
10 *Liverpool Mercury*, 22 November 1881, 6; *The Stage*, 2 December 1881, 11–12.
11 *The Stage*, 2 December 1881, 11–12.
12 *Liverpool Mercury*, 19 January 1885, 5.
13 Paul Rodmell, *Opera in the British Isles 1875–1918* (Farnham: Ashgate, 2013), 32.
14 *Liverpool Mercury*, 1 May 1889, 7.
15 Rodmell, *Opera in the British Isles*, 33.
16 *Liverpool Mercury*, 30 July 1884, 5.
17 *Liverpool Mercury*, 1 May 1889, 5.
18 *Liverpool Mercury*, 6 May 1889, 7.
19 *The Era*, 8 August 1896, 12.
20 *The Stage*, 23 June 1882, 11.
21 *Liverpool Mercury*, 12 January 1897, 6.
22 *Liverpool Mercury*, 28 January 1897, 6.
23 *Liverpool Mercury*, 1897, 8.
24 Iles, 'Issues in Theatrical Management', 50–1.
25 *The Era*, 15 March 1913, 13.

1881

10 September	*The Lancashire Witches or King James's Frolics*	music by F. Stanislaus and R. T. Gurton	light opera
25 September	*The King's Dragoons*	J. Wilton Jones; music by John Crook	opera
8 October	*The Sultan of Mocha*	Alfred Cellier	popular comic opera.
24 October	*Faust and Marguerite*	with music from Mendelssohn and Gounod	romantic drama
7 November	*The Corsican Brothers*	Dion Boucicault	Mr Hermann Vezin
21 November	*Caste*	T. W. Robertson	T. W. Robertson and Bruce Company
	School	T. W. Robertson	
	Ours	T. W. Robertson	
28 November	*The Guv'nor*	E. G. Lancaster	T. W. Robertson and Bruce Company
5 December	*Proof*	F. C. Burnaud	
12 December	*Ninon*	W. C. Wills	Miss Wallis and specially organised company
	The Lady of Lyons	Bulwer Lytton	
	Cymbeline	Shakespeare	
24 December	*Babes in the Wood*	John F. McArdle; music by John Crook	George Capel as King Juculose and Alice Cook as Prince Choquot, his only son.

The 1881 opening night performance of Stanislaus and Gurton's light opera *The Lancashire Witches or King James's Frolics* (*Illustrated London News*)

Christmas, 1881–1913

1881 *Babes in the Wood* by J. F. McArdle

The return of the pantomime was heralded as a return to the days of old when,

> [a]mong the many theatres in the provinces where pantomime is produced with exceptional beauty and completeness, the Liverpool Amphitheatre was for a long period notably the foremost and old playgoers look back upon the Amphi pantomimes with pleasure. Mr R.B. Bainbridge ... has wisely adopted these lines; and everything that taste, a lavish expenditure, experience, and skilful management can effect has been put forth in this year's pantomime. (*Liverpool Mercury*, 26 December 1881, 7)

Having started out with a pantomime, the Royal Court then abandoned the traditional Christmas entertainment for over ten years.

1882 Carl Rosa Opera Company

> This year there will be no pantomime produced at the Court Theatre but a series of most interesting performances will be given by the Carl Rosa Opera Company ... On Christmas Day, the company will give a grand sacred concert; on Tuesday *The Bohemian Girl* will be given, and in the evening *Maritana*. (*Liverpool Mercury*, 23 December 1882)

1883 Barry Sullivan Tour including ***Richard III*** and ***Hamlet***

> It had been extensively announced that Mr Barry Sullivan would, on Christmas Eve, begin an engagement at the Royal Court Theatre, and that building was occupied last night by a large audience who had assembled to witness this popular tragedian's performance of a part with which his name is particularly identified, viz., *Richard III*. Half-past seven was the hour fixed for the rising of the curtain, but eight o'clock came without any sign being shown of a fulfilment of the promise of the programme. Naturally the audience became impatient, and there were loud demands for an explanation of the delay. At this juncture, the acting manager of the theatre (Mr. John Atkinson) came before the curtain and said, 'I regret to announce there will be no performance to-night. Any person wishing to have his or her money back can get it on applying at the box-office; or seats will be given for Boxing Night when Mr Sullivan will appear as *Richard III*.' ... the audience became demonstrative in their impatience ... Angry things were said in the

auditorium, but, happily, the theatre was cleared of its occupants without serious disturbance. Several reasons for the disappointment caused by Mr Sullivan's non-appearance were afterwards mentioned. We were, however, given to understand that Mr Sullivan declined to play on the ground that scenic and other accessories provided for *Richard III* were not of the extent and quality which he deemed requisite on such an occasion. (*Liverpool Mercury*, 25 December 1883, 6)

1884 Carl Rosa Opera Company

1885 D'Oyly Carte Opera Company, ***The Mikado***

1886 Carl Rosa Opera Company

The thickest and blackest fog which has enveloped Liverpool, continuing from early morning until late at night, greatly affected the attendance at the Royal Court Theatre last night, when Lecoq's *Peptia* was performed for the first time in England. Notwithstanding the untoward atmospheric drawback however, there was considerable enthusiasm on the part of those who braved the streets to assist at the initial representation here of a work which adds considerably to the reputation of a composer and librettist ... although the lines were occasionally a little Frenchy and suggestive, the reception accorded to the work was of the heartiest kind. (*The Era*, 1 January 1887, 14)

1887 ***Held by the Enemy*** by William Gillette

While conceding the necessity of pantomime to the circle of Christmas entertainments, there is something agreeable in the knowledge that the stage of at least one theatre in the city is occupied by drama. (*Liverpool Mercury*, 27 December 1887, 6)

1888–91 Carl Rosa Opera Company

1892 ***The Shaughraun*** by Dion Boucicault with J. Pitt-Hardacre's company

Mirth that ends in moping melancholy
Is found in Pantomime – that Pinchbeck King.
Its wit is worthless, and its fun but folly.
Real laughter hath a true and sterling ring.
One week at least let's shun King Holly
For humour true – Shaughraun's the thing
To make folk jolly (*Liverpool Mercury*, 21 December 1892, 1)

1893 *The Shaughraun* by Dion Boucicault

1894 *East Lynne*

1895 *Dick Whittington* by Sir Augustus Harris with Cecil Raleigh and Henry Hamilton

The excitement at the return of pantomime, enabled by the shortening of the Carl Rosa season to four weeks, produced a long and enthusiastic response in the local papers which emphasised the lavishness and scale of the production, with a cast of over 240 – no surprise when the pantomime had come from the stage of Drury Lane. In Dick's dream scene

> he sees a vision ... Fairy after fairy, clad in gossamer-like folds, appears and when all the aerial group is present, graceful evolutions make the exquisite colours of the costumes and the flowers which the airy dancers carry harmonise and flash and flash again. Then several of the fairies soar above their fellows, their hands meanwhile waving flowing streamers of roses. One ascends higher than the rest, and they cluster beneath her as with magic toe, she poises herself upon a posy of flowers. (*Liverpool Mercury*, 27 December 1895, 5)

1896 *Cinderella* by Fred Locke

> *Cinderella* ... will be staged before Christmas [and] promises to afford genuine delight to old and young alike as Mr Robert Arthur, the popular lessee, has evidently spared no pains in connection with his first pantomime to maintain and even exceed the prestige attaching to last year's annual... (*Liverpool Mercury*, 10 December 1896, 8)

> The transformation scene ... is entitled 'The World of Fleeting Fancies' ... Also the harlequinade is a part of the Christmas annual by which the children lay great store and it will be found that the 'Exterior of a Museum' and 'The Sands and Pier at Blackpool' serve as excellent backgrounds while the members of the Levi troupe amuse those who fill the theatre. (*Liverpool Mercury*, 24 December 1896, 6)

1897 *Robinson Crusoe* by Wilton Jones with J. Levey

> The Sisters Levey – a trio of exceptional prowess in both singing and dancing – are hosts in themselves, their rollicking songs entitled 'We Represent the Leaders of the Jolly Tar Brigades' and 'The Soldiers of the Queen' evoking

The Levey Sisters (Adele, May Lillian and Carlotta), here shown dressed for their ostrich dance, appeared as the three daughters of Captain Mainbrace in the 1897 production of *Robinson Crusoe*. (*The Sketch*, 22 August 1894)

> storms of applause. As Captain Mainbrace – the diminutive father of the three stately daughters Henrietta, Arethusa and Majestic, represented by the Leveys – Mr H. H. Douglass displays an irresistible fund of humour, his eccentric entries and exits to the tune of 'I left the girl behind me' always being the signal for a burst of merriment... (*Liverpool Mercury*, 28 December 1897, 5)

1898 *Aladdin* by Walter Summers[1]

> Mr Arthur was first in the Liverpool field with his third annual pantomime ... Following the general practice, the chief of the establishment again takes a familiar and well-worn 'text' for his pantomime 'sermon.' Thanks, however to the ingenuity of the author, the art of the scenic artist, the picturesqueness of the stage groupings, and the unstinted liberality of the leading director,

> *Aladdin and His Lamp* as the annual is styled, comes with a freshness and attractiveness ... described as an 'operatic pantomime' ... With ample scope for comical business, Little Tich, whose make-up was a wonderful study, fairly revels in the broad fun of Wishee-Washee, intensely Chinee-Chinee, of the true George Thornish type of characterisation. All his business is intensely funny, his quips, cranks and petit foibles causing much merriment. (*The Era*, 24 December 1898, 20)

1899 *Babes in the Wood* by Walter Summers

Walter Summers was seen as '[a]n author of no little experience in the moulding of an up-to-date extravaganza on a fabric of a time-honoured fairy tale'.

> The opening scene is called 'The Swamp,' a locale of sufficient indefiniteness [serving] to introduce the forces of good and evil, inseparable from any well-regulated pantomime. As Good has it all her own way at the finish, it is only fair, perhaps, that Evil should begin well; so, to the 'Witch' are the first honours of speech, loudly accompanied by 'thunder, lightning and rain' not forgetting tempestuous wind. Surrounded by toads, frogs, adders, and other gruesome crawling creatures, she shrieks her accord with 'elemental strife', vows vengeance on humanity, and finally invokes the Oracle, which is in the form of an over-grown Owl, with blinking red eyes. Elfinella – the good sprite – is evolved from a flame, and Vice and Virtue commence their combat. (*Liverpool Mercury*, 22 December 1899, 8)

1900 *The Forty Thieves* by Walter Summers

> [T]he annual affords fresh evidence of unstinted liberality and enterprise associated with superior taste and keen discernment of popular requirements ... Little Tich comes first on the list of competents, his Abdallah, chief of the robber gang, being quaint, comical and original in every aspect, his dancing once more mirth-provoking, and his singing marked by the humour which he knows so well how to employ to the best advantage. (*The Era*, 29 December 1900, 22)

1901 *Oberine, or the Nymph of the Adriatic* by Walter Summers

In 1896 the *Liverpool Mercury* complained about the limited pantomime plots, bemoaning the fact that 'year after year one is called upon to notice representations of the same old historical nursery legends'. It would take a bold manager, it thought, to 'step outside this magic limit' (*Liverpool Mercury*, 23 December 1896, 5). This year

Little Tich in the 1900 *Aladdin* from the first edition of the *Liverpool Pantomime Annual*, a short-lived publication produced by Will A. Bradley (Liverpool Record Office)

Robert Arthur obliged and

> [p]roduced a fairy extravaganza, 'fresh from the mint', prominently spectacular and somewhat classic in style ... The first scene is laid in a peaceful island named Contesime, 'not marked down in the chart' which is governed by the Duke of Ciquanta. In the gardens of the palace stand a statue to which is attached a legend. Centuries before, a youth beloved by a sorceress was turned into stone by her out of revenge for his refusal to give her his love, and the reigning monarch of the time gave the inhabitants of the island strict injunctions that the ossified prince should be carefully watched night and day to prevent his being stolen. (*The Era*, 28 December 1901, 14)

The stand-out performer was Stella Gastelle:

> Quite an ovation, repeated again and again during the evening, was given to Miss Stella Gastelle ... Her reputation ... was most materially advanced on this occasion by the irresistible charm of her acting as well as by the supreme excellency of her vocalisation in her delineation of Oberine. The delightful earnestness of the clever artiste impressed the whole of the audience, and in one instance triple encore was insisted upon of one of the numerous charming songs which come within the scope of the part. (*The Era*, 28 December 1901, 14)

Stella Gastelle as Oberine (1901)

1902 *Santa Claus Jr* by Walter Summers

Buoyed by his success with the unfamiliar, 1902 saw Robert Arthur present another new 'fairy fancy', clearly showing

> his masterly development of a new line of Christmas entertainment ... He ignores in fullest measure the old-time fun and frolic of the comical clown, the often silly patter of the pantaloons, the somewhat wearisome posturing and gyrations of columbine and harlequin, not to mention the always conflicting personages of the demon king and fairy queen ... and he gives, instead, as seasonable and attractive entertainment ... which, in picturesqueness and brilliancy have never been equalled at the 'Court'. (*The Era*, 27 December 1902, 8)

1903 *The Scarlet Goblin; or The Legend of the Golden Key* by Frank Dix

> [O]n the shore, headed by the Red Goblin, are gathered a motley crew of smugglers, wreckers, storm fiends ... fiercely gloating over the rapid wrecking and fast approaching foundering of a distressed vessel in the offing, while the thunders roll and the lightenings flash. In the midst of their devilish glee there enters the Earl of Chatswood, who is distraught in view of the loss of his vessel, as he has an only child on board, who he lovingly dotes on. His princely offer to the gleeful wreckers and smugglers if they will only try to save his daughter are laughed to scorn and after telling the story of the golden key which is hung around the child's neck, which can only open a treasure chest which has been washed ashore, the heart-broken father vows that he will retire from the life of the world, become a recluse, and thus remain till the end of his days, unless his child be saved and returned to him. (*The Era*, 26 December 1902, 10)

1904 *Dick Whittington* by Frank Dix

> To the accompaniment of sprightly music the rise of the curtain discloses the belfry of Bow Church, with a party of smocked-men ringing the bells and singing a swinging chorus. Here the Demon Rat announces his intention of injuring Alice, daughter of Alderman Fitzwarren, a universal provider and a director of the Anti-rat Crusade but, as is customary, the Spirit and Fairies of the Chimes appear in time to intervene ... Hetty King as Dick Whittington found favour with her audience. Vivacious and sprightly, she quite suited her part, her sand-dancing earning for her an encore, and her singing of 'When a fellow is twenty-one' and 'Bluebell' being warmly applauded. (*The Era*, 31 December 1904, 8)

Hetty King as Dick Whittington (1904)

1905 *The Queen of Hearts* by Frank Dix

> [I]t would be difficult to imagine a more charming production than that presented under the uncommon title of *The Queen of Hearts* ... The story, which is set forth in two acts ... opens in the city of Kardallah, where, fronting the King's Palace, are assembled peasants, guards &c., to celebrate the natal day of Prince Florinzel, and, to present to his Majesty an illuminated scroll on his marriage to his cook. Estrella, the adopted daughter of the witch Armida. (*The Era*, 30 December 1905, 24)

1906 *Aladdin*

> Fun predominates throughout the whole of the pantomime. Mr Malcolm Scott as the Widow Twankey found many opportunities for exhibiting his humour and his patter and his assumption of the Gibson Girl à la Miss

Fanny Fields as Gretchen and M. A. Morand as Widow Twankey in *Aladdin* (1906)

A scene from *Aladdin* (1906) (Alun Pugh/Matthew Lloyd)

Clifford proved a capital caricature. His song relative to a coon tune raised many a broad smile ... Happy Fanny Fields, as Gretchen, a Dutch laundry maid, was highly amusing, her special style of dancing gaining her much favour; Miss Hetty King threw a deal of spirit into the part of Aladdin, and among her songs were 'It's a different girl again', 'I want to be a Gibson Girl' and 'Back to Piccadilly' ... For the first time in Liverpool, the cinematograph ... was made use of in pantomime, and with excellent effect. On Abanazar and Aladdin escaping from the wrath of the Emperor by means of the motor car, the theatre was suddenly plunged into darkness, and on a front cloth was shown a continuation of the fugitives' flight. Uphill and down dale raced the car, careering over mountains and peaks, reaching to the moon with the utmost ease, leaping from crag to crag, and even turning somersaults, until when the lights go up again the motorists are discovered sprawling on the ground of a Chinese laundry. (*The Era*, 29 December 1906, 10)

1907 *Cinderella* by Frank Dix

The Baron, having received an intimation that the Prince is coming to breakfast, starts out to catch a fish, and here a funny scene is witnessed. His first attempt brings up a scotch cap and his second results in Wee Rab (Harry Lauder), the son of the gamekeeper appearing through the bulrushes entangled in the line. The Baron explains his non-success at fishing, whereupon Rab, procuring a branch from a tree, attaches a string and a large hook to it ... His initial essay brings a large salmon, which he 'makes lie down' by vigorously banging its head upon the ground; a moment later, an enormous flying fish shows itself on his string, quickly followed by three great salmon at one try. The Baron is delighted, and immediately engages him as his body-servant, at the same time giving him a handbell which he instructs him to ring whenever he finds anyone telling a lie. The many occasions upon which Lauder had to sound the instrument when the Baron is boasting of his fishing exploits provoked much merriment ... Mr Lauder came in for a great reception, and at one period, after rendering a Scotch wedding song, the action of the pantomime was interrupted for several minutes owing to the demand for an encore. (*The Era*, 28 December 1908, 10)

1908 *Humpty Dumpty* by Frank Dix

Each succeeding year Mr Arthur principally aims at spectacular effect, and his latest production certainly lacks naught in this respect ... the curtain rises upon a nursery situated locally, where we find a mother endeavouring to explain to her questioning boy the story of Humpty Dumpty's downfall. The lad drops asleep over his book, when the Queen of Humpty Land appeared from the fireplace, and transports him, along with his two Gollywogs, who have become animated, to the realms of Fairydom ... Miss Lily Morris made a handsome and dashing Humpty ... her song 'A tiny seed of love' was joined in by her hearers, who demanded encores... (*The Era*, 2 January 1909, 14)

1909 *Red Riding Hood* by Frank Dix

The book is remarkable for two features – first, that it contains a deal of the spirit nursery ... and, secondly, the up-to-date allusions, political and otherwise, are such as to be appreciated by the grown-up members of the audience ... Briefly, the story is that the Squire of Dingle ... desires to gain the lands and fortune of Red Riding Hood, who is in charge of Mother Hubbard at Liverpool, 'a peaceful village close to Warrington,' and in order to do so makes a compact with the King of the Wolves to destroy her ... Of course, a Budget song, concerning taxes must be introduced. (*The Era*, 1 January 1910, 13)

1910 *Ali Baba; Or The Forty Thieves*

Mark Sheridan (Ali Baba) is, of course, the mainstay of the whole pantomime ... There is not a dull moment while the lively comedian is on the stage, his quips and funniosities being rattled off with a speed and point that keep the audience in continuous laughter. The well-known hat, with the equally well-known tilt, is there, accompanied by the ever-moving switch in hand. Of course, Mark Sheridan's costume would be incomplete without the ludicrous wide-spreading attachment to his nether-garments. It is likewise present. (*The Era*, 31 December 1910, 12)

1911 *Puss in Boots* by James J. Hewson

Puss in Boots is making records for Mr Arthur in Liverpool. From the opening night the pantomime has run with great smoothness. The theatre is crowded at each performance despite the vagaries of the weather ... There are at the moment from twelve to fifteen pantomimes in the neighbourhood and all are flourishing. (*The Stage*, 11 January 1912, 21)

Dorothy Ward, who was a popular Tommy Tucker (1912)

Topsey Sinden was much praised for her dancing as Princess Priscilla in *Tommy Tucker* (1912)

1912 *Tommy Tucker*

> Undoubtedly *Tommy Tucker* is out for a run. He has now settled down to a steady pace, and his course is a clear one ... Miss Dorothy Ward, the principal boy, has a voice rich and tuneful, and she is making many of the refrains of her songs exceedingly popular. Miss Topsy Sinden is a dancer in whose praise little needs to be said. Her art in incomparable, and she is backed up with ripe experience and a name as a dancer which she long since earned. (*Liverpool Echo*, 21 January 1913, 7)

> Miss Ward closed her career as Tommy Tucker at Liverpool Court in a blaze of glory. Her benefit night broke all records for the house, and it took 28 of the London chorus ladies to carry on at the close the collection of bouquets which had been presented to Miss Dorothy. There were huge floral tokens of goodwill from the chorus ladies themselves, the chorus gentlemen, the theatre staff and stage hands, one from the Lord Mayor and Lady Mayoress of Liverpool and another from a Merseyside admirer who sent specially to London for a bouquet of 10,000 Parma violets, Miss Ward's favourite flower. (*Preston Herald*, 22 March 1913, 7)

1913 *The House That Jack Built* by J. Hickory Wood and James J. Hewson

> The curtain went up on Wednesday evening last, and until it descended, long after eleven o'clock, a large audience who will certainly tell their friends enjoyed a glorious time ... The opening scene showing the exterior of Durden's farm, commands the full extent of the vast Royal Court stage ... while in the concluding scene, entitled the Wedgewood Palace, the dialogue was stopped while the painter came upon the stage in response to the general plaudits ... It may be mentioned that among the many attractive processions that representing vegetables was particularly effective. (*The Era*, 31 December 1913, 25)

Notes

1 Walter Summers also provided the libretto for three other Robert Arthur pantomimes that year; *Dick Whittington* for Newcastle, *Little Red Riding Hood* for Nottingham and *Cinderella* for Kennington. As well as writing pantomimes, Summers was a principal comedian with the D'Oyly Carte Opera Company between 1894 and 1897. His last pantomime was Fred Karno's *Cinderella* at the Alexandra Theatre, Stoke Newington, before his death in 1905 at the age of 38.

1895

4 March	*Dorcas*	Harry and E. A. Paulton	musical comedy
11 March	*Arms and the Man*	George Bernard Shaw	from the Avenue Theatre
18 March	*A New Woman*	Sydney Grundy	J. Comyns Carr's company
25 March	*Dick Sheridan*	Robert Buchanan	J. Comyns Carr's company
	Topsyturveydom	Roy Byford	premiere of farcical comedy
1 April	*Dorothy*	B. C. Stephenson; music by Alfred Cellier	comic opera
8 April	*The New Boy*	Ralph R. Lumley	comedy drama
15 April	*Charley's Aunt*	Brandon Thomas	with Stanley Cooke
22 April	*The Gaiety Girl*	Owen Hall; music by Sidney Jones	George Edwardes Gaiety Company in a musical comedy
29 April	*Qwong Hi*	F. Mackay	farcical comedy with Willie Edouin
6 May	*His Excellency*	W. S. Gilbert and F. Osmond Carr	comic opera
13 May	*A Bunch of Violets*	Sydney Grundy	Herbert Beerbohm Tree's principal company
20 May	*The Chieftan*	F. C. Burnard; music by A. Sullivan	comic opera
27 May	*Mirette*	Michel Carre and Messager	opera
3 June	*Don Juan*	J. T. Tanner	burlesque
10 June	Gilbert and Sullivan	D'Oyly Carte	
17 June	*Buttercup and Daisy*	George Dance	William Greet's company in a musical comedy

Frank Benson as Petruchio in *The Taming of the Shrew*, a role he performed at the Royal Court in December 1895 in a week of Shakespeare performances that also included *Romeo and Juliet*, *The Merchant of Venice* and *Macbeth*

24 June–3 August	closed		
5 August	*Proof*	F. C. Burnand	with Louis Calvert
12 August	*The Passport*	B. C. Stephenson	comedy
19 August	*The Circus Boy*	George R. Sims; music by Ivan Caryll	burlesque opera with the full Avenue Theatre company with over fifty performers.
26 August	*The Shop Girl*	H. J. W. Dam; music by Ivan Caryll	George Edwardes Gaiety Company in a musical comedy
2 September	*The Prodigal Daughter*	Henry Pettit and Sir Augustus Harris	sporting drama with six blood horses including the Grand National winner, Voluptuary
9 September	*Charley's Aunt*	Brandon Thomas	with Stanley Cooke
16 September	*The Fatal Card*	G. Haddon Chambers and B. C. Stephenson	drama with Fred G. Latham's company
23 September	*The Prude's Progress*	J. K. Jerome and Eden Philpotts	H. H. Morrell's company
30 September	*Trilby*	Paul M. Potter	Beerbohm Tree and Dorothea Baird
	Hamlet	Shakespeare	
7 October	*The Ironmaster*	Pinero from a French play	Mr and Mrs Kendal
	The Queen's Shilling	G. W. Godfrey	comedy
	All for Her	Herman Merivale	
	A Scrap of Paper	Victorien Sardou	

	The Greatest of These	Sydney Grundy		
14 October	*The Shop Girl*	H. J. W. Dam; music by Ivan Caryll		
21 October	*Fedora*	Victorien Sardou	Mrs Bernard-Beere	
	Adrienne Lecouveeur	adapted by H. Herman from Scribe and Lecouve		

Mr and Mrs Kendal in *The Ironmaster*, adapted by Pinero from a play by George Olinot. They performed it at the Royal Court seven times between 1891 and 1907.

	As in a looking Glass	adapted by F. C. Grove from a novel by F. C. Phillips	
	Masks and Faces	Charles Reade and Tom Taylor	historical comedy
28 October	Gilbert and Sullivan	D'Oyly Carte	
4 November	*An Artist's Model*	Owen Hall; music by Sidney Jones	George Edwardes Company
11 November	*Thorough-bred*	Ralph R. Lumley	comedy with J. L. Toole
	Dot	Dion Boucicault	
	Paul Pry	John Poole	farce
18 November	*The Sign of the Cross*	Wilson Barrett	melodrama with Wilson Barrett's company
25 November	Gilbert and Sullivan	D'Oyly Carte	
2 December	*His Excellency*	W. S. Gilbert and F. Osmond Carr	opera with Sidney Harcourt
9 December	*Romeo & Juliet*	Shakespeare	F. R. Benson's company
	The Merchant of Venice	Shakespeare	
	The Taming of the Shrew	Shakespeare	
	Macbeth	Shakespeare	
15–23 December	closed		
24 December–22 February 1896	*Dick Whittington*		

Wilson Barrett in *The Sign of the Cross*

That a Liverpool audience is a critical one, I have some reason to believe; but there is criticism and criticism; there is the criticism that comes to carp, and there is the criticism which ... is criticism of the highest order, the criticism of sympathy.

Programme cover from the 1920s

4 Popular Plays and Familiar Faces, 1880s–1920s

John Martin-Harvey played the role of Sydney Carton in *The Only Way* 22 times at the Royal Court. He first appeared in the role in 1899 at the age of 36. His last performance there as Carton was in 1939 at the age of 75.[1] This was in no sense an exceptional feat in Martin-Harvey's career: he also appeared in *The Breed of the Treshams* 15 times and in *The Cigarette Maker's Romance* 12 times, with these performances of his most popular plays interspersed with others including *The Bells*, *David Garrick* and *The Corsican Brothers*. Other companies and other actors were little different in the regularity of their appearances and in their choice of a repeating repertoire. From Mr and Mrs Kendal, who performed frequently at the Court between 1882 and 1908, to Fred Terry and Julia Neilson, who toured there almost every year between 1900 and 1928, familiar plays and familiar actors were welcomed on to the stage of the Royal Court. Other well-known faces included the comedian J. L. Toole, Wilson Barrett (especially with *The Silver King*) and John Hare. Some were actors and companies mostly reliant on a London base, the stars of their day such as Henry Irving and George Alexander. Others were actor-managers who had tried to make a name in London but had failed or found it too costly, such as Edward Compton, who with his Compton Comedy Company pursued 'with vigour ... the mission which he undertook ... of maintaining the public interest in the comedies of the last century'.[2] Others, such as the Shakespearean Frank Benson, found it better 'to reign in the provinces than to serve "backer" for fifteen years or so for an uneasy position as a London manager'.[3] Some held London seasons when they could but spent most of their time on the road. These touring companies, joined by productions of London successes either after they finished in the capital or as a second (or third or fourth) touring company while the London run continued, were the mainstay of the Court's programme from 1881. The original stock companies had disappeared from the 1860s as transport allowed for easier touring, and from its reopening in 1881 the Court relied totally on touring companies and their actor-managers.

Many of these performers are no longer well known, but in their time they were household names. By the time John Martin-Harvey set out on his second national tour in 1900, fans had started to gather at stage doors pressing gifts into his hands, including a posy of flowers that always appeared when he went to Liverpool from 'Little Valentine', who never missed a performance of *The Only Way*.[4] By 1901, in Maurice Wilson Disher's flamboyant prose,

> [p]raise of 'The Martin-Harveys' could be heard in the streets ... Where enthusiasm had fired a dozen breasts among scanty audiences on the first tour, thousands now came to see what the few had raved about – or merely affirmed faith in their quiet way ... It was the young who swore by Martin-Harvey, very much more especially the young men and women of the day ... he was an intoxication and a passion, awakening half-formed desires, hidden longings and impulses, secret enthusiasms, and wielding sway more imperiously over heart and sense and soul than any other man of his time did over the intellect of the reason of his disciples.[5]

Martin-Harvey would go on to be knighted in 1921. Another star was Wilson Barrett, whose biographer claimed that by the end of 1896 his most popular play,

The Sign of the Cross, had been seen by 70,000 a week in Britain alone, and Dennis Kennedy adds that it may have been the most popular play of the nineteenth century; by the time of Barrett's death in 1904 it had been performed over 10,000 times across the globe and seen by over 15 million spectators.[6] Lewis Waller was something of a matinee idol and Hesketh Pearson notes that

> [t]he scenes at his first and last nights had to be seen and heard to be believed. The pit and gallery, mostly filled with women, went completely mad. These ladies banded themselves into a club or society vulgarly known as K.O.W. (Keen on Waller) Brigade and they packed the pit at almost every performance.

Lewis Waller as Robin Hood, performed at the Royal Court in October 1907

> Waller's first appearance in a play was received with such a storm of shouts and yells and hand-clapping and foot-stamping that the action was often held up for several minutes.[7]

Fred Terry's obituary in *The Times* suggests that the Terrys drew the public of London and the provinces in their thousands,[8] and in her autobiography, Julia Neilson maintains that one of their plays, *Sweet Nell of Drury Lane*, which they performed regularly between 1900 and 1929, made them well known to three generations of playgoers:

> The Edwardians came and beamed on us; their children made something very like a cult of us – I recall one woman, now middle-aged who saw *Sweet Nell* no less than thirty-six times. The tough post-war generation was, rightly and reasonably, sceptical of their parents' and its grandparents' raptures, but were constrained by politeness not to refuse when invited to accompany a family party to see these strange famous Terrys 'doing their stuff' … Critical tongues well in their cheeks, they took their places in the stalls, and it seems that their criticism faded away.[9]

All of these companies had a number of key plays or roles, a personal vehicle (or two) that they were associated with in the eyes of their audiences and which could ensure a full house and a profit. For Lewis Waller it was *Monsieur Beaucaire*, an eighteenth-century Bath barber. For Edward Compton it was *Davy Garrick*. For Wilson Barrett it was *The Silver King*. For the Kendals it was *The Elder Mrs Blossom*, *The Ironmaster* and *A Scrap of Paper*. For the Terrys it was *Sweet Nell* and *Henry of Navarre*, but above all it was Baroness Orczy's *The Scarlet Pimpernel*, which they performed at the Court ten times between 1905 and 1928. They established its popular status in Edwardian England (the novel was published after the stage version) and '[t]o a considerable extent they *were* Sir Percy and Lady Blakeney', creating the 'phenomenon that was to become "The Scarlet Pimpernel"'.[10]

Popular Companies 1: John Martin-Harvey

Described by Disher as 'the last romantic', John Martin-Harvey was just setting out on his career as an actor-manager when he first arrived in Liverpool in 1899. The play he performed that year, and in 1939 on his farewell tour (after some 35 visits by his company), was *The Only Way*, an adaptation of Dickens's *A Tale of Two Cities*. Martin-Harvey had already spent some thirteen years working with Henry Irving and, as Jim Davies notes, this long exposure to Irving's 'strong visual sense and ability to create a stage picture' contributed to Martin-Harvey's approach to

John Martin-Harvey as Lieutenant Ned Reresby, 'the Rat', and his wife, Nina de Silva, as Batty in *The Breed of the Treshams*, which was performed at the theatre 15 times between September 1904 and September 1925.

creating a performance.[11] *The Only Way* was replete with tableaux and stage pictures, most notably the Revolutionary Tribunal scene where Martin-Harvey, in his role as Sidney Carton, defends Charles Darnay, a scene *The Stage* considered the most striking and grandly melodramatic moment of the play:

> the mad crowd, the concentrated calmness of Carton, the helpless prisoner, the distracted Lucie, and the sorrowful Dr Manette all go to form a strong picture. But it is a picture of life and action … It is a great scene, where yelling, half-crazy men and women, thirsting for blood, give full vent to their animal desire. Inspired by the old hag known as The vengeance, the howling mob grows frantic in its madness, and reeling with excitement, it follows at her nod…[12]

This was matched by what was to become the most famous image in the play, as Carton, having swapped clothes with the condemned Darnay, mounted the scaffold, an image described by *The Stage* as 'beautiful and significant', as Sydney Carton, 'bareheaded and alone, standing calm and resolute ... behind him is a lurid and troubled sky, and in front are the soldiers and the mob, eager for the end'. It was 'a beautiful picture of ... a pure and holy love – a picture that fills the heart with sadness and regret'.[13] It was, according to Davies, to become such a popular part of the play that Martin-Harvey could calm unruly mobs by threatening not to play it.[14] But the force of Martin-Harvey's romantic acting also relied on the art of oratory to move the audience – to tears, to fear, to joy – and *The Only Way* offered the actor-manager plenty of opportunities to achieve this end. The rousing speech, delivered at the Tribunal and written by Martin-Harvey for himself, was the key to winning the audience:

> CARTON: Citizens all, hear me. Whatever sacrifice a man can make, that man has made for France. He heard the cursed story of his house, and he renounced his name: title, wealth, estate – he flung them to the wind. Stripped of all – one of the poor himself – he went to seek his bread in a strange land. That was like a man –
>
> *Aye the crowd murmurs reluctantly*
>
> – A true man –
>
> *Aye murmurs the crowd less reluctantly*
>
> – A man who loves his country much, but liberty and manhood more.
>
> *Applause mingled with cries of dissent*
>
> Citizens, you who are building up the ruins of France into a temple of glorious liberty, will you not forgive the man his birth for the sake of his deeds? His fault is a name, his atonement is a life ... I read your hearts like an open book. Tell you of tyranny and you burn to avenge it; tell you of generosity and you burn to outdo it. You will say: 'This man is one of ourselves.' You will make him welcome to the new heritage of man, the young great world, born of the old world's sorrow, above which floats the tricolour of France.
>
> *All salute the tricolour rapturously. Murmurs which are continued through the next speech, with a steady crescendo culminating in the words:*
>
> This day and this deed will fill a noble page in history. All down the ages, brave eyes will grow dim as they read this story, the story of how the father sinned and the child suffered, and France took pity and forgave.[15]

It was a moment praised by *The Era* as 'a masterpiece of expression and delivery. We were made to understand the power of the voice, the gesture, and the well-chosen word over a mass of hearers. We felt that it was impossible that the jury should not be convinced.'[16] The power of Martin-Harvey's popularity therefore lay in a combination of sentimental drama, visual spectacle and powerful, almost sermonising oratory.

Although Sidney Carton was the character with whom Martin-Harvey was most associated, two other plays were regularly performed as part of his week's visit to the city, both of which were also 'stuff and fustian of the romantic kind'.[17] The first, *The Cigarette Maker's Romance*, an adaptation of Marion Crawford's novel, was 'cheap sentimental stuff', a story of a Russian nobleman, Count Skariatine, who loses his memory and wanders to Munich where he is employed in a cigarette factory. Every Wednesday he is convinced that his friends will come for him and remind him who he is, but they never do. Instead he is befriended by those who work at the factory and, in particular, by Vera, who he promises to marry. His cousin, who has stolen his estates, tries to have the Count sent to an asylum, but all is saved when Skariatine sees his name on a piece of plaster rescued from a broken doll. In a flash his memory comes back and he ends the play by telling the audience

> There is a greater thing than riches upon earth. With it the poor man is wealthy, without it the rich man is poor; beggars may possess it, it is not to be bought by kings. The greatest thing in all the world – Love. Gentlemen, let me present you to Vera, my Countess. My love for all time![18]

The 1903 play *The Breed of the Treshams* by John Rutherford (in reality Beulah Marie Dix and Evelyn Greenleaf Sutherland), performed at the Royal Court some 12 times, was set in a mythical Midlands town at the time of the English Civil War. This play gave Martin-Harvey a chance to play a character who was different to Sydney Carton or Count Skariatine. The hero was Lieutenant Ned Reresby, a tough, gambling soldier of fortune known as The Rat who, at the start of the play, is to be found with a Cavalier troop caught in the middle of enemy territory with a leader looking to defect to the Parliamentarians. Amid much duelling and treachery, Reresby seeks to redeem his wasted life and ends up ensuring that the young lovers are saved and coming out firmly on the side of King Charles. Despite the roughness of the character, it was still a part that appealed overwhelmingly to the sentiment of the audience, as this unnamed reviewer quoted by Disher makes clear:

> The hero, it is true, does not lay down his life in the sacred cause of sentiment, as in *The Only Way*, but he is whipped, and stabbed, and burnt for the sake of a young lady who has no further claim upon him than her eyes happen to resemble the eyes of a lady with whom he was once in love.[19]

John Martin-Harvey as Sydney Carton in *The Only Way*, a role he played some 22 times at the Royal Court. On his final performance as Carton in Liverpool in May 1939, when he was 75, the *Daily Post* remarked that it remained 'one of the performances that has to be seen by every connoisseur of English acting' (2 May 1939, 8).

Unsurprisingly, Martin-Harvey was often criticised for his choice of sensational and sentimental drama. Max Beerbohm took him to task after watching *The Cigarette Maker's Romance*:

> Mr Martin Harvey, with upturned eyes and wearing ever that ethereally mystic smile, is proceeding steadily on his sentimental journey from bad to worse, 'Halt!' I cry to him. For is it not a thousand pities that so important a young mime as he should persist in wasting his gifts on quite worthless plays? *The Only Way* was a dull melodrama, which 'ran' by reason of Mr Harvey's glamour ... *A Cigarette-Maker's Romance* ... is ... pitiably old-fashioned balderdash ... Thirty years ago, in the more remote parts of the provinces, it might have had some measure of success. But in London, and the present century, the public really has no use for it.[20]

Martin-Harvey did bring other plays with him over the years, including *Hamlet* and *Oedipus Rex* (in which he had been directed by Max Reinhardt), as well as some plays by Maeterlinck. But the Liverpool audience seemed unperturbed by the 'worthless' plays which were always their favourites, and Martin-Harvey continued to be a popular and much welcomed visitor to the city. On the occasion of his final tour in May 1939, he was entertained to a civic lunch at the Adelphi Hotel, and the *Daily Post* bemoaned his retirement as marking the end of 'the last survivors of the great tradition of actor-management', remarking that his portrait of Sydney Carton was 'an outstanding feature of the English stage for many years; and it remains to-day one of the performances that was to be seen by every connoisseur of English acting'.[21]

There was only one occasion when Martin-Harvey might have been a little less welcome in the city. During 1924 he became embroiled in a dispute with the Actors' Association, a forerunner of the British Actors' Equity Association, which had imposed a boycott on his company (and others) over a long-running dispute involving touring contracts. Martin-Harvey, a member of the rival Stage Guild, was not unsympathetic to their demand that contracts should only allow managers to put their company out of work for one week in ten. What he was opposed to was trade unionism in the acting profession and being forced into using 'a form of contract dictated by them and coerce all my artists into joining the Actors' Association. I refuse to allow my artists to be coerced and intimidated in this manner and will afford them every protection.'[22] The week before the company arrived in Liverpool, they had been in Glasgow where, following a private meeting between the two sides, Martin-Harvey's company members had voted (18 to 3) to suggest that the Stage Guild and the Actors' Association work together to resolve the problem. The Stage Guild accepted this. The Actors' Association did not. At the evening performance, sandwichmen had patrolled the streets outside the theatre advising the public to stay away in view of this 'deliberate attempt to smash trade unionism in the theatre'.[23] At the end of that week, when his set arrived ahead of the company at Liverpool Exchange station, the carters at first refused to move it if it was touched by non-union labour. When this problem was overcome, stagehands refused to take the set into the theatre. Martin-Harvey threatened to perform *Richard III* on a bare stage but was saved from this by members of the orchestra who helped move the set. In the evening, Martin-Harvey gathered a group of people, mainly rugby players, to prevent interruptions from the audience and they produced their own broadsheet informing the public that

> [a] dispute in the Theatrical Profession has been seized by the Communists as an opportunity to stir up trouble amongst scene-shifters and other employees who are not directly affected. A vendetta has been started against

> Sir John Martin Harvey, who has taken a strong stand against them, and it is anticipated that organised interruption will be practised at the Royal Court Theatre on at least one night this week. Although we have nothing to do with the Trade Union dispute, it is felt that, as this is a deliberate attempt on the part of Communist hooligans to attack the present social system, it is a cause which comes within our ken…[24]

In the event there were no interruptions, and the audience numbers suggested that the 'old favourite' had 'lost little of its popular appeal'.[25] At the end of the evening, Martin-Harvey made a speech from the stage, thanking the audience for their support and expressing pleasure that 'the old play' had gone without a hitch.

Popular Companies 2: Fred Terry and Julia Neilson

In what was to become known as 'The First Company on the Road', the husband and wife team of Fred Terry and Julia Neilson toured the country from 1900 until Terry's illness forced his retirement in 1929, bringing with them 'pseudo-historical melodrama' and romantic comedy.[26] Their style of performance is captured by a review in the *Illustrated London News* of one of their less popular plays, Kester and Major's *Dorothy o' the Hall* (September 1906), which suggested that

> picturesque melodrama such as this affords a pseudo-historical setting to an adventurous, happily-ending love story and sufficiently riots in all the time-honoured conventions of personal misunderstandings, false impersonations, gallant sword-play, eavesdropping, hiding behind curtains and the like will always have its votaries among our unsophisticated playgoers.[27]

Continuing to belittle the audience who came to see such plays, the review went on to suggest that because the play was 'adorned with such charming stage-pictures of lattice-windowed, ivy walled, rose embowered and "typically English" manor … its defiance of tradition and its patchwork of hackneyed scenes will not disturb theatre-goers of unexacting tastes'.[28] At a fast and furious pace, it told a story typical of many of the Terrys' plays. Here the focus is Sir John Manners and his faithful sweetheart, Dorothy Vernon, who conquers her villainous cousin in a broadsword fight and acts as a substitute for the Queen of the Scots when she finds she has betrayed her secret hiding place and imperilled the safety of her lover. Along with the plots, Neilson's acting was often criticised as sentimental, mannered and over-emphatic, although she was praised for her archness, vivacity, animation and, of course, for her beauty. But none of these criticisms deterred the Court audience and the Terrys paid some thirty visits to the theatre.

Julia Neilson as Nell Gwynn in Paul Kester's *Sweet Nell of Drury Lane*, a play that appeared at the Royal Court regularly between 1900 and 1929.

Terry's driving ideal in choosing plays came from the belief that 'after working all day in the office, a man likes to see on the stage an ideal hero, with the glamour of fine clothes and finer deeds upon him'.[29] John Gielgud, Fred Terry's great-nephew, went so far as to suggest that he 'would be violent about anything in a play that he did not think was manly and noble. The heroines were white and the villains were black and that was that.'[30] This attitude is illustrated by the change made, at Terry's insistence, to the original ending of *The Scarlet Pimpernel*, which had Sir Percy disguised as a Jewish horse-trader being thrashed by the French villain of the piece, Chauvelin. Orczy claimed that Terry did not like the idea of making his final bow to the public in the unattractive disguise of an old Jew, and Neilson suggests that the receipt of an anonymous letter from a galleryite put them on the right track:

> 'For Gawd's sake,' wrote our unknown correspondent, 'don't let Blakeney be thrashed by a "froggy."' This suggestion immediately gave us the clue. Chauvelin, the villain, was overcome, the Pimpernel triumphant, and after that the audiences were able to cheer heartily.[31]

The Scarlet Pimpernel was the play most favoured by their audiences, cashing in on the popularity of stories of the French Revolution on stage. However, unlike Martin-Harvey, who had focused on noble self-sacrifice, here the emphasis was on national pride and a conservative, patriotic agenda, as Sir Percy rescues royalists from revolutionary France. Throughout, the French are cowardly and emaciated, the English are resourceful, daring and well-fed, and the blood-soaked Parisian streets are contrasted with the genteel ballrooms and gardens of England. Similarly, *Sweet Nell of Old Drury*, as popular in their repertoire as *The Scarlet Pimpernel* and performed at the Court 11 times between 1900 and 1929, was a swashbuckling costume drama that valorised the monarchy and the aristocracy.[32] Described by Marguerite Stein in *A Pride of Terrys* as a piece of theatrical twaddle but one which was to prove a money-spinner for thirty years, and by Neilson as not a great play, but 'certainly ... grand entertainment', this time the plot centred on Charles II and Nell Gwyn. It had a long, involved and, according to Neilson, 'wholly fictitious story' which involved Nell Gwyn using her relationship with the king and her ingenuity in disguise to save the life of Fairfax (an earlier love) who has been, wrongly, accused of treason.[33] Following all the traditions of romantic comedy, it has a happy ending. Similarly, *Henry of Navarre* by William Devereux offered excitement and drama which reached a climax on St Bartholomew's Eve and the ensuing massacre, and moved the Terrys to France where they played Henri de Bourbon and Marguerite de Valois taking on the villainy of Catherine de Medici and Charles IX.

Julia Neilson as Marguerite de Valois and Fred Terry as Henri de Bourbon in the first appearance of *Henry of Navarre* at the Royal Court in 1909. When the play returned in 1918, the *Liverpool Echo* declared it was 'a play that grows upon one – those who have seen it want to see it again, and enjoy the second performance better than the first' (1 November 1918, 2).

Alongside the excitement of the plots, one reason for the Terrys' continued success seems to have been their unerring sense for the spectacular drama these plays demanded. While Stein suggests that Terry, unlike his mentor Henry Irving, had no artistic sense but unerring commercial sense, his artistic sensibility led him to rewrite and rework several of the texts he was presented with to emphasise the action. Unhappy with Orczy's original opening scene for *The Scarlet Pimpernel*, which she had set in a pub in Kent where Sir Percy's daring rescues were discussed, Fred Terry determined that the audience must see one of his exploits for themselves in order to accept his later daring acts and take him to their hearts as the hero for the evening. Accordingly, and by all accounts with Louis Calvert, one of the actors in the company, he rewrote the opening scene. This now showed Sir Percy Blakeney, disguised as an old hag, rescuing the Comtesse de Tournal and her daughter from the guillotine, driving them through the West Barricade in Paris while singing the revolutionary song 'Ça ira', and telling the guards he was driving a cartload of plague victims. Equally, the entrance of Julia Neilson as Mary Queen of Scots in *The Borderer*, a play of 'plots and counter-plots, of swaggering soldiers and the clash of steel',[34] gives a sense of their understanding of the theatrical, as described by Donald Wolfit who joined the company for a tour in the 1920s:

> The build-up began from the rise of the curtain; everyone who came on referred to the approaching procession. A piper was travelled throughout the tour for this one scene. He commenced to play far down the street outside the theatre, and as he entered the stage-door shouts, murmurs and cheering joined the skirl of the pipes. The volume of sound gradually swelled until it became almost deafening as he mounted the stairs to the stage; and then a covey of maids-in-waiting fluttered to the ground as Julia literally floated on to such a storm of applause that it stopped the play.[35]

Wolfit also suggests something of the care the two actors took in rehearsing, even if they were approaching a play they had been working on for years. At the outset of rehearsals for *The Borderer* and *The Scarlet Pimpernel*, he wondered what they would do during the two weeks' rehearsal period:

> after all there were only two plays to rehearse and more than half the company were old hands in their parts. I soon learned the answer. Rigid discipline, small scenes taken ten and twenty times and rehearsed to a hair's breadth; it was as if *The Pimpernel* had never been played before but it was a new play ... Little readjustments to suit the personalities of the new actors were carefully made. The setting and cleaning of the supper-table in the first act became a miracle of timing under the hand of the genius, for Fred Terry was that in costume comedy.[36]

This attention to detail and to freshness in performance was also noted by another actor in the company, who wrote that 'repetition was no more to Fred than a challenge each time to utter a certain phrase or word in such a fashion that it did more than ring freshly on the listener's ear, but started an entirely new train of thought, struck a fresh note of comedy or tragedy'.[37] Trying to recapture the performance and its appeal at this distance is inevitably difficult, especially given the often dismissive reviews of popular plays, but the same actor's description of Terry provides a glimpse of the appeal of this husband and wife team, who in their heyday, Wolfit was told, used to be met by a crowd at the railway station on their arrival in a city, who would remove the horse from the cab and haul it to their hotel:[38]

> In watching Fred Terry act ... I have often been reminded of the fallacious popular conception of cloak-and-sword drama as an affair of bluster, of swagger, of outcry and flourish. I have yet to see a scene in a modern comedy invested by its protagonists with one-tenth of the subtlety he brought to what might almost be described as a stock Terry 'situation' ... There was a moment in the Third Act of *The Scarlet Pimpernel*, when Fred's hands flickered above his wife's head, a speechless moment that was informed with all the elements of tragedy by the movement of those hands: the premonition of betrayal, the despair of love wasted on an unworthy object, the longing for confidence ... all blown out like candle-flame by the studied coolness of his voice.[39]

The Terrys were also renowned for their attention to detail and accuracy in terms of costume, wigs and props, despite the pseudo-historicism of the plays' plots. Nothing was allowed to disturb the harmony of the stage picture, and Fred Terry was also well known for his elaborate use of props and fondness for stage business, which in *The Scarlet Pimpernel* involved a quizzing glass and a cane. But for all the attention to detail and historical accuracy in the stage picture, Neilson was convinced that the success of the plays was reliant on their acting:

> Looked at coldly, these old romantic comedies were no truer to nature than the musicals that followed them; the plots were almost always artificial, loaded with coincidence and woefully lacking in common logic. It was the characters that saved them. I think we both possessed ... the art of building a character that our public could understand, with which it could sympathise, and whose thought and reactions in some way reflected their own.[40]

Summing up their careers, Walter MacQueen-Pope described them as 'perhaps the best stage couple of their time'. Fred Terry, in particular, 'should have led the stage' but 'he preferred to keep the flag flying in the provinces, to see that the playgoers of the great cities were not starved of the best'.[41]

We Know You – And You Like Us

The enduring appeal of all of these companies (and John Martin-Harvey and the Terrys could have been replaced here by the Kendals or Lewis Waller or Wilson Barrett) lay in the ease and familiarity of their work, which 'gave one rather a jolly nursery feeling', and there are innumerable similarities between *Sweet Nell* of the Terrys and *The Elder Mrs Blossom* of the Kendals.[42] It was an appeal summed up by the *Telegraph* in a review of *The Scarlet Pimpernel*:

Fred Terry as Sir Percy Blakeney in disguise rescuing the Comtesse de Tournal and her daughter from the guillotine in the opening scene of *The Scarlet Pimpernel.*

> There are some melodramas which disarm criticism. They are not usually of the highest rank, but they make so few demands on the imagination or the thought of the spectator, that he finds himself instinctively applauding them – almost as if they were old friends. And, indeed, old friends they generally are, if not in their main design, at all events in their incidents ... They are all formed in the same mould, full of exciting incidents, crammed with glaring effects, a little tawdry, it may be, and, if we may dare say so, a little common. But how satisfactory they are from the point of view of the public! ... How honest and undisguised and devoid of all complexity they are! Straightforward melodrama? Yes, melodrama so straightforward and so frank that it jumps to the eyes...[43]

Audiences seemed unperturbed by the ageing of their favourites, who were still performing the same roles in their sixties and seventies. Julia Neilson was 61 when she played Nell Gwyn at the Royal Court for the last time in 1929, and nobody seemed to bat an eyelid when a 75-year-old John Martin-Harvey mounted the guillotine at the end of *The Only Way* in 1939. But it was more than the ease and familiarity of their work that appealed to the audiences. These actors became 'friends' and worked hard to woo and win their audiences, to make them feel loved and special. This could be part of the performance itself, as Wilson Disher suggests about Lewis Waller, who 'represented the kind of romance which has no use for subtlety':

> Directly the proscenium loomed in his sight he went for it like a bull at an open gate with a red-flannel petticoat on the other side. Whatever he meant was for the audience; he never played to the gallery – he fixed it, stalls, boxes, dress circle, pit, upper gallery and amphitheatre as well, with his fiery eyes. If the English Army had to be exhorted to do battle he ignored his eighteen penny supers as men he paid and attended strictly to the people who paid him. With the loveliest of actresses waiting at his side to be wooed he would ignore her, and instead of pouring out his honeyed words to one devoted heart addressed them to a palpitating thousand. Critically, it was penny gaff. Emotionally, it was magnificent, not to be coldly withstood, not to be heard without a strong desire to throw hats in the air and cheer.[44]

These actors were also adept at making speeches after the show aimed at wooing the audience. Edward Compton, in particular, had a way of making any audience feel that their particular town or city was the one place he had wanted to return to since he had last been there, 'and his speeches from the stage, although the same in every

Queen Square, opposite the theatre, in 1920 showing the Stork Hotel, a popular venue for pre- and post-theatre drinks and meals.

town, were full of local references and figures of speech'.[45] Martin-Harvey was also adept at wooing and flattering the audience wherever he was. His curtain speech at the Court, after the first night of *The Only Way*, was designed to make the audience feel not only special but also intelligent:

> Ladies and gentlemen, we have all known that you formed a very critical audience. 'Ah,' my friends said, 'wait till you get to Liverpool; you'll have to mind your P's and Q's' ... I hope we have come out unscathed (Applause). That a Liverpool audience is a critical one, I have some reason to believe; but there is criticism and criticism; there is the criticism that comes to carp, and there is the criticism which ... is criticism of the highest order, the criticism of sympathy. After the welcome you have given us to-night, and the sympathetic attention with which you have followed our efforts, I think I may thank you most heartily on behalf of my fellow-workers and myself, for that highest order of criticism which tonight you have brought to bear upon my work.[46]

It may even be possible to suggest that the actors and the companies that appealed most to provincial audiences, that made the strongest connections with them, were those who focused more on touring outside London. As Disher says of Martin-Harvey, the niche he filled was 'staying in the provinces because the provinces, all of them, were his home. The masters of St James's and His Majesty's never bestrode England as securely as he. They merely visited where he addressed his own public.'[47]

Popular Companies 3: The D'Oyly Carte Opera Company and Gilbert and Sullivan

In opera, by far the longest 'serving' company was D'Oyly Carte, its regular performances of the Gilbert and Sullivan canon (sometimes for three weeks in a year) between 1892 and 1975 by far eclipsing performances by any other company. With a repertoire limited to 12 'popular' operas, the company's works would have been well known to the Court audience, and many would have been word perfect, bringing with them the scores which they followed during the show. As early as 1887 (and before their arrival at the Royal Court), Gilbert boasted to Sullivan that they were 'as much an institution as Westminster Abbey' and much of their continued success lay with Richard D'Oyly Carte, who in 1875 established a company to perform their works.[48] The company was to continue until 1982, almost ceaselessly touring and holding a monopoly on the professional performance of these works. Overall, their appeal is summed up by David Cannadine, in a way that explains this continued attraction for a Court audience:

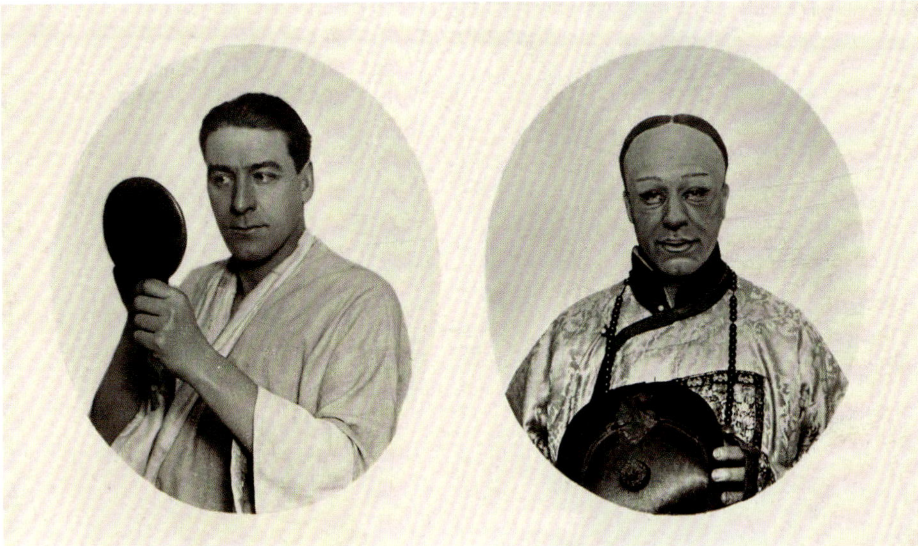

Matheson Lang before and after his make-up to play the title role in *Mr Wu*, which was performed at the Royal Court in May 1915.

> They deliberately sought to make their work appealing to the well-educated middle classes, and they triumphantly succeeded. They created a new form of entertainment, precisely pitched between the music hall and the concert hall, which was intelligent but not intellectual, tasteful but not pretentious, tuneful but not cloying. They took the theatrical conventions of the lower classes and made them acceptable to the bourgeoisie.[49]

The specific appeal of Gilbert and Sullivan inevitably changed over this period. In their early days, despite being an expression of theatrical revolution, the wholesomeness of the operas (the works were wholly devoid of anything likely to offend a Victorian audience), their wit, the spectacle of the productions, which gave prominence to costume, props and set, and their topicality were paramount. This was coupled with the fact that the operas were also 'a paean of praise to national pride and to the established order', particularly important in the last decades of the nineteenth century, which were 'the most crowded, tumultuous and disturbing of the century with deepening economic uncertainty and the scramble for power and control abroad'.[50] In particular, for the audience of theatres such as the Royal Court who, Cannadine suggests, were 'bewildered by Irish Home Rule, worried by the depression of prices, profits and interest rates and concerned about a working class that was better educated and partially enfranchised, yet sometimes seemed

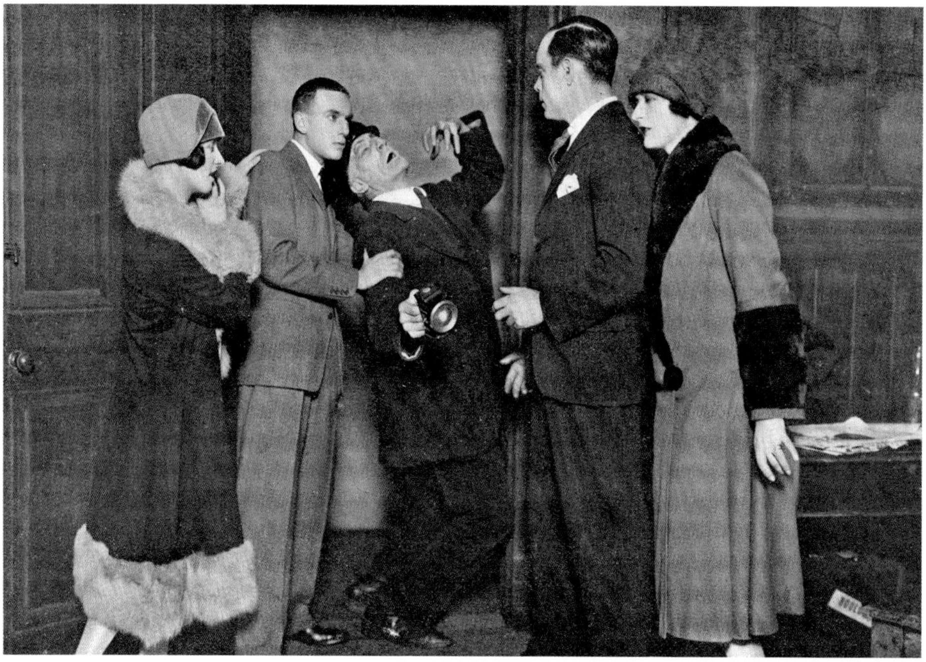

A scene from Arnold Ridley's *The Ghost Train*, one of the popular post First World War thrillers (*Play Pictorial*)

ominously discontented', this appeal to national pride was comforting.[51] By the twentieth century the works of Gilbert and Sullivan were far less topical. D'Oyly Carte might have ensured the survival of their work, but they also ensured that the operas were performed in their original form without any attempt to bring them up to date. As a result, they came to stand, not for innovation and contemporaneity, but for tradition. They had become a national institution. Their 'pageantry, their stirring marches, their gorgeous costumes, and their robust loyalty to crown and nation' were still comforting and, in the interwar years, their work

> found a ready response among the many members of the 'flag-saluting, foreigner-hating, peer-respecting' working classes. Their undemanding tunefulness appealed with equal success to the increasingly philistine members of the upper classes ... Their refusal to address social problems, and their light-hearted escapism, which had made them such a tonic during the gloomy decade of the 1880s, were of even greater value at the time of the inter-war depression. And their disdain for 'abroad', their inability to take foreigners seriously, and their determination not to bow down to continental dictators ... gave them a new and reassuring relevance during the First World War – and again during the 1930s.[52]

Popular Plays

Certain plays too were very regular visitors. Some, such as H. A. Jones's *The Silver King*, an 1882 melodrama about the plight of a man who wrongly believes himself to be a murderer, were associated with individual actors, in this case Wilson Barrett. Although this was the role most keenly connected with Barrett, *The Sign of the Cross*, in which he played Marcus Superbus, a pagan Roman patrician at the time of Nero, was a more frequent visitor to the Court in the last decade of the nineteenth century – although not always with Barrett in the cast. The story was of Superbus's conversion to Christianity through his love of Mercia and their subsequent death in the arena. Having attacked *The Silver King*, which it thought a most dismal melodrama deficient in incident and dull in dialogue, the *Liverpool Mercury* was much happier leaping to the defence of *The Sign of the Cross*, being seemingly unimpressed by other critical responses:

> The attack of the leopard which, by its spring and bite destroyed the life of St Pancratius in the Coliseum was less aggressive than the strictures which tongue and pen have invented to decry Mr Wilson Barrett's piece which, as an amalgam of the arts and literature, of music, of painting, and of acting, is admirable.[53]

The unmasking of the Ringer in Edgar Wallace's thriller of the same name (*Play Pictorial*)

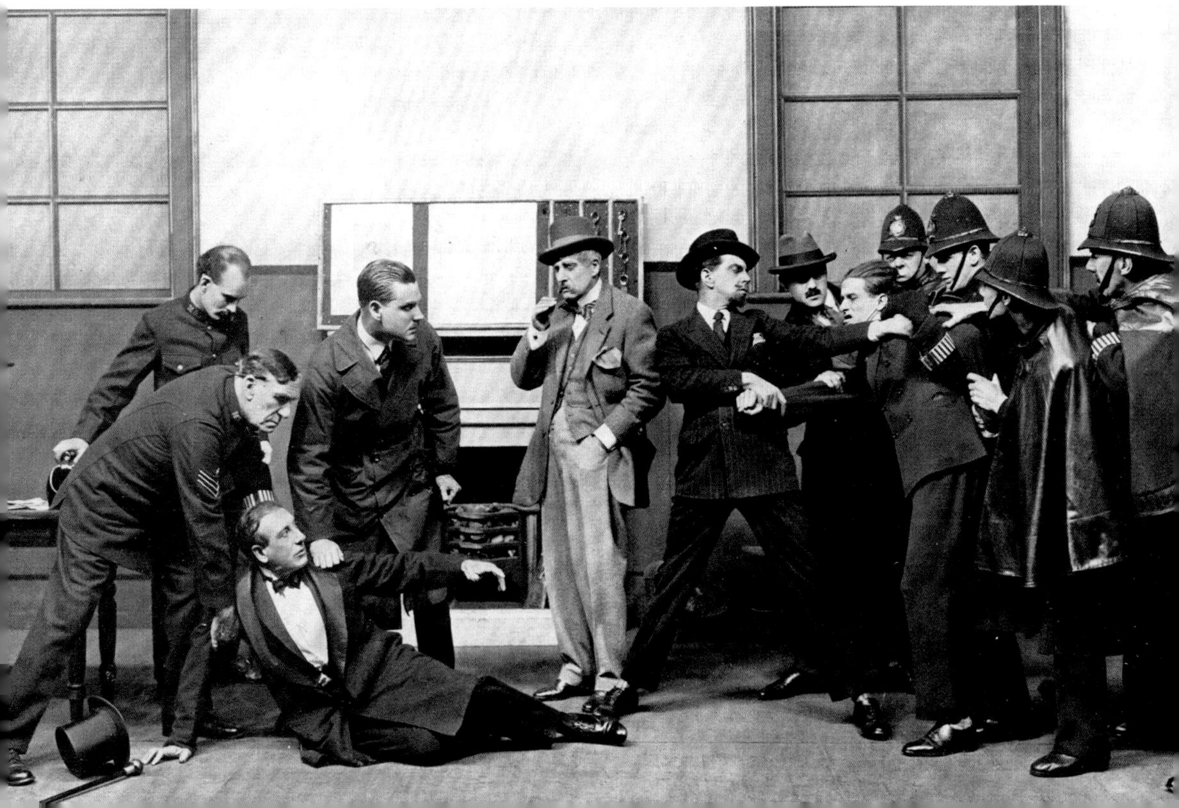

The Court audience too seemed unperturbed by criticisms of the play and on this, its fourth visit in two years, the theatre was crowded and 'the audience surrendered themselves without reserve'.[54]

In the early twentieth century two plays vied for being the most performed. *When Knights Were Bold* by Charles Marlowe (a pseudonym for Harriet Jay), which premiered in 1906 and arrived for the first of ten appearances at the Royal Court in 1908, was 'a delightful piece of fooling' about Sir Guy who arrives home from India to inherit his title and his estates.[55] He has been little bothered about his ancestry until he meets and falls in love with Lady Rowena Eggington, who has her head full of tales of knights and their chivalrous deeds and is carried away by the talk of a twentieth-century Irish 'knight'. Suffering from a cold, Sir Guy has an extra glass of hot whisky and falls asleep, finding himself transported some 720 odd years into the past and, still wearing his dinner jacket, surrounded by knights who address him in the language of the twelfth century.

Equally as light-hearted and popular was *Paddy, The Next Best Thing* by Gayer Mackay and Robert Ord, which made seven appearances at the Court during the 1920s. General Adair had always wanted a son, but not having managed to produce one, Paddy, his youngest daughter, is declared to be 'the next best thing' and brought up as a tomboy. This means that as a young woman her 'biting, kicking, fighting' nature gets her into trouble, and also leads her to keep her potential lover at arm's length 'with a persistence worthy of Shakespeare's Katherine'. *The Stage,* as well as likening it to J. Hartley Manners's *Peg o' My Heart,* another play that was popular at the Court, also declared that it was 'full of what is called the more popular aspect of Irish wit and sentiment'.[56]

Another persistent visitor was *Peter Pan,* which between 1916 and 2003 made nearly twenty appearances. Many of these (up to 1961) were courtesy of the Daniel Mayer Company which, from 1915, regularly performed the show in London and then toured, with March or April becoming a traditional month for the show to arrive at the Royal Court. It brought with it a host of famous names including Eva Embury (1916), Celia Lipton (1944) and Margaret Lockwood (1950), and some famous Captain Hooks including Alistair Sim (1943). The most popular play on the Court's stage, and on stages all round the world, was, however, the evergreen farce *Charley's Aunt.* Written by Liverpool-born Brandon Thomas, it first arrived with Stanley Cooke in the title role in 1893 and made over twenty appearances between then and 1971, when Tom Courtenay played the part of Lord Fancourt Babberley. In between it had fallen to (amongst others) Percy Crawford, Lenton Murray, William Kershaw, Leslie Phillips and Frankie Howerd, allowing some theatregoers plenty of opportunities to compare the success of different actors in the role.

Popular Forms

Alongside a continued liking for the sentimental and the melodramatic, the well-made plays of Tom Robertson and H. A. Jones were popular choices in the first two decades of the Royal Court's existence. Some well-made plays continued to surface into the 1920s, particularly from the pen of Frederick Lonsdale, even though it was 'a genre now sniffed at'. Henry Bernstein's 1907 play *The Thief*, for example, was revived in the 1920s (appearing at the Court in 1924) and condemned by *The Stage* for the insistence on updating it with 'modern instances', referring to the wireless and the crossword craze and its 'up-to-date "confections" to take the place of what we are ridiculously bidden to regard as the old-style "costumes of 1907"'.[57] But gradually, three particular forms came to dominate these decades. Farce was well represented, from the Court farces of Pinero in the last two decades of the nineteenth century to the arrival of the Aldwych farces (mostly penned by Ben Travers) in the 1920s. These latter added a different dimension to the Court's repertoire. Although, as Clive Barker points out, they were designed to amuse a middle-class audience, over time the class dominance of the characters changed:

> The three central male characters are the aristocratic blithering idiot, played by Ralph Lynn, the bullying and corrupt bourgeois played by Tom Walls and the much put-upon lower middle-class worm, played by Robertson Hare. In the early plays, the pecking order runs Walls, Lynn and Hare, but as the period develops Robertson Hare moves more into the centre of the plotting until, towards the end of the 1930s he plays the major character around whom the plot revolves.[58]

Travers's plays also offered less settling conclusions than those of Martin-Harvey or the Terrys or even of the Pinero farces where, at the end of Act III, respectability and normality are regained. Although his farces do have some sense of resolution (the couple are reconciled in *Rookery Nook*, Ronny gets the girl in *Thark*), 'the stifling forces of convention are put to rout at the end'[59] and the stage is often left in chaos, as at the end of *Thark*, in a classic farcically confused bedroom scene:

> *Whittle is at the window; as he pulls the curtains aside the lightning flashes through, lighting up his face – he disappears through the window, leaving them open; the wind is howling furiously, blowing the curtains across the room – an enormous clap of thunder is heard, blankets and quilt are blown off the bed.*
>
> *Ronny puts the light on and Benbow gets his gun and is pointing it towards the window – at that moment the force of the storm blows the brass candlesticks from*

FRANKIE HOWERD in

CHARLEY'S AUNT

by BRANDON THOMAS

"Oh, what an Aunt is Frankie Howerd"

— Milton Shulman - Evening Standard

Frankie Howerd in the 1956 visit of *Charley's Aunt* to the Court

> *the mantelpiece* R., *also the huge picture falls from above the fireplace – which makes Benbow turn quickly and point the gun that way. Ronny jumps out of bed and starts to beat the gong ... Mrs Frush, Lady Benbow and Kitty rush into the room followed by Jones and Hook ... a huge branch of tree has fallen through the window – they are all scared. Ronny is still hitting the gong while Benbow is on the bed pointing the gun round the room from the window to the door.*[60]

By far the most popular genre, and one which seemed to sit more comfortably with the sentimental dramas of the Terrys, was musical comedy. These were dominated by the 'girl' musicals from George Edwardes and his imitators, and the first decade of the twentieth century had more than 13 musicals with girl in the title, encompassing everything from *The Runaway Girl* and *The Dancing Girl* at the start of the decade to *The Earl and the Girl* and *The Girls of Gottenburg* towards the end. Equally popular were those musical comedies that offered 'fantasy versions' of a foreign world.[61] These included works set in Europe, such as *Miss Hook of Holland,* but increasingly focused on the orient in shows such as *The Geisha, San Toy* and *The Cingalee*. However, the form that came to challenge the prevalence of musical comedy as the theatre moved through the early twentieth century was the thriller. This form covered a multitude of kinds of plays, including the first dramatisation, by Michael Morton, of an Agatha Christie play. *Alibi* (February 1929) was a stage version of *The Murder of Roger Ackroyd,* complete with Poirot (played by Charles Laughton), who does not appear in the book. There were also comedy thrillers; Frank Vosper's *Murder on the Second Floor* (November 1929) turns the inhabitants of an ordinary boarding house into characters in a murder mystery when Sylvia, the daughter of the landlady, accuses him of being a 'highbrow'. The characters include a respectable middle-aged retired salesman who is transformed into Reynolds, the head of a dope-smuggling ring. Such an imaginary transformation touched on a common theme in many of the thrillers, many of which played with the idea that anyone could be a criminal. Names might vary from The Ringer, The Terror and The Cat to The Black Spider and The Gorilla, but they all encouraged the audience to engage in solving the puzzle of the criminal's identity as the show unfolded. In Carlton Daws's *The Black Spider* the programme even carried a question mark in place of the name of the actor playing the role. One of the earliest incarnations of this newly popular form was *Raffles,* written in 1904 but not to arrive at the Court until 1928. Raffles was 'a man of taste and education' who preyed 'secretly upon the county society that delights to do him honour in his public capacity of a famous slow bowler. He systematically robs his own class, which gives him its unsuspecting hospitality…'[62] But Raffles was far more gentlemanly than the kinds of criminals who were to follow the First World War, when 'the dramatic interest was unashamedly spurred by violence' which held centre stage 'as a release for the frustrations of a wounded officer class fighting hard to claim its place in a modern world'.[63]

The form that really came to dominate in the 1920s was the hard-boiled 'crook' drama or what Gerald du Maurier was to describe as the 'thick-ear play'.[64] The play du Maurier was describing was *Bull-Dog Drummond* (October 1921), in which a returning officer tries to alleviate post-war boredom by advertising in a newspaper:

> Demobilised officer, finding peace incredibly tedious, would welcome diversion. Legitimate, if possible, but crime, if of a humorous description, no objection. Excitement essential. Reply at once Box X 10.[65]

He does not have to wait long before Phyllis Benson, the sister of an old comrade whose life he saved in the trenches, arrives at his door with the story of some strange goings-on in the nursing home next to where she lives, with which she is worried her uncle has unwittingly become embroiled. In actuality, the proprietor of the home, Dr Lakington, and his blackmailing associates, Carl and Irma Peterson, are keeping the millionaire Hiram G. Travers 'doped' and bleeding him of his money and valuables. Drummond succeeds in spiriting the drugged millionaire out of the nursing home, but the crooks are on to him and send Irma to try to persuade him that this is all a practical joke and that he could be in serious trouble. Carl Peterson's men arrive, and there is 'a tremendous dust-up' from which the crooks depart, happy once again to have the millionaire in their possession. However, the 'millionaire' this time is really Drummond in disguise, though he has unfortunately managed to leave his gun behind, and he now finds himself held captive by the crooks along with Phyllis, who has been kidnapped. 'Phyllis is subjected to insults from Doctor Lakington – with Drummond, like a trussed fowl, looking on – while Peterson goes off post haste' for the real millionaire. 'Drummond, eventually set free by Phyllis, throttles the doctor to death after a tremendous fight', and the returning Peterson walks into a trap set by Drummond. Scotland Yard are sent for, but after they have left with Peterson and Irma, Drummond discovers that the police were actually Peterson's men – so he has in fact escaped.[66] Du Maurier thought the success of the play lay in its appeal to the youth of the country, 'because they can recognise the sort of leadership they badly needed and aren't getting anymore'.[67] There were more sophisticated arguments about the universal fascination with violence and brutality, from the need for the kinds of ritualistic events that the modern world no longer seemed to provide, to the essayist Pellizzi's assertion that the thrills that Edgar Wallace provided sent a

> slight shiver to the bones, which is desired, waited for, and received with relief; it is a slight intoxication of which we rid ourselves with a little internal electrical discharge – something like a sneeze ... [a] reacting with the nerves against the heaviness and boredom of the environment.[68]

The Era preferred to see the play as a moral story:

> There are thousands of Captain Hugh Drummonds about in real life so the play in question has an extra usefulness ... It shows the real Drummonds what may happen if they advertise in the same way as the fictitious one did. It shows them they'll as likely as not get a 'thick ear' though they may, to their consolation, quite possibly manage, before getting it, to do some good in some direction or other.[69]

Patrick Hamilton's *Rope* also touched on the impact of the First World War on attitudes to murder and violence. It is the story of Wyndham Brandon and Charles Granillo who have murdered a third man, hiding his body in a chest. Unlike many

The Royal Court in 1924 by H. Haughton Ward (Liverpool Record Office)

of these plays, the audience was aware from the outset who the murderers were, and the thrill came from whether they would get away with it or not, as they audaciously invite the murdered man's friends and family to a party where the chest serves as a buffet table. But it is towards the end of the play, when Rupert, one of the dinner guests, uncovers the truth, that the heart of Hamilton's argument comes out. Rupert has earlier admitted to committing murder himself, but in a very different context. 'It is all simply a question of scale', he tells the assembled party:

> You, my friends, have, paradoxically a horror of murder on a small scale, a veneration for it on a large. That is the difference between what we call murder and war. One gentleman murders another in a back alleyway in London for, let us say … the gold fillings in his teeth, and all society shrieks out for

> revenge upon the miscreant. They call that murder. But when the entire youth and manhood of a whole nation rises up to slaughter the entire youth and manhood of another, not even for the gold fillings in each other's teeth, then society condones and applauds the outrage and calls it war. How then can I say I disapprove of murder, seeing that I have, in the last Great War, acted on these assumptions myself? ... The point is that I have proved that I don't disapprove of murder.[70]

Later, when Rupert has uncovered the body, Brandon explains to him that they committed the crime

> for adventure. For adventure and danger. You read Nietzsche, don't you Rupert? ... And you know that he tells us to live dangerously ... And you know that he's no more respect for individual life than you, and tells us – to – live dangerously. We thought we would do so – that's all. We have done so. We have only *done the* thing. Others have talked. We have done.[71]

Brandon thinks he will understand, but confronted with the reality, Rupert goes back on his earlier philosophical logic and condemns them for committing 'a sin and a blasphemy', rotting the lives of people 'to whom he was dear'. He looks forward to the punishment that society will now impose on them, the play ending with him telling Brandon, 'You are going to hang, you swine! Hang! – both of you! – hang!', as he leans out of the window to summon the police who wait below.[72]

Hamilton's conclusion may have started to mark a shift in post-war attitudes towards murder, but in the years after the First World War the stage had been filled with thrills and spills, with violence and vengeance in a spate of 'thrilling, killing and chilling' plays.[73] Harold Owen and Harry M. Vernon's *Mr Wu* (May 1915) included the murder of his daughter, the torture of her seducer with thumbscrews, the threatened dishonouring of a mother and finally the poisoning of Mr Wu himself who dies painfully on stage. *The Cat and the Canary* (August 1923) involved house guests staying overnight in a remote house after the late-night reading of a will, with an escaped 'criminal lunatic, whose homicidal mania takes the form of ripping with a claw like grip', in the neighbourhood. Predictably, this leads to scenes of clawed hands appearing through sliding panels in the walls, grabbing at the heroine. Arthur Ridley's *The Ghost Train* (September 1930) featured a supposedly phantom train that runs once a year through the remote south Cornwall station of Fal Vale, 'with signal bell sounding, brakes creaking, and whistle piercing the air', complete with 'bright and dazzling lights of the train with body cunningly concealed', and was a 'non-stop thriller'. *The Stage* noted that it would be hard to 'imagine anything of a more eerie and blood-curdling character' with the play offering 'three acts of hair-raising returns of the spirit world – and a startling denouement'.[74] Charles Bennett's *The Last Hour* (April 1930) involved 'eye-dazzling Death Ray illusions', the Death Ray in question having been stolen by Prince Nichola de Kovatch, a secret agent from a foreign country, and the illusions included the prince's turning one of his own men to little more than charred remains.[75] *The Last Hour* also had a lot of fun at the expense of the rural police sergeant who trusses up the stalwart hero (who is thought to be an escaped convict) and

> accepts as Gospel, every word uttered by the two most palpable looking foreigners you ever saw.
>
> 'They are foreign spies' cries Peter Byron.
>
> 'Vot, us? – Ach no. Impossible,' comes the guttural rejoinder and the Policeman beams an endorsement of the latter speaker's remark.[76]

In many of these plays, the police, whether rural sergeant or Scotland Yard inspector, are not shown as being very capable. Indeed, Edgar Wallace's *The Ringer* (so called because he rings the changes in his appearance; September 1926, November 1927) has managed, undetected, to disguise himself as Lomond, a Scottish doctor and criminologist, the divisional surgeon of Flander's Lane police station. Wallace was the king of the hard-boiled crook drama and The Ringer comes to London seeking revenge for the seduction of his sister. Wallace sets up Meister, a fence and a receiver, as the real villain of the piece who, together with seducing the sister, has 'nearly all the vices' and 'will thoroughly deserve what he gets when he gets it'.[77] The scene where Meister is cornered by The Ringer suggests much about the complexity of the staging and the playing and atmosphere of these plays.

> [*The lights go out. There is complete darkness except for a red light glowing over the door. We hear a strange voice, rather weird tone. It is really* LOMOND, *The Ringer.*]
>
> THE RINGER: Where are you Meister?
>
> [*The piano ends on a discord and Meister gurgles*]
>
> The Ringer's come for you.
>
> [*There is a stifled groan from Meister*]
>
> [*Loudly*] That's for Gwenda!

[*A woman's scream is heard. Then there is much confusion in the darkness. The red light goes out.*]

WEMBURY: Stand by that door.

LOMOND: Put up those lights! Who was it screamed? Put up those lights, you damned fool!

[*The policeman puts up the lights. Positions are the same as except for* WEMBURY *who is in front of panel* L. *of door* C., *and* MEISTER *who is leaning with his back to the door with the sword part of his own sword-stick through his breast with a green light on him.*]

[NOTE – What is supposed to have happened. *The Ringer has murdered* MEISTER. *The red light is supposed to have been put on by* MARY LENLEY *who is presumed to have come into the room in the darkness to get the cheque forged by her brother, and to have knocked into* WEMBURY *and screamed and gone out again. As the whole thing is in complete darkness, of course nothing is seen.*]

[What does happen. *As soon as the lights are out, the property man and* ATKINS *fix an arrangement made of the front of a white dress waistcoat and dress shirt front on a corset of flexible flat steel with the handle of a sword-stick and about four inches of the blade sticking in the breast in front of it.* MEISTER *then goes up to door* C. *and gets in position. The girl outside opens a panel, screams after* 'That's for Gwenda!' *and closes the panel again.* LOMOND *has moved up to* C. *to enable his voice to come from there, and immediately gone back to his position before the lights went out…*][78]

Later, Lomond is unmasked:

WEMBURY: Lomond, I – I can tell you who is The Ringer.

[BLISS *has come down to back of* LOMOND *with an automatic in his hand.*]

LOMOND: You can tell me, eh! Then who is The Ringer?

BLISS: [*pointing pistol at* LOMOND''s *back*]. You're The Ringer!

[BLISS *moves in front of* LOMOND and *whips off his hat and throws it upstage. This is a trick affair, a distinctive hat, the replica of the one* LOMOND *has worn and carried through the play, but with a false fringe of grey hair fixed inside, so that the whole lot comes off together. At the same time* LOMOND *whips off his moustache* ... THE RINGER *stands revealed, a young man.*][79]

Having set up some sympathy with The Ringer, and perhaps with an eye on a sequel, as with *Bull-Dog Drummond* he manages to escape, this time disguised (once again) as a policeman.

The Ringer was just one of several Wallace plays that appeared at the Court and was followed by *Double Dan* (April 1927) and *The Terror* (May 1930), which had a 'ghost' dressed as hooded monk who plays the organ and walks the night, stalking the corridors of Monkshall Priory in a 'sensational play of startling thrills and blood-curdling horrors'.[80] The performance was 'received with alternating raptures and shudders' and the play illuminated a key idea behind many of the thrillers – nothing is quite what it seems and no one is quite who they claim to be. *The Stage* review continued,

> that an apparently blameless retired tea merchant was really the arch-criminal and lunatic with many lucid intervals ... and that a supposedly drunken young waster, who bores most of the people on whose society he forces himself, was really a famous detective, who finally brings The Terror to bay, were but two of the surprises.[81]

It is worth noting, however, that for all the popular visits and revisits of plays and companies and for all the staging of new popular plays, the theatre did operate a mixed repertoire. While the London hits on tour were also likely to be money-spinners for the management, they did, very occasionally decide to give over a week to a more risky venture. 1920 brought Ernest Hutchinson's *The Right to Strike*, a play that focused on a railwaymen's strike and the battle between labour and capital, including the death of a doctor, killed by strikers while trying to bring food into the village by motor car, and the subsequent implications of this death for the pregnant wife of one of the strikers. On its London premiere, *The Era* announced that it was a relief to sit through a play in which the prevailing topic was social rather than amorous.[82] In Liverpool, *The Stage* noted 'the tumult of applause bestowed upon the play', suggesting that while 'it may not be a classic of literature' it was 'a good, tingling, tense and moving play'.[83] In October 1923 there was a staging of Karel Capek's science fiction play *RUR*, a parable about robots styled in the press as a fantastic melodrama. 1930 brought Paul Robeson in an evening of songs along with the first act of Eugene O'Neill's *The Emperor Jones*. But these shows were little more than pinpricks in what was a much more conventional, popular and well-known repertoire that dominated the Court's stage during these decades.

Notes

1 He claimed to have performed the role some 3,000 times during his career, and the *Liverpool Echo* in 1939 was putting the figure at 4,999 (26 April 1939, 14). Butler suggests that the total number was 2,475. Nicholas Butler, *John Martin-Harvey: The Biography of an Actor-Manager* (Colchester: Nicholas Butler, 1997), 135.
2 *Liverpool Mercury*, 16 June 1885, 8.
3 G. B. Shaw, quoted in Ralph Berry, 'Benson's Shakespeare', in Richard Foulkes (ed.), *British Theatre in the 1890s: Essays on Drama and the Stage* (Cambridge: Cambridge University Press, 1992), 184.
4 Butler, *John Martin-Harvey*, 61.
5 Maurice Wilson Disher, *The Last Romantic: The Authorised Biography of Sir John Martin-Harvey* (London: Hutchinson, 1948), 157.
6 Dennis Kennedy, 'British Theatre, 1895–1946: Arts, Entertainment, Audiences – an Introduction', in Baz Kershaw (ed.), *The Cambridge History of British Theatre. Volume 3: Since 1895* (Cambridge: Cambridge University Press, 2004), 10.
7 Hesketh Pearson, *The Last Actor Managers* (London: White Lion, 1950), 41.
8 *The Times*, 18 April 1933, 12.
9 Julia Neilson, *This for Remembrance* (London: Hurst and Blacklett, 1940), 173. Many claim that Fred Terry, who died in 1933, retired in 1927, but he appeared at the Royal Court in 1928 and 1929.
10 Sally Duggan, *Baroness Orczy's The Scarlet Pimpernel* (Farnham: Ashgate, 2012), 83.
11 Jim Davies, '*The Only Way* and the Other Way: a Dickens Adaptation for the 1890s', in Richard Foulkes (ed.), *British Theatre in the 1890s: Essays on Drama and the Stage* (Cambridge: Cambridge University Press, 1992), 61.
12 *The Stage*, 23 February 1899, 14.
13 Ibid., 14
14 Davies, '*The Only Way* and the Other Way', 62.
15 Quoted in Butler, *John Martin-Harvey*, 142.
16 *The Era*, 18 February 1899, 15.
17 A. E. Wilson, *Edwardian Theatre* (London: Arthur Barker, 1951), 106.
18 Quoted in Butler, *John Martin-Harvey*, 61.
19 Disher, *The Last Romantic*, 168.
20 *Saturday Review*, 16 February 1901; quoted in Butler, *John Martin-Harvey*, 63.
21 *Daily Post*, 2 May 1939, 8.
22 *The Stage*, 25 September 1924, 20.
23 Ibid., 20.
24 *The Stage*, 2 October 1924, 19; Butler, *John Martin-Harvey*, 121–2.
25 *The Stage*, 2 October 1924, 10.
26 *The Times*, 18 April 1933, 12.
27 *Illustrated London News*, 21 April 1906, 2.
28 *Illustrated London News*, 21 April 1906, 2.
29 *Strand Magazine*, 49 (1915), 640.
30 Quoted in Duggan, *Baroness Orczy's The Scarlet Pimpernel*, 88.
31 Neilson, *This for Remembrance*, 193; Duggan, *Baroness Orczy's The Scarlet Pimpernel*, 88.
32 Duggan, *Baroness Orczy's The Scarlet Pimpernel*, 88.
33 Neilson, *This for Remembrance*, 171.
34 Neilson, *This for Remembrance*, 218.
35 Donald Wolfit, *First Interval: The Autobiography of Donald Wolfit* (London: Odhams Press, 1954), 100.
36 Ibid., 97.
37 Neilson, *This for Remembrance*, 205.
38 Wolfit, *First Interval*, 98.
39 Neilson, *This for Remembrance*, 208.
40 Ibid., 174.
41 Walter MacQueen-Pope, *Carriages at Eleven: The Story of Edwardian Theatre* (London: Robert Hale, 1947), 204.
42 Neilson, *This for Remembrance*, 173.
43 *Daily Telegraph*, 6 January 1905, 7.
44 Disher, *The Last Romantic*, 134–5.
45 Lou Warwick, *The Mackenzies Called Compton* (Northampton: Lou Warwick, 1977), 185.
46 *Liverpool Mercury*, 19 September 1899, 8.

47 Disher, *The Last Romantic*, 163.
48 David Cannadine, 'Gilbert and Sullivan: The Making and Un-Making of a British "Tradition"', in Roy Porter (ed.), *Myths of the English* (Oxford: Polity Press, 1993), 13.
49 Ibid., 18.
50 Ibid., 19.
51 Ibid., 19.
52 Ibid., 25–8.
53 *Liverpool Mercury*, 27 February 1883, 5; 14 September 1897, 8.
54 *Liverpool Mercury*, 14 September 1897, 8.
55 *Play Pictorial*, vol. IX, no. 55, 1907, 254.
56 *The Stage*, 8 April 1920, 16.
57 *The Stage*, 29 January 1925, 18.
58 Clive Barker, 'Theatre and Society: The Edwardian Legacy, the First World War and the Inter-war Years', in Clive Barker and Maggie B. Gale (eds), *British Theatre between the Wars, 1918–1939* (Cambridge: Cambridge University Press, 2000), 31.
59 Leslie Smith, *Modern British Farce: A Selective Study of British Farce from Pinero to the Present Day* (Basingstoke: Macmillan, 1989), 69.
60 Ben Travers, *Five Plays* (London: W.H. Allen, 1977), 244–5.
61 Len Platt, *Musical Comedy on the West End Stage, 1890–1939* (Basingstoke: Palgrave Macmillan, 2004), 70.
62 *The Stage*, 17 May 1904, 16.
63 John Stokes, 'Body Parts: The Success of the Thriller in the Inter-war Years', in Clive Barker and Maggie B. Gale (eds), *British Theatre between the Wars, 1918–1939* (Cambridge: Cambridge University Press, 2000), 42, 46–7.
64 *The Era*, 30 March 1921, 5.
65 Stokes, 'Body Parts', 42.
66 *The Stage*, 31 March 1921, 16.
67 Quoted in Stokes, 'Body Parts', 46.
68 Barker, 'Theatre and Society', 30; Stokes, 'Body Parts', 47.
69 *The Era*, 30 March 1921, 5.
70 Patrick Hamilton, *Rope* (1929) (London: Constable, 1985), 60–1.
71 Ibid., 84.
72 Ibid., 86.
73 *The Stage*, 2 July 1925, 14.
74 *The Stage*, 25 June 1925, 21; 26 November 1925, 20. The 'ghost train' turns out not to be quite so ghostly, but rather the cover for a Bolshevik gang smuggling machine guns into the country.
75 *The Stage*, 28 December 1928, 26.
76 *The Era*, 26 December 1928, 1.
77 *The Times*, 3 May 1926, 12.
78 Edgar Wallace, *The Ringer* (London: Samuel French, 1926), 67–8.
79 Ibid., 71–2.
80 *The Stage*, 19 May 1927, 16.
81 Ibid., 16.
82 *The Era*, 6 October 1920, 12.
83 *The Stage*, 9 December 1920, 17.

1904

29 February	*Amorelle*	Barton White; music by Gaston Serpette	comic opera
7 March	*Whitewashing Julia*	Henry A. Jones	comedy
14 March	*The Orchid*	J. T. Tanner; music by Ivan Caryll and Lionel Monckton	musical play
21 March	*The New Barmaid*	F. Bowyer and W. Edward Sprange; music by John Crook	musical play
28 March	*A Country Girl*	James T. Tanner; music by Lionel Monckton and Paul Ruebens	musical play
4 April	*Davy Garrick*	William Muskerry	Edward Compton Comedy Company
	She Stoops to Conquer	Oliver Goldsmith	
	A Reformed Rake	Walter E. Grogan and Pelham Hardwicke	
	The School for Scandal	Richard Brinsley Sheridan	
	To-Morrow		
	The Rivals	Richard Brinsley Sheridan	
11 April	*The Belle of New York*	Hugh Morton; music by Gustave Kerker	musical comedy
18 April	*The School Girl*	Henry Hamilton and Paul M. Potter; music by Leslie Stewart	musical comedy
25 April	*In Dahomey*	Jesse A. Shipp; music by Will Marion Cook	Negro musical comedy with Bert A. Williams, George Walker and Ada Overton Walker
2 May	Gilbert and Sullivan	D'Oyly Carte	
9 May	*Winnie Brook, Widow*	M. Watson and H. Fordwych	comedy

16 May	*The Good Hope*	Heijerman	with Ellen Terry and Matheson Lang
23 May	*The Bells*	Leopold Davis Lewis	Henry Irving
	Becket	Tennyson	
	The Merchant of Venice	Shakespeare	
	Louis XI	Adapted by Dion Boucicault from the French	
CLOSED			
1 August	*San Toy*	Edward Morton; music by Sidney Jones	musical play
8 August	*A Country Mouse*	Arthur Law	satirical comedy
15 August	*Joseph Entangled*	Henry A. Jones	comedy
22 August	*A Chinese Honeymoon*	George Dance; music by Howard Talbot	musical play
29 August	*The Girl From Kays*	Owen Hall; music by Ivan Caryll and Cecil Cook	musical comedy
5 September	*Boy Bob*	Stephen Bond and B. Soane-Roby	military play
12 September	*The Cingalee; or Sunny Ceylon*	James Tanner; music by Lionel Monckton and Paul Ruebens	musical play
19 September	*The Fairy's Dilemma*	W. S. Gilbert	domestic pantomime
26 September	*The Breed of the Treshams*	John Rutherford (Evelyn Greenleaf and Beulah Marie Dix)	John Martin Harvey
3 October	*Marguerite*	Michael Morton	with Lena Ashwell
10 October	*The Orchid*	J. T. Tanner; music by Ivan Caryll and Lionel Monckton	musical play with Lawrence Grossmith
17 October	*A Scrap of Paper*	Adapted by J. Palgrave Simpson from Victorien Sardou	Mr and Mrs Kendal
	The Elder Mrs Blossom	Ernest Hendrie and Metcalfe Wood	

Edward Compton as David Garrick

Henry Irving as Shylock, a role he played on his last appearance at the Royal Court in November 1904. He was due to appear at the theatre in October 1905 but died in Bradford the previous week.

	Still Waters Run Deep	Charles Wyndham	
	Dick Hope	Ernest Hendrie	
24 October	*Sunday*	Thomas Raceward	Fred Terry and Julia Neilson
31 October	*The New Clown*	H. M. Paull	farce with James Welch
7 November	*The Earl and the Girl*	Seymour Hicks; music by Ivan Caryll	musical comedy
14 November	*The Duchess of Dantzic*	Henry Hamilton; music by Ivan Caryll	romantic opera
21 November	*Mrs Dering's Divorce*	Henry A. Jones	with Mrs Langtry
28 November	*The Merchant of Venice*	Shakespeare	Henry Irving
	Becket	Tennyson	
	The Bells	Leopold Davis Lewis	
	The Lyons Mail	Charles Reade	
5 December	*A Country Girl*	James T. Tanner; music by Lionel Monckton and Paul Ruebens	
19 December	*Dick Whittington*		

A good play, well-acted, engrosses all our sense. We are once more as children listening to the story, be it tragic or comic. Our tears may yet glisten on our cheeks, but the troubles are forgotten as we listen to the tale. Is it not a worthy task, a necessary one, to cheer the leisure of those who work and to give an anodyne to such as sit in the shadows of great grief?

5 Lifting the Burden of Care: The First World War

To all and each,
Where sin is rife,
We go to teach
The simple life.
To banish lies,
The wrong to right,
To darkened eyes
To bring the light,
To all on earth,
To teach the truth,
The song of mirth,
The dance of youth.
So shall they be
In true accord
With Arcadee,
Where love is lord.[1]

On the day war was declared, a city about to be changed forever was presented with an image of a perfect and magical world, as the Royal Court played host to Robert Courtneidge's number one touring company in a production of *The Arcadians*, the show's fourth visit to the theatre. The musical fantasy starts in Arcadia, where they know nothing of buying and selling or eating meat or telling lies. The inhabitants believe that England is a land peopled by savages who crowd together and live in cages. Visited accidentally by Smith, a failing caterer whose plane crashes, they transform him into Simplicitas by throwing him into the well of Truth when he is discovered to be lying, and they set off to transform the whole of England into a place where virtue triumphs and the simple life is victorious. Inevitably, this does not work. Smith establishes a fake Arcadian restaurant and becomes the wealthy toast of the town. In disgust, the Arcadians return home, leaving the English to 'the Thing That is Not' and berating the people for not accepting 'the truth without making a show of it'.[2] Back in Arcady, they can enjoy life where

Summer never passes,
Warm the wind that wanders free
Thro' the bending grasses;

Sunbeams peeping through the shade
Mint a golden treasure;
Dimpled Youth goes down the glade
Hand in Hand with pleasure![3]

In Liverpool, the summer did pass and the impact of war was felt throughout the city from the first day. At Lime Street station, large crowds gathered to greet Territorials hastily recalled from distant annual training camps and to say farewell to large numbers of navy reservists. The *Daily Post* captured the scene, painting a picture of '[w]ives and children, with tears streaming down their faces' clinging 'to husbands and fathers in passionate farewell. Young girls flung themselves into the

Programme cover 1914

The end of September 1914 saw the arrival on stage of Raleigh and Hamilton's *Sealed Orders*, a play welcomed by the *Liverpool Echo* as 'a warlike play, full of patriotic sentiments' which threw interesting 'sidelights' on international political intrigue and the secret service (26 September 1914, 4).

arms of sweethearts whom, in their over-wrought state of mind, they imagined they would never see again. The horror of approaching war had already laid its cold grip on their hearts.'[4] Local battalions could be seen training in Knowsley, Croxteth and Sefton parks or guarding the coast. Financial institutions were closed for a week amid concerns about a run on the banks and the Stock Exchange. Liverpool stores were crowded with people panic buying foodstuffs; Coopers on Church Street was so full that it closed its doors, allowing in only one customer at a time. Leigh's on Byrom Street was besieged when it was discovered that sugar was on sale at 2d a pound, 7d a pound cheaper than Cooper's.[5] As the days wore on, the effect of the war spread through the city. Military law could mean being stopped by sentries on the road. People signed up for first aid training or responded to appeals for beds, bedding, pyjamas, clothing and cash for the new hospitals that were springing up through the city in expectation of the arrivals of casualties. The Earl of Derby offered the use of Knowsley Hall. The Liverpool industrialist Holbrook-Gaskell placed his 62-acre estate at Woolton Woods at the disposal of the War Office. The trustees of the late Sir Alfred Jones turned his Aigburth Road property, Oaklands, into a military hospital. The first wounded arrived on 22 September on board a steamer, with more following by train to Aintree station. Other new arrivals included Belgian refugees, 400 arriving in mid-October to be greeted at Lime Street by the Liverpool Consul for Belgian Refugees and Other Allies with the band of the 79th Brigade of Scouts playing the Belgian national anthem. By the end of October, when the Chief Constable announced that there would be no more refugees coming to the

The battle in the Zeppelin from *Sealed Orders*
(*Play Pictorial*)

city because of its protected nature, there were between 1,100 and 1,200 Belgians in Liverpool.[6]

Seemingly undeterred by the arrival of the wounded, men rushed to enlist. The recruiting office headquarters in the Old Haymarket was besieged and when, on 8 August, Lord Kitchener called for 100,000 army volunteers, the city 'made every effort … to be able to report that Liverpool was the first to place a new 800 strong battalion in the field'.[7] An appeal by Lord Derby in the newspapers on 27 August resulted in 1,500 recruits from commercial offices, and on

> Saturday morning, Liverpool had their first opportunity of seeing the comrades en masse. After mustering in their trade sections at their respective exchanges or on Exchange Flags, the men marched through the city to Ivy Farm, Tramway Road, Aigburth where a general parade took place before their commander. After a crash course in drill, the recruits marched in four columns along thoroughfares lined with cheering crowds to be reviewed on the steps of St George's Hall by General Sir Henry Mackinnon Commander in Chief (CIC) Western Command…[8]

By 14 November 1914 there were four pals battalions, an entire brigade to fulfil Lord Derby's ambitions. For those men too old to be army recruits, the Liverpool Civic Service League Committee, formed during the 1911 strike and consequently resented by many in the city, announced it would dedicate itself to the war effort. By the end of August 1,500 men between the ages of 35 and 50 had signed up for duties as special constables or to work with the St John's Ambulance Brigade.

As the war progressed there were very real fears of Zeppelin raids and invasion. As a result, air raid precaution lighting restrictions were implemented in February 1915 and public illuminations were dimmed. Buildings considered to be potential German targets were left in total darkness and the *Liverpool Echo* reported that while Lord Street and Church Street were 'thronged as they always are on a Saturday night with arm-linked promenaders and people hurrying to and from theatres', they had 'an air of unwanted glumness'. Lime Street 'took on an eerie character in the partial eclipse'.[9] Lighting was forced to dim further in 1916, following an abortive attempt by German Zeppelins to reach Liverpool on a bombing mission (they mistook the lights of Derby, Tipton and Wednesbury for Manchester, Birkenhead and Liverpool, and 61 people in the Midlands were killed). As a result, in Liverpool, all external or externally seen lights had to be extinguished unless the Chief of Police thought them necessary for safety. As Stephen McGreal notes, shop lighting was dimmed, tram lighting was reduced to a level 'sufficient only for collecting fares' and households were advised to fit blackout blinds and to keep buckets of sand and water upstairs in case of incendiary bombs. The population was informed that in the event of approaching aircraft, the electricity and gas would be shut off.[10]

The escalation of fighting in the Western Approaches brought the war even closer as the Atlantic became 'the graveyard of merchant ships and Liverpool mercantile marine personnel'.[11] The workforce and the nature of work also changed. By mid-1915 twenty local firms were engaged in the manufacture of shells, and from the end of 1915 women entered the workforce in growing numbers – from working in munitions factories to collecting train tickets or delivering the post. By 1917 shortages were beginning to bite. On 1 January sugar was rationed to half a pound a person (when it was available) and white bread disappeared with the introduction of the 'national loaf'. There was also a potato famine, with the city holding only 20 tons of potatoes as opposed to the usual 200 tons, and, according to Lee Ruddin, hundreds of chip shops had closed down in the city.[12] Prolonged bad weather also led to coal shortages and McGreal reports that in Crown Street, 'hundreds of people of all classes attempted to get coal and one firm was forced to call in the police'.[13] Accompanying the shortages were price rises. Food prices had risen by 100 per cent in the previous two and a half years and wages lagged well behind. One response to this was to grow your own, and allotments started to spring up across the city, including in Sefton Park where the football pitches were ploughed up.

In June 1917 the population of the city changed with the arrival of the first American, the commander of the American Expeditionary Force, who was greeted at the Pier Head by a huge crowd. He was followed by some 840,000 American troops in 1918 who disembarked at ports on the River Mersey, the vast majority then marching through the streets to the American Camp at Knotty Ash. The marking of Independence Day that year with celebrations in St George's Square attracted some 50,000 people who 'thronged the route, collected in windows and perched even on the roofs' to cheer the American troops.[14] But as much as war changed the face of the city and the reality of people's day-to-day lives, on the whole the Royal Court chose to look the other way.

Stealing an Hour from Sorrow

> So far … from feeling that theatrical performances are vicious at the present moment, I cannot think when they were more urgently needed. This is an hour when all aids to cheerfulness are assets of priceless value. Everything that can steal an hour from sorrow, or lift the burden of care from the depressed or overworked shoulders, deserves the commendation and support

of the community. A good play, well-acted, engrosses all our sense. We are once more as children listening to the story, be it tragic or comic. Our tears may yet glisten on our cheeks, but the troubles are forgotten as we listen to the tale. Is it not a worthy task, a necessary one, to cheer the leisure of those who work and to give an anodyne to such as sit in the shadows of great grief?[15]

Robert Courtneidge's words could sum up the philosophy of most of the work at the Royal Court during the war years. In common with theatres around the country, the aim seemed to be to 'provide a space or a brief moment where the grief and sorrow of wartime could be kept outdoors'.[16] Consequently, shows were predominantly advertised and reviewed as 'a welcome relaxation at the present strenuous time' (*The Marriage Market*)[17] or as 'full of light trifles' (*A Little Bit of Fluff*)[18] or as a way 'to brighten the hours when one can escape from war's alarms' (*The Girl in the Taxi*).[19] Musical comedy dominated the stage of the Court between 1914 and 1918, and although one of the biggest war hits, *Chu Chin Chow,* did not make it to the theatre until 1921, the other big success, *Maid of the Mountains,* a love story of mountain bandits, made three appearances in 1917 and 1918. Many of the musicals were revivals of shows staged before the war, such as J. T. Tanner's *A Country Girl,* first staged at the Court in 1904, or else were musicals 'built unashamedly in the traditional model' such as Basil Hood's *The Pearl Girl* which had cashed in on the notoriety of a court case involving a stolen pearl necklace.[20] Kurt Ganzl's outline of what he describes as the 'well-used' plot of Hicks's *The Earl and the Girl* (originally written in 1903 and staged at the Court in 1904, 1905 and 1907 before returning in 1915) gives a flavour of the kind of musicals seen most often during the war by the Royal Court audience:

Jim Cheese, a dog trainer, cannot pay his hotel bill and wishes he was someone else. David Wargrave has got engaged to £3m heiress Elphin Haye and has heard that her fearsome uncle, A. Bunker Bliss, is after him and he, too, wishes he were, at least ostensibly, someone else. In good musical comedy fashion, the two swap identities with the complicity of their respective young ladies. But other people are after Dick as well: an English solicitor and an American attorney with the news that he has inherited the Earldom of Stole. In the circumstances it is Jim Cheese who receives both the brickbats of Bunker Bliss and the coronet. Therewith, everyone repairs to the increasingly popular second act location of Nice where the sorting-out motions are gone through.[21]

Less evident were revues. The theatre did see *To-night's the Night* (September 1915 and March 1916), *The Bing Boys Are Here* (March and October 1917) and *Bric-*

a-Brac (June 1917), but the faster-paced, brasher form was not much in evidence, despite the fact that by 1915 Edgar White found revue sharing 'with Charlie Chaplin and the war the chief attention of the British public'.[22] Nor did the Royal Court see much of what Herbert Farjeon described as the 'gloom boom', and Eugene Brieux's *Damaged Goods*, a thesis on sexually transmitted diseases, which became a 'theatrical money-spinner' and brought a spate of propaganda plays in its wake, did not appear on its stage, though it was seen in Liverpool at the Olympia in 1917.[23] However, in June 1917, more than a decade before it appeared on the main stage of the much more radical Playhouse, the war did bring the first performance of Ibsen's *Ghosts*, a play which also dealt with syphilis and the idea of the sins of the father being visited on the son. The *Daily Post* was 'more impressed with it' than any play it had seen for years and suggested that 'every soul in the crowded audience seemed to feel the same'. The paper encouraged people to go if they could 'face life seriously at a serious time'.[24]

Much more apparent were comedies and farces, the latter, according to Gordon Williams, particularly popular because of the need created by the war for people to 'escape from moral responsibility' and a growing sense of 'moral dislocation'.[25] But the Royal Court audience seemed to have a keener taste for sentimental comedies that represented little sense of moral dislocation. J. Hartley Manners's *Peg o' My Heart* (which appeared five times during the war) was 'welcomed by all those who like their laughter to tremble on the brink of tears'.[26] The story of Peg, an Irish girl who will come into an inheritance if she can only get a suitable education, is a sentimental one. Newly arrived from New York at her pretentious but impecunious English relatives, Peg's innocence and innate wisdom win out against the snobbery of her new family. Likewise, Horace Vachell's *Quinney's* (September 1915, April 1917 and May 1918) was a family comedy, with a self-made Yorkshire father at the helm, which pitted affection against standing in society. The *Liverpool Echo* described it as a play that posed no moral questions but was just 'splendid entertainment'.[27]

Detective plays started to appear, although these were often comic, as in the case of *Grumpy*, the story of an eccentric criminal lawyer caught up in finding a diamond stolen from his nephew. The Royal Court had to wait until August 1918, with a performance of Eugene Walters's *The Knife*, for the arrival of the hard-boiled American 'crook drama' which came to dominate the genre during the war. As with the previous era, the Court liked to stick with what it knew, and even a surfeit of 'piquant, palpitating and picturesque' musical comedies could lead the *Daily Post* to welcome with a real sense of relief the return of the 'restful and refreshing … older order of things' with the arrival of *Caste* in March 1915.[28] Given that *Caste* had been produced by the Edward Compton Comedy Company (with his 1,864th appearance as Garrick), an event that was 'always sure to awaken agreeable recollections in the minds of old playgoers', it could be argued that the war made little difference to the taste of the Royal Court audience.[29] Indeed, the stress of war may have strengthened the hold of older values at the Court.

But inevitably, the war made some of the old favourites take on new resonances. Swashbuckling heroes rescuing people, or whole countries, from despotic tyrants, from Lewis Waller's *The Three Musketeers* (April 1915) and the Terrys' *Scarlet Pimpernel* (October 1916 and November 1917) to Baroness Orczy's *The Legion of Honour* (June 1918), were uniformly proclaimed apposite for the times. Plays rooted in history reminded audiences both of what was being fought for as well as allowing for some nostalgia. Arnold Bennett and Edward Knoblock's *Milestones* (making its fourth appearance at the theatre in December 1914), with its story set across three generation in 1860, 1885 and 1912, suggested continuity. Charles Marlowe's dream fantasy *When Knights Were Bold* made a welcome wartime appearance in August 1916, evoking notions of chivalry and valour. Shakespeare clearly could be seen to speak for the times; the arrival of F. R. Benson in February was particularly welcomed in 'these days of boasted patriotism'.[30] But for all these reverberations, the theatre's face seemed firmly turned against the realities of war either at the front or at home. It was an era of escape – to the mystery of the Orient in *Mr Wu*, to the colour and breeziness of California in *The Marriage Market* and to rollicking adventures with pirates in *The Spanish Main*.

The War Creeps In

However much the theatre might have tried to encourage its audience to escape from the war, the war changed the theatre. This was noticeable in the make-up of the audience, from the large audience for George Edwardes's *Gipsy Love* in November 1914, which was 'freely besprinkled' with representatives of the forces, to the many Belgian refugees in attendance at John Martin-Harvey's performance of *The Taming of the Shrew* in October of the same year. Closing the show, 'speaking in French and to enthusiastic applause', Martin-Harvey addressed 'some words of cheer, assuring them of Britain's determination to see them restored to their own country'.[31] Martin-Harvey also took a leading role in using the theatre to raise funds, holding a Sunday concert in aid of the Officers War Hospital Fund and becoming renowned for his Sunday lectures and curtain speeches which urged men to join up. In October 1914 the stage of the Royal Court was adorned with the Union Jack and the flags of allied nations while Martin-Harvey addressed a large audience on war issues and enlistment; the climax of the evening was the theatre orchestra playing all the allied national anthems.[32] Martin-Harvey invited young men who had not yet joined up to meet him at the stage door, hinting that he could secure them postings to the regiment of their choice. He often recited Helen Gray Cone's 'An American Chant of Love for England', both in the theatre and at special concerts for the wounded, which the *Daily Post* suggested was a worthy reply to Germany's 'Hymn of Hate':

> A song of hate is a song of Hell;
> Some there be that sing it well.
> Let them sing it loud and long.
> We lift our hearts in a loftier song;
> We lift our hearts to heaven above,
> Singing the glory of her we love – England!
>
> Glory of thought and glory of deed,
> Glory of Hamden and Runnymeade;
> Glory of ships that sought far goals,
> Glory of swords and glory of souls!
> Glory of songs mounting as birds,
> Glory immortal of magical words;
> Glory of Milton, Glory of Nelson,
> Tragical glory of Gordon and Scott,
> Glory of Shelley, Glory of Sidney,
> Glory transcendent that perishes not, –
> Hers is the story, hers be the glory,
> *England!*[33]

Other companies made less rhetorical contributions. The proceeds from a matinee of *The Fantastics* were donated to the Home Service Corps by the Esme Percy and Kirsten Graeme Company, and in 1916, at a tea held in the Town Hall by the mayor and mayoress for 500 wounded servicemen, the entertainment was provided by artistes from the Royal Court including Little Tich.[34] Like Martin-Harvey, Lewis Waller took part in recruitment activities in the city while on tour to the Royal Court and spoke at Exchange Flags in early October 1915, telling those present that 'England needs you to maintain the freedom of Europe against the most notorious bully in the world'.[35] The speech finished with Henry V's rousing speech at Agincourt which was met with loud and prolonged applause and which prompted the *Daily Post* reporter to write that 'one will not readily forget the note of scorn with which the actor emphasised the reference to "gentlemen in England now abed"'.[36]

Not all actors were seemingly as welcome on stage. At the end of 1915 the Liverpool theatres followed the example of London, where, after some long and loud hooting at the 'supposed slackers of the footlights', notices had been put up announcing that all male members of the companies were ineligible for the Army. The *Liverpool Echo* was also moved to mount its own defence of the profession which had 'done wonders in connection with recruiting efforts, help for the wounded, enlivening the Tommie at the Front and in subscribing members of the profession to the colours'. To make the point even more clearly, the article was accompanied by a letter from Jack Roberts, a repertory actor, who was at the Front.[37] While some actors had volunteered, the introduction of conscription for healthy single men aged 18 to 41 in March 1916 (with married men added in May 1916 and men up to the age of 51 in 1918) had an influence on the availability of male performers. *The Stage* did argue that actors were of vital economic importance to the country, with amusements being 'among the necessities of life', but gaps started to appear, especially in opera choruses and orchestras.[38] When the Moody-Manners Opera Company appeared at Kelly's Theatre, Liverpool in 1916, Charles Manners told the audience that

> [a] difficulty lay in the fact that so many men were being called up for Army Service. Last week the orchestra had had to do its parts without the assistance of a cello or a flute and it was probable that as many as eight or ten members of the company might have to go at one rush ... Unlike the modern revue, men were essential in opera; they could not, for example, represent Valentine or Mephistopheles with ladies.[39]

The arrival of conscription also made places of entertainment potentially dangerous for those eluding military service, and local raids targeted popular public places including cafés and theatres.

Rising taxes, including the 1916 Entertainment Tax which added to the cost of tickets, and rising living costs created further problems. Transport, too, was an increasingly challenging difficulty for touring companies. Pressure on the railways was enormous and theatre companies were not a high priority. Fares increased and restrictions were placed on luggage, leading to immense difficulties in travelling with scenery and props, as *The Stage* leader noted:

> It is one thing to bring the play, the company, the wardrobe and a reasonable amount of printing, and another thing to bring the whole production, often with tons of scenery and properties, and sometimes with extra working staff and musicians ... So far, the railway companies profess their ability to get a company into a town in time for the opening on the Monday night, but they accept no responsibility for the due delivery of scenery etc. As an official of one of the great railway companies said ... last week: "War traffic ... must have precedence of all else and the manager must not expect that he will be

> able to get his scenery over a long stretch of country on Sunday and unload it on Sunday night…"[40]

In order to ensure that people moved as quickly as possible, goods wagons not containing war necessities could be uncoupled and left in sidings. Such restrictions put more pressure on the local theatres to provide scenery, and also meant that some of the productions that boasted that they had come straight from a London success may not have boasted the same scale of production. *The Stage* argued, anyway, that spectacular shows were an 'incubus' in wartime and 'should be avoided accordingly'. The combination of hardships in finding male actors and transport shortages caused problems for theatres in finding productions. Some touring managers decided to 'go off the road for the time being' or to curtail their operations and *The Stage* appealed to theatres to help companies 'to travel light and travel less' by organising longer engagements and by better coordination between venues. There was even a suggestion that some theatres should contemplate returning to stock seasons, putting on their own shows with the help of touring managers.[41]

The theatre people who had some of the most difficult times in the early days of the war were the foreign musicians. A wave of xenophobia swept through the country at the outbreak of the war and 'residents were encouraged to assist the police and military authorities by reporting any suspicious movements of foreigners'.[42] From the start of the war a 'self-imposed "purification" boycott of all plays originating in enemy states' was in operation, backed up by a policy of banning operas by living German composers.[43] In the early days, some German work slipped through; *The Cinema Star* (September 1914 and March 1915), with Jack Hulbert and Cicely Courtneidge, was based on a German show, *Kino-Königen*. Starting to do bad business in London, where 'everything Germanic was anathema', it was sent on the road 'where the thought of boycotting German-written music had not yet taken hold'.[44] The sinking of the *Lusitania* in 1915 with its predominantly Liverpool crew 'awoke sharper tempers' and 200 German shops in the city were wrecked in three days, with 'the outbreak of hostility towards German residents and shopkeepers … so determined the police were powerless to check the depredations of indignant people'.[45] The Cotton Association, which had already expelled enemy aliens, resolved that no member should trade directly or indirectly with Britain's enemies for ten years after an armistice and Liverpool's Conservative MPs looked to root out alien directors and shareholders from British companies. The introduction of a National Restriction Order as early as 5 August 1914 (with three further orders following in quick succession) meant that any 'enemy alien' had to register at the central police station. In Liverpool, they required special police permits to live in a port city and could not travel more than five miles from their residence without police permission, an order that was also accompanied by a host of other restrictions. Spy fever (accompanied by an argument about protecting the safety of enemy aliens) had led the Home Office to order a round-up of Germans and Austrians to be sent to detention camps. In Liverpool, according to McGreal, the police arrested every German, Hungarian and Austrian male between the ages of 17 and 45, including the Liver Bird sculptor Carl Bernard Bartels.[46]

All of this impacted on the many foreign musicians in the city who were playing in theatre and music hall orchestras, encouraging those who were looking to undermine what they perceived as a foreign takeover of orchestras. In October 1914, under the chairmanship of Sir Frederick Cowen, a committee was set up seeking to 'inaugurate a central bureau for the purpose of supplying information to employers and others as to British musicians, British music and British musical commodities' and to 'start a campaign for enforcing a preference in every direction for native orchestral players'.[47] Concerns were raised not just about 'undue preference' being given to European musicians and composers but also their possible connections with spying, a 'well-known Liverpool musician' telling the *Daily Post* that one foreign musician 'who had played at most of our local seaside resorts was found in possession of a motor-cycle and a camera long after the proclamation was made forbidding aliens possession of such articles'.[48] At the same time, Sir Thomas Beecham was writing to the conductor at the Royal Court promising to preside over a meeting in Liverpool to discuss the matter. There is no evidence that he kept this promise, but a large gathering of local musicians did take place in November 1914. The musicians attending were principally drawn from theatre and music hall orchestras (including Joe Sheppard, the recent conductor at the Royal Court, along with Julian H. Wilson who had replaced him). Held at the Marlborough Hall on Hardman Street, James M. Glover, musical director at Drury Lane, spoke on 'The Alien Musician Question'. He started by talking about his memories of first coming to Liverpool thirty-four years previously as a touring conductor. Then, at the old Prince of Wales Theatre, 'he found that the foreign musician was not a serious element'. Since then, however, the increase in places of entertainment had led to 'cheap foreign players', particularly those who were now the enemy, cutting 'the feet from under the Britishers'. He suggested that foreign musicians had earned £19,700 while many 'able Britishers were walking about looking for work', and concluded by saying that if the musicians of the country 'intended to seize hold that which belonged to them, now was the time to do so before the war ended'.[49] There is no evidence of what happened as a result, but the *Post* claimed that not a single German or Austrian musician was employed in Lancashire, and the same 'well-known Liverpool musician' suggested that all the Belgian musicians of fighting age had returned to Belgium and the German musicians had either left for Germany prior to the start of the war or were interned.[50]

The War on Stage

Nationally, there was debate throughout the war about the appropriateness of staging war plays. *The Era* leader-writer of August 1914 thought the audience would resent both flippancy and chauvinism in war plays, that writers needed to 'avoid boastfulness and brag' and at the same time maintain 'a tone of quiet confidence'.[51] Two years later, the same paper addressed the problem of bringing the real tragedy of war to the stage, especially when actors were resistant to appearing on stage to spout 'cheap patriotism as a khaki hero'.[52] One of the problems facing the theatre was balancing what was staged with the realities that people were facing both through their own lives and losses and through what they were reading on the pages of the local paper about the truth of life at the Front. Despite tight regulations on what could be printed in newspapers, Michael Finn has shown that local papers were openly asking for letters from soldiers, which were printed on their pages and which often offered graphic descriptions of life at the Front. The retreat from Mons, for example, was depicted in the Liverpool press in 'cataclysmic terms' through a letter from Private William Ball from Birkdale, who was serving with the South Lancashires when he was shot and wounded in Belgium. A letter to his wife was 'syndicated' in most of the north Liverpool papers and printed with a heading 'Men fell dead just like sheep'. Ball told his wife:

> [o]ur regiment was first in the firing line, and we were simply cut up. Very few escaped, so I think I was lucky, for I was nearly half a mile creeping over nothing but dead men in the trenches. Bullets and shells came down on us like rain. I even had to lift up dead men and get under them for safety.[53]

The realities of the Front were also brought home in the cinema with the arrival in August 1916 of the documentary *The Battle of the Somme*. Released in an attempt to 'bridge the divide between the lives of soldiers on the Western Front and civilians on the Home Front', people were encouraged by royalty and politicians to watch the film.[54] It fast became the talk of Liverpool that month and there was a great demand for seats, a demand met by it being shown in three city-centre cinemas. Ruddin suggests that 'as appreciative as civilians were for accounts of soldier life, the silent black and white images left many initially speechless and after animated', conveying, as they did, a much greater sense of reality than the lengthy lists of casualties.[55]

Responses in the papers included the following from the *Evening Express*, which observed that

> [u]ntil *The Battle of the Somme* was put up on the screen English people at home had merely an imaginative idea of what war mean[t]. [The film] show[s] much of devastation that modern conflict entails ... an entire countryside reduced to a wilderness ... British soldiers falling dead in the act of charging over the parapets ... huddled heaps of killed, and groups of prisoners ... Yesterday I watched the onlookers ... little gasps of pity were heard as our wounded were carried past, and there was an awe-stricken silence as the pictures rested for a moment on the figure of a British soldier seated dead – poor fellow – in a trench ... The attitude was one of weariness, like that of a man overcome with fatigue fallen asleep. They were pictures that produced a new gravity, a new sense of what war news really means, and of what is to be read between the lines of the daily communiques.[56]

In the same month the Royal Court was showing *Charley's Aunt, Peg o' My Heart, When Knights Were Bold* and the musical *Mr Manhattan*. But, given the letters and the film and people's lived experience, the theatre could not entirely ignore the war or simply offer ways to escape from it. Although there was no evidence of 'a wild scamper after topicality', there were a few moments that touched on the outside world, although none that touched on life at the Front or that moved far from the realms of melodrama.[57]

Possibly the harshest and most uncompromising war play staged between 1914 and 1918 was John Martin-Harvey's *Armageddon* (October 1915). Written by Stephen Phillips, it was, according to Butler, 'propaganda, bigoted, crude and humourless'.[58] It opened with a Prologue set in Hell and with Martin-Harvey playing Satan, wearing a pair of large wings and little else, the 'very spirit of Milton's devil'.[59] He is smarting from his defeat and decides to unleash a holocaust, sending Attila the Hun back to earth accompanied by the sound of wailing women and children. The first scene showed German officers in Rheims wanting to destroy the cathedral even though it was flying the Red Cross flag. They threaten a peasant with death and his girlfriend with dishonour if they do not help. The peasant is shot; the girlfriend manages to shoot herself. The Abbé of the cathedral (also played by Martin-Harvey) is dismissed when he comes to beg for his church to be saved. The German commander invokes the spirit of Attila and bids his fellow officers to banish pity. As they sit drinking and singing 'Deutschland über Alles', a shell explodes, killing them all. In an English orchard at sunset, Lady Carteret and her son's fiancée Nell talk of the glories of war where it is 'Splendid to stand against the leaden hail!/ Or in the mowed war-line to give no inch./ How fine the grapple in the very heaven!/ Or go back for a friend through gaping death!'[60] But as women these joys are forbidden them, so they wait and hope, only to be brought the news of the death of the son. In Germany, the head of the German Press Bureau listens to lies made up by his staff, dismissing one who inadvertently publishes a fact that is true. In Cologne, the cathedral is likely to be flattened by the Allies in revenge for the destruction of the cathedral in Rheims. Three generals, English, French and Belgian, debate the matter. Beneath a portrait of Joan of Arc, the English general (played by Martin-Harvey) argues in favour of sparing the cathedral, even when news of the death of his son is brought to him. Joan of Arc comes to life, asking for the cathedral to be spared. The whole finishes back in Hell where Satan is congratulating Attila for his success when suddenly a shaft of light appears and Satan cowers beneath 'a dreadful fall of gentleness, a flower-soft influence omnipotent'.[61] Not successful when it opened in London in June 1915, the play stayed in Martin-Harvey's repertoire until the spring of 1916 and then quietly disappeared, although not before the *Liverpool Echo* declared it was 'one of the most important contributions to war literature since the outbreak of the hostilities'.[62]

The first war play to reach the Royal Court stage was *Sealed Orders* (September 1914), advertised as the 'Great Patriotic Naval Play' and welcomed by the local press as being 'full of patriotic sentiments' in depicting Britain at war with a foreign country 'whose people bear singularly German names'.[63] In reality, Cecil Raleigh and Henry Hamilton's play had first appeared at Drury Lane in 1913 and rather than being a 'great, patriotic naval play', it was a melodramatic adventure with plenty of splendid scenery that ranged from Christie's auction room to a Zeppelin, in the basket of which the protagonists fight only for it to be shot down by a naval gun, becoming, in front of the audience's eyes, 'a weird and tangled mass of falling debris'.[64] The convoluted story starts with a bungled jewel robbery, the clerk involved ending up working for the suspiciously named Baron Kurdman, who is determined to acquire the sealed orders of the title upon which the safety of the Empire depends. To this are added incriminating gambling debts and two small Chinese idols that carry a dire curse for anyone who buys or sells them. But it seemed to catch something of the mood of the early war years and a sense of adventure, with the *Liverpool Echo* praising it for throwing insight on international political intrigue as well as demonstrating 'the use of aircraft and motor cars in times of stress, the importance of the Navy to England and the advantages of big guns over airships'.[65] Similar in melodramatic tone was the play that arrived towards the end of the war. Lawrence Cowen's *The Hidden Hand* was premiered at the Royal Court (27 May 1918) and focused on the dangers that those in prominent social positions could pose. Set at the beginning of the war, Sir Charles Rosenbaum MP has, from 'patriotic motives', assumed a Scottish name, and his frequent and emphatic expressions of abhorrence at Germany's crimes convinces everyone of his loyalty to Britain. In reality, he is stirring up strikes in his own shipbuilding firm, securing government secrets through bribery, signalling to enemy aircraft and scattering bacteria germs among people. He is stopped by the heroine, Mary Marshall, with the aid of a patriotic soldier clergyman called St George. Although the dialogue 'not infrequently' approached 'what in ordinary life would be condemned as ranting', the bombastic journalist and leading propagandist in the war effort, Horatio Bottomley, declared it to be 'far and away the finest war play ever written'. He hoped it would 'rouse the country to a proper realisation of our true position'.[66] The play was presented under the auspices of the Theatrical Propaganda Department, to which the union leader Ben Tillett had been appointed director in May, and despite 'the marked extremes of "good" and "bad" people all ... prone to loudly uttered sentiments', it was greeted in Liverpool by frequent applause, close attention and hearty cheers.[67]

Less melodramatic was what was seen as the stirring story told in Gladys Unger and A. Neil Lyons's *London Pride* (October 1917 and April 1918). Described by *The Stage* as 'a cockney idyll seen through war spectacles', it was the story of Cuthbert Tunks and included scenes in France and in an English hospital, as well as 'the final decoration of the coster soldier with the V.C.' Unfortunately, in order to get home to help his girlfriend, he is impersonating a dead soldier, so is not a real war hero, but the *Liverpool Echo* still praised it for 'possessing patriotic fervour'.[68] The most popular war play was J. E. Harold Terry and Lechmere Worrall's *The Man Who Stayed at Home* (April and November 1915). It is dismissed by Williams as a 'solid second-rater', but was greeted in the local press as a 'play of the moment' and one of 'the very few war-plays written for this war time that have achieved and deserve to achieve real success'.[69] The play exploited the East Coast spy terror in the country, but the fear (and reality) of spies was also very real in Liverpool. In the same year the play was performed, Carl Hans Lody, a German who spoke fluent English and travelled on an American passport, was arrested. On his way to Ireland, and unaware his messages were being intercepted by Military Intelligence, he wrote a detailed letter about the ships in the port of Liverpool and other military matters, and was arrested in Dublin.[70] *The Man Who Stayed at Home* confronted the audience with the idea that things are not always what they seem and people are not always who they say they are. It is set in an undefined seaside resort at Wave Crest, a hotel which '*requires no description*' as '[*its*] *like must be familiar to at least fifty out of every men and women in the country*' being '*more of less comfortable, more or less pretentious and chiefly more than less furnished on the hire purchase system*'.[71] But the hotel proves to be much more than this, harbouring no fewer than four German spies who covered 'most of the permutations and combinations and transfigurations' of the spy.[72] There is Fritz, the German waiter, allegedly Dutch and clearly above suspicion as he whistles the Marseillaise and is in charge of the carrier pigeons roosting in the garden. He is aided by the German governess, Fraulein Schroeder, who speaks immaculate English and has impeccable references but who also turns out to be a dab hand at producing drawings of the harbour defences. In charge is the English-sounding Mrs Sanderson, owner of the hotel, who in reality was born in Dresden and, though hiding behind her second husband's English name, is the widow of General von Mantel, the greatest German expert in the art of espionage. The quartet is completed by her son Carl, who has managed to get himself a job at the Admiralty, providing him with ample opportunity for unearthing information. The fireplace, which never has a fire in it, contains a Marconi wireless and other transmitting and receiving equipment. Eventually, with the radio disabled and the last carrier pigeon shot, the Germans send a signal by setting the hotel on fire, rejoicing in the thought of roasting the English visitors in their beds. They have to be stopped and on their trail is Christopher Brent, 'a particular sort of idiot' and a 'pseudo Johnny' on the surface, but who proves himself to be a super spy, 'a military Sherlock Holmes'.[73] The play also touches on a number of other war issues, from 'those Russians' to the proffering of white feathers and uniforms that do not fit, but for all its comedy, melodrama and stereotypes, it was a play that J. T. Grein declared was 'the real article', conjuring up no pictures of war and 'looking on the situation at home with a sense of humour'.[74] In Liverpool, its return was welcomed.

On the day war ended the theatre was opening with George Grossmith and Edward Laurillard's *Arlette,* described variously as an operetta and a musical comedy. Set in the mythical country of Pirania, it was a work much more in keeping with the theatre's repertoire. While there is a sub-plot involving spying and a plan to assassinate Prince Paul, it was really a 'lovely and light-hearted show', a 'very pleasing light entertainment'.[75] With the country bankrupt, ministers advertise for an heiress to marry the prince, a call responded to by an American millionaire and his daughter Cherry. In the meantime, the prince has fallen in love with Arlette, who works at the palace, and decides he would rather spend his life in poverty and obscurity with her. Everything is neatly tied up when he abdicates in favour of his cousin, who Cherry seems just as happy with. From the start to the end of the war, it might appear as if little had changed on the stage of the Court.

Notes

1 Mark Ambient, A. M. Thompson and Robert Courtneidge, *The Arcadians* (London: Samuel French, 1909; repr. 1945), 20.
2 Ibid., 8.
3 Ibid., 32.
4 *Daily Post*, 4 August 1914, quoted in Stephen McGreal, *Liverpool in the Great War* (Barnsley: Pen and Sword Military, 2014), 19.
5 McGreal, *Liverpool in the Great War*, 24.
6 *Daily Post*, 30 October 1914, 3.
7 McGreal, *Liverpool in the Great War*, 31.
8 Ibid., 35.
9 Ibid., 50.
10 Ibid., 88.
11 Ibid., 48.
12 Lee P. Ruddin, 'The "Firsts" World War: A History of the Morale of Liverpudlians as Told through Letters to Liverpool Editors, 1915–1918', *International Journal of Regional and Local History* 9.2 (2014), 85.
13 McGreal, *Liverpool in the Great War*, 110.
14 Ruddin, 'The "Firsts" World War', 88.
15 *The Stage*, 20 May 1915, 18.
16 Eva Krivanec, 'Staging War. Theatre 1914–1918', in *1914–1918 online: International Encyclopaedia of the First World War* (2014), 2, https://encyclopedia.1914-1918-online.net/article/staging_war_theatre_1914-1918 (accessed 27 November 2018). Helen Brook's Great War Theatre Project (https://www.greatwartheatre.org.uk/, accessed 27 November 2018) suggests that far more plays performed and written during the war did reflect life on the front line than has previously been thought.
17 *Liverpool Echo*, 6 October 1914, 3.
18 *Liverpool Echo*, 22 September 1916, 3.
19 *Liverpool Echo*, 1 September 1914, 4.
20 Ganzl, *British Musical Theatre*, vol. I, 1092.
21 Ibid., vol. I, 840.
22 *The Era*, 22 December 1915, 21.
23 *Era Annual* 1918, 37.
24 *Daily Post*, 7 May 1917, 2.
25 Gordon Williams, *British Theatre in the Great War: A Revaluation* (London: Continuum, 2003), 161–2.
26 *Daily Post*, 8 August 1916, 8.
27 *Liverpool Echo*, 14 September 1915, 7.
28 *Daily Post*, 30 March 1915, 9.
29 *Daily Post*, 2 March 1915, 6.
30 *Liverpool Echo*, 22 February 1916, 4.
31 *Liverpool Echo*, 27 October 1914, 3; 10 November 1914, 4.
32 *Daily Post*, 26 October 1914, 4.
33 Butler, *John Martin-Harvey*, 205, 99; *Daily Post*, 8 October 1915, 3.
34 *Daily Post*, 16 August 1915, 8; McGreal, *Liverpool in the Great War*, 86.
35 *Daily Post*, 4 October 1915, 3.
36 Lewis Waller died of pneumonia three weeks later, which some suggest was as a result of speaking outside at the meeting.
37 *Liverpool Echo*, 17 December 1915, 6.
38 *The Stage*, 11 May 1916, 16.
39 *The Stage*, 9 March 1916, 17.
40 *The Stage*, 8 February 1917, 14.
41 Ibid., 14.
42 McGreal, *Liverpool in the Great War*, 30.
43 Krivanec, 'Staging War. Theatre 1914–1918', 4; Rodmell, *Opera in the British Isles*, 178.
44 Ganzl, *British Musical Theatre*, vol. I, 1108.
45 McGreal, *Liverpool in the Great War*, 57.
46 Ibid., 42.
47 *Daily Post*, 1 October 1914, 6.
48 *Daily Post*, 28 October 1914, 3.
49 *Daily Post*, 30 November 1914, 4.
50 *Daily Post*, 1 October 1914, 6; 28 October 1914, 3.
51 *The Era*, 26 August 1914, 9.
52 *The Era*, 8 March 1916, 15.
53 *Waterloo and Crosby Herald*, 12 September 1914, quoted in Michael Finn, 'Local Heroes: War News and the Construction of "Community" in Britain, 1914–1918', *Historical Research* 83.221 (2010), 525.
54 Ruddin, 'The "Firsts" World War', 83.
55 Ibid., 83.

56 *Evening Express*, 29 August 1916, 2.
57 Williams, *British Theatre in the Great War*, 177.
58 Butler, *John Martin-Harvey*, 101.
59 Disher, *The Last Romantic*, 225.
60 Butler, *John Martin-Harvey*, 101.
61 Ibid., 101.
62 *Liverpool Echo*, 7 October 1915, 4.
63 *Liverpool Echo*, 26 September 1914, 4.
64 *The Stage*, 18 September 1913, 22.
65 *Liverpool Echo*, 26 September 1914, 4.
66 *Daily Post*, 4 June 1918, 3; *Liverpool Echo*, 3 June 198, 3.
67 *Liverpool Echo*, 4 June 1918, 3; 28 May 1918, 3; *The Era*, 29 May 1918, 6.
68 *The Stage*, 7 December 1916, 19; *Liverpool Echo*, 16 October 1917, 3.
69 Williams, *British Theatre in the Great War*, 151; *Liverpool Echo*, 17 April 1915, 3.
70 McGreal, *Liverpool in the Great War*, 42; *Liverpool Echo*, 17 April 1915, 3.
71 J. E. Harold Terry and Lechmere Worrall, *The Man Who Stayed at Home* (London: Samuel French, 1916), 9.
72 *Daily Telegraph*, 11 December 1914, 11.
73 Terry and Worrall, *The Man Who Stayed at Home*, 66; *Liverpool Echo*, 23 November 1915, 6.
74 *Sunday Times*, 13 December 191, 2.
75 *The Era*, 12 September 1917, 8; *The Stage*, 13 September 1917, 16.

1915

5 January	*The Double Mystery*	Jose G. Levy, after L. Forest and H. de Gorsse	with Arthur Bourchier and Violet Vanbrugh; one performance only
22 February	*The Earl and the Girl*	Seymour Hicks; music by Ivan Caryll	musical comedy with Dorothy Monkman
1 March	*Davy Garrick*	William Muskerry	Edward Compton Comedy Company
	Richelieu	Edward Bulwer Lytton	historical drama
	Sir Roger de Coverley	Justin Huntley McCarthy	comedy
8 March	*A Country Girl*	James T. Tanner; music by Lionel Monckton and Paul Rubens.	musical play
15 March	*The Cinema Star*	Jack Hulbert (adapted from *Die Kino-Konigen)*	farcical musical comedy with Jack Hulbert and Cecily Courtneidge
22 March	*Betty*	Fredrick Lonsdale and Gladys Unger; music by Paul A. Ruebens and Ernest Steffan	musical play
29 March	*Caste*	T. W. Robertson	
5 April	*The Three Musketeers*	adapted from Dumas by Henry Hamilton	Lewis Waller in a swashbuckling drama
12 April	*Land of Promise*	W. Somerset Maugham	with Irene Vanbrugh
19 April	*The Man Who Stayed at Home*	J. E. Harold Terry and Lechmere Worrall	spy play
26 April	Gilbert and Sullivan	D'Oyly Carte	two weeks
10 May	*Brewster's Millions*	G. B. McCutcheon; adapted by Winchell Smith and Byron Ongley	comedy
17 May	*Mr Wu*	Harold Owen and Harry M. Vernon	thriller with Matheson Lang
24 May	*Charley's Aunt*	Brandon Thomas	with Percy Crawford

31 May	*The Girl in the Taxi*	adapted by Frederick Fenn and Arthur Wimperis from *Die Keusche Susanne*; music by Jean Gilbert	musical
7 June–31 July	closed		
2 August	*Peg o'My Heart*	J. Hartley Manners	comedy
9 August	*The Importance of Being Earnest*	Oscar Wilde	Esme Percy and Company
	The Gay Lord Quex	Arthur Pinero	comedy
16 August	*East Lynne*	adapted from novel by Ellen Wood	J. Pitt Hardacre's company
23 August	*The Pearl Girl*	Basil Hood; music by Howard Talbot and Hugo Felix	musical comedy
30 August	*The Laughter of Fools*	H. F. Maltby	Edwin T. Heys Company
6 September	*Countess Coquette*	Roberto Bracco; adapted by Gilbert Canaan	comedy
13 September	*Quinneys*	Horace Annesley Vachell	comedy drama
20 September	*To-Night's the Night*		revue
27 September	*Gamblers All*	May Martindale	melodrama with Lewis Waller,
4 October	*The Only Way*	adapted by Freeman Willis from *A Tale of Two Cities*	John Martin Harvey; in aid of War Hospital Fund for Officers
	The Breed of the Treshams	John Rutherford (Beulah Dix and Evelyn Sutherland)	
	Hamlet	Shakespeare	
	Armageddon	Stephen Phillips	
11 October	*Betty*	Frederick Lonsdale and Gladys Unger; music by Paul A. Ruebens	musical play from Daly's Theatre, London
18 October	*Grumpy*	Horace Hodges and T. Wigney-Perceval	comic detective story
25 October	*Find the Woman*	Charles Klein	American drama with Arthur Bourchier and Violet Vanbrugh

1 November	*The Spanish Main*	Vasco Marena	historical adventure drama with Oscar Asche and Lily Brayton
8 November	*On Trial*	Elmer E. Reizenstein (Elmer Rice)	melodramatic murder mystery
15 November	*Floradora*	Owen Hall; music by Leslie Stewart and Paul Ruebens	musical comedy
22 November	*The Man Who Stayed at Home*	J. E. Harold Terry and Lechmere Worrall	return of spy drama
29 November	Carl Rosa Opera Company		productions included *Faust*, *Mignon* and *Aida*
6 December	*Potash and Perlmutter*	Montague Glass and Charles Klein	comedy
13–25 December	closed		
27 December	*Sinbad the Sailor*	J. Hickory Wood and J. James Hewson	

The discovery of the radio hidden in the fireplace in Terry and Worrall's *The Man Who Stayed at Home*

Christmas in Wartime

1914 *Old King Cole* by Hickory Wood and J. J. Hewson
On the first Christmas of the war, the *Liverpool Echo* thanked the theatre managers and high public spirits for making 'no difference whatsoever in either the volume or the quality of our Christmas fare' hoping that 'if the miseries of the time can be forgotten by any of us, then theatres are doing their best to bring about that result' (26 December 1914, 2). It was a sentiment echoed by the *Daily Post*, quick to praise 'the courage and the public spirit of local theatrical managements' (11 December 1914, 7). Its review suggested

> [i]f some person with a patient German capacity for laboriously collecting useless information were to make a round of all the pantomimes in the kingdom and time all the laughs with a stopwatch he would surely find that *Old King Cole*'s aggregate of merry moments stood somewhere near the top of the list. At any rate, there is just about as much laughter in *Old King Cole* as any one pantomime can hold without hurting itself. (*Daily Post*, 28 December 1914, 3)

Nor was the war completely forgotten:

> You see [John Humphrey's] capacity as a comedian best illustrated in the coffee-stall incident, where with a chunk of bread, a spoon, and a teacup, he explains with the misty elaborateness of the war expert how the British Force ought to outflank the Germans and cut off their retreat. 'And then where's your blooming German Army?' he asks with beaming confidence and conclusiveness. (*Daily Post*, 28 December 1914, 3)

Clara Beck, who played the principal boy in the first wartime pantomime *Old King Cole*

1915 *Sinbad the Sailor*

By December 1915 the *Liverpool Echo* felt confident enough to raise an issue that had been discussed the previous year, but not on the pages of the paper. In an article entitled 'Should We Go to the Pantomime?' it wrote

> a year ago people were perplexed as to whether we ought to go to the pantomime and enjoy ourselves for an hour or so ... some cranks raved ... against people taking a quiet time of recreation by watching theatrical shows. There was grave danger that the hardy annual 'pantomime' would receive the same knockout blow as that which the Grand National has suffered. Fortunately, sense prevailed, and the Christmas fare was served up without any scene and with much good result to the wracked nerves of the populace of the country. (*Liverpool Echo,* 17 December 1915, 6)

This year there had not been even a whimper against the prospect of the pantomimes, but the paper noticed other ways in which the war impacted on them, complaining that

> one effect of the growth of revue productions during the past eighteen months or so has been to divert in that hybrid form of entertainment the service of many eligible artistes who under former conditions found useful employment in the Christmas pantomimes. For this reason it may be assumed the theatrical managers generally have this year experienced some difficulty in finding adequate exponents for their pantomime characters. The difficulty seems to have confronted the management of the Court Theatre for it cannot pretend that the latest 'annual' quite reaches the standard attained for some of the Court pantomimes of previous years. (*Liverpool Echo,* 28 December 1915, 3)

Despite these concerns, the Court had managed to attract Little Tich, that 'great humourist in miniature', back to pantomime after a break of fifteen years, and he proved to be a big draw, 'a pantomime in himself', in a role usually reserved for the principal boy, raising

> ready laughter by his quaint methods and irresistible eccentricity. He calls the tune of the fun, and those associated with him readily respond. As Sinbad, Little Tich has ample opportunity for the display of the versatility and broad humour which have made his name so prominent as a comedian. (*Liverpool Echo,* 18 January 1916, 8; 28 December 1915, 3)

1916 *Babes in the Wood* by Frank Dix

The war still impacted on the theatre's twenty-first pantomime but the issue this year was not the company, which offered 'as good a band of principals as one could ever wish to see in a pantomime', but the need for economy in the staging of the show.[1]

> Not a little fun is made in one scene of the object of economy and as to what constitutes a luxury or a necessity. The producers themselves have been false to the teaching of economy. Gay and lively diversion is surely a necessity in these anxious days, but brilliance of spectacle must be classed as a luxury, and in these times sumptuousness would be both wasteful and unpatriotic. That *The Babes* is not elaborately staged really adds to its merits… (*Daily Post*, 26 December 1916, 3)

While the war and war topics were almost banished from the dialogue, the songs brought it back into people's minds.

> Sprightly numbers there are about the khaki lads and their yearning for home, but the only time we get 'into the thick of it' is when a familiar old tune is revived to extol the tanks that strolled along with an independent air – 'the tanks that broke the ranks out in Picardy-dy' … the popular imagination will be attracted chiefly by 'It's a Long, Long Way to My Home in Kentucky' [which] incidentally makes one wonder why the ideal home is always in the States and never in England! (*Daily Post*, 26 December 1916, 3)

1917 *Red Riding Hood*

The fourth year of the war encouraged a sense of nostalgia, and the Royal Court, while still not making pretensions to elaborate scenery (or 'the cultivation of a commanding cast') included 'the happy revival of an old-time tradition' – albeit not in the place one would expect to find it conventionally. Following a scene in the village of Nick-Nock where 'a stream of boisterous mirth' has been set out

> there is ingeniously introduced a harlequinade – wonderfully well played by children – in which many memories of the good old times are recalled, and the rollicking 'rally', in which clown, pantaloons, harlequin and columbine are inextricably mixed is followed by a shadowgraph display of whimsical adroitness. (*Daily Post*, 26 December 1917, 2)

The paper finishes its review by offering a word about the wonderful electrical display called 'The Giant Chicken' and praising the dancing of the Mersey Mites, a local children's dance group which had become a feature of the pantomime.

Notes

1 The cast included Dorothy Craske as Robin Hood and Fred Colley as Baron Blighty.

1928

30 January	*The Student Prince*	Dorothy Donnelly; music by Sigmund Romberg	operetta
6 February	*When Knights Were Bold*	Charles Marlowe (Harriet Gray)	farce
13 February	*Mary's Ankle*	May Tully	American comedy
20 February	*Paddy the Next Best Thing*	W. G. Mackay and Robert Ord	comedy based on novel by Gertrude Page
27 February	*The Silent House*	G. Brandow and G. Pickett	play
5 March	*And So To Bed*	J. B. Fagan	comedy
12 March	*Rose Marie*	Otto Harbach and Oscar Hammerstein; music by Rudolf Friml and Herbert Stothart	operetta
26 March	*Rookery Nook*	Ben Travers	farce
2 April	*The Father*	August Strindberg	drama
9 April	*Such Men Are Dangerous*	Alfred Neumann, adapted by Ashley Dukes	historical drama with Matheson Lang and Donald Wolfit
16 April	*The Temptation of Eve*	Desiree Welby and Christopher Sandeman	drama
23 April	*The Letter*	W. Somerset Maugham	drama with Gladys Cooper
7 May	*The Silver Cord*	Sidney Howard	American drama with Peggy Ashcroft
14 May	*Holding Out the Apple*	Betty Wynne-Bower	comedy with John Gielgud
21 May	*Lord Babs*	Keble Howard (John Keble Bell)	farce

28 May	*The Rat*	David L'Estrange (Ivor Novello and Constance Collier)	thriller
4 June	*None But the Brave*	Bernard Merivale and Brendon Fleming	farcical melodrama
11 June	*Plus Fours*	H. A. Vachell and Harold Simpson	comedy
18 June	*Thunder in the Air*	Robins Millar	drama
25 June	*Just Married*	Adelaide Matthews and Ann Nichols	farcical comedy
2 July	*Rookery Nook*	Ben Travers	farce
9 July	*Biffy*	Vera Beringer and William Ray	farcical comedy

The popular farce *When Knights Were Bold* by Charles Marlowe, the pen name of Harriet Gray

16 July	*Tons of Money*	Will Evans and Valentine (Archibald Thomas Pechey)	farce
23 July	*It Pays to Advertise*	Roi Cooper Megrue and Walter Hackett	American farce
30 July–4 August	closed		
6 August	*Thark*	Ben Travers	farce
13 August	*The Revolt of Christopher*	George Arthurs and A. Miller	comedy from a novel by Mabel Barnes-Grundy
20 August	*The Soul of Nicholas Snyder*	Jerome K. Jerome	fantasy
27 August	*Bow Wows*		musical revue

3 September	*Lumber Love*	Leslie Stiles; music by Berté and Archie Emmett Adams	musical play
10 September	*Two White Arms*	Harold Dearden	farce with Owen Nares
17 September	*The Real McCoy*	J. J. Mackeown	mystery play
24 September	*The Lyons Mail*	Charles Reade	melodrama with John Martin Harvey
1 October	*The Mystery of the Red Tavern*	John Floyd	melodrama with George Zucco Roberts
8 October	*Baby Cyclone*	George M. Cohan	comedy
15 October	*The Man Who Changed His Name*	Edgar Wallace	thriller
22 October	*Raffles*	W. Hornung and E. W. Presbrey	thriller
29 October	*Trial of Mary Duggan*	Veiller	melodrama
5 November	*The Scarlet Pimpernel*	Baroness Orczy and Montague Barstow	with Julia Neilson and Fred Terry
12 November	*So This Is Love*	Stanley Lupino and Arthur Rigby; music by Hal Brody, Guy Fane and Teddy Fox	musical play
19 November	*The Farmer's Wife*	Eden Philpotts	comedy
25 November	*The Acquittal*	Rita Wieman	with Hesketh Pearson and Godfrey Tearle
3 December	*A Bird in the Hand*	John Drinkwater	
10 December	*He Walked in Her Sleep*	Norman Cannon	farce
17–25 December	closed		
26 December	*The Yellow Mask*	Edgar Wallace; music by Vernon Duke	musical comedy drama

Christmas, 1918–1929

1918 *Cinderella*

During the passage of time the stories of Cinderella and her immediate associates have undergone many changes. The little slave of the kitchen, unlike Peter Pan, has grown with the times, and has acquired habits of the time, even to the extent of indulging in ragtime ditties. At the Royal Court, 'Cinders' is ever within hearing of tuneful airs very closely allied to the numbers made conversant by the periodical visits of American cousins. The pantomime, let it be said, loses nothing by the use of imported quavers and semi-demi-quavers ... Brightness and briskness reign throughout. (*Liverpool Echo*, 23 December 1918, 3)

1919 *Humpty Dumpty*

This is not the first time that this subject has been chosen, as Mr Robert Arthur made out of the same theme, a remarkably fine show during the latter period of his proprietorship of the theatre. Probably, the present is a little broader in treatment than was displayed by Mr Arthur, whose artistic conception of theatrical production was always in a refined and delicate vein, which is not always the prevailing note in pantomime ... The presence of Scotch Kelly, who dominates the cast; of George Jackley, of the Jackley Troupe; of Ray Holgate, the clear, sparkling Mozelles, Lila Wood and Florence Helm should make for perfection in their multifarious lines. (*The Stage*, 25 December 1919, 3)

1920 *Robinson Crusoe*

A heavy task has been laid upon Stanley Shuter in providing the elaborate scenery which enfolds and illustrates what of the story there is, for that talented artist has provided no fewer than ten of the thirteen scenes staged. Mr Shuter has put some bold painted pictures before us, very effective in their broad and striking treatment, several of them rather heavily barbaric, and one could not but have wished for a trifle more gossamer and lightly graceful treatment in several of them ... Among the most elaborate are what will be regarded as the gigantic lobster scene and that illustrating the effective cracker or bon-bon Carnival ... The Storm scene and the drowning of Robinson Crusoe are strikingly done, and fully deserved the attention

The Christmas pantomime for 1919 with Scotch Kelly as the Queen of Humptiland, Florence Relm as Humpty Dumpty and the Sparkling Mozelles as Jack and Jill, with specialities by Cliff Berzac's Circus

The Christmas pantomime for 1920 with Lottie Collins Jr as Robinson Crusoe, Winnie Collins as Polly and including a fire dance by La Pia

> bestowed upon the two-part scene, mechanically in the tossing submarine – we trust it is a submarine – and in the kinema, pictorially… (*The Stage*, 20 December 1920, 14)

1921 *The Gipsy Princess*
Kalman's Viennese operetta was the story of a famous cabaret star in love with a prince who she cannot marry because she is a commoner. All is saved at the end when his mother reveals that she was once an entertainer herself.

> Not since the time of Carl Rosa Opera company, to our memory, have we been denied our pantomime here but this year we fall back upon comic opera in *The Gipsy Princess*. A crowded audience at the first performance here manifested at times considerable enthusiasm. (*The Stage*, 5 January 1922, 2)

> It is gratifying to find how welcome *The Gipsy Princess* has been made. It was somewhat a leap in the dark to substitute this work in place of the pantomime, which has always been such a marked feature in the Christmas entertainment at the Court. (*The Stage*, 19 January 1922, 2)

1922–25 D'Oyly Carte Gilbert and Sullivan seasons

1926 *The Blue Kitten* by Otto Harbach
This musical comedy had not been received with great enthusiasm in London earlier in the year, but

> Macdonald and Young's *The Blue Kitten* opened a season here on December 27, and proved very enjoyable. It has music – Friml at his most fascinating – dancing, humour, and colour to commend it, and what musical comedy could desire more? (*The Stage*, 31 December 1925, 41)

1927 D'Oyly Carte: Gilbert and Sullivan

1928 *The Yellow Mask* by Edgar Wallace

> Mr Edgar Wallace's excursion into the realm of musical comedy ensures an effectively strong book with dashes of melodrama with which to eke out the spectacle and rather better humour than is usual in this class of entertainments … Master Hale, three hundred years ago, stole for his sovereign a famous diamond which adorned one of Li-San's ancestors. The opening episodes reveal Li-San's plot to regain possession of the jewel which reposes in the Tower. The Chinaman, here supposedly on a friendly

mission, arranges for an ex-Guards officer to knock out his brother – the hero – and take his place at the changing of the guard. The jewel procured is brought on board the China mail by a special seaplane and later the hero, in pursuit, drops through the roof of the saloon from another 'plane. On the ship ... are most of the members of the party. Sylvia Main, who has had a taste of Li-San's villainy, is there, also the comic detective who was drugged and smuggled on board, and the pretty little schoolmistress – a useful dancing partner at odd moments. Once in China, things move with great rapidity ... The principal excitement is the drugging of the heroine, who is taken to Li-San's castle and is about to be tortured before her lover's eyes when the image of the famous ancestor turns out to be ... the funny little detective, who heralds the appearance of the Dowager-Empress's Imperial Guard and the Royal Executioner. As the curtain falls, we are led to suppose that in a few minutes Master Li-San will himself become an ancestor. (*The Era*, 15 February 1928, 1)

1929 *La Vie Parisienne* by A. P. Herbert
The show was originally produced in April 1929 by Sir Nigel Playfair at the Hammersmith Lyric, where *The Graphic* declared

> The period ... is 1863, which means pork-pie hats and capes and Victorian crinolines. And when these are accompanied by music from Offenbach ... the battle is half won ... nobody could want anything better than the dialogue and the verses furnished by Mr Herbert, who has managed this story of an English sight-seeing family in Gay Paree not only with wit, but with grace and variety and distinction.
>
> At first I was afraid that it was all going to be just a little too jolly and bright. I was anxious when I found some of Offenbach's most serious airs supplied with lines such as 'Can it be right to drink all night?' ... But when we passed – via the Customs Barrier – from the deck of a packet boat (an Ugly scene) to the Café des Etrangers at night (a little paradise of a scene) all was well. Here the melting tunes were allowed to melt us, and vivacity was in fine fettle, with the ladies of the café dancing the can-can as French as they could make it for the very English English husband, and then doing the same thing like a minuet for his no less English English wife ... I predict an Offenbach boom. We may enjoy ragtime on our off nights. But, after all, good composers were the best. (Herbert Farjeon, *The Graphic*, 27 April 1929, 29)

Slumps don't end overnight.
One's jolly lucky if one can see
a little daylight ...

6 Troubled Times: The 1930s

The Royal Court faced an uphill struggle as it entered the 1930s. Touring theatre was starting to struggle, and as J. C. Trewin noted, theatres were facing increasing competition from the cinema as it became 'all-talking, all-singing, all-dancing'. The talkies might have been 'crude and blaring, but they were new' and they were cheaper than the theatre.[1] Against the economic background of the decade, this was not an inconsiderable consideration, for the biggest problem that faced the theatre was the Depression. The decision by Harrods in 1920 to drop its plans for a Liverpool store was just a symbolic precursor to what quickly spiralled into a major decline. As the main export port in Britain, dependent on trade rather than manufacturing, Liverpool was hit disproportionately hard, and in 1931 the overall volume of trade in the city was 42 per cent of the 1924 figure. Throughout the 1930s

Arthur Denville's repertory company

A view of the theatre looking along Great Charlotte Street, 1930 (Liverpool Record Office)

unemployment remained resolutely above 18 per cent, double the national average. In 1932, the worst year of the Depression, it totalled 28 per cent, nearly one in three of the workforce, and many others who did not appear in those figures could only find work for a few days a week. Workers in the port were particularly hard hit. Passenger trade across the Atlantic declined and, to make matters worse, this trade was starting to move to Southampton. From the port, the ripples of unemployment spread throughout the city. Shipping lines were entering a period of fierce competition and rationalisation. Companies were swallowed up and others moved their headquarters to London. As a consequence, clerks, book-keepers, typists and secretaries found themselves without work in services ranging from shipping lines to insurance and banking. By the winter of 1932–33, nearly half of the 34,000 workers in the shipping industry were unemployed. Even in manufacturing, the picture was grim. In the 'new' industries, such as the manufacture of fibres, there was a decline in the number of available jobs, and workers in established industries on Merseyside (from tobacco to food and drink) faced streamlining and mechanisation. Despite all of this, Merseyside was not designated a depressed area in the 1934 legislation when priority was given to the industrial north.[2]

Against this background the Royal Court managed to carry on through the first three years of the decade, but things were not easy. In an attempt to cut costs, 1931 bought an experiment, when Robert Arthur engaged Alfred Denville's Repertory Company for a thirteen-week season. The programme explained that

> [t]he high standard invariably aimed at by the Royal Court Theatre and their energetic Management with regard to first-class entertainment is abundantly maintained by their engagement of a Stock Company to be run by Mr Alfred Denville, who has for so many years held the position of Premier Stock manager in the British Isles. Mr Denville is bringing his best and most

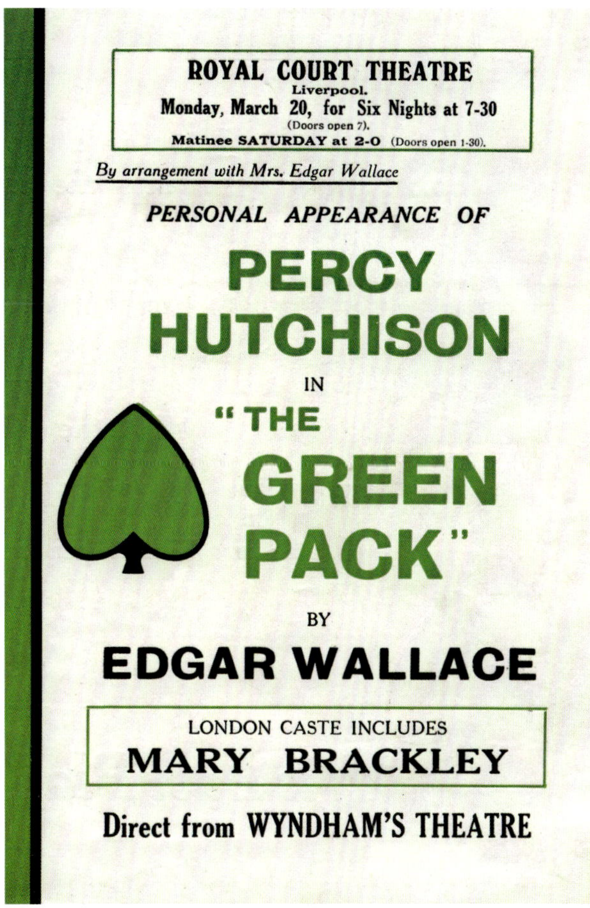

The Green Pack was Edgar Wallace's last murder mystery and played at the Royal Court in March 1933

carefully selected company to the Royal Court Theatre. The magnitude of Mr Denville's activities will be understood when it is realised that he has companies playing Stock at the present time in Portsmouth, Southampton, Swansea, Newcastle, Hull and Sheffield … He has also had seasons at Birkenhead, Wallasey and New Brighton.

The experiment was not repeated nor was the season deemed a success by Harold Ackroyd, who calls the twice-nightly trial 'a disastrous policy'.[3] The change in the status of the Royal Court is shown starkly when the idea of a stock company season is compared to Robert Arthur's success in the 1890s, when the theatre

> saw its palmiest days as Liverpool's leading theatre. All the famous generations of actor-managers – Irving, Tree, Alexander, Forbes-Robertson, Wilson Barrett, Edward Compton and – until a year or two ago – Martin Harvey – paid regular visits to the theatre, and in those days queues often extended for a quarter of a mile.[4]

Aimée and Philip Stuart's all-female drama, *9 Till 6*, set in a dressmaker's shop, which raised issues about the plight of female workers, played in January 1931

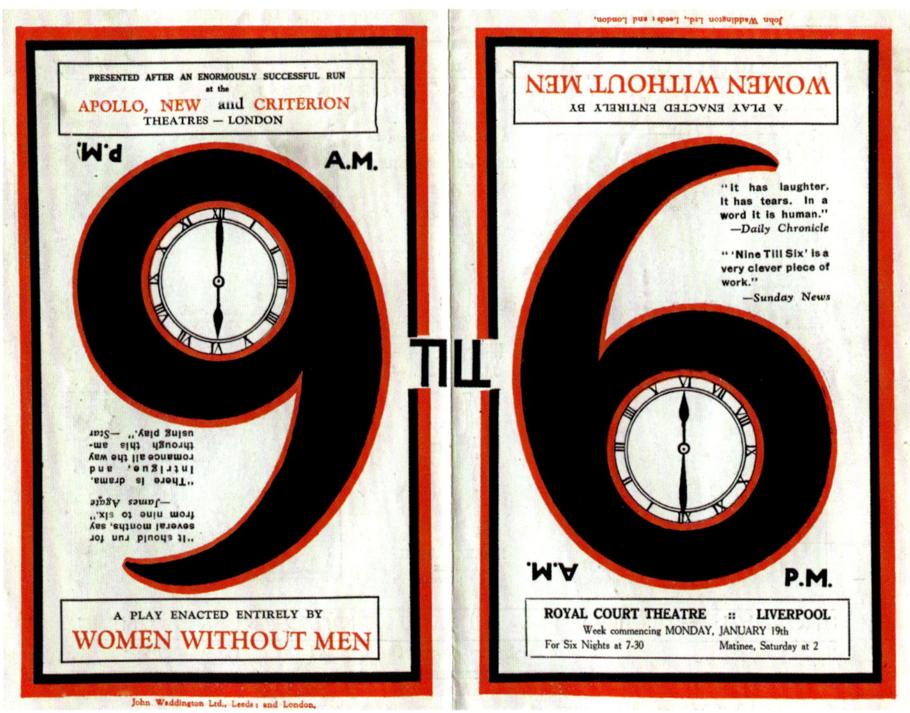

R. W. Thomas's watercolour of the Royal Court, n.d. (Liverpool Record Office)

Now the queues were forming at the nearby Empire Theatre (previously the Prince of Wales) which Moss Empires had taken over in the early 1890s. This was the Royal Court's main competition. Moss Empires had made some serious investment in the building, employing the renowned theatre architect Frank Matcham to add glamour and comfort. In 1925 the company had pulled the theatre down entirely and reopened it with the widest auditorium in Europe, the largest stage in Britain and an audience capacity of 2,500, claimed to be larger than the London Palladium.[5] This meant it could offer the biggest, the most lavish and the newest shows, many of them musicals, and the attraction of headlining stars, including Fred and Adele Astaire and Tallulah Bankhead.

The Royal Court struggled to compete, and Howard and Wyndham, in the face of rapidly declining business, when 'it was difficult to get the right attraction, difficult to coax the public into the theatre', looked for outside help.[6] The company turned to Harry Tennent, at that time engaged in revitalising the fortunes of the Moss Empires, which despite all outward appearances were also finding the 1930s a challenging time. Tennent resigned from Moss Empires and for a year became booking manager for Howard and Wyndham. By 1933 he had persuaded the two companies to amalgamate 'for the promotion of legitimate theatre' through the establishment of Moss Empire and Howard and Wyndham Tours Ltd. He was joined by Binkie Beaumont, who had also been a booking agent for Moss Empires, and between them they revitalised Howard and Wyndham with 'good, pleasant commercial plays ... usually comedies which would attract one of two stars and which would appeal to the middle-brow audiences on the provincial circuit'.[7] There was some local concern that the amalgamation would lead to a loss of competition, with local playgoers being offered not what they wanted, but those plays that the company decided to present.[8] But Howard and Wyndham pressed ahead, the 'amalgamation' being more important to it than simply ensuring successful bookings and a full theatre in Liverpool. It was also trying to 'shed any vestige of ... a provincial image' and was looking to establish a London office. In order to make the move, the company needed to find 'insiders from the West End' to help it, and Beaumont and Tennent, who established their own company, H. M. Tennent, in 1936, were good connections to have.[9] One of their other allies was showman and impresario Charles B. Cochran. He was taken on to the board two months after Wyndham's death in 1930 because A. Stewart Cruikshank, who took over the business, was seen to be a 'sober business mind' in need of more artistic judgement.[10]

Some of this success lay in the future. While the establishment of a company with Moss Empires must have looked on paper to be a good, maybe the only, prospect of reviving its fortunes, something went wrong. Suddenly, following the Easter show in 1933, the Royal Court announced, without any advance warning, that it was closing. As Ackroyd notes, 'the suddenness of the decision to close' was indicated by the fact that the local press and playbills had already announced *Le Chauve Souris* as the attraction for the following week.[11] It is possible that the closure was contrived by Moss Empires to eliminate competition, but whatever the reason, Robert Arthur, still managing the theatre for Howard and Wyndham, was faced with a problem, one that he managed to resolve by leasing the theatre to a new company. In May 1933 *The Stage* announced that the theatre was to be taken over by the British Theatre Corporation, the new proprietors of the Pavilion on Lodge Lane.[12] While being run jointly to enable the company to 'use the joint interest of the two theatres in order to bring to Liverpool such leading stars as can be attracted by the offer of a double nightly appearance at both houses', the Royal Court was to be headed by its own management.[13] Running under the name of the Royal Court Theatre Co. (Liverpool) Ltd, the theatre was to be managed by Maurice Voss (of Voss Motors Ltd) with the help of Alderman J. C. Cross. The biggest shock to theatregoers was the fact that it was to become a twice-nightly variety house.

This new page in the Royal Court's history opened on the August Bank Holiday. Top of the bill, for the first time in Liverpool, was Geraldo and his Gaucho Tango

Band from the Savoy Hotel in London, supported by the tap dancing of Richard Castle and Rosalind Wade and the comedians Max Wall and Billy Matchett. In the following weeks, the stage was graced by acts including the impressionists Cingalee and A. C. Astor, the mimic Ann Perry, the skating act of Mary and Eric, the clever young juggler Boy Foy and Jean Florian, praised by *The Stage* for 'manipulating bouncing balls with skill and grace'.[14] But, 'as if in the nature of a punishment by the Muses of Comedy and Tragedy upon the management who had dared turn the historic theatre into a music hall', disaster struck.[15] On the night of 22 September, after the theatre had been emptied of the largest audience it had seen since it had been turned over to variety, fire broke out, destroying the roof and causing £20,000 worth of damage, mainly to the auditorium. Rebuilding was to be the responsibility of Robert Arthur Theatres but, although he kept promising an early reopening, a series of arguments with the insurance company meant the theatre would remain closed until 1938.

The 1933 Season and Dodie Smith's Service

While the last year in which the Royal Court ran as a legitimate theatre for over five years was a short one, it was also one that tackled some difficult and morally challenging plays exploring inter-generational conflicts, the stifling of youth (with a nod to lesbianism) and the Depression itself. The year started with the internationally renowned American actor Ruth Draper offering a series of comic character sketches including 'On a Porch in a Maine Coast Village' and 'In a Church in Florence'.[16] In the latter, and using nothing more than a few props and some costumes, she presented a series of sketches evoking six women visiting the painting of La Madonna della Misericordia, who also conjured up over twenty other characters. They included two in Italian (an old beggar and a young girl who has arranged to secretly meet her lover) and one in German, depicting a tourist bedecked in a green loden cape,

> Bavarian felt hat, metal framed glasses, cane, bundles in string bags, large purse. Slowly, she walks down the aisle, confronts the Madonna, and points it out to her party – Gretl, Frieda and Willy: 'Schokolade? Heir, in der Kirche? Nein Willy!' Impressed and nodding, she gazes respectfully at the painting: 'Der kaiser was heir? Ach so. Und Goethe auch?' That they stand where the great men stood reduces her to satisfied silence. Expressing disgust with Italian food – 'Macaroni – macaroni – macaroni!' – they go off in search of Münchener Bier.[17]

In between, she also evoked an American tour leader reading from her Baedeker while chaperoning a group of wayward young girls and a linen-smocked amateur English painter struggling to make a copy of the Madonna but finding herself discouraged:

> I simply cannot get it! … Oh, it's frightfully bad – it's the worst thing I've done … You see, the trouble is I started all wrong, and it's so terribly difficult to get a thing right if one starts all wrong. It's very badly drawn and I started to paint too soon, and now it's too late! No, you see – it's all so *flat* … There's no perspective at all … Those mountains should be miles and miles away – and I've got my mountains under my arch.[18]

Jealous of her friend's perfect sky and exactly right highlights, she borrows a tube of paint from her (she never gets 'tired of squeezing paint') before giving up in despair to go and buy 'one of those lovely rich chocolate cakes in the Toranbuoni' and have tea at Fiesole. The evening prompted *The Stage* to praise the wealth of effects produced 'with such rigid economy of means'.[19]

Equally at home on the stage of the Court was a revival in April of the 'long-popular and epoch making' musical *The Belle of New York*, first performed at the Royal Court in 1898, in which a Salvation Army girl reforms a spendthrift and falls in love.[20] The year also included two plays with local connections. *The Flaming Torch* was a pageant play by Percy Corkhill, civic impresario and secretary to the Lord Mayor, staged by amateurs in aid of Liverpool hospitals and preceded by Corkhill's one-act play *The New Member*. It was previously performed at the Court on a Sunday in 1932 and it was Corkhill's third local pageant play, part of a wider series of pageants and civic weeks held in the city during the 1930s aimed at boosting the city 'not only as the greatest shipping centre in the country, but also as a rising industrial centre'.[21] The other play with local connections came from the pen of Itak Goller, an adaptation of his novel *The Five Books of Mr Moses*. Goller had been a minister of the New Hebrew Congregation in Hope Place, later teaching from his own home, and *Cohen and Son* presented a comic look at the conflict between Judaism and Christianity, looking at religious fanaticism and at finding peace between religions.

Other plays were more challenging. Joan Temple's *The Cage* was a gloomy picture of a suburban family stifled by a selfish mother where youth revolted against strait-laced parental control. *The Firebird* was a high-society melodrama that also dealt with the conflict between generations, but in this case it was turned on its head. The mother, claiming to be an adulteress and murderer, tries to protect her daughter, an ultra-modern 'bad girl'. In the end, it is the daughter who is proved to be the lover and murderer of the dead man and who is 'an utterly un-moral product of this age of shameless precocity'.[22] The premiere of *Your Money or Your Wife* (quickly renamed

Vernon's visit to the Royal Court in 1939 (Vernon's House Journal)

Doctor's Orders) was a translation from the French of Louis Verneuil, offering the audience a particularly French view on marriage and marital affairs. Helene Lorimer, the half-French wife of wealthy Alfred Lorimer, is kidnapped and held to ransom. She believes she has been kidnapped by a young man because he is in love with her. At the outset he is not, but then he does fall for her. When the kidnap gang is caught, he manages to escape capture only to reappear in the final scene, and he ends up, on the suggestion of the husband, going off with Helene to Melrose for a few days, leading *The Stage* to suggest that the play ended in 'a very un-English frankness'.[23] Radical attitudes to marriage also run through Rachel Crothers's *When Ladies Meet*. Mary is writing a novel about a single woman in love with a married man, which proposes that she live with him for a year to see if it is, indeed, true love. If this is the case, she will go to the wife and explain it all, assuming the wife will give him a divorce. In actuality, this story reflects Mary's own position. She is in love with her married publisher and at a party meets his wife. Unaware at first who the other is, the scene between the two women is pivotal to the play as they discuss marriage, promiscuity and virginity. While, at its heart, the play is not a plea for the sexual freedom of women but rather for an end to adultery and seduction by men, the women, realising they are suffering through the husband's selfishness, both reject him.

One of the most challenging plays of the year was Christa Winsloe's *Children in Uniform*. Set in a Prussian school for the daughters of military officers, the harsh regime which prizes 'self-denial, discipline and hunger' leads one of the young girls to fall in love with a mistress who shows her kindness.[24] Manuela is ecstatic when Fraulein von Bernberg replaces her worn-out underwear with one of her own chemises and on a drunken evening with some of the other girls she can no longer keep her joy to herself. 'I am so happy', she tells them, 'so blissfully happy ... because, now, I know for certain – SHE LOVES ME (*Laughs.*) She loves me.'[25] Unfortunately, she is overheard by the headmistress, who sends her to isolation, and on finding out that she will never see Frau von Bernberg again, who tells her she must not love her so much for 'it is harmful – it is a sin', Manuela throws herself out of a window.[26] While the 'morbid, exaggerated passion' of the young girl was seen by many as being the main focus of the story, the play was as much a satire of the old Prussian ideals of 'discipline, order, self-control, and obedience' and a warning about the return of these ideals to Germany.[27] In a last argument with the headmistress, Frau von Bernberg tells her that the house is 'a rat-trap ... a house of death ... This galvanised suppression is spiritual death. Only women can do such terrible things to women!'[28] The headmistress is resolute. 'Church, kitchen, children' is what the school must teach the girls.[29]

The play that touched most closely on the world of the 1930s and that drew big crowds to the Royal Court was Dodie Smith's *Service*. Writing under the pen name of C. L. Anthony, Smith saw her mission as making 'life more hopeful for her fellow creatures' and *Service*, while telling a story of a department store threatened with closure because of the Depression, did have a positive ending.[30] Service's is an old family business looking to celebrate its 200th birthday but struggling to survive. It is a luxury shop whose customers 'have been hit more than anyone'.[31] While it used to sell Genoa, Dutch and English velvets, now what people want 'is an announcement of "Colossal Bargain Sale – everything 100 per cent below cost" and even then, they will not buy anything'.[32] Things are looking bleak, and while Gabriel Service hopes that things will improve, as the outcome for everyone is inconceivable if they do not, staff are laid off and the firm faces bankruptcy. The only solution seems to be to sell to Stoner, a 'nasty little tyke' who owns a string of shops where 'every floor's a bargain floor'.[33] *Service* paints a picture that suggests that everyone is struggling and suffering as a result of the Depression. If the staff have to take a pay cut or be laid off, then Gabriel Service has to make economies too. Thus he walks to the station instead of getting a taxi, although he does understand that, when he tells his wife that this means hardship for the Service family, it is 'the sort of hardship that would be luxury to most of my poor devils of a staff'.[34] Gabriel's young wife leaves him. His children seem unconcerned about impending bankruptcy (at least at first), preferring their dinners on the lawn or tennis parties, and Caroline is first seen coming to see her father because she needs money to get her hair waved and her nails done. In comparison, when Benton, who has worked for the company for over ten years, returns home to tell his family he has been let go, they are more sympathetic. 'It'll come right, Dad', says his daughter Elsie. 'We'll all pull together.'[35] However, his sacking has implications. Mrs Benton has to tell her charlady, Mrs Munsey (who has a sick child at home), that she will no longer need her, but that if she cares to come round 'there might be – perhaps a little food over – for the children'.[36] Just as Benton does not blame Service, Mrs Munsey does not blame the Bentons. 'It's bad times for all of us', she says as she leaves.[37]

Dodie Smith was looking for a happy ending, so eventually everyone does follow Elsie's advice and pull together. Benton's wife encourages him and he sets up a bakery and café in their front room. For the Services, it is the younger generation who come good. Michael, the son, who has supposedly been on holiday, has in reality been in Paris studying new furniture designs made from steel. As a result, the shop gets the possibility of fitting out a liner and then – maybe – a whole fleet of liners. The family get a note about the monthly sales figures which are up – just a fraction. It is not a miracle. They are not saved. According to Service, 'slumps don't end overnight. One's jolly lucky if one can see a little daylight…'[38] As the play draws towards its end, it is still raining outside but the clouds are breaking:

> Michael: Here comes the sun –
> *A gleam of pale yellow sunlight shines on the painting of the first* GABRIEL SERVICE…
> Caroline: Oh, please God, do let there be a rainbow.
> Geoffrey: There – it's starting. Right over St Mary's – see?
> Caroline: Oh, how lovely! Angel – our own special rainbow!
> Service: It won't be much use if it's only for us, Caro; the first rainbow was for the whole world. Let's hope this one is.
>
> *They are grouped round the window, watching the arc as it grows stronger. The room is at last flooded with late afternoon sunlight. St Mary's-in-the Meadow chimes six as the –*
>
> CURTAIN FALLS[39]

As *Service* closed its week's run, the Royal Court, with no such glimmer of the sun, closed its doors. There must have been those at the theatre and in the city who were hoping that the rainbow might also be shining for them.

Notes

1 J. C. Trewin, *The Turbulent Thirties: A Further Decade of the Theatre* (London: Macdonald, 1960), 17.

2 Belchem, 'The New Livercool', 226; Sam Davies et al., *Genuinely Seeking Work: Mass Unemployment on Merseyside in the 1930s* (Birkenhead: Liver Press, 1992), 13–22.

3 Harold Ackroyd, *The Liverpool Stage* (Erdington: Amber Valley, 1996), 25.

4 *The Stage*, 28 September 1938, 8.

5 Ackroyd, *Liverpool Stage*, 100–3; Barrett, 'Fish out of Water', 90.

6 Richard Huggett, *Binkie Beaumont: Eminence Grise of the West End Theatre 1933–1973* (London: Hodder and Stoughton, 1989), 98.

7 Iles, 'Issues in Theatrical Management', 58; Huggett, *Binkie Beaumont*, 98.

8 Ackroyd, *Liverpool Stage*, 25.

9 Huggett, *Binkie Beaumont*, 57.

10 Iles, 'Issues in Theatrical Management', 56–8.

11 Ackroyd, *Liverpool Stage*, 25.

12 *The Stage*, 18 May 1933, 4.

13 *The Era*, 17 May 1933, 14.

14 *The Stage*, 24 August 1933, 2.

15 Ackroyd, *Liverpool Stage*, 26.

16 Draper, who had been performing in England since 1920, made her first appearance at the Royal Court the previous year and was to return in 1946.

17 Dorothy Warren, *The World of Ruth Draper: A Portrait of an Actress* (Carbondale, IL: Southern Illinois University Press, 1999), 2.

18 Ruth Draper, *The Art of Ruth Draper: Her Dramas and Her Characters* (Oxford: Oxford University Press, 1960), 283.

19 *The Stage*, 19 January 1933, 1.

20 *The Stage*, 10 August 1933, 10.

21 *Liverpool Echo*, 28 July 1926; Belchem, 'Celebrating Liverpool', 29–36. Corkhill's other pageant plays included one for the pageant in Sefton Park in 1928 to mark George Audley's gift of a replica statue of Peter Pan, and one for the Great Rail Pageant of 1930 to mark the centenary of the Manchester–Liverpool railway. In 1934, as part of Royal Tunnel Week, Corkhill contributed a mime play optimistically entitled 'The Turning of the Tide' (Belchem, 'Celebrating Liverpool', 37–8).

22 *The Stage*, 1 September 1933, 12.

23 *The Stage*, 26 January 1933, 15.

24 Christa Winsloe, *Children in Uniform*, in *Famous Plays of 1932–33* (London: Victor Gollancz, 1933), 44.

25 Ibid., 77.

26 Ibid., 99.

27 *The Stage*, 16 February 1933, 2; Winsloe, *Children in Uniform*, 102.

28 Winsloe, *Children in Uniform*, 103.

29 Ibid., 103.

30 *The Era*, 19 October 1932, 2.

31 Dodie Smith, *Service*, in *Three Plays* (London: Samuel French, 1939), 132.

32 Ibid., 133.

33 Ibid., 198.

34 Ibid., 179.

35 Ibid., 161.

36 Ibid., 160.

37 Ibid., 160.

38 Ibid., 241.

39 Ibid., 242.

1933

16 January	Original Character Sketches	Ruth Draper	
23 January	*Your Money or Your Wife* (renamed *Doctor's Orders*)	Louis Verneuil (trans Harry Graham)	premiere with Yvonne Arnaud and Raymond Massey
30 January	*Strange Orchestra*	Rodney Ackland	play
6 February	*The Cage*	Joan Temple	drama of suburban life
13 February	*Children in Uniform*	Christa Winsloe; adapted by Barbara Burnham	
20 February	*The Flaming Torch*	Percy F. Corkhill	pageant play for Hospital Week
27 February	*The Firebird*	Jeffrey Dell	Viennese drama
6 March	*Cohen and Son*	Izak Goller	comedy drama with Selma vas Diaz
13 March	*Othello*	Shakespeare	H. V. Neilson's Shakespearean Company
20 March	*The Green Pack*	Edgar Wallace	murder mystery
27 March	*When Ladies Meet*	Rachel Crothers	with Marie Tempest, Robert Donat and Owen Nares
3 April	*The Belle of New York*	book and lyrics by Hugh Morton; music by Gustave Kerker	musical comedy
10 April	*Unto Us a Son is Given*	Monseigneur Gonne	a Passion play performed by Liverpool University Catholic Society
17 April	*Service*	Dodie Smith	

Christmas, 1930s

1930 *The Love Race* by Stanley Lupino
The first Christmas show of the decade was a musical comedy from the Gaiety Theatre with a story that never lapsed 'into solemnity' and twisted 'itself into incredible complexities'.

> They are, perhaps, best of all at the breakfast table where they do those ridiculous things that die in print, but live for a moment of glorious absurdity in the theatre: the shuffling of a pack of toast, the friendly entanglement of the toast rack, the desperate dicing with loaf sugar. (*The Times*, 26 June 1930, 14)

1931 *Bitter Sweet* by Noel Coward

> The charming music and romantic plot of Noel Coward's *Bitter Sweet* continues to draw large audiences to this theatre, which has recently been very attractively redecorated. (*The Stage*, 14 January 1932, 16)

1932 ***Tell Her the Truth***, a play with tunes by R. P. Weston and Bert Lee, adapted from ***Nothing but the Truth*** by James Montgomery
When Bobbie takes on a bet for £1,000 that he can go twenty-four hours without telling anything but the truth, the consequences are, inevitably, farcical.

> [T]o judge by the enthusiasm with which the opening performance was greeted, the piece is likely to have a successful run. This excellent adaptation ... is an admirable mixture of gaiety and music, with a general air of light-hearted happiness. (*The Stage*, 30 December 1932, 11)

1933–37 closed

1938 ***Humpty Dumpty*** by Emile Littler

> The story of Humpty Dumpty opens in the fair land of Eggville. Nobody worries much in Eggville. It's all very 'Hey Nonny Nonny.' The girls tell you that at the start of the Pantomime. They tell it you in song, like this:
>
> Hoorah for the fair land of Eggville,
> A Country that's made of shell!

Bobbie Comber as Agatha Applepip in the 1938 *Humpty Dumpty*

Where villagers merry
Sing 'Derry down Derry,'
(And Fol dol de rol dol as well!)

And nothing could be clearer than that, could it? But wait! There is a cloud lurking somewhere on the horizon. There always is. In this case it's none other than the ancient legend of the Egg on the Wall. For an evil destiny will overtake this fair land should this egg ever fall. Eggville has a very, very, *very* good King named Good King Yolk, and that old legend says that on the day the egg falls from the wall, King Yolk falls from his high estate...

So, when they're not singing 'Hey Nonny Nonny,' the inhabitants of Eggville spend their time guarding the egg. And that's what they're doing when the Pantomime opens. (Programme)

The roller-skating Resusa Sisters provided the speciality act for the 1938 pantomime

1939 *Goody Two Shoes* by Emile Littler

> There was a really happy note about the opening of Emile Littler's pantomime ... Young and old, alike, in the audience fell under the cheerful spell of the company, echoing Robin's 'Little Sir Echo' with zest, assuring him that his 'flower' grew apace each time he came on the stage and 'Boomps a Daisy'ing with Dame Prunella in the most joyous and hearty fashion ... Jack Stanford's interpretations of the foundations of several ballroom dances are a sheer delight; the speciality numbers of Michel and Arnova a combination of artistry and skill; the ballet burlesque of Betty Jumel extremely funny; the juggling of Eddie Gray clever and slick, and not least in the list was the feat of the Tiller Girls in which all sixteen weave and pattern the stage for several minutes on top of rolling balls, with hardly a fault... (*The Stage*, 28 December 1939, 21)

1938

17 October	*Under Your Hat*	Archie Menzies, Arthur Macrae and Jack Hulbert; music by Vivien Ellis	with Cecily Courtneidge and Jack Hubert
24 October	*Operette*	Noel Coward	
7 November	*St Moritz: the original ice musical spectacular*	Music by Herbert Griffiths	with Pamela Prior, professional champion skater 1937, and a vast real ice stage
21 November	*Plan for a Hostess*	Thomas Browne	comedy with Yvonne Arnaud
28 November	*Victoria Regina*	John Houseman	from the Lyric Theatre
24 December	*Humpty Dumpty*	Emile Littler	

Cecily Courtneidge and Jack Hulbert disguised as Colonel and Mrs Sheepshanks of Poona in *Under Your Hat*, trying to convince the headmistress in a girls' school that they are prospective parents so that they can get to the aeroplane parked on the school's playing field to prevent the theft of a secret carburettor by the villainous Boris (*Theatre World*)

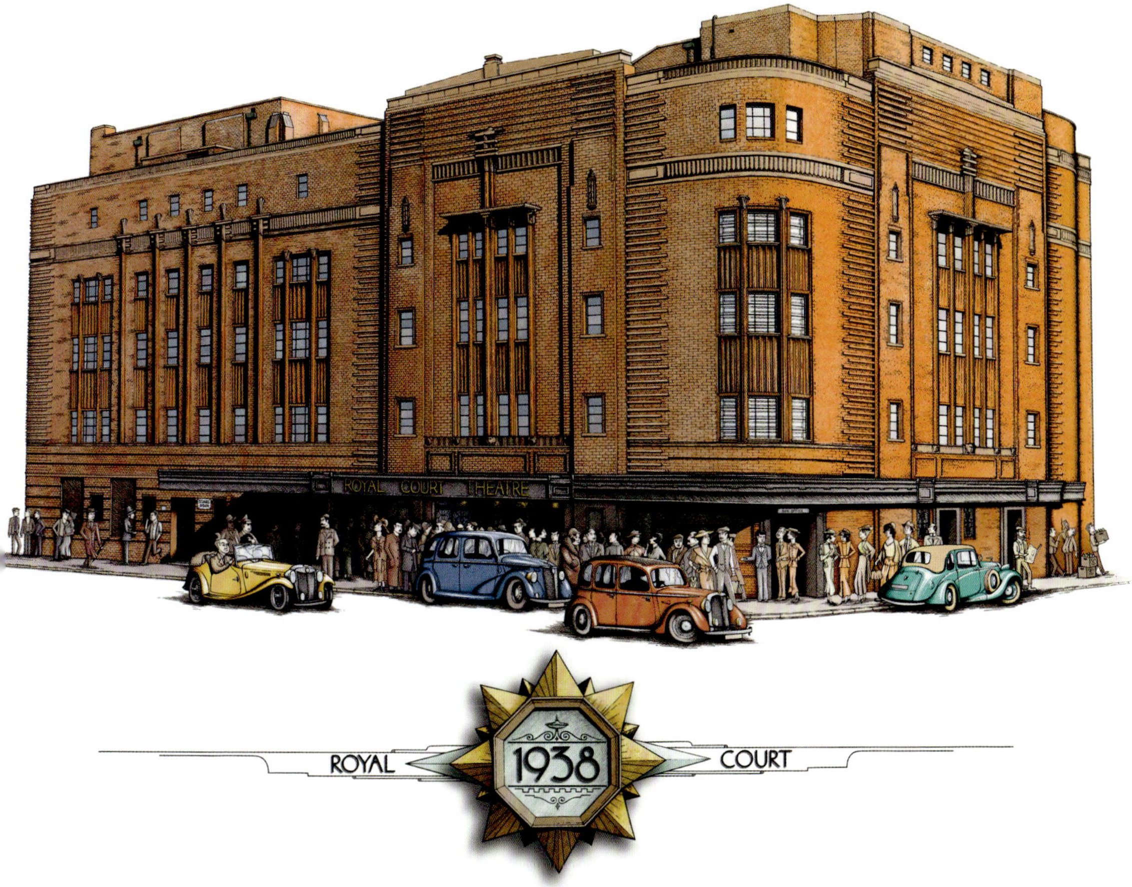

The Royal Court, 1938 (Paul Imrie)

Entertainment is Essential:
Let us preserve our balance. ENTERTAINMENT IS AN ESSENTIAL WAR INDUSTRY. It gives much needed relief to strained nerves and tired minds. It gives relaxation to fighting men on leave.

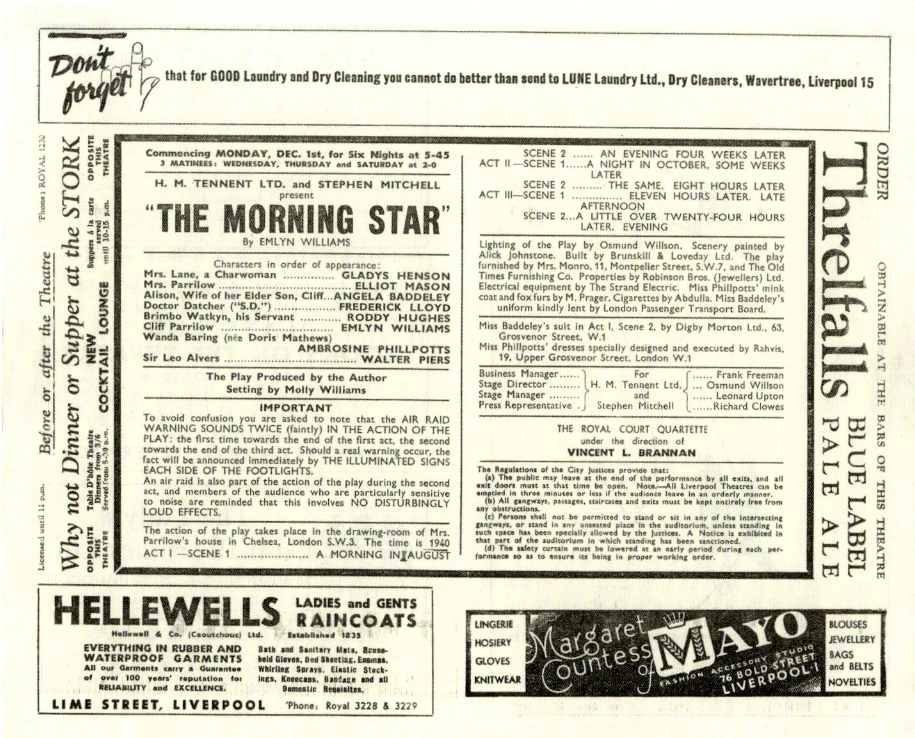
Don't forget that for GOOD Laundry and Dry Cleaning you cannot do better than send to LUNE Laundry Ltd., Dry Cleaners, Wavertree, Liverpool 15

'Phone: ROYAL 1230

Licensed until 11 p.m.

Before or after the Theatre

Why not Dinner or Supper at the STORK

OPPOSITE THIS THEATRE

Table D'hôte Theatre Dinners from 3/6 Served from 5.30 p.m.

NEW COCKTAIL LOUNGE

Suppers à la carte served until 10-15 p.m.

OPPOSITE THIS THEATRE

Commencing MONDAY, DEC. 1st, for Six Nights at 5-45
3 MATINEES: WEDNESDAY, THURSDAY and SATURDAY at 2-0

H. M. TENNENT LTD. and STEPHEN MITCHELL
present
"THE MORNING STAR"
By EMLYN WILLIAMS

Characters in order of appearance:

Mrs. Lane, a Charwoman .... GLADYS HENSON
Mrs. Parrilow .... ELLIOT MASON
Alison, Wife of her Elder Son, Cliff...ANGELA BADDELEY
Doctor Datcher ("S.D.") .... FREDERICK LLOYD
Brimbo Watkyn, his Servant .... RODDY HUGHES
Cliff Parrilow .... EMLYN WILLIAMS
Wanda Baring (née Doris Mathews)
AMBROSINE PHILLPOTTS
Sir Leo Alvers .... WALTER PIERS

The Play Produced by the Author
Setting by Molly Williams

IMPORTANT

To avoid confusion you are asked to note that the AIR RAID WARNING SOUNDS TWICE (faintly) IN THE ACTION OF THE PLAY: the first time towards the end of the first act, the second towards the end of the third act. Should a real warning occur, the fact will be announced immediately by THE ILLUMINATED SIGNS EACH SIDE OF THE FOOTLIGHTS.

An air raid is also part of the action of the play during the second act, and members of the audience who are particularly sensitive to noise are reminded that this involves NO DISTURBINGLY LOUD EFFECTS.

The action of the play takes place in the drawing-room of Mrs. Parrilow's house in Chelsea, London S.W.3. The time is 1940

ACT I —SCENE 1 .... A MORNING IN AUGUST
SCENE 2 ...... AN EVENING FOUR WEEKS LATER
ACT II —SCENE 1......A NIGHT IN OCTOBER, SOME WEEKS LATER
SCENE 2 .... THE SAME. EIGHT HOURS LATER
ACT III—SCENE 1 .... ELEVEN HOURS LATER. LATE AFTERNOON
SCENE 2...A LITTLE OVER TWENTY-FOUR HOURS LATER. EVENING

Lighting of the Play by Osmund Willson. Scenery painted by Alick Johnstone. Built by Brunskill & Loveday Ltd. The play furnished by Mrs. Monro, 11, Montpelier Street, S.W.7, and The Old Times Furnishing Co. Properties by Robinson Bros. (Jewellers) Ltd. Electrical equipment by The Strand Electric. Miss Phillpotts' mink coat and fox furs by M. Prager. Cigarettes by Abdulla. Miss Baddeley's uniform kindly lent by London Passenger Transport Board.

Miss Baddeley's suit in Act I, Scene 2, by Digby Morton Ltd., 63, Grosvenor Street, W.1

Miss Phillpotts' dresses specially designed and executed by Rahvis, 19, Upper Grosvenor Street, London W.1

Business Manager...... For H. M. Tennent Ltd. and Stephen Mitchell ...... Frank Freeman
Stage Director .... Osmund Willson
Stage Manager .... Leonard Upton
Press Representative . ...Richard Clowes

THE ROYAL COURT QUARTETTE
under the direction of
VINCENT L. BRANNAN

The Regulations of the City Justices provide that:

(a) The public may leave at the end of the performance by all exits, and all exit doors must at that time be open. Note.—All Liverpool Theatres can be emptied in three minutes or less if the audience leave in an orderly manner.

(b) All gangways, passages, staircases and exits must be kept entirely free from any obstructions.

(c) Persons shall not be permitted to stand or sit in any of the intersecting gangways, or stand in any unseated place in the auditorium, unless standing in such space has been specially allowed by the Justices. A Notice is exhibited in that part of the auditorium in which standing has been sanctioned.

(d) The safety curtain must be lowered at an early period during each performance so as to ensure its being in proper working order.

Threlfalls BLUE LABEL PALE ALE

ORDER OBTAINABLE AT THE BARS OF THIS THEATRE

HELLEWELLS LADIES and GENTS RAINCOATS

Hellewell & Co. (Caoutchouc) Ltd. Established 1835

EVERYTHING IN RUBBER AND WATERPROOF GARMENTS
All our Garments carry a Guarantee of over 100 years' reputation for RELIABILITY and EXCELLENCE.

Bath and Sanitary Mats, Household Gloves, Bed Sheeting, Enemas, Whirling Sprays, Elastic Stockings, Kneecaps, Bandage and all Domestic Requisites.

LIME STREET, LIVERPOOL 'Phone: Royal 3228 & 3229

LINGERIE
HOSIERY
GLOVES
KNITWEAR

Margaret Countess of MAYO
FASHION ACCESSORY STUDIO
76 BOLD STREET LIVERPOOL·1

BLOUSES
JEWELLERY
BAGS and BELTS
NOVELTIES

7 Providing Relief for Strained Nerves and Tired Minds: The Second World War

The government's decision to close all places of entertainment at the outset of the war amid concerns of imminent air raids was greeted with apprehension. The *Daily Post* argued that this would have a far-reaching effect in the city, 'which is a great seat of the entertainment industry and caters for large numbers from beyond its own boundaries'.[1] The city had 14 theatres and music halls together with 79 cinemas, with an estimated weekly capacity of three million seats. The paper was anxious that nearly 4,000 jobs would be lost. While Smiths of Lord Street were quick to advertise Player Pianos for home entertainment to fill the gap, nationally many protested against the closure, including Sir Oswald Stoll, who in a letter to *The Times* declared entertainment to be necessary to the morale of the people, pointing out that it was 'not logical to close theatres and cinemas and to open churches to crowds. None can foresee where bombs will fall and whether by night or day.'[2] George Bernard Shaw declared the closure to be 'a master-stroke of unimaginative stupidity':

> During the last war we had 80,000 soldiers on leave to amuse every night … Are there to be no theatres for them this time? We have hundreds of thousands of evacuated children to be kept out of mischief and traffic dangers. Are there to be no pictures for them? … What agent of Chancellor Hitler is it who suggested that we should all cower in darkness and terror for the duration?[3]

In the end the fears were unfounded as places of entertainment were quickly allowed to reopen. By 15 September cinemas in Liverpool were welcoming customers, and the Royal Court started business again on 9 October with Emlyn Williams's *The Corn is Green*, later than many theatres in the city as companies struggled with rearranging tours and with travel restrictions. Apart from a month towards the end of 1940, the theatre remained open for the duration, despite the fact that, after London, Liverpool suffered from more air raids than any other city in the country, enduring over 80 nights of bombing which reached their peak in May 1941. By the end of the war over 4,000 people had lost their lives and only 15 per cent of the housing stock in Bootle was undamaged. Some theatres were destroyed. The Rotunda on Stanley Road and the Argyle in Birkenhead were both bombed in September 1940, and the Metropole in Bootle, which had reopened with a Gala performance on 5 May 1941, was destroyed two days later. The Royal Court was never directly hit. It did, however, suffer a near miss in December 1940 when a bomb fell in Roe Street between the theatre and the Victoria Hotel. As Richard Whittington-Egan observes, neither building was seriously damaged, but the bomb made a huge crater 'into which a fire engine which was responding to an urgent call was driven, and its entire crew of seven was killed'.[4]

Despite the fact that the building suffered no serious damage, the war made an impression on the theatre straight away, most obviously in the make-up of the audience. Some stopped going to the theatre because of the war, as a Liverpool typist told the 1940 Mass Observation report on women in wartime. She used to go to the theatre a lot with friends, but now 'many of them are away' and, with the blackout, it was difficult to go with people who you knew would have to go home alone a different way from yourself.[5] Writing about the Playhouse, the manager, Maud Carpenter, noted,

> [t]he wartime audience was mainly composed of young people in uniform, the majority of them strangers to the city, and, in many cases, seeing 'live' plays for the first time. Many of the 'regulars' had been bombed out of their

homes and evacuated, others were engaged on important war work which left them with little time for theatre-going, especially with transport difficulties and early openings.[6]

Liverpool was a city full of service personnel, some drawn from the RAF base in Speke and some from the Royal Navy, which made the city its home in 1941. These were joined by merchant seamen, Liverpool becoming the main port of entry for imports during the war. Bryan Perrett estimates that 4.7 million troops passed through the city during the war, including 1.2 million Americans, and he offers a picture of the city centre

> crowded with servicemen and women on leave or duty. Amid the throng there were men from Canada, France, Belgium, Holland, Norway, Czechoslovakia and Poland, a moving kaleidoscope of peaked caps, forage caps, berets, kepis, Polish mortar boards, French pom-poms, naval cap ribbons, uniform khaki, dark or light blue, polished Sam Browne belts, gleaming brass buttons, gold lace, medal ribbons, service insignia and badges of rank.[7]

Specially opened clubs, including the Ocean Club in Lord Street for the Royal and Merchant Navies and two floors of the North Western Hotel in Lime Street for officers in the armed services, provided some social space for these servicemen. Theatres, too, offered a place for them to spend their free time. Nor was it was just service personnel who filled the theatres. Many women discovered that the war meant they had money to spend. Employment opportunities for women, as well as for men in protected industries, expanded during the war. The Rootes Factory in Speke, Littlewoods' 14 factories making shells, parachutes and barrage balloons and the two Royal Ordnance factories in Kirkby and Fazakerley employed between them in excess of 50,000 people, the majority of whom were women. These were joined by the women in the auxiliary forces. Across the board, a rise in living standards, full employment and a steady rise in real wages, accompanied by a shortage of luxury goods for sale, meant that money was more available for cultural activities.

Other aspects of theatregoing also changed. In 1942 the actress Cicely Courtneidge noted that going to the theatre 'was no longer the social occasion which began with dressing up, a few drinks, dinner, followed by the theatre at 8.30pm and then home at leisure'.[8] The wearing of evening dress gradually disappeared and earlier starting times (anywhere between 5.30 and 7 p.m. at the Royal Court) in the hope of getting the audience home before the raids started meant there was no time for dinner and drinks. Most importantly, however much it was emphasised that theatre was an escape from the war, 'however much they laughed at that world, in the comfort of theatre seats, they still had to reckon with it'.[9] In the theatre itself, there were reminders of the realities and dangers, and opening the programme, audiences found the following (calming) advice:

> An Air Raid Warning does not necessarily mean a raid.
>
> You will be notified if the Warning is given.
>
> DO NOT BE ALARMED, because the Warning does not mean that a raid will take place, and it is not likely to occur for at least seven minutes.
>
> If you wish to leave for home or shelter near at hand, you are at liberty to do so – the Staff will guide you. If not, you should remain in the building which is much safer than on the streets.
>
> If you wish to leave the auditorium, the Staff will guide you to shelter accommodation in the Theatre.
>
> Shelter accommodation in the Theatre is clearly indicated by signs in the auditorium – the Staff will guide you.
>
> Keep Calm, it may not happen. The Programme will continue.

Getting to the theatre often meant negotiating bomb-damaged streets and dealing with transport problems. While the theatre remained unscathed, much of the area around it took direct hits. The Adelphi Hotel was bombed in 1940 as were St John's fishmarket and St George's Hall. In 1941 the museum and central library were hit as were the department stores Lewis's and Blackler's (situated on Great Charlotte Street). Getting home could mean being caught in a raid, as one woman visiting the theatre in August 1941 remembers:

> One night a friend and I went to see Richard Tauber in *Land of Smiles* and an air-raid started half-way through the performance. The manager came on stage and warned the audience, but said the show would go on, so the audience stayed put. When we left the theatre, everyone singing or humming 'You Are My Heart's Delight' the searchlights were still criss-crossing the sky, and the anti-aircraft guns were "ack-acking" away, but we walked home to Edge Lane…[10]

And if the audience and getting to and from the theatre had changed, the war also impacted on what happened on stage.

Maintaining Morale?

The Listener in 1940 suggested that 'the maintenance of morale' was of the first importance, so 'if a dose of light entertainment helps us to forget our troubles even momentarily, there is no need to begrudge ourselves that pleasure: refreshment of this kind strengthens us to face the grimmer tasks...'[11] In the same year, *The Stage* argued that 'the bulk of the public wants entertainment ... and wants it light', going on to maintain that theatre should 'offer a passing means of escape from the anxious preoccupations' of war.[12] The Royal Court itself added to the idea that its role was primarily to entertain. Audiences were met with the following notice in their programmes headed 'Entertainment is Essential': 'Let us preserve our balance. ENTERTAINMENT IS AN ESSENTIAL WAR INDUSTRY. It gives much needed relief to strained nerves and tired minds. It gives relaxation to fighting men on leave.' In contrast to this picture of a population in need of escape from their anxious preoccupations, the Mass Observation reports on Liverpool suggested that morale in the city was appreciably higher than in other blitzed cities. There was a 'large amount of singing and whistling in the streets' (the most popular number being 'Bless 'em all'), suggested the December 1940 report on Liverpool and Manchester. The 'town does not shut down directly there is an alert', it continued, and to a casual visitor the city centre at night represented 'a mixture of a bump supper night at Cambridge and a bank holiday at Blackpool', with dance halls still holding 500 people when an enemy plane was overhead.[13]

Despite the apparently high morale in Liverpool, the perception that wartime theatres were dominated by the light entertainment required to raise spirits is one that has entered popular thinking. In common with many contemporary historians, Juliet Gardiner was still stating in 2005 that

> theatre audiences seemed not to want to see the war on stage ... in general American musicals such as Cole Porter's *Something for the Boys* and *Dubarry Was a Lady*, and comedies such as Noel Coward's *Blithe Spirit* and Rattigan's *Whilst the Sun Shines*, were what wartime audiences flocked to see as the all-too-real spectacle of war played in the surrounding streets.[14]

While only the two comedies on her list made it to the stage of the Royal Court, several other shows from the period suggest that there is some truth in this assessment. Max Catto's *Punch Without Judy* (February 1940), set in a make-believe Bohemian world 'where everybody is nice ... and nobody feels rancour against anyone else', was, in the eyes of *The Stage*, 'consistent in its resilient lightness'.[15] Peter Blackmore's 'ideal war-time comedy', *The Blue Goose* (August 1940), was a story about an amateur dramatic performance of *The Mikado* in a seaside opera house complete with a drunken admiral's widow and a yachtsman who keeps slipping on the dead Michaelmas daisies on his boat deck.[16] Many of the newer musicals too, including Stanley Lupino's *Lady Behave* (February 1942) and *Tonight's the Night* (June 1943; a revival from the First World War), chose to bypass reality by way of a Hollywood film studio and a masked ball. And the play being performed on the day peace was declared in Europe, Norman Ginsbury's *The First Gentleman* (May 1945), was a Regency pageant about 'our most flamboyant, self-satisfied, grandiloquent, debauched, mistress ridden prince'.[17]

Emlyn Williams as Cliff Parrilow, Elliott Mason as Mrs Parrilow and Angela Baddeley as Alison in *Morning Star*

Yet many of the lighter plays did not ignore the world outside, and even comedies and farces often situated themselves in the present, allowing the audience a chance of shared problems and the laughter of recognition. In Walter Ellis's farce *Sleeping Out* (October 1942), the audience encounters Freda having trouble with the blackout and worried because the window cleaner 'has joined the balloons and has to go up with them tomorrow'. When her husband evacuates his business to the countryside, she is worried because he employs Gipsy, 'a very attractive little refugee stenographer', who is periodically trailed as a potential spy by a Secret Service man. This was 'whimsical fun', but fun rooted in some sense of the everyday realities of a country at war.[18] Equally, Barbara Cartland and Bruce Woodhouse's *French Dressing* (December 1943), while described as a trivial comedy of 'the fluffy type', also had a French woman seeking a job as a cook who falls under suspicion of being a spy.[19]

In comparison to Gardiner's assessment of wartime theatre, W. A. Darlington, for many years drama critic of the *Daily Telegraph*, suggested that while there was a liking for 'light, gay pieces', the audience 'did not close its mind to the serious or unhappy things'. He noted that 'it soon became clear that a play-going population which was, or might at any moment be, in imminent danger of death … was willing, and at times, eager to face truth'. This he thought especially true for those in areas of acute danger (which included Liverpool), but he also noted that as all of England 'even the areas regarded as comparatively safe, *was* a part of the battlefield', the same 'readiness to like serious entertainment' manifested itself around the country.[20] Echoing Darlington's words, many of the plays and musicals that made it to the stage of the Royal Court did not avoid the situation in the outside world or the concerns of the audience, although they reflected it in a variety of ways.

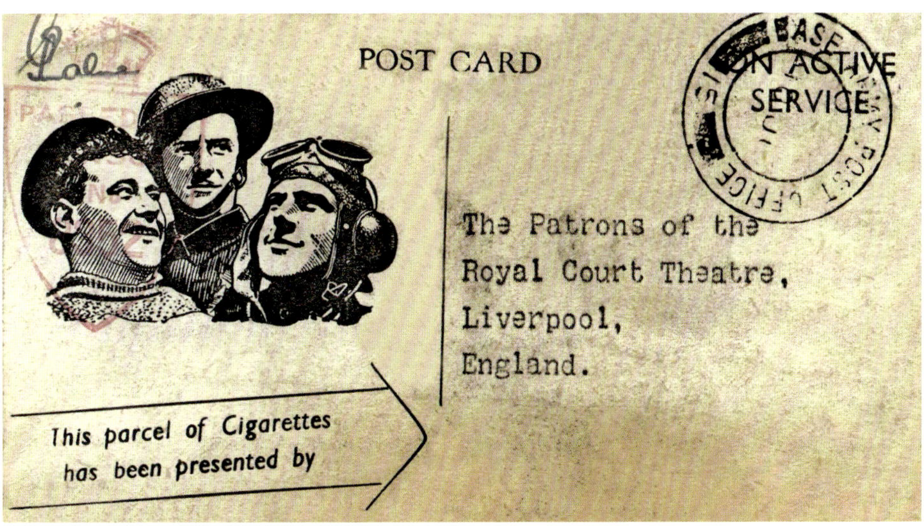

Musicals and Revues

On the surface, musicals might appear to be the form least likely to speak to the times, but many did. Cicely Courtneidge and Jack Hubert's follow-on from *Under Your Hat*, *Full Swing* (February 1942), used the same characters and a similar plot line, with Kay Porter and Jack Millett being sent on another secret mission by the War Office. This time they are on an assignment to track down Dr Caro and their friend Charlie, a member of the British Secret Service, whom the doctor has kidnapped and taken to South America. In the process, they also manage to mistakenly post a dossier full of the wicked doctor's crimes to him, so this too, with the help of a myriad disguises, has to be rescued. The most successful musical of the war years was Ivor Novello's *The Dancing Years* (January 1942). Although premiered in March 1939, it went on to play on tour and in London for ten years. Set in Vienna, it is the story of Rudi, a poor musician who becomes famous and wealthy, only to find himself under threat of death for helping those refused passports by the Nazis. As a consequence, his music is banned. Faced with an intransigent Nazi officer, he tells him,

> Do you think this silly embargo on my music here in our poor country has killed it for the world outside? That's where my fortune is – outside and you can't touch it. It's there for them to use, to keep them in comfort, to teach them to remember there was once a place called Vienna, where the only crime was to be unhappy – not this city of the dead.[21]

In a final scene, Rudi is saved by the woman he loves but cannot have, and who tells him, with certainty, that 'the dancing years' will come again.

Much of *The Dancing Years* is set in the time before the annexation of Austria, offering, as *The Times* noted, a picture of an untroubled Vienna, that 'city where gaiety was golden'.[22] Along with revivals of a multitude of earlier musicals (from *The Chocolate Soldier* and *The Desert Song* to *Lilac Time* and *Chu Chin Chow*), which far outnumbered new musicals at the Royal Court during the war, this underscored some important anxieties. One was a 'deep concern with old-time (pre-Fascist) Europe', so they can be seen as both 'nostalgic of a world without Nazism' and also as a way of 'keeping the plight of Europe to the fore', just as Rudi sees his music as a way that people will remember the old Vienna.[23] At the same time, some of the musical revivals had straightforward messages for a contemporary audience. In Lehar's *Land of Smiles* (August 1941), a countess marries a Chinese prince and goes to live with him in China. She cannot reconcile herself to life there and returns home. Despite being heartbroken, he respects his country's rule that, however he feels, he

Week commencing MONDAY, SEPTEMBER 22nd, 1941
NIGHTLY at 6-0
MATINEES: WEDNESDAY, THURSDAY and SATURDAY at 2-0

H. M. TENNENT LTD.
presents

VIVIEN LEIGH
in
"THE DOCTOR'S DILEMMA"
By BERNARD SHAW

Characters in order of their appearance:

Redpenny	COURTNEY BROMET
Emmy	MARGARET MURRAY
Sir Colenso Ridgeon	FRANK ALLENBY
Dr. Leo Schutzmacher	CHARLES GOLDNER
Sir Patrick Cullen	MORLAND GRAHAM
Cutler Walpole	JOHN TURNBULL
Sir Ralph Bloomfield Bonington	AUSTIN TREVOR
Dr. Blenkinsop	GEORGE RELPH
Mrs. Dubedat	VIVIEN LEIGH
Louis Dubedat	CYRIL CUSACK
The Maid	JOAN LANG
The Newspaper Man	GEOFFREY EDWARDS
The Secretary	DOROTHY HAMILTON

ACT I
Sir Colenso Ridgeon's Consulting Room. June 15th, 1903
ACT II
Scene I.........The Terrace at The Star and Garter Hotel, Richmond

One of the theatre's two programme designs used in the 1940s

must always smile. Similarly in *The Student Prince* (June 1940), the young prince eventually learns that duty to his country and family is more important than love.

Revues too offered a wartime audience a balance between nostalgia, escapism and comment on the contemporary world. Tom Arnold's *Sky High* (May 1942) was, despite wartime economies, a 'sweeping panoramic production' with 32 scenes, including a nostalgic paddle-boat dream with the whole cast on board a Thames steamer in mid-Victorian costume singing popular songs of the period. But it also included a seabed discussion between two mermaids about the current problems of the war, reflecting concerns about 'making do'. The sketch 'For Ladies Only' told the audience how to get the most out of their coupons in 'an undressing talk'. In 'Bicycling', Hermione Gingold offered advice on making your own bicycle, including the use of pram wheels, piano pedals and a home-crocheted chain made from cast iron. C. B. Cochran, in *Top Hat* (March 1942), specially written for the Royal Court following a promise he made after the reopening in 1938, included, amid the wit and Cochran's famous ladies, a moving moment when Marcel de Haes sang a song as a Free French soldier. Ronald Jeans, born in Liverpool and known to a Liverpool audience for his First World War revues at the Playhouse, produced *Green for Piccadilly* (December 1942) in which *The Stage* noted that wartime allusions were paramount. Sketches included a sergeant major faced with 'a bevy of athletic looking beauties to drill' who fell victim to their tendency to swing, Mr and Mrs Perfect Citizen intent on doing everything they were told by the authorities, and a blitzed-out hotel resident sighing for the 'Old Familiar Things' of her lost home. In 'A Barnyard Tragedy', hens and a cockerel lament the sacrifice one of their number will have to make to meet the wartime reduction of feeding stuffs.[24] Jeans particularly delighted the audience with his 'terse comment ... on the fish shortage now affecting Liverpool'.[25]

At other times revues missed the target. The *Liverpool Echo*, while applauding the satire that hit the mark such as the lampooning of the 'red-tape mind' in 'Letter from the Ministry', chastised *Rise Above It* (March 1941) for losing 'touch with the temper of the times', asking 'are there not more suitable targets for ridicule than railwaymen – in days when they tackle fire-bombs in trucks full of explosives – phone girls, taxi drivers and waitresses?'[26] Overall, however, revues served the purpose of enabling the audience to face the trials and tribulations of war on the home front with a lighter heart. As Cicely Courtneidge noted, people laughed easily in those early wartime revues, 'at the blackout, the bombs, the Germans, the Italians, gas-masks, air-raid wardens and all the problems of wartime living'.[27]

While musicals and revues (alongside continuing visits from opera and ballet companies) liberally peppered the Royal Court stage during the war, it was straight plays, from comedies and farces to dramas and thrillers, that dominated. The Royal Court audience were offered few classic plays; Donald Wolfit toured with one Shakespeare production (*The Merchant of Venice* in October 1943) and John Gielgud with two (*Macbeth* in April 1942 and *Hamlet* in July 1944) alongside his production of Congreve's *Love for Love* (March 1943), an unlikely wartime hit.

This lack of classic plays may be attributed to the arrival of the Old Vic company, which made the Liverpool Playhouse its home from 1942 until June 1946, offering a programme which, while also including newer plays and newer 'classics' such as Shaw, Ibsen and Pirandello, embraced Shakespeare, Goldsmith, Sheridan and Marlowe. At the Court, what dominated were new plays with a handful of revivals, a picture that contradicts Andrew Davies's assertion that 'most of the productions seen during the war were of classics – Shaw, Shakespeare and Ibsen – and there were few opportunities for new writers'.[28] Revivals, though, were not always welcome or in tune with the times. Commenting on *Smilin' Through*, a play originally performed in 1919, the *Liverpool Echo* found its sweet nostalgia for the days after the First World War a trifle cloying in 'these harsh days'.[29]

Stage Thrills

The Stage noted in September 1942 that 'at a time when fact is so much more blood curdling than any fiction', thrillers, crime and murder remained popular genres, and Rebecca D'Monté notes that in 1944, at 'a time when it would be expected that audiences required escapism', 25 per cent of West End plays were concerned with murder.[30] The Royal Court hosted many thrillers during the war, some focusing directly in terms of subject matter on the war itself, where inevitably the Germans were foiled. In *Cottage to Let* (September 1941), Geoffrey Kerr told a story of spies attempting to steal a secret from a scientist, reflecting fears of invasion and concerns with fifth columnists. Frank Lauder and Sidney Gilliat's comedy thriller *The Body Was Well Nourished* (June 1940 and April 1941)[31] dealt with attempts by Gestapo agents to kill a Cabinet minister, the only person who can pull off a vital pact with the Balkans. The agents have failed to kill his secretary, whose 'corpse' is left in a grand piano and who revives for long enough to reveal her fragmentary knowledge that he is to be blown up at the Green Man in an unknown town at a fast-approaching time. Other comedy thrillers included Frank Harvey Jr's *Saloon Bar* (October 1939) and Claire Booth's *Margin for Error* (July 1940). The latter was set in New York's German consulate where the Consul, thought to have been murdered by three different people but later found to have poisoned himself, is guarded by Jewish policemen. It offered the audience a first half which, according to the *Liverpool Echo,* dissected 'fanaticism with … considerable insight'.[32]

The popularity of thrillers may have had a number of causes, not least of which were the fearful, darkened streets where people 'blundered about' as if 'suddenly blinded' and there was no knowing what lay around the corner.[33] The war also led to a dislocated, transient population living in cities and towns where they had no ties, with no one to watch over them but no one to look out for them either. It may also have reflected the real rise in crime rates. In 1939 there were 303,771 reported crimes in England and Wales. By 1945, that number had risen by 57 per cent. In part this was due to the fact that in wartime there were simply more laws to break, and many crimes were connected to the black market. However, there were also popular wartime stories of more 'thrilling' crimes to feed people's imaginations, from the short-lived notoriety of the 'Blackouts Ripper' who murdered three women, to the story of Harry Dobkin, who killed his wife, leaving her mutilated body in a bomb-damaged building in the hope that she would become one more unidentifiable victim of the Blitz.[34] The popularity of detective plays especially continued a trend that had started in the decades after the First World War when they served as 'a sedative for the nerves'.[35] In the interwar decades, the nerves of those from the First World War,

> who had undergone the privations of war at home – rationing, black-out, cold, the influenza epidemic, bereavement and the long, long hours of waiting to hear the worst were … jarred. Pitting their wits in a struggle that was cerebral without involving strain, this was the generation that made the crossword puzzle the national pastime of the middle class … whodunits were perhaps the literature of emotional invalids, shock-absorbing and rehabilitating, like playing endless rounds of clock patience.[36]

The bombings and privations of the home front during the Second World War seemed to demand the same soothing of the nerves, the same desire to be preoccupied by 'the mental equivalent of pottering', and it was during the war that Agatha Christie's first play appeared at the Royal Court.[37] Performed twice during the war, *Ten Little Niggers* (November 1943, in the week prior to its London opening, and June 1944) used a murder mystery to touch on concerns facing the audience. Here, an apparently random group of strangers are lured to an island with the promise of a free holiday, but what promises to be a relaxing break away from the pressures of everyday life quickly becomes fearful, as guests start to fall victim to an unknown murderer. Privacy and isolation compound the terror, as anyone can potentially be the murderer or the next victim. Alison Light sees it as 'a metaphor for the corruptions of insularity' with the 'security of the island rapidly becoming claustrophobic and imprisoning'.[38] Even worse, as D'Monté points out, the island represents Britain not as a country where everyone is working together, but as a place where there is no kinship.[39] It is a society of strangers, all fearful of each other, and all harbouring a secret crime. Playing on Christie's familiar themes of guilt and the nature of justice, it does not 'take a huge leap of the imagination to see how this scenario might have resonated with the vulnerable inhabitants of an island state at war with a powerful enemy'.[40] In some attempt to ameliorate the gloom, Christie changed the ending from the original novel, offering wartime theatregoers a happier conclusion. In the original, all ten are dead and Wargrave gets away with his lifelong desire to avenge himself on those he thinks have got away with their crimes. On stage, two survive, in a comic twist involving a woman who is unable to shoot straight, and Christie turned the play into a 'morale booster'.[41]

In a slightly different vein, dissecting the workings of evil was also a recurring theme, reflecting a population's concern with the perceived mentality of the enemy. The revival of Benn W. Levy's *The Man With Red Hair* (August 1942) explored the psychology of Crispin, a man obsessed with the pleasure of pain, who believes that only through pain do we reach happiness and power. The psychology of evil was also at the heart of Cyril Campion's *The Devil's Sanctuary* (August 1941). Set in a crumbling abbey, Campion's play focused on the prevalence of a strange form of hysteria among women in a village, coupled with the disappearance of a French doctor on the eve of perfecting a cure for cancer. It transpires that Sir Francis Farquharson has fallen into evil ways and, as a student of religious sects, has taken to performing black magic rites in the chapel under the abbey ruins. In Russell Thorndike's *The House of Jeffreys* (August 1942), Georgina falls under the spell of the portrait of 'The Hanging Judge' from whom the publishing family are descended in a macabre tale of cannibalism.[42] The best-known of these plays was Emlyn Williams's *Night Must Fall* (March 1943), 'a play about a charmer ... who cuts up women'.[43] He had found himself 'wanting to write a play in which the audience knew as the curtain rose, that the murderer had not only "done it", but was to be hanged for his crime', and the play opens in the Court of Criminal Appeal where the Lord Chief Justice dismisses the murderer's appeal and declares that his sanity 'has never been called into question'.[44] In what follows we see the story of Dan, the chirpy page boy who has got housemaid Dora pregnant on a Bank Holiday jaunt and who moves into the isolated house in the woods complete with a hat box later discovered to contain his first victim's head. His second victim is Mrs Bramson, the tyrannical 'invalid' he is looking after. Williams's main concerns are with how the rest of the characters perceive Dan, from the housekeeper's pronouncement that he is 'such an ordinary boy' to Mrs Bramson's niece Olivia's dawning realisation that there is something wrong with him.[45] Beginning to sense that something is awry, she muses on how frightening it is to think what faces can hide. 'I sometimes catch sight of one looking at me. Careful lips and blank eyes ... And then I find I am staring at myself in the glass ... and I realise how successfully I'm hiding the thoughts I know so well ... and then I know we're all ... strangers.'[46] There is a deep sense of insecurity in the idea that anyone could be a murderer (or a spy) and you would never know by looking at their face, and a sense of insecurity in a realisation that murder (like war) can happen to you. 'Murder's a thing we read about in the papers; it isn't real life', says Olivia. 'It can't touch us ... but it can. And it's here. All round us. In the forest ... in this house. We're ... living with it.'[47]

War on Stage

It took until 1945 for a play to arrive on the Royal Court stage that dealt with the front line of war. The success of Wallasey-born Captain Colin Morris's *Desert Rats* (May 1945) *was* a big surprise. 'Who could prophesy', *Variety* asked,

> that such a big critical welcome would be given to a war play ... at the present time when all smart men of show business have thought nothing but a hundred percent escapist fare would click? It was five years after the First World War before the British public wanted to ... see war plays like *Journey's End*.[48]

Praised by *The Stage* as the best picture of war so far, it was an adventure story about the rescue of the remnants of a small squadron from the Tripoli coast road. Thrilling, noisy, performed by an ex-servicemen cast and with each scene introduced by 'Lili Marlene', they are eventually saved by the Highlanders who arrive marching along to the tune of 'Cock o' the North', a moment described by *The Stage* reviewer as 'emotionally' stirring.[49] It was, though, one of a kind at the Court, and while the Home Guard were at the heart of Bernard Miles's comedy *They Also Serve* (November 1944) and the theatre hosted the War Office-backed historical pageant *Salute the Soldiers* (May 1944) aimed at raising funds as part of Help the Soldier Week (and complete with a cast of 250), most plays avoided the battlefield.

Instead, the themes that did well were 'concerned with the home front and domestic readjustments' that had arisen from the upheaval of the war.[50] It is a world captured by Helen Forrester, who traces the journey for many in the city from the fear and pessimism of the early years to the drudgery of the later years. 1940 and 1941 were times of 'quiet despair',

> a period when the Merchant Navy was decimated by German submarines and aircraft. Once a man was at sea, there was not a moment when he was not in acute danger. Over the bar, in Liverpool Bay, the U-boats waited, like cats at a mouse hole, for the slow, ill-defended freighters entering and leaving the ports of Liverpool and Birkenhead. If they survived the submarines, they could strike acoustic mines, magnetic mines and other menaces plopping about in the heaving waves.[51]

At her work in Bootle, 'the names of ships whispered by weeping women became a monotonous litany'.[52] Later, it was the small irritations of war that irked the most,

> the blackout, the inability to fight one's way down a packed corridor of a long distance train, simply to get off or go to the lavatory; the problem of obtaining even a cup of tea on a long journey; trying to find a cobbler to mend shoes or an electrician, or a plumber; or a washer or a switch in order to do a repair oneself. But gradually we got so used to people looking grey, shabby and untended, to buildings being left unpainted, to taps that dripped and appliances which did not work, to furniture with seats worn thin, to shopkeepers like bully boys, that we did not even notice them.[53]

Strap-hanging in packed trains and trams for a couple of hours a day to get to work was wearing 'and one could end a journey to and from work bruised and exhausted'.[54] The greatest hardship was the lack of fuel. 'We queued for coal at the railway stations', she wrote. 'Gas jets flickered down to a tiny, almost useless flame; and, despite dropping shillings into the electric meter, the lights often went off.'[55] Local newspapers wrote of shortages of everything from eggs, beer, blankets and soap to potatoes, prams and chimney sweeps. The everyday hardship of queues and getting food on to the table were also a perennial concern as this 1943 column from the *Liverpool Echo* highlights:

> On numerous occasions since the outbreak of war and queuing has become the fashion, it has been said that our hard-working British housewives revel in the habit as it provides ample opportunity for a gossip. Such however, is by no means the case ... I cannot offer anything but praise and admiration, along with sympathy for the housewife who stands in queues endeavouring to get something fresh for the family. I do not suppose for a moment that when the family arrive home for dinner or tea and find tomatoes on the menu, and perhaps a strawberry, gooseberry or cherry pie they realise how much it cost in patience and weariness.[56]

It was these local concerns that many of the plays came to address. J. C. Trewin suggested that Esther McCracken's *No Medals* (September 1944 and July 1946) was 'about the cares of a housewife in wartime (and, for that matter, in time of peace). It is about marmalade and vacuum-cleaners and charwomen and plum-bottling and fish-queues...'[57] Yet it is also a play about how war challenged and changed the roles that women played, a theme reflected as well in Daphne du Maurier's *The Years Between* (December 1944). In McCracken's play, Martha finds herself taken for granted by her extended family, being 'an unpaid nanny, messenger boy, house keeper and general servant' as well as fire watching, working in a canteen and selling Savings Stamps to people who do not particularly want them.[58] She sees herself as a frustrated heroine longing 'to sweep through the seas protecting the convoys, or to sweep through the skies protecting England'. Yet all she can do 'is sweep through the flues once a week…'[59] In an argument with her sister, who works in a war office, her frustration, exhaustion and boredom explode into a tirade against those who do not seem to value what the housewife does. In Liverpool, the play was warmly welcomed. The *Liverpool Echo*, which saw it as 'a happy blend of acid comment on housekeeping' and 'Superior Persons in Uniform', thought that 'all mothers will bless Esther McCracken who has stated their case so amusingly'.[60] The following day the newspaper took the almost unprecedented step of publishing the scene from the play when Martha finally has enough of her sister's attitude, commenting afterwards that 'the audience's applause showed that the case for the housewife had "got home" and that many home-workers did deserve a medal'. It also noted the great laugh of recognition when 'in the midst of trying to do several thing at once, Martha's neighbour shouts at the door, "The fishmonger's got fish" and she drops everything to go into the queue'.[61]

For other women in McCracken's play, the greatest curse of the war is waiting, 'waiting for someone, waiting for letters, waiting for news – and just plain waiting for it all to end'.[62] As Monica, whose husband is away fighting, tells Martha,

> [y]ou go through a numb misery phase. I remember in the middle of it thinking that my face had expressed nothing for so long that it must be doing the wrinkles a bit of good. I smiled faintly after I'd thought it, so I suppose that was the first stage of recovery to more or less normal. I'm afraid it never gets better than 'more or less'.[63]

Waiting is also central to Terence Rattigan's *Flare Path* (November 1944), which although set near an RAF base and touching on issues of heroism and working-class stoicism, is ostensibly about the women (and men) who wait for the fliers to return from a raid. In this instance the audience waits with them through the long night and suffers with the Duchess as her Polish airman is not among the returning number. In a play that offers, as Dan Rebellato suggests, 'a kind of resistant affirmation of life against the constant possibility of imminent death', Flying Officer Count Skriczevinsky does eventually return, enabling the play to finish with a rousing chorus of 'We don't want to join the Air Force'.[64] Rebellato suggests that London audiences (and by inference audiences in all cities that had experienced direct attack) 'had a strong affinity with the play because they were placed in precisely the same position as the characters in Act Two. Listening for the offstage sounds of battle, waiting for news, hoping for the best.'[65]

The real sense of danger from the world was even more evident in Emlyn Williams's *The Morning Star*, which premiered at the Royal Court in December 1941. Opening their programmes, audiences were confronted with the following notice:

> To avoid confusion you are asked to note that the AIR RAID WARNING SOUNDS TWICE (faintly) IN THE ACTION OF THE PLAY, the first time towards the end of the first act, the second towards the end of the third act. Should a real warning occur, the fact will be announced immediately by THE ILLUMINATED SIGNS EACH SIDE OF THE FOOTLIGHTS.
>
> An air raid is also part of the action of the play during the second act, and members of the audience who are particularly sensitive to noise are reminded that this involves NO DISTURBINGLY LOUD EFFECTS.

It was a necessary warning in the bombed-out city, and throughout *The Morning Star* the action is accompanied by insistent sirens, bombs and gunfire. Mrs Parrilow's Chelsea house is hit twice. By the start of Act II, the drawing room boasts a broken window and a door blown off its hinges. The furniture from the damaged upstairs rooms is piled up and beds have been moved in. The grand piano, now known as the fortress, provides a refuge in the raids. At the end of first scene in Act II, the house is hit again. There is, as the stage directions tells us,

> *a muffled roar; and simultaneously several things happen: the front door crashes open, ornaments and pictures fall over, articles of furniture piled in the corner tumble to the floor, the curtains billow, the windows splinter and break; the rumble of falling masonry, then silence, broken by the distant noise of glass – and more glass – smashing to the ground, dying into an endless sinister tinkle. Silence.*[66]

Into this is brought the body of a badly injured man, Brimbo, who has been lodging in the house, looking after Dr Datcher. Despite being operated on by Mrs Parrilow's doctor son, Cliff, he later dies. Offstage, the woman who has been heard drunkenly singing on the streets is killed and her body laid out in the bathroom upstairs. A telegram arrives to tell Mrs Parrilow that one of her sons, a pilot, has been killed. Throughout the play the radio announcer relays stories about the world outside, detailing the nights of bombing and the number of casualties. The lady typist buried under the bombed flats across the road is never found. Mrs Lane, the Cockney charlady, finds her house destroyed, leaving only a fragment of bedroom wallpaper exposed to the gaze of passers-by, 'such a strange thing to 'appen to respectable people'.[67] But she does not want Mrs Parrilow to tell anybody about it as 'these things don't cheer nobody up, and with the flats fallin' on the shelter and the fires and a lot of people gone dead…' there was plenty to be going on with.[68]

For many in the Liverpool audience, this was a play set on the hard edge of their everyday lives, but Williams included much that might keep people's spirits up as well. Both Mrs Parrilow and Mrs Lane exhibit a stiff upper lip in the face of adversity, with Mrs Parrilow announcing she will only leave the house 'feet first, dead or drunk'.[69] The ending is also an optimistic one. Throughout the play Cliff has been depressed, and in the face of bureaucratic lack of interest in his attempt to try out a new technique for saving people whose hearts have stopped because of shock, he is nearly lured away to Hollywood as a propaganda writer, contemplating leaving his wife for an ex-model. But he is 'saved' when the hospital he works in is hit. Spending the night trying to dig people out, he finally comes across a small boy, O.K. Toots (so called because those were the only words he had said apart from swearing), who he has been trying to cure.

> I started tapping about four; just as it was getting light, he began to tap back, and in another hour he was talking to me. His leg was pinned ... Then he started singing. I thought that only happened in the papers. 'Over the Rainbow' over and over again, getting weaker, I knew he was delirious. Then I got at him. He was sitting up in his night-shirt. I didn't know him, he wasn't my little tough at all, he was out of the Bible, a cherub or something. Same old formula, 'how arc you, pal,' I said, and he said 'O.K. toots'; and then as I scrambled through, I saw him fall forward, and die... (*He weeps*).[70]

Pulling himself together, he declares that he just needs some food, a sleeping draught and twelve hours' sleep and he will be better. He warns 'we'd all better be, because there's a lot of work to do, clearing up, a little headway every day, not much but onwards, mending, mending'.[71] Coming home from the hospital,

> I suddenly thought ... – behind this welter of smashing up there must be *something* ... otherwise it is just insane ... and I thought, there *is* something, very high up, very far away, high up over the balloon barrage, high up over the Jerry planes, watching us hard and saying ... 'Stop asking why it all has to be, you'll know in my own time, the only thing that interests me, is ... are you going to lie down, or are you going to stick together and fight?' ... The time has come, I told myself, for you to go home to that house and say aloud to them there, something you've been ashamed to whisper before but now life's too short ... You'll tell them that your heart is bursting with love for them, and theirs with love for you; and hospitals can burn and our lives can crash before our eyes, there'll be that we can be sure of, for ever – our love, and trust, and courage – as long as we stick together and fight.[72]

The play ends with the news that Cliff's wife, Alison, is pregnant and with Cliff vowing that the children will have their chance because he is going to fight, as against a clap of gunfire Mrs Parrilow pours glasses of celebratory wine and the '*wail of the siren merges into a crescendo of fanfare music which fills the theatre as the lights dim slowly into darkness*'.[73] The *Liverpool Echo* suggested that the play had an enthusiastic reception in the city and, while some of the speeches were overlong and the play 'wins the heart without always quite satisfying the head', it was 'emphatically a play to be grateful for'.[74]

What Are We Fighting For?

Alongside the realities of home front life, plays also addressed what the war was being fought for. As D'Monté points out, 'scenes of the English countryside continued to proliferate as a kind of pastoral idyll of pre-industrial life', and if all plays were not set in the countryside or were not pre-industrial, a strong sense of nostalgia was present.[75] Esther McCracken's *A Quiet Weekend* (November 1945, but first performed in July 1941) presented a chaotic jumble of village life, family recipes for making blackberry jam, fishing and the dying art of tying flies, poaching and the village organ fund, all set in a ramshackle house held together by string. Dodie Smith's *Dear Octopus* (December 1939), set over the weekend of a golden wedding celebration, was a hymn of praise for the family, 'that dear octopus from whose tentacles we never quite escape, nor, in our inmost hearts, ever quite wish to'.[76] It focused on 'a very ordinary family', as Nicholas, the son, makes clear in the grand toast to the happy couple:

> We own no crests, no heirlooms and our few ancestors are very badly painted. I wonder what they would think of us, great grandfather with his twinkle and grandmamma who wasn't quite as fierce as that. But she was fierce. I think she might shake her head and say: 'The family isn't what it was.' And there, most honoured grandmamma, lies its strength. It is, like nearly every British institution, adaptable. It bends, it stretches – but it never breaks.[77]

The 'ordinariness' of family life with its sense of continuity was becoming something to celebrate. Noel Coward's *This Happy Breed* (November 1942), a domestic *Cavalcade* set at number 17 Sycamore Road, Clapham Common, was a play about 'the importance of knowing one's place'.[78] Spanning the years from 1919 to 1939, the trials, tribulations and pleasures of the Gibbons family presented ordinary, suburban people who were, by the time the play was staged, fighting the war. It spelled out the everyday values being fought for. The *Scotsman*'s review was at pains to point out the commonality of the characters' lives with those of the audience:

> They are ordinary with no vaulting ambitions ... and the groundwork of their lives is that of millions of other people like them ... The dozen people of the play one might meet anywhere in London and but for the dialect, almost anywhere else in Britain. The incidents of this twenty years are the stuff of common experience.[79]

Frank Gibbons presented, according to the *Liverpool Echo*, 'the best qualities of our race'.[80] He resolutely argues throughout that 'there are worse things than being ordinary and respectable', and while some things might need changing, change needs to come slowly. As he tells his wife, 'We've got our own way of settling things, it may be slow and it may be dull, but it suits us all right and it always will.'[81] His children, who try and stray from the fold (Reg with his youthful Bolshevism and Queenie who runs off to France with a married man, hating living in a house that is exactly the same as a hundred others), are brought back into line. The play ends in June 1939 with a hymn of praise to the ordinary man; Frank tells his grandson that while 'life isn't all jam for anybody' and the country has been on its knees a bit, 'letting people who've trusted us down and allowing noisy little men to bully us', it will be all right because

> the people themselves, the ordinary people like you and me, know something better than all the fussy old politicians put together – we know what we belong to, where we come from, and where we are going. We may not know it with our brains, but we know it with our roots ... We 'aven't lived and died and struggled all these hundreds of years to get decency and justice and freedom for ourselves without being prepared to fight fifty wars if needs be – to keep 'em.[82]

The same sense of ordinary life and the values being fought for were present in Mabel and Denis Constandurous's *Acacia Avenue* (August 1943), a play that the *Liverpool Echo* pronounced 'the season's best antidote to the blackout'.[83] Set in a pre-war 1939, no mention is made of the war, and this appears to be a small, insular and domestic world. The Robinsons are about to go abroad for the first time in their lives on a Mediterranean cruise, but because of a series of setbacks they end up going back (rather gratefully) to dear old Bognor. Any sense of the outside world is limited. Mrs Robinson is not even sure where the Mediterranean is. Their next-door neighbours, who, smugly, have already been on a cruise, did not like Athens because it was just a lot of old buildings without a golf course or a decent cup of tea, and anyway the most important parts of cruising were the deck games, the bridge, the dancing or having a 'tiddley' in the bar. As

Mrs Wilson remarks, 'I shall never forget the time Tommykins kept on at me to look at Vesuvius in the middle of playing bridge. Made me miss a Little Slam.'[84] Underneath the insularity, however, is a defence of everything the family stands for. As the daughter Joan announces that she will marry Michael without going through a long engagement because she is not concerned by 'the ordinary cheap, conventional things like everybody else', her father responds: 'Just being ordinary isn't being cheap, Joanny – though sometimes I think it is the best way to be happy ... I wonder how the country would get on without us ordinary people, who run their little homes and dig their little gardens and pay their little taxes.'[85] While Joan is concerned that marriage is dull and steady, he tells her that 'a quiet steady affection like your mother's and mine can make an ordinary home into one of the best things in the world'.[86]

But far from a sense of 'ordinary' people all pulling together uncomplainingly, tensions and challenges to the fabric of society are also underlined by these plays. Many of them reflected the changes in the make-up of the 'family' and how people were now living. The household in *No Medals* included Martha and her two daughters, one of their husbands home on leave, Geoffrey Radcliffe (a friend of Martha's dead husband), an airman billeted on the family and a seaman staying for a few days, all living in furnished rooms in a port somewhere in England, and later joined by Phyllis Malling whose husband has been sent overseas and who needs the comfort and company of others. It is a long way from the nuclear family wistfully praised in *Dear Octopus*. *Acacia Avenue* also asked difficult questions about class and about sex outside marriage. The young people left home alone all face the difficult question of sex. Michael wants to spend the night with Joan to whom he is engaged and she agrees. Reg wants to take the rather fast and flashy blonde Estelle to a hotel for the weekend, and the maid, Shirley, is propositioned by Fred, who she rebuts but who makes her reflect thoughtfully on the question:

> 'Ere we are, all shoved into the world together' – Fred said. Very reasonable 'e spoke, reely ... 'life doesn't last long,' 'e said. 'At least not the kind that's any use! Youth's the only thing that can ever give life a kick,' Fred said – and 'im and me can't afford the things that sort of trims life up, so's you can see the bare bones underneath. With rich people they're 'idden, under luxuries, but with pore people they're always jest under the surface, ready to poke up – There's a lot in what 'e said, don't you think?[87]

As far as Fred is concerned, all people like him and Shirley have got are their bodies, which 'was given to us for something besides wearin' 'em out workin' for other people'. According to Fred, 'they can give us what very little else in the world can – esstacy! 'Ave you known esstacy, my girl?' ... And of course I 'ad to say I never

’ad – beyond being given a penny for an ice-cream cornet when I was a kid.’[88] While none of them do actually have sex, the question dominates the second half of the play, alongside questions of class, as Joan, unlike Queenie in *This Happy Breed* who is horrified of being thought common, mounts a lively defence of drinking wine out of a Bakelite mug when her fiancée objects. Storming off to get a proper glass, she demands to know if it matters if the glass comes from Woolworths or Marks and Spencer’s, while all Michael can do is throw his hands up in horror when she returns with a port glass. It is an argument about pretensions and class that rumbles on through the question of wedding present cutlery (the new plate canteen bought by Joan’s Aunt Edith or the real silver passed down through Michael’s family) and wine choices (the white wine with the pretty label that Michael thinks tastes like pear juice or the best burgundy that Joan thinks tastes like post office ink). Everything nearly falls apart but is eventually resolved through compromise.

Questions of class and attitudes to sex before marriage also run through Reginald Beckwith’s *A Soldier for Christmas* (August 1944) when a Canadian private is invited to the Fergusons for the holidays and Mrs Ferguson’s attachment to notions of a classless society and having tea once a week with the maid in the kitchen are challenged by realities. While she is delighted that ‘bombs break down any class distinctions’, seeing the Blitz as a great leveller, she is less pleased when she thinks her daughter may have spent the night with the soldier. Into the mix, Beckwith also adds two servants who behave in ways that challenge perceptions of their roles. The cook, Mrs Jones, has been found from the pages of the *New Statesman*, Mrs Ferguson thinking that when ‘it said “Cook, Progressive,” it meant she was used to electric ovens and vacuum cleaners’.[89] Instead, it turns out that Mrs Jones is a member of the Oxford Group with a minor talent for disappearing upstairs to write lengthy essays.[90] The Fergusons also have a charlady, the formidable, ancient and belligerent Mrs Jarvis, who demands to be addressed as comrade and whose tricycle basket is full of copies of the *Daily Worker* and political pamphlets.

Not all plays were focused on the home front in England, and a more international perspective was found in a handful of American plays. Both John Steinbeck’s *The Moon is Down* (September 1943) and Robert E. Sherwood’s *There Shall Be No Night* (November 1943) engaged with countries under occupation and the resilience and resistance of the inhabitants. The latter was originally set in Finland at the onset of the Soviet invasion of 1939, but later moved to Greece which had been invaded by the Germans in 1941. Sherwood’s hero is a Nobel Prize winner concerned with humanity’s loss of resistance. By the end of the play both he and his son are dead, his daughter-in-law and her son have been sent to safety in America, and his wife and aged uncle are left prepared to defend their house and their country to the bitter end. Both of these plays were ostensibly aimed at encouraging America to enter the war, as was Lillian Hellman's *Watch on the Rhine* (January 1943), but they all found resonances with an English audience, albeit being shown after America had become involved in the war. In Hellman's play, the daughter arrives at the family home with her German husband, Kurt, an anti-Nazi who is collecting funds to help the war against Hitler in Europe. The reality of their life over the past few years lived in hiding and on the run is contrasted to the comfort and distance of America. For them, the time for polite political conversations is over. 'By this time', Sara tells her mother, 'all of us must know where we are and what we have to do. It's an indulgence to sit in a room and discuss your beliefs as if they were a juicy piece of gossip.'[91] There is also another house guest, Teck de Brancovis, an impoverished Romanian count, in league with the German Ambassador, who on discovering that Kurt has $23,000 and a gun threatens to tell the Germans unless he gives him the money. As Teck threatens Kurt, the innocence of the Americans is still evident, the son, David, telling Kurt that he is safe in America where 'they can't do anything to you ... You're a political refugee. We don't turn back people like you. People who are in danger.'[92] Kurt, unconvinced, kills Teck and determines to go back to Germany to help the fight. For him, there can be no excuse not to be involved. 'Each could find a reason. And many find it', he tells Fanny, the matriarch of the house. But for him, 'my children are not the only children in the world'.[93] Gradually, the Americans start to understand the world differently and are moved to help Kurt escape, to give him money and to see that they too have to find a way to be part of the fight. They have been, as Fanny tells her son David, 'shaken out of the magnolias' and discover that they are not 'put together with flour and paste'.[94] For audiences at the Court, all of these would have chimed with the reality of the world they found themselves in during the war.

The Future

In December 1942, amid all the 'shortages and making do and daily grind', the first vision of a better future was made with the publication of what Tommy Handley in his *ITMA* role of 'His Fatuity the Minister of Social Hilarity' called 'Gone With the Want'.[95] The Beveridge Report was an instant bestseller and newspapers gave it saturation coverage. It promised an attack on the five 'giants ... on the road to a just society, those of Want, Disease, Ignorance, Squalor and Idleness'.[96] Beveridge insisted that 'the purpose of victory is to live in a better world than the old world', adding that people were also more likely to focus on the war effort if they felt that the government was already planning for a better world.[97] In the wake of Beveridge, Churchill too turned his eyes to the future, establishing a Ministry of

Reconstruction in 1943. With the government looking forward, the theatre too started to ask what a world after the war might look like. J. B. Priestley's *They Came to a City* (April 1943) offered a picture of a brave new world. It gathered together a disparate group of people, ranging through all walks of life, who find themselves outside the walls of a city, all arriving there through mysterious accidents. In this 'utopian excursion', the audience never get to see inside the city walls, having to rely on the reports from the characters who, in the end, fall into two groups – those who find it hateful and those who find it beautiful.[98] There are those who want to leave, including the capitalist Cudworth, Lady Loxfield, the wife of a now deceased pillar of the Empire, and the conventionally minded Mrs Stritten. They don't like the dancing, the lack of interest in wealth and the equality between people. As Mrs Stritten tells her husband, an idealistic bank manager, 'I don't like any of it. It's silly. It's – common … they've no decent manners. They don't know how to behave properly.'[99] Those who, having seen the city, want to stay include an overworked charlady from Wandsworth, the repressed but rebellious daughter of Lady Loxfield who feels stifled by her mother's way of life, Joe, an itinerant mechanic, who at the outset has lost his revolutionary zeal, and Alice, a waitress and barmaid, who has had enough of people thinking 'they were buying you along with their pot of tea and toast'.[100] In the city, she

> was having the best day of my life. I was among people who were happy and I was happy. I was in a wonderful place at last … I've always hoped, in a silly sort of way for something wonderful just around the corner. But I never thought there was a place as good as this. I didn't think people had it in them to build a city like this. I never really thought that people could work and play together like these people can. I'll do anything for these people, I'd die for this place.[101]

It was a place she had always believed might be around the corner, always knowing that 'life hadn't to be a dog fight round a dustbin. We'd made it like that, but it didn't need to be like that. Here they start every morning feeling as we only feel for about half an hour every two years, half lit at somebody's birthday party.'[102] The city also rekindles Joe's revolutionary passion and he determines to go back to tell the people it is possible to build a world where machines and money work for men and women, not the other way around,

> where greed and envy and hate have no place – where want and disease and fear have vanished – where nobody carries a whip and nobody rattles a chain. Where men have at last stopped mumbling and gnawing and scratching in dark caves and have come out into the sunlight.[103]

The play was welcomed by the local press. The *Liverpool Echo* saw it as 'throwing out a challenge to thoughtful people', making the point that 'justice and plenty are ours if we can stamp out sloth and selfishness'.[104] The *Liverpool Evening Express* judged it was 'a play much needed today'.[105]

On a less utopian level, Daphne du Maurier's *The Years Between* (December 1944, August 1946) offered a domestic drama focusing on the hopes that women harboured for a different world after the war. Diana's husband, Michael, is missing, presumed dead, following a plane crash, and after a year, Diana determines to take over his role as an MP and is duly elected. He had been at the heart of everything she did since they got married, but now she is starting to realise that her life 'doesn't belong to him anymore, it's mine, I can do what I like with it. And oh ... that sudden sense of freedom – almost as if the years had rolled away and I was young again.'[106] But her sense of freedom is curtailed by the reappearance of Michael, who has been on a secret mission in Europe. His 'death' was simply a cover to keep him safe. The two are pitted against each in other in terms of what they think is being fought for, a battle the *Liverpool Echo* summed up:

> A home-brewed brave new world may seem too new to tired warriors, who, no longer feeling so brave, crave only the old, and tried, the memories of which kept them going in the darkest hours. On the other hand, not all wives just sit and weep, or even stand and work to fill in the time. Some find outlets for newly-realised ambitions, and the warriors home-coming brings not peace, but a clash of outlooks, a test of love, a threat of lasting sorrow.[107]

Du Maurier offered no happy ending. Diana lets her chance of happiness in marrying Richard, a nearby farmer, go in order to stay with Michael. They are both going to fight for the future, Diana in the House of Commons and Michael by returning to Europe. The point is to make a world for their son, Robin, and to do that 'there must be no sitting back for a while. Not for our generation.'[108] So they set out to work for peace separately. Maggie Gale suggests that the final image of Diana with her child and the nanny, physically and emotionally separated from her husband and therefore 'effectively a single working mother', shows that they 'will play an important role in the re-building of Britain'. At the same time, the 'overall imperative' was 'to sacrifice one's own wishes to the greater good of the nation. Individual choice is inevitably ruled by national need.'[109]

The appearance of the war and of future hopes on the stage of the Royal Court should not be surprising. This was the first time, as Winston Churchill said, that '[t]he whole of the warring nations [were] engaged, not only soldiers, but the entire population, men, women and children'.[110] There was nowhere to escape, as Lionel

Birch, a soldier dreaming of how he was going to spend his 48-hour leave, discovers 'the revolutionary truth: [in this war] there is no such thing as leave…':

> [t]oday war follows you around. On the platform of the London terminus it is waiting there to meet you; and as you round the bend of the village main street, you come face to face with it again … There is no relief from the imperatives of war, restrictions and shortages, no let-up from the fear of death or injury in enemy action.[111]

The specific experience of individuals, even within one city, might have been different, but the war was all-pervasive and theatre did not simply turn away from the lived reality of its audience, a point reflected on the pages of *The Stage*. While it had argued in 1940 that the bulk of theatre audiences wanted entertainment and not 'furiously to think in the theatre', as there was quite enough 'hard thinking to do from day to day outside the theatre', by 1944 things were very different.[112] By then people had shown 'a remarkable liking for really good plays about the war'. They had 'flocked to *There Shall Be No Night*, *Flare Path* … not forgetting the social side of the service-man's life, touched on in gay comedies like *A Soldier for Christmas*'. The war had shown that theatre, at a time when 'petty tyrannies seem to dominate life', was the home of individual freedom, an essential part of 'our imaginative life which is more important than cabbages and vegetable marrows'.[113] In programming theatres up and down the country, like the Royal Court, Howard and Wyndham seemed to agree.

Notes

1 *Daily Post*, 1 September 1939, 6.
2 *The Stage*, 7 September 1939, 5.
3 Quoted in Richard Fawkes, *Fighting for a Laugh* (London: Macdonald and Jane's, 1978), 12.
4 Richard Whittington-Egan, *Liverpool Roundabout* (Manchester: E. J. Morten, 1976), 363.
5 Mass Observation, *Women in Wartime* (1940), 166.
6 Ros Merkin, *Liverpool Playhouse: A Theatre and Its City* (Liverpool: Liverpool University Press, 2011), 56.
7 Bryan Perrett, *Liverpool: A City at War* (Burscough: Hugo Press, 1990), 136–7.
8 Courtneidge, *Cicely*, 133.
9 Ibid., 133.
10 Liverpool City Library, *Liverpool Women at War* (Liverpool: Picton Press, 1991), 134.
11 Juliet Gardiner, *Wartime: Britain 1939–1945* (London: Headline Review, 2005), 132.
12 *The Stage*, 4 January 1940, 6.
13 Mass Observation, *Liverpool and Manchester Morale* (December 1940), 7, 4.
14 Gardiner, *Wartime*, 141.
15 *The Stage*, 7 December 1939, 10.
16 *Spectator*, 31 January 1941, 11.
17 *Liverpool Echo*, 8 May 1945, 2.
18 *The Stage*, 1 October 1942, 1.
19 *The Stage*, 4 November 1943, 5.
20 W. A. Darlington, *The Actor and His Audience* (London: Phoenix House, 1949), 170–1.
21 Ivor Novello, *The Dancing Years* (London: Samuel French, 1939; repr. 1953), 64.
22 *The Times*, 24 March 1939, 12.
23 Rebecca D'Monté, *British Theatre and Performance 1900–1950* (London: Bloomsbury, 2015), 171–2.
24 *The Stage*, 24 December 1942, 1.
25 *Liverpool Echo*, 16 December 1942, 3.
26 *Liverpool Echo*, 4 March 1941, 3.
27 Courtneidge, *Cicely*, 133.
28 Andrew Davies, 'The War Years', in Michael Balfour (ed.), *Theatre and War 1933–1945* (Oxford: Berghahn Books, 2001), 64.
29 *Liverpool Echo*, 9 October 1940, 5.
30 *The Stage*, 24 September 1942, 4; D'Monté, *British Theatre and Performance*, 173.
31 It was later renamed *Meet a Body* and filmed in 1956 as *The Green Man*.
32 *Liverpool Echo*, 23 July 1940, 2.
33 Helen Forrester, *By the Waters of Liverpool and Lime Street at Two* (London: Harper, 2010), 107.
34 Gardiner, *Wartime*, 595.
35 C. H. B. Kitchin, quoted in Alison Light, *Forever England: Femininity, Literature and Conservatism between the Wars* (London: Routledge, 1991), 71.
36 Light, *Forever England*, 71.
37 Ibid., 71.
38 Ibid., 96.
39 D'Monté, *British Theatre and Performance*, 173.
40 Julius Green, *Curtain Up: Agatha Christie – A Life in Theatre* (London: Harper Collins, 2015), 180.
41 Ibid., 181.
42 *The Stage*, 20 August 1942, 4.
43 Emlyn Williams, *Emlyn: An Early Autobiography 1927–1935* (London: Bodley Head, 1973), 384.
44 Emlyn Williams, *The Collected Plays of Emlyn Williams, Volume 1* (London: Heinemann, 1961), xvi, 5.
45 Ibid., 51.
46 Ibid., 48.
47 Ibid., 51.
48 *Variety*, 9 May 1945, 6.
49 *The Stage*, 3 May 1945, 1.
50 Edgar Ralph, 'Are War Plays Wanted?', *The Stage*, 6 June 1946, 1.
51 Forrester, *By the Waters of Liverpool*, 204.
52 Ibid., 242.
53 Ibid., 341.
54 Ibid., 394.
55 Ibid., 405.

56 *Liverpool Echo*, 23 June 1943, 2.
57 *John O'London's Weekly News*, 2 November 1945.
58 Esther McCracken, *No Medals* (London: Samuel French, 1947), 36.
59 Ibid., 44.
60 *Liverpool Echo*, 26 September 1994, 2.
61 *Liverpool Echo*, 27 September 1944, 3.
62 McCracken, *No Medals*, 63.
63 Ibid, 49.
64 Terence Rattigan, *Flare Path* (1944) (London: Nick Hern, 2011), xxxv.
65 Ibid., xxxiv.
66 Emlyn Williams, *The Morning Star* (London: Heinemann, 1942), 63.
67 Ibid., 74.
68 Ibid., 74.
69 Ibid., 52.
70 Ibid., 96–7.
71 Ibid., 98.
72 Ibid., 98–9.
73 Ibid., 101.
74 *Liverpool Echo*, 2 December 1941, 4.
75 D'Monté, *British Theatre and Performance*, 185.
76 Dodie Smith, *Dear Octopus*, in *Plays of the Thirties Volume 1* (London: Pan, 1966), 379.
77 Ibid., 378.
78 Philip Hoare, *Noel Coward: A Biography* (London: Mandarin, 1995), 300.
79 *The Scotsman*, 1 December 1942, 3.
80 *Liverpool Echo*, 3 November 1942, 3.
81 Noel Coward, *This Happy Breed* (1943), in *Coward. Plays: Four* (London: Methuen Drama, 1979), 280.
82 Ibid., 372.
83 *Liverpool Echo*, 7 September 1943, 2.
84 Mabel and Denis Constanduros, *Acacia Avenue* (London: Samuel French, 1944), 21.
85 Ibid., 80–1.
86 Ibid., 81.
87 Ibid., 53.
88 Ibid., 53.
89 Reginald Beckwith, *A Soldier for Christmas* (London: Samuel French, 1946), 7.
90 The Oxford Group was a radical group popular in the 1930s which sought to bring the nation under God's control while not believing in the Church.
91 Lillian Hellman, *Watch on the Rhine* (1941), in *Six Plays by Lillian Hellman* (New York: Vintage Books, 1979), 260.
92 Ibid., 279.
93 Ibid., 284.
94 Ibid., 301.
95 Gardiner, *Wartime*, 581.
96 Ibid., 582.
97 Ibid., 583.
98 *The Times*, 22 April 1943, 6.
99 J. B. Priestley, *Three Plays* (London: William Heinemann, 1943), 202.
100 Ibid., 158.
101 Ibid., 192–3.
102 Ibid., 210.
103 Ibid., 215.
104 *Liverpool Echo*, 9 April 1943, 2.
105 *Liverpool Evening Express*, 13 April 1943, 3.
106 Daphne du Maurier, *The Years Between* (1945), in Fidelis Morgan (ed.), *The Years Between: Plays by Women on the London Stage 1900–1950* (London: Virago, 1994), 346.
107 *Liverpool Echo*, 5 December 1944, 4.
108 Du Maurier, *The Years Between*, 395.
109 Maggie B. Gale, *West End Women: Women and the London Stage 1918–1962* (London: Routledge, 1996), 165.
110 Angus Calder, *The People's War: Britain 1939–1945* (1969) (London: Pimlico, 1992), 17.
111 Quoted in Gardiner, *Wartime*, 2.
112 *The Stage*, 4 January 1940, 6.
113 *The Stage*, 17 August 1944, 4.

1943

18 January	*Watch on the Rhine*	Lillian Hellman	with Zena Dare
26 January	*Peter Pan*	J. M. Barrie	Daniel Mayer Company, with Alistair Sim and Ann Todd
2 February	*Roll Away Clouds: A Cavalcade of Musical Comedies*		Songs and scenes from hit musical comedies
9 February	*The Merry Widow*	Viktor Léon and Leo Stein; music by Franz Lehár.	operetta
15 February	Sadlers Wells Opera		including *Madame Butterfly, Marriage of Figaro* and *La Boheme*
1 March	*The Morning Star*	Emlyn Williams	drama
8 March	*Night Must Fall*	Emlyn Williams	thriller
15 March	*Love for Love*	Congreve	with John Gielgud
22 March	Ballet Jooss		
29 March	*The Devil's Own*	Walter Ellis	play
5 April	*Moon Madness*	Philip King	farce; later renamed *See How They Run.*
12 April	*They Came to a City*	J. B. Priestley	with Googie Withers
19 April	*The Desert Song*	Oscar Hammerstein; music by Sigmund Romberg	operetta
26 April	Sadlers Wells Opera		two weeks
10 May	*The Racketeers*	Monckton Hoffe	A new play with Will Fyffe
17 May	*It's Time to Dance*	Douglas Furber and L. Arthur Rose; music by Kenneth Leslie-Smith	with Jack Buchanan
31 May	*Kiss the Girls*	Harriet Jay, Emile Littler and Tomas Browne; music by Harry Parr-Davies	musical adventure based on the play *When Knights Were Bold*

7 June	*To-Night's the Night*	Fred Thompson; music by Paul Rubens	Gaiety Theatre musical originally performed in 1915
14 June	*The Petrified Forest*	Robert E. Sherwood	with Owen Nares and Constance Cummings
21 June	*Flying Colours*	Ronald Jeans and Eric Maschwitz	with Binnie Hale and Douglas Byng
28 June	*The Count of Luxembourg*	Franz Lehar	operetta
5 July	*Tons of Money*	Will Evans and Arthur Valentine	Shaftesbury Theatre farce with Ralph Lynn
12 July	*The Wind and the Rain*	Merton Hodge	comedy set in students' study in Scottish university city
19 July	*She Follows Me About*	Ben Travers	farce with Robertson Hare

26 July	*This Time It's Love*	Louis Verneuil	light comedy adapted from the French
2 August	The International Circus		featuring the Six Superbs (rhythmic dancers) and Cooke's Famous Ponies
9 August	*Floradora*	Own Hall; music by Leslie Stuart	musical comedy originally performed in 1890s
16 August	Gilbert and Sullivan	D'Oyly Carte	two weeks
30 August	*Three Men on a Horse*	John Cecil Holm and George Abbott	American farce
6 September	*Acacia Avenue*	Mabel and Denis Constandurous	comedy
13 September	*The Admirable Crichton*	J. M. Barrie	with Diana Churchill
20 September	*The Moon is Down*	John Steinbeck	direct from Whitehall Theatre; with Lewis Casson
27 September	*The Love Racket*	Stanley Lupino; music by Noel Gay	musical comedy with Arthur Askey
4 October	*The Chocolate Soldier*	Rudolf Bernauer and Leopold Jacobson; music by Oscar Strauss	operetta, originally performed in 1909
11 October	*Wuthering Heights*	Emily Bronte, adapted by John Davison	
18 October	*The Merchant of Venice*	Shakespeare	with Donald Wolfit
25 October	*The Man Who Came to Dinner*	George S. Kauffman and Moss Hart	comedy
1 November	*There Shall Be No Night*	Robert E. Sherwood	with Alfred Lunt
8 November	*Ten Little Niggers*	Agatha Christie	
15 November	*A Month in the Country*	Turgenev; adapted by Emlyn Williams	with Michael Redgrave
22 November	*The Druid's Rest*	Emlyn Williams	with Richard Burton

29 November	*Where the Rainbow Ends*	Clifford Mills and John Ramsay	Talia Conti's production
6 December	*French Dressing*	Barbara Cartland and Bruce Woodhouse	comedy
25 December	*Babes in the Wood*	Charles Ross	

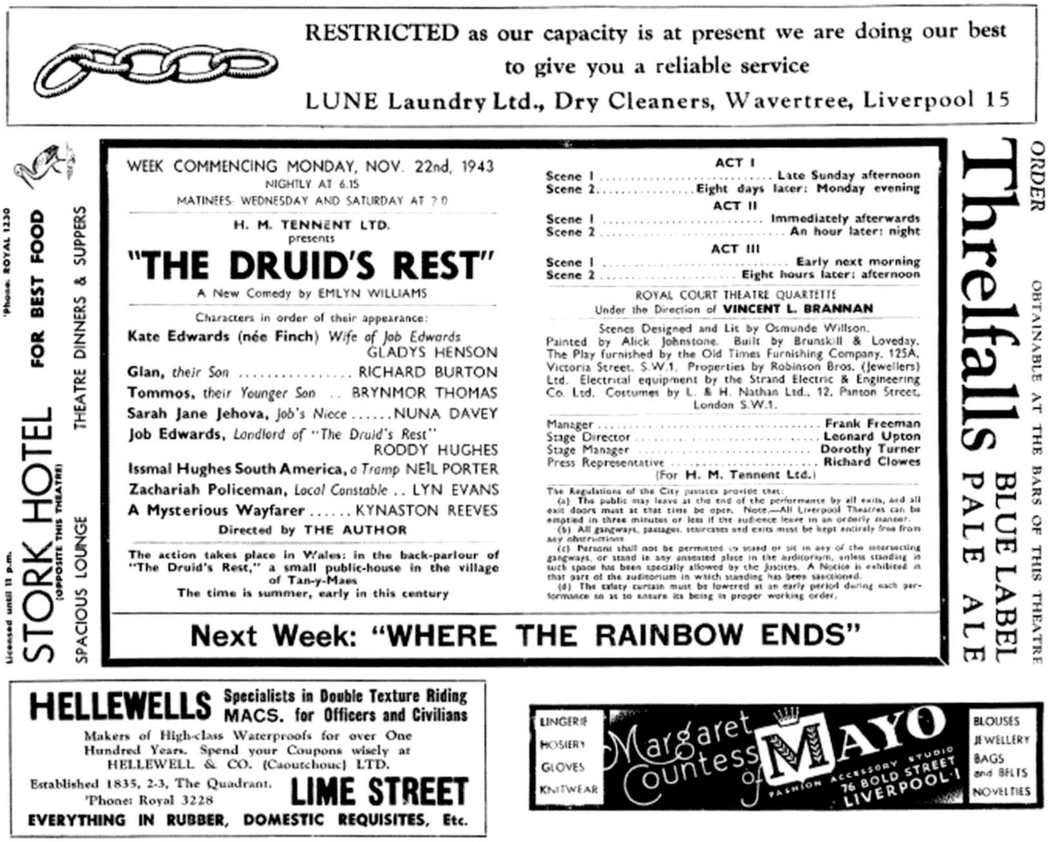

RESTRICTED as our capacity is at present we are doing our best to give you a reliable service

LUNE Laundry Ltd., Dry Cleaners, Wavertree, Liverpool 15

Licensed until 11 p.m. 'Phone: ROYAL 1230

STORK HOTEL (OPPOSITE THIS THEATRE) FOR BEST FOOD

SPACIOUS LOUNGE THEATRE DINNERS & SUPPERS

WEEK COMMENCING MONDAY, NOV. 22nd, 1943

NIGHTLY AT 6.15

MATINEES: WEDNESDAY AND SATURDAY AT 2.0

H. M. TENNENT LTD.

presents

"THE DRUID'S REST"

A New Comedy by EMLYN WILLIAMS

Characters in order of their appearance:

Kate Edwards (née Finch) *Wife of Job Edwards* GLADYS HENSON

Glan, *their Son* .... RICHARD BURTON

Tommos, *their Younger Son* .. BRYNMOR THOMAS

Sarah Jane Jehova, *Job's Niece* ...... NUNA DAVEY

Job Edwards, *Landlord of "The Druid's Rest"* RODDY HUGHES

Issmal Hughes South America, *a Tramp* NEIL PORTER

Zachariah Policeman, *Local Constable* .. LYN EVANS

A Mysterious Wayfarer ...... KYNASTON REEVES

Directed by **THE AUTHOR**

The action takes place in Wales: in the back-parlour of "The Druid's Rest," a small public-house in the village of Tan-y-Maes

The time is summer, early in this century

ACT I

Scene 1 .... **Late Sunday afternoon**

Scene 2................ **Eight days later: Monday evening**

ACT II

Scene 1 .... **Immediately afterwards**

Scene 2 .... **An hour later: night**

ACT III

Scene 1 .... **Early next morning**

Scene 2 .... **Eight hours later: afternoon**

ROYAL COURT THEATRE QUARTETTE

Under the Direction of **VINCENT L. BRANNAN**

Scenes Designed and Lit by Osmunde Willson. Painted by Alick Johnstone. Built by Brunskill & Loveday. The Play furnished by the Old Times Furnishing Company, 125A, Victoria Street, S.W.1. Properties by Robinson Bros. (Jewellers) Ltd. Electrical equipment by the Strand Electric & Engineering Co. Ltd. Costumes by L. & H. Nathan Ltd., 12, Panton Street, London S.W.1.

Manager .... **Frank Freeman**

Stage Director .... **Leonard Upton**

Stage Manager .... **Dorothy Turner**

Press Representative .... **Richard Clowes**

(For **H. M. Tennent Ltd.**)

The Regulations of the City Justices provide that:

(a) The public may leave at the end of the performance by all exits, and all exit doors must at that time be open. Note.—All Liverpool Theatres can be emptied in three minutes or less if the audience leave in an orderly manner.

(b) All gangways, passages, staircases and exits must be kept entirely free from any obstructions.

(c) Persons shall not be permitted to stand or sit in any of the intersecting gangways, or stand in any unseated place in the auditorium, unless standing in such space has been specially allowed by the Justices. A Notice is exhibited in that part of the auditorium in which standing has been sanctioned.

(d) The safety curtain must be lowered at an early period during each performance so as to ensure its being in proper working order.

Next Week: "WHERE THE RAINBOW ENDS"

ORDER Threlfalls BLUE LABEL PALE ALE OBTAINABLE AT THE BARS OF THIS THEATRE

HELLEWELLS Specialists in Double Texture Riding MACS. for Officers and Civilians

Makers of High-class Waterproofs for over One Hundred Years. Spend your Coupons wisely at HELLEWELL & CO. (Caoutchouc) LTD.

Established 1835, 2-3, The Quadrant. 'Phone: Royal 3228 **LIME STREET**

EVERYTHING IN RUBBER, DOMESTIC REQUISITES, Etc.

LINGERIE HOSIERY GLOVES KNITWEAR

Margaret Countess of MAYO

FASHION ACCESSORY STUDIO 76 BOLD STREET LIVERPOOL 1

BLOUSES JEWELLERY BAGS and BELTS NOVELTIES

The Druid's Rest, which opened at the Royal Court on 22 November 1943, marked the first professional stage appearance of Richard Burton.

Christmas, 1940s

1940 ***New Faces*** with book and lyrics by Eric Maschwitz and music by Jack Strachey
Bombed out of the Comedy Theatre in London, this revue found a home in Liverpool, making it one of only two Christmas shows staged in the city that year.

> When the company of the revue *New Faces* ... arrived over the weekend, they felt they were bringing the show to its real home. It was while he was in Liverpool on Government work that Eric Maschwitz hit on the idea and wrote much of the material, having as co-author of one sketch Jenny Nicholson, then at the Playhouse. The sponsor, Mr Jack Davies ... is a Liverpool man. And the players have many Liverpool links. Judy Campbell ... was enlisted by Mr Maschwitz after he had seen her in last year's Playhouse revue. Betty Ann Davies, another of the principals, is the daughter of Mr Jack Davies.
>
> Then José Noman, who wrote the ballet music and also appears, was known as a brilliant young pianist under the name of Norman Henderson, in Liverpool, some ten years ago. (*Liverpool Echo*, 24 December 1940, 2)

1941 D'Oyly Carte: Gilbert and Sullivan

1942 ***The Maid of the Mountains*** by Frederick Lonsdale

> Born during a war-time Christmas 26 years ago, the *Maid of the Mountains* is now appropriately reincarnated at another war time festival. Time has not staled its appeal, as was obvious from the reception which the crowded audience gave it on Christmas Eve. Emile Littler's company is a talented one and brings out to the full all the appeal of Fraser-Simpson's music and the romanticism of the story. (*Liverpool Echo*, 28 December 1942, 3)

1943 ***Babes in the Wood***

> There are several catchy numbers, notably 'What's at the Top of a Sunbeam?' and 'In My Wee Gas Mask.' (*The Stage*, 30 December 1943, 2)

> Austerity must be reckoned with when considering the new pantomime shows. To the grown-ups the chill hand of quotas, control and the National Service Act becomes evident at the rise of the curtain when it is found the stage is peopled mainly by juveniles. One may miss the glamour imparted on these occasions by the high-stepping ladies of the chorus; there may be sighs

Royal Court, July 1947 (Liverpool Record Office)

at the absence of the traditional transformation ... It is every bit as good as the times allow. (*Daily Post*, 28 December 1943, 4)

1944 *Cinderella*

The romantic story of the glass slipper lends itself to imaginative treatment and war-time limitations demand added ingenuity. The best tribute to John Roker's production was the hysterical delight of the children and the hearty appreciation of their elders. (*Liverpool Echo*, 27 December 1944, 2)

1945 *Goldilocks and the Three Bears* by John Roker

John Roker has made a grand job of writing and producing the Court pantomime ... he has gone back to the old story; Howard and Wyndham have gathered a remarkable company and provided dresses and sets which take the breath by their beauty and grandeur. Dave Morris, full of local lore and topical targets – especially the Civil Service – convulses the grown-ups. (*Liverpool Echo*, 24 December 1945, 2)

The Tarzan-like character of Orson must appeal strongly to the youngsters and the not-too-unexpected revelation that this ugly duckling is really the long-lost brother of the gallant prince is a climax in the true tradition of fairy stories. (*Daily Post*, 24 December 1945, 3)

1946 *Goody Two Shoes* by Julius E. Day

Cast
Goody Two Shoe, Dame's Adopted Daughter: Carol Decy
Prince Peerless: Nancy Brown
Lady Love-Bird, a lady in waiting: Betty Dayne
Lord Lustre, the Prince's Steward: Wyn Gifford
Dame Hubbard: Mickie Renton
Billy Hubbard, her son: Syd Stuart
Sir Brownlow Hill, Squire of Jitterbug: Dave Morris
Fazakerley, Squire's Valet: Billy Smith
Andy and Sandy, Two Dog fanciers: Eddie Davies & Ronnie Ross
Mischief: Fred Fredericks
Twinkletoes, a Good Fairy: Sheila de Haan
Dog Tray: Jack Chugg
Specialities: Four Nemecs, Betty Hobbs Troupe of Twelve

Dave Morris' … Sir Brownlow Hill has an intimate knowledge of Liverpool which he uses with freedom in many gags with local flavour. (*The Stage*, 2 January 1947, 6)

1947 *Jack and the Beanstalk*

It will be a pity if any trimming must be done to Howard and Wyndham's production … for it was three and a half hours of sheer delight. Clean and wholesome, it is as rich in talent as it is in material … The comedy, of which there is a prodigality, has topical ripeness but is never over-ripe, with the expressive-eyed, whimsical, and clownish Dave Willis leading a capital team. (*The Stage*, 1 January 1948, 9)

Edna Squire Brown and her doves provided the novelty act in the 1944 *Cinderella*.

The 1939 pantomime included Kitty Reidy as Robin Goodfellow, Monsewer Eddie Gray, formerly of the Crazy Gang, as Monsewer de Grabbo and Jack Stanford as Muddles.

1948 *Mother Goose*

Freddie Carpenter has produced another successful pantomime which maintains with ease the high standard that has characterised post-war pantomimes here. For three and a half hours it runs a smooth and amusing course ... An outstanding feature is the fresh youthfulness of the majority of the company ... and in Beryl Reid the show has a perky and amusing soubrette with a distinct flair for mimicry. Among the numerous solos and duets are 'Bounce-y, Bounce-y. Ball-y', 'I'm Looking Over a Fourleaf Clover', 'Singing a Dicky-Bird Song' ... and the 'Pussy Cat Serenade' in which Miss Reid and Jack Edge cleverly combine. The Liverpool born comedian also leads the children's song of 'Fuzzy-Wuzzy.' (*The Stage*, 31 December 1948, 15)

1949 *Sleeping Beauty*

Few pantomime producers will be busier than Freddie Carpenter this Christmas. He is at present in Edinburgh directing *The Queen of Hearts* for Howard and Wyndham at the King's, opening on Friday week. The next day Mr Carpenter goes to Liverpool to direct *The Sleeping Beauty* for Howard and Wyndham opening on December 24 at the Royal Court. He will just have time to dash down to the Victoria Palace to supervise the dress rehearsal of *Snow White and the Seven Dwarfs* opening there on Christmas Eve. (*The Stage*, 8 December 1949)

Roe Street, November 1947
(Liverpool Record Office)

All members of staff will stand upright in their posts. Any lounging about or unnecessary talking on duty is strictly forbidden. Smoking or the eating of sweets or the chewing of gum will render the offender liable to instant dismissal.

8 A Golden-tinted Era of Lost Content: The 1950s and 1960s

Robert Arthur finally gave up his connection with the theatre in 1941, leaving Howard and Wyndham in charge. By the 1950s the company also owned the Grand Theatre in Leeds, the King's Theatre and the Royal Lyceum Theatre in Edinburgh, the Alhambra and the King's Theatre in Glasgow, and the Opera House and the Theatre Royal in Manchester.[1] Extending the reach of the company even further, these theatres were also booked in conjunction with

Aberdeen: His Majesty's Theatre
Belfast: Grand Opera House
Blackpool: Grand Theatre and Opera House
Bournemouth: Pavilion Theatre
Bristol: Hippodrome
Cardiff: New Theatre and Prince of Wales
Coventry: Coventry Theatre
Derby: Hippodrome
Dublin: Gaiety Theatre
Dudley: Hippodrome and Palace Theatre
Leicester: Opera House
Northampton: New Theatre
Sheffield: Lyceum Theatre

This meant that the company was booking over twenty No. 1 touring venues, putting the balance of negotiating power into its hands. The company would be assured of the best attractions at the times best suited to it and, moreover, the West End directors on Howard and Wyndham's board would be guaranteed the most favourable bookings for pre- and post-West End tours.[2] However, a simple listing of the venues controlled by the company does not really give a full picture of the growing monopoly in theatre management and the number of key companies increasingly meshed together to run theatres and stage productions. Once Howard and Wyndham made the move to London, it built on its connections, enmeshing the company with the others known as The Group, the key players in theatre management and production from 1942. These included Stoll Theatre Corporation, Prince Littler, Associated Theatre Properties and Moss Empires. A measure of how far the theatre managers were caught up in a net of associations can be seen from the number of boards that Stewart Cruikshank, by then the managing director of Howard and Wyndham, was on. For 1953, Sandison lists 26 directorships for Cruikshank, including H. M. Tennent, Associated and Tennent Plays Ltd, all the members of The Group (sometimes in more than one guise), the Apollo Theatre Co. Ltd, Theatre and Opera House (Leeds) Ltd and Coliseum Syndicate Ltd.[3] By the mid-1950s Howard and Wyndham had become, as Claire Cochrane notes, 'a monopolistic model of theatre management', and as one of only two companies operating in the provinces (the other being Moss Empires, which controlled over twenty theatres), it had enormous leverage over the choice of plays, operating in essence as theatre managers and (with the exception of the pantomime) not producers.[4] This was a very long way from Cooke and Copeland.

Having established 'a national infrastructure' with a head office in London, Howard and Wyndham ran its theatres as a single, standardised, uniform entity, producing a 200-page 'bible' covering every aspect of running the theatre, issued

This was a pre-London tour in which Ralph Richardson played a Ruritanian king. Writing to Laurence Olivier and Vivien Leigh, John Gielgud bemoaned the fact that '[p]oor old Ralph had a really horrid play – he is on stage from beginning to end but with neither conflict, characters nor situation to keep one interested or give him any chance to be amusing. Mu [Meriel Forbes] is quite good in a poor part. In fact it is quite well played by everyone. Even Lilian [Braithwaite], who staggered on occasionally like a terrifying scarecrow, managed to waft a few faint laughs out, but there simply isn't a play.' (*Sir John Gielgud: A Life in Letters*, (Arcade, 2004), 118–19)

Flora Robson as Alicia Christie in Lesley Storm's *Black Chiffon*, at the Royal Court in June 1950

'solely for the use of theatre managers'. In 1935 advice on front of house staff included:

> It is essential to engage girls smart, intelligent, and of a good appearance. Middle-aged women cannot be engaged. Ushers must wear black stockings.
>
> Only young men of good appearance to be engaged. Fingernails to be inspected before opening the house. They should be kept well-trimmed. Hands should be washed before proceeding on duty.
>
> All members of staff will stand upright in their posts. Any lounging about or unnecessary talking on duty is strictly forbidden. Smoking or the eating of sweets or the chewing of gum will render the offender liable to instant dismissal.
>
> Uniforms must be kept scrupulously clean. On no account should polish be used on buttons. They should be rubbed with a clean cloth.
>
> All attendants must be at their posts a quarter of an hour before the House opens. They must not leave until the whistle is blown.[5]

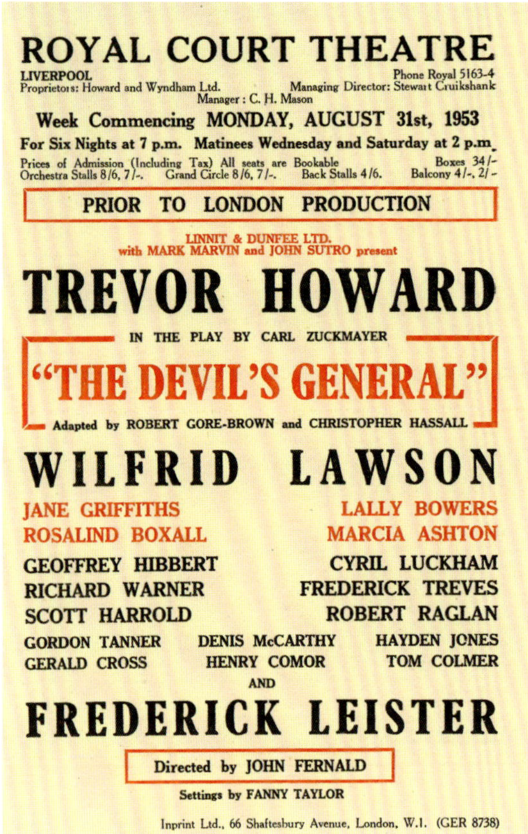

The emphasis was on 'discreet and polite contact with the public', as Cruikshank senior wrote in the preface, and Iles notes that this management style continued into the 1960s, as shown in a programme from the Manchester Opera House in 1968:

> Any INCIVILITY or INATTENTION on a part of an attaché of the establishment or OVERCHARGING FOR SERVICE OR REFRESHMENTS should be reported to the Manager. INFRACTIONS of ANY of the foregoing rules may be communicated to the Management, who will gladly summarily dismiss the same.[6]

As late as 1967 Howard and Wyndham was still writing to the manager of the Royal Court reminding him that managers and assistant managers were expected to 'strictly comply' with the wearing of dinner jackets for all evening performances. For matinees, lounge suits were permitted, but for any shows starting at 5 p.m., they were instructed to change into a dinner jacket for the first interval. The London management also demanded detailed records, with a plethora of forms covering everything from attendance and receipts to overtime payments and the minutiae of box office postage for correspondence to be sent to Head Office for Cruikshank's personal approval. Any discrepancies led to letters of enquiry and demands that these be accounted for. In January 1962 the manager was being quizzed by Head Office about the amount of soft soap being ordered for cleaning and was issued with a warning that the company did not consider it to be good policy to order large quantities of any type of cleaning materials, as 'cleaners may be inclined to be extravagant in the use of such materials'.

This air of gentility, standardisation and central control suggests a programme on stage to match, and many of the plays and performances cheerfully obliged. The annual calendar throughout these decades made plenty of space for regular appearances of opera and ballet, many from companies that were favourites of the Royal Court audience. D'Oyly Carte was still performing the same Gilbert and Sullivan operas almost every year for two weeks. Carl Rosa was still appearing in the 1950s and was joined by performances of Italian opera companies boasting stars from La Scala and Rome, although as the theatre moved into the 1960s, with the exception of D'Oyly Carte, opera was all but replaced by ballet. Here, different seasons offered different companies, from Sadlers Wells to the Royal Ballet, but what remained the same was the repertoire, generally drawn from well-known classical ballets. Occasionally more international offerings appeared. 1957 brought the New

Ronald Shiner in Hugh Hasting's naval comedy *Seagulls Over Sorrento*

ROYAL COURT THEATRE LIVERPOOL
Proprietors: Howard & Wyndham Ltd.
Managing Director: Stewart Cruikshank
Manager: C. H. Mason
Phone: Royal 5163-4
Week commencing MONDAY, MAY 3rd, 1954
Evenings at 7-0
Matinees Wednesday and Saturday at 2-30
Prices of Admission (All Seats Bookable): Boxes 34/-, Grand Circle and Stalls 8/6 7/-, Balcony 4/- 2/-, Back Stalls 4/6
RIX THEATRICAL PRODUCTIONS
present
JOHN SLATER
in
"RELUCTANT HEROES"
A FARCE
by
COLIN MORRIS
with
BERNARD FOX
MICHAEL EARL
TIMOTHY HEALE
MARTIN BRADLEY
WILLIAM DOUGLAS
JOHN ARM
SHIRLEY BUSH
BETTY IMPEY
DEIRDRE DAY
JOHN CHAPMAN
Directed by
THE AUTHOR
(An adaptation from the original production by FRANK DERMODY)
"A MIRTHQUAKE" SUNDAY PICTORIAL
NOW IN ITS 4th YEAR AT LONDON'S WHITEHALL THEATRE

York Negro Ballet, the Urals Ensemble and Inbal, the national dance company of Israel. The 1965 Commonwealth Arts Festival provided the opportunity to stage the Nigerian Folk Opera, Australian Ballet and the National Dance Theatre of Jamaica. Increasingly, weeks were given over to local amateur companies (the Birkenhead Amateur Operatic Society, the Waterloo and Crosby Amateur Operatic Society and the Wallasey Operatic Society) which between them would fill four weeks a year with musicals. Space was also made on a regular basis for Shakespeare, often performed by the Old Vic Company and occasionally by the Shakespeare Memorial Theatre. These provided the opportunity for appearances by star performers, and you could see Michael Redgrave in *Love's Labour's Lost* (May 1950), Laurence Olivier and Vivien Leigh in *Antony and Cleopatra* (November 1951), Peggy Ashcroft, John Gielgud and Moira Lister in *Much Ado About Nothing* (November 1955), Judi Dench's first professional stage performance as Ophelia (September 1957) or Alistair Sim as Prospero (November 1962). Sitting just beyond the end of the 1960s, Peter Brook's production of *A Midsummer Night's Dream* (December 1972), with Patrick Stewart, appeared at the Court on a special engagement as part of its world tour.

Stars didn't appear only in Shakespeare productions, and these were the decades during which it was possible to see a bevy of well-known actors in a variety of different shows. In 1952 alone (not an unusual season in this respect), the Royal Court welcomed Michael Redgrave, Googie Withers, Flora Robson, Katherine Hepburn, Richard Attenborough (in both *Sweet Madness* and *The Mousetrap*), Geraldine McEwan and Joyce Grenfell. Vivien Leigh appeared in seven shows between 1941 and 1965, including two alongside her then husband Laurence Olivier. Other stars (many appearing regularly) who added to the sense of glittering occasion included Alec Guinness, Celia Johnson, Ralph Richardson, Edith Evans, Jean Simmons, Margaret Rutherford, Margaret Lockwood, Anna Massey, Trevor Howard, Rex Harrison, Ian Carmichael and, on one occasion, Julie Andrews, at the start of her career in an ill-fated musical called *Mountain Fire* (May 1954). Moving into the 1960s, these famous names of stage and screen were replaced by those from television, from *Emergency Ward 10* stars in *Doctor in the House* (May 1962) to Kathleen Harrison, television's Mrs Thursday, in *All for Mary* (June 1968). The proliferation of stars led J. B. Priestley to scathingly condemn 'the half-witted mobs in provincial cities' who visited theatres 'only to see film stars in the flesh', going on to suggest that the success of a tour in the larger provincial theatres

> depends more and more on the touring company having at least one star who is known to the provincial film audiences. One film star, who may be an indifferent stage performer, will attract far bigger audiences in most

> provincial cities than a really first-class team of stage players. This is a shocking state of affairs, but of course the blame lies with the Press and public of the provinces ...[7]

Trite and Flimsy

By implication, Priestley's comments also suggest that many of the plays on offer were not very good. Indeed the overall perception of the commercial stage offerings of the 1950s and 1960s is rather damning. The output was seen, in almost all accounts, as trite, flimsy and artificial, dominated by The Group and in particular by Tennents, which John Elsom painted as 'the Fortnum and Mason of British theatre, a supplier of quality goods to the gentry and those of a similar disposition'.[8] Dan Rebellato offers a tongue-in-cheek picture of the period, suggesting that, by 1956, British theatre was in a terrible state:

> The West End was dominated by a few philistine theatre managers, cranking out emotionally repressed, middle-class plays, all set in drawing rooms with French windows, as vehicles for stars whose only talent was to wield a cigarette holder and a cocktail glass while wearing a dinner jacket. While war and suffering raged around it, the theatre continued to reflect a tiny segment of society, and ignore the rest. Reluctant Debutantes held Cocktail Parties in Pink Rooms and Confidential Clerks spent Saints Days in Living Rooms at Separate Tables, all of them talking Dry Rot.[9]

Most famously, the era was lambasted by Kenneth Tynan, then the *Observer* critic, suggesting there was nothing in the commercial theatre 'that one dares discuss with an intelligent man for more than five minutes'. He defined drama's prevalent genre as the Loamshire play with its country house setting where, with the exception of someone sneezing or being murdered, the sun always shines. The inhabitants 'belong to a social class derived partly from romantic novels' and 'the crash of denunciation' had dwindled into 'Oh, stuff, Mummy!' and 'Oh, really, Daddy!'[10]

On the surface, Royal Court plays seem to fit perfectly into this picture. Almost all of the plays named by Rebellato appeared, from Rattigan's *Separate Tables* (August 1954) and John Chapman's horse-racing farce *Dry Rot* (October 1956) to T. S. Eliot's *The Cocktail Party* (which had three appearances – two in 1951 and one in October 1968). William Douglas Home's *The Reluctant Debutante* (April and July 1957) focused on an aristocratic family during the debutantes' season, with a mother trying desperately to avoid a scandal after she confuses two men, both called David, accidentally setting her daughter up with a philanderer rather than the perfect match. Plenty of plays drew descriptions from reviewers that suggested that they were light and fluffy. *Affairs of State* by Louis Verneuil (April 1954) was 'a shoe-string tale with a multitude of sparkling lines' and Ted Willis's *Doctor in the House* 'offered nothing for the seriously minded patron of drama'.[11] Michael Clayton Hutton's *Silver Wedding* (May 1957), concerning a philandering ambassador whose wife announces that she is going to leave him and take a lover on their 25th wedding anniversary, had dialogue 'as realistic as numerous references to Harrods, Marshall and Snellgrove, Swan and Edgar, the Café de Paris and Fortnum and Mason can make it'.[12] *Man of Distinction* (September 1957) earned its author praise for 'a pretty tasselled roundabout' that was an 'entire trifle'.[13]

The plays of husband-and-wife playwright team Hugh and Margaret Williams have come to stand for much of this work, and five of their plays appeared at the Royal Court between 1957 and 1968. *The Times* suggested that they produced plays that marked 'a thin red line in defence of conventional' comedy; they stood guard

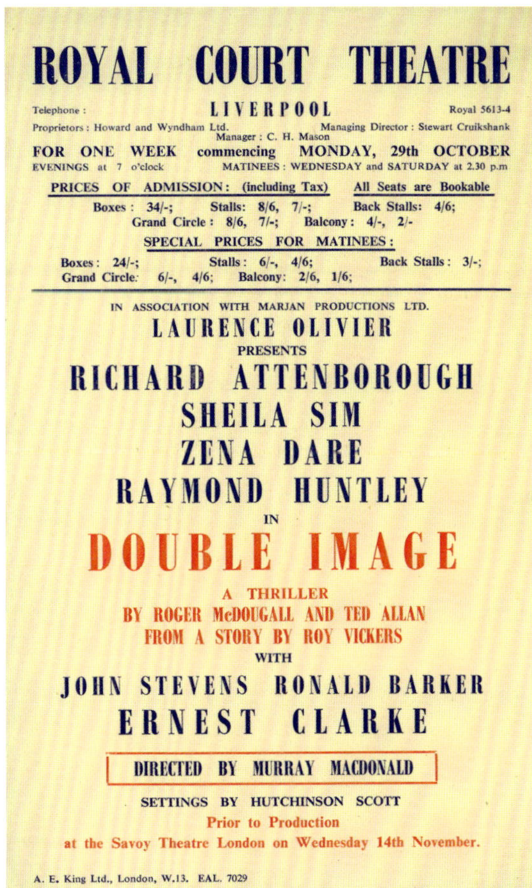

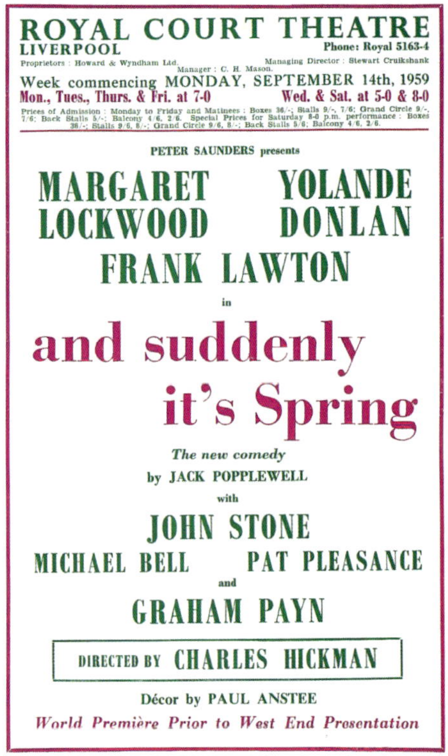

The Remarkable Mr Pennypacker provided Easter entertainment in 1955 with a comedy set in 1890, featuring a father who has seven children in Wilmington and seven in Philadelphia and who tries to make a case for polygamy, only to find himself being judged in the final scene by all of his children.

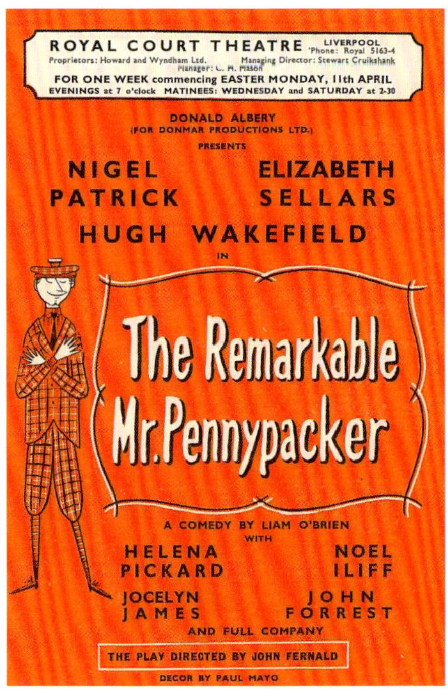

Ira Levin's comedy, performed for two weeks in April 1958, presented the Royal Court stagehands with one of their the most complicated sets. Much of the action took place on board a bomber in full flight, and the performance also included a parachute descent by the hero.

Five years after the defection of Burgess and Maclean to Russia, Lesley Storm's *The Long Echo* (July 1956) explored the problems of those left at home when a diplomat leaves for Eastern Europe.

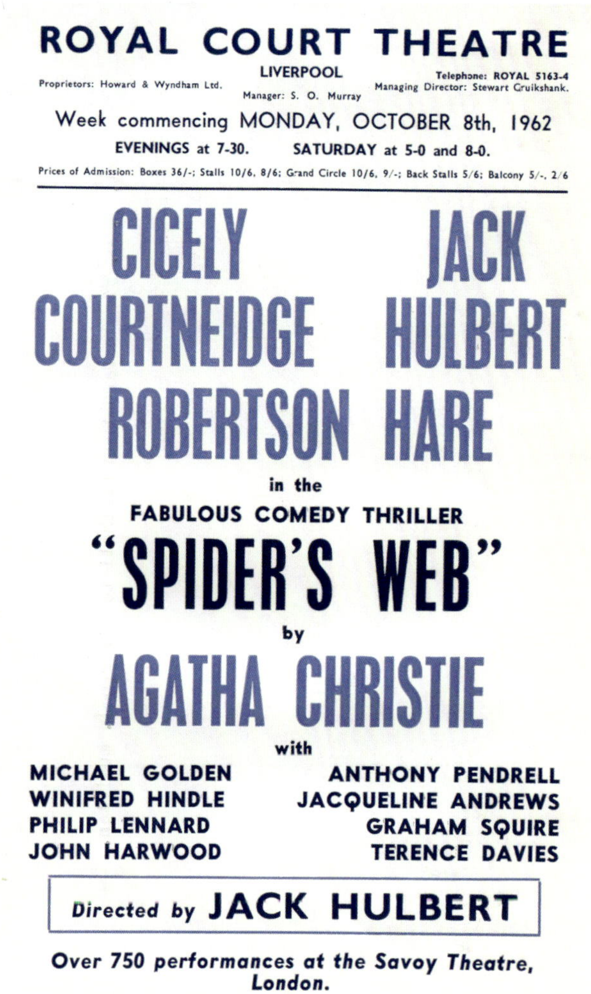

over this 'mild evening pastime as if, in some way, it embodied the moral fibre of the nation'. Their plays were variously pronounced as being 'scenes of a bloodlessly inert romance' and 'a go as you please ramble … where every fresh step leads to the recognition of the familiar'. The first of these, 'a charming trifle in the Lonsdale style of gilded comedy', was *Plantiff in a Pretty Hat* (August 1957), about a man who finds the right woman to marry after nearly marrying the wrong one and is taken to court by the 'wrong' woman for breach of promise. Luckily, she finds a peer to marry instead. It was 'as light as a hydrogen balloon' with a plot less important than the trimmings.[14] They are all set in 'a world of wealth, status and wit', offering a 'perfect amalgam of the old and the new'. Using a marketable formula, the 'plays always ended with the world put back to rights, the fleeting independence of the female characters abandoned in a sensible desire to comply with the will of the paternalistically conceived male leads'.[15]

Unquestionably, the Court favoured plays set firmly inside the home. Howard and Wyndham chose shows that were domestic, increasingly middle class in setting, increasingly focused on middle-aged characters. Drawing on classic plots, usually of extra-marital affairs (increasingly carried on by women), these often concentrated, as with *Silver Wedding*, on couples who had been married for a number of years. Hugh and Margaret Williams's *The Grass is Greener* (March 1960) found the wife of a solidly reliable but impoverished Earl, married for twelve years, tempted to leave him for the uncertain excitement of a lover. The Earl is equal to the challenge, invites the lover to stay in their stately home, but then

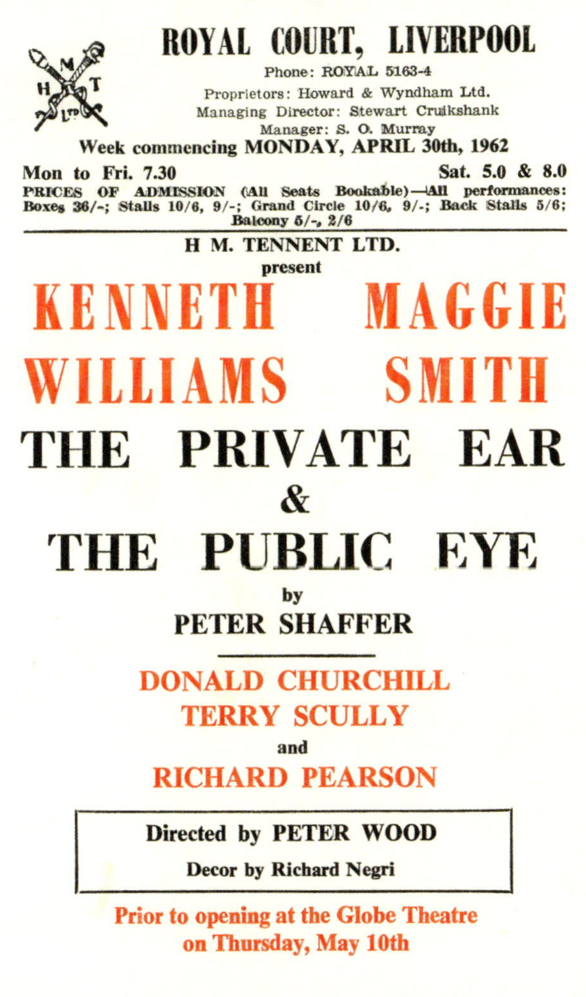

challenges him to a duel, resulting in a bullet in his arm and a wife who discovers that she does really love him. *Irregular Verb to Love* (March 1961), again by Hugh and Margaret Williams, had a mother returning from prison following her latest protest against the fur trade, and followed what *The Stage* by then was describing as 'the familiar formula of the twenty-year-married couple having their domestic ups and downs'.[16] So prevalent was the theme that by 1968 William Douglas Home's *The Secretary Bird* (September 1968) was described by Marriott as 'yet another tale of adultery and would-be or might-be adultery', once again instigated by the younger wife who is tempted by the exciting and glamorous lover only to come back to the older husband.[17] *Irregular Verb to Love* also included another favourite

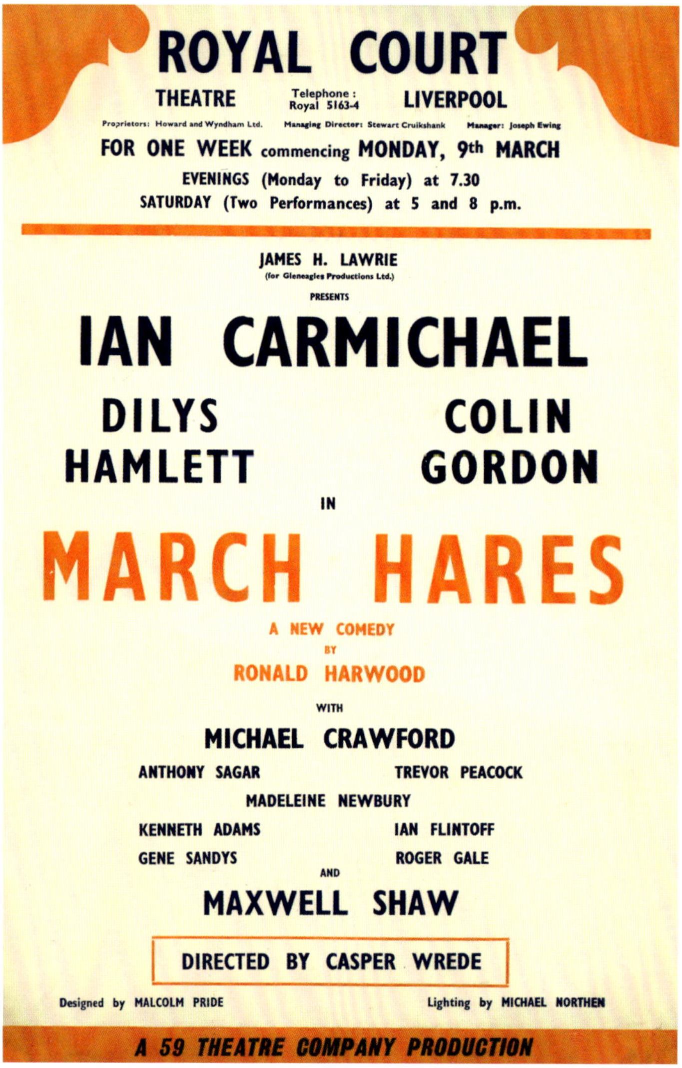

theme, inter-generational conflicts and misunderstandings. Here, Mrs Rankin discovers that in her absence, her son has returned from a walking holiday with a girlfriend who only speaks Greek and that her daughter is pregnant and unwilling to get married. But as with the issue of adultery, these differences were resolved with a light heart.

Occasional plays dealt more darkly with divorce and disillusionment. *The Tulip Tree* by N. C. Hunter was 'a play about middle-age, firmly addressed to a middle-aged audience'. Youth and old age appear, 'romantically lit on the margin of the drama', but they

> hold no position on the central battlefield where a married couple wage their fight against mortality. To distract themselves from the process of growing old the husband has taken refuge in work and the wife has buried herself in the country, idealizing her dead son.

Their marriage is partly saved when the husband suffers a heart attack and is forced to convalesce in the country, 'where both characters are at leisure to analyse their predicament. Callousness, narrowness and refusal to face unpleasant realities are well-known failings of middle life'.[18] Brought back together, Colin and Clare 'find themselves lonely, afraid and empty' as they sit, stroll and talk beneath the tulip tree in a garden that reflects their own decay.[19] But the darkness of *The Tulip Tree* was exceptional, and for all the misunderstandings, these were generally comedies with happy endings where disagreements were ironed out and new beginnings embarked on, with husband and wife happily back together.

Marlene Dietrich appeared at the Royal Court in July 1965 as part of a six-week national tour

Farce and the Decline of Straight Plays

However, there are things that the description of theatres dominated by Loamshire does not reflect. One of these was the continued popularity of farce, which offered a very different approach to the world, and through the 1950s and 1960s this became dominated by the Whitehall shows of Brian Rix. From his first major touring production, *Reluctant Heroes* (June 1950) through John Chapman's *Dry Rot* (October 1956) to Ray Cooney and Tony Hilton's *Chase Me Comrade* and *Bang Bang Beirut* (October 1966), the Royal Court's stage was home to surrealist absurdity in which ordinary people were caught up in an extraordinary chain of events. Here the impossible seemed possible, the deranged normal, and silliness was a substitute for sense. Mistaken identity was essential (including plenty of men dressed as women) and authority was often mocked, as farce allowed the audience 'a holiday from normal behaviour'.[20] Vicars were a staple of these farces and often to be found trouserless. In Philip King's *Pools Paradise* (April 1961), they found themselves caught up with the football pools. In King's *See How They Run* (November 1964, though first performed at the Court as *Moon Madness* in April 1943), the five vicars included two imposters, one a German internee, and the play also involved a love-starved, cycling spinster who was having a little trouble with her inner tube. Cooney and Hilton's *One for the Pot* (September 1964) had Brian Rix playing four identical quadruplets (an innocent country lad, a suave man-of-the world, a slippery Irish rogue and a slick Frenchman), all trying to claim a £10,000 inheritance. The problem is that the inheritance will only be given to a sole survivor, so all four brothers have to claim to be one, leading to confusions of identity summed up by Rupert, the posh brother, as he tries to explain the situation:

> I've been trying to explain all evening, darling, I'm not who I said I was ... When I first arrived I said I was who I was. When I met you I had to say I was who I wasn't. Then I had to be who I said I was when I wasn't when I really wanted to be who I was when I said I was. Now I want you to know that I'm not who I said I was when I wasn't but who I was when I said I was who I was. (*There is a pause*)[21]

Bang Bang Beirut, subsequently retitled *Stand By Your Bedouin*, was a jumble of spies and double agents set in a Middle Eastern hotel requisitioned by the army, which has just staged a coup, and involved a variety artist finding himself embroiled in a plot to spirit away the young king before the revolutionaries get him. *Chase Me Comrade*, the last of the Whitehall farces, was loosely based on Nureyev's 1961 defection to the West, and included a civil servant who,

Marti Webb with Fagin's gang from the cast of *Oliver* gathered together around the GPO advertising machine at the Royal Court theatre to record on tape an advert for the show, May 1966 (Mirrorpix)

endeavouring for reasons too numerous to mention to delude his future father-in-law, an irascible naval commander, by simulating a BBC news bulletin, conceals himself and a microphone beneath a tiger-skin rug by the radio. The stratagem succeeds up to a point. The frustrated officer, thunderous but preoccupied, has abandoned the gibbering apparatus and is striding back to his study when he encounters the skin crawling furtively toward another door. He stares. The skin halts. Tentatively it rubs its head against his flank. Persuasively, it lays a paw upon his sleeve. Hopefully, long after hope has fled, it rises to gaze into his crimson features, its glass eyes beseeching him to continue as if nothing has happened, to say it has not been found out, that he accepts unquestioningly and casually the presence in his drawing-room of an affectionate Indian man-eater wearing naval trousers... But as the animated pelt, a bellowing officer at its heels, scrambles off-stage in a whirlwind of slamming doors, the piece achieves that moment for which ... the cast, with fingers crossed, nightly hold back: the 'take-off', the hysterical consummation when actors and audiences, throwing off restraint and calculation, mutually surrender to the mingled idiocy and ingenuity which is the specific pleasure of farce.[22]

Such a moment represents for the audience a pleasure shared with each other and also with the performers, just as do the moments in *One for the Pot* when one actor frantically changes from brother to brother, with the audience unsure at times which is the actual performer and which a stand-in.

The *New Statesman* also makes a telling point about the perception of farce, asking why 'no-one wholeheartedly speaks up' for the Whitehall Company, one of the most successful British theatrical enterprises of its time. The writer is particularly curious about this, 'considering the current intellectual agitation for a theatre of the masses, a true working class drama' which drew on 'boisterous, extrovert playing, the integrated teamwork, the Cockney irreverence of an unselfconscious

Roe Street, 1963. E. M. Cooper (Liverpool Record Office)

unacademic audience bent purely on pleasure'. While the Royal Court audience of the time might have been less than flattered at being perceived as un-selfconscious, un-academic and Cockney, the popularity of these farces, with their appeal to irreverent laughter, suggests another side to the theatre at the time.

Another thing overlooked by the characterisation of theatres such the Court as the home of the Loamshire play is the decline of straight plays through the 1960s, which were increasingly replaced by comedies and farces or musicals and variety. By 1969, of the seventeen shows presented, seven were not plays. The London Festival Ballet opened the year in February and there were visits from the Welsh National Opera, Glyndebourne Touring Opera and D'Oyly Carte. Three weeks were given over to amateur productions of musicals and two professional musicals visited,

Lionel Blair's production of the 1920s musical *No, No Nanette* and (an oddity) Alan Plater's mining musical set in the north-east, *Close the Coalhouse Door.* Don Ellis offered what was becoming a regular feature, a week of 'Olde Tyme' Music Hall. Of the non-musical offerings, five shows were comedies or farces, including two (*She's Done It Again!* by Michael Pertwee and *Let Sleeping Wives Lie* by Harold Brooks and Kay Bannerman) from the Whitehall stable. The two straight plays included only one new work, a quartet on the familiar theme of marital and extra-marital relationships by John Mortimer, which was packed with stars including Glynis Johns, Denholm Elliot and Joss Ackland. The other, *Trio,* was a trilogy of short plays from the older pens of J. M. Barrie, Noel Coward and George Bernard Shaw.

The Problems of the World

Clearly the theatre did try very hard to close the door on the outside world and certainly to keep the new at bay. In theatre terms, this meant that almost nothing of the theatrical explosion happening at London's Royal Court appeared. There were no Angry Young Men in Liverpool's Royal Court. Osborne's *Look Back in Anger* was never performed there (its first Liverpool performance was at the Playhouse in 1958). Nor were the works of Brecht or Samuel Beckett. Occasional pinpricks were felt – Brendan Behan's *The Hostage* (August 1960), Shelagh Delaney's *A Taste of Honey* (February 1960) and John Osborne's *The Entertainer* (August 1958). Occasionally this world did appear, but as the butt of comedy. Frank Harvey's title character in *Norman* (April 1963) was up from Essex for the production of his first play at a theatre in Sloane Square, and the whole was a parody of kitchen sink drama, including a line much applauded on its London performance when Dora, the mother of the London family Norman stays with, makes a plea for the theatre of the good old days, the theatre that provided 'only light entertainment ... demanding no thought and contributing nothing to the serious culture and progress of the nation'.[23] The Court determinedly ignored teenagers, rock and roll and the Beatles, none of which were allowed to cross the threshold. The closest they came was with two variety shows headed by The Bachelors (April 1966 and December 1967) or the occasional mocking of new ways, as in Peter Ustinov's *Halfway Up the Tree* (October 1967), a send-up of 'the effect of flower-powered hippy children on home and parents'.[24] When General Sir Mallalieu Fitzbuttress returns home

> from four years in the Malayan jungle he finds his son a beatnik and a long-haired Oxford reject, looking like what he describes as 'Something left over from the Last Supper' and his daughter brazenly and unrepentantly pregnant. In the first act, the children expound their philosophy and he is converted. In the second act the play changes course from comedy to absurdity, the General discarding his bowler hat for Red Indian feathers and costume.[25]

The serious argument between the generations is lost in a growing preoccupation with sex, as the General makes occasional descents from the walnut tree in his garden where he decides to hold forth about the changing times.

However, for all the light comedies and old-fashioned domestic dramas and mockery that graced the Royal Court's stage at this time, there were also plays that, although yielding to the pressure to bend ideas into a 'pre-existing, stale, tired shape', did not inhabit Loamshire, and that raised more complicated and challenging issues, issues of concern in a world that was not as tranquil as it appeared on the surface.[26]

As Michael Billington notes, England in the 1950s 'was not quite the homogenous, socially stable, blandly contended place' that it is often painted.[27] It was rather, in Andrew Marr's words, a 'golden-tinted era of lost content'.[28] Concerns abounded about the Cold War and the proliferation of nuclear weapons and spies, and about the national debt accrued through the Depression and the cost of winning the war. Concerns also surfaced about the loss of Empire and the implications this had for Britain's global position. As Elsom notes, by the 1950s there was a difference from the early part of the century when the gentry who dominated the stage 'were at the heart of an empire. Their codes were of consequence from Delhi to Timbuktu.' Then the audience did not ask 'Why am I watching these boring people?' because these people were running the world. Now, 'nobody knew what would happen to the Empire. It was a source of much anxiety. Could it be revived?' It was of little 'comfort to watch people behaving as if they ruled the world, if you knew that they did not, or rather (since nothing in those days was certain) thought that they might not'.[29]

All this underlying doubt and insecurity might explain the theatre's predilection for closing the door and staying inside. The world itself was

> so full of vital, pressing problems, which no class or kind of person can easily escape, that playwrights, managers and audiences are inclined to fight shy of thoughts in the theatre … It is bad enough, people seem to say, reading about the dangers and horrors of modern life in our newspapers, or talking of them at home, without having to 'enjoy' them in the theatre.[30]

But Howard and Wyndham could not prevent the door from blowing open occasionally. Uncertainty and anxiety were played out on the stage, and while John Osborne's angry shout of 1956 was not heard loudly, fainter echoes could be found in some of the plays that reached the stage of the Royal Court; as another reviewer in *The Stage* asked, 'Is it a question of the writer today being unable to avoid such matters as bombs and universal fear, unrest and intolerance?', concluding 'he cannot ignore the widespread battle of faith against darkness, violence against understanding'.[31]

Inevitably, the war still threw its shadow over the 1950s and beyond. Some of these plays conjured up nostalgia for the all-male camaraderie of army life. Anthony Kimmins's *The Angry Deep* (February 1961) was an adventure story set on a submarine in Malta, complete with daring raids, the destruction of an enemy tanker and the awarding of the VC to a brave lieutenant. *No Time for Sergeants* by Ira Levin (April 1958) was a comedy about American forces, *The Stage* commenting that it was 'yet another stage variation on the theme of the tribulations of recruits' where the little man triumphs over the figure of authority, suggesting that this had become a common sight.[32] Other plays, such as Colin Morris's popular *Reluctant Heroes* (June 1955, May 1954, November 1955), also picked up on this theme, but this time in connection with National Service, introduced in 1947 and to run until 1963. Morris's 'excuse for antics and uproar' showed three defenceless, gullible National Servicemen subjected to a variety of physical and psychological humiliations by the authority figure. Sergeant Bell, known to them as Tinkerbell, ruthlessly bullies them through a series of bureaucratic army manoeuvres from kit issue to morning inspection. Inevitably, the little men win and Bell gets his come-uppance. By the end of the play he is left grovelling around on his hands and knees having caused a massive explosion. The battle of the little man with authority was also coupled with plenty of 'fun with undressing' involving a WRAC officer and her two attractive privates.[33] Slated by many of the critics as nothing more than a series of well-worn music hall jokes and routines, Rix attributed the play's popularity to 'that indefinable quality of identification':

> EVERYONE who had ever been called to attention by a bawling NCO recognised something of their own lives – and as most of the male population (and much of the female one too) had served in the war or been called up for National Service – we had a ready-made audience of millions.[34]

The all-male *Seagulls Over Sorrento* by Hugh Hastings (November 1953 and July 1954) also focused on National Service, with men working in a disused wartime naval fortress at Scapa Flow, now an experimental base.[35] Here, the reminder was that in peacetime, military life could still be dangerous, as they carried out secret experiments with explosives, but otherwise the formula was much the same – men recalling stories of absent women and fighting with bullying authority.

As the distance from the war increased, plays started to deal with more troubling questions. Mary Hayley Bell's *Foreign Field* (September 1953) questioned the nature of heroism, as a young war widow grieved for her husband reported dead in 1940. With his death finally confirmed, she visits his grave in France, only to have her illusions shattered when she meets a young French boy who is obviously her husband's son. Increasingly, plays tackled the issue of war crimes and guilt. The German son in Sartre's *The Condemned of Altona* (April 1961; also staged as *Loser Wins*) locks himself in his room on his return, struggling with guilt for what he has done in the war. It is a struggle that ends in suicide. Rupert Forster, in John Whiting's *Marching Song* (March 1954), has spent seven years in prison at the end of the war, guilty of failing to carry out an attack and, in the process, killing 400 children. Finally released, he is faced with the prospect of a trial so that the country can lay the blame for losing the war on his shoulders and everyone else can shrug off the collective blame. He is offered the choice of suicide instead, encouraged by a Chancellor desperate not to have the trial, which has been called for by the liberal opposition. It is a play that also asks difficult questions about what it is to be a hero (Forster was a hero to the young before the war), what it is to be a soldier and what it is to fight and win wars. For Whiting, it is a never-ending question, something Rupert comes to realise when

> I found this helmet beneath the tracks of my carrier in battle. I picked it up and a skull rattled inside. After hundreds of years he'd come to the surface, and we're still fighting over the same ground. Nothing had been gained since the day he'd fallen. I was attempting with my armoured vehicle only to do what he'd tried to do with his armoured head and his antique sword. His end on that field was death, mine was disgrace. But I was left as surely and eternally in that clay-cold earth as this comrade-in-arms of mine.[36]

Questions about war also fed into questions about the Cold War. In *The Prisoner* by Bridget Boland (March 1954), a cardinal, once a leader of the Resistance, is accused of war crimes by the new revolutionary state. Set in an unnamed European capital, echoes of the Russian show trials were all too apparent, and everyone knew 'that the episodes enacted in this medieval castle represent only too truly the kind of episodes that are being enacted almost every day in this twentieth century in more than one European capital'.[37] Other plays, from *The Delegate* by Roger McDougal (July 1955) to Lesley Storm's *The Long Echo* (July 1956), were more explicit in their criticism and satire of the Soviets, as well as dealing with the issue of Soviet spies. Storm's play was not quite the story of Donald and Melinda Maclean, but the similarities were obvious in a play written from the point of view of the women left behind as a diplomat defects to the East, and raising questions about loyalty and the personal impact of such choices. Inevitably, plays also dealt with nuclear weapons – sometimes seriously and sometimes as farce. Robert Bolt's *The Tiger and the Horse* (August 1960) brought Michael Redgrave on to the stage alongside his daughter Vanessa in a play that took an academic who had hidden behind the grey walls of his college into the world of anti-nuclear protests. In *The Burning Glass* by Charles Morgan (June 1954), Terriford invents a way to control the weather and concentrate the sun's rays on the earth. He is hoping for 'rain on parched land and … well, sunshine on derby day'.[38] It is a harmless invention, or so he thinks. Other people have different ideas. The Prime Minister arrives at his home determined to use the celestial flame thrower as a weapon or at least as a deterrent. Terriford refuses to give him the code. Later, foreign agents, helped by Terriford's assistant, kidnap him to try and get the secret. At its heart, the play is a debate about the use of science for the common good rather than the destruction of humanity, as Terriford explains near the end:

> The Wonders of Applied Science have become much less wonderful than they were. Only half-baked minds any longer worship that particular Golden Calf. Men of science themselves do not ... They have great dread of their own miracles ... For example, supersonic speed. It gets the headlines and it gets the movies. But who for a moment believes that *that*, or atomic energy, or the Burning Glass, is anything else than a monstrous gadget.[39]

More comically, John Chapman's *Simple Spymen* (November 1961) was a slapstick drama, with foreign agent Max chasing Grobchick and his secret Atomic Pile Restorer, and George and Percy (two street musicians who have mistakenly become embroiled) also chasing Grobchick, and in turn being chased by Colonel Gray-Balding and Lieutenant Fosgrove. Working through a series of disguises and confusions of identity as George and Percy move from street musicians to secret agents to French waiters to private detectives (by way of a vicar, an organist, a widow and a colonel and including at one time three men disguised as stage Turks), the whole turns out to have been a waste of time, as the Atomic Pile Restorer is a carpet cleaner rather than a nuclear secret.

Rarely, the world abroad crept on to the stage. Most famously Osborne's *The Entertainer* (August 1958) used a family as a microcosm of Britain and the Empire in decline. Storm's *Time and Yellow Roses* (April 1961) was set against the background of the Congo crisis but was actually played out in the penthouse suite of a luxury hotel. Madame Rouarte has hurriedly brought her daughter to London to get her away from the Brussels demonstration that she has been involved in against Belgian policy in the Congo. What transpires is that all three women (they have brought with them Madame Rouarte's elderly mother) have been rebels – a suffragette, a Second World War resistance fighter and now an opponent of colonialism.

However, the overwhelming majority of plays remained firmly at home, where, for all those that managed to resolve domestic problems, there were many that suggested that things could not be so neatly tied up. In many of the plays of Lesley Storm, a regular visitor to the Royal Court stage, the unhappiness, misery and destructive nature of family life and marriage for women was the focus of an evening's entertainment. In *Black Chiffon* (June 1950 and September 1963), Mrs Christie, a wealthy woman, steals a black chiffon nightgown a few days before her son's wedding. During the ensuing investigation into this uncharacteristic act, conducted by her family and the psychiatrist whom they summon, they propose that she mounts a defence based on her close relationship with her son and her fear of his impending marriage, but she would rather go to prison than drag her son's name through the courts. Gale suggests that the play shows that 'the family is a complex and unhappy environment and that when children leave, the dysfunctions are revealed'.[40] The play is, variously, an exploration of the 'emotional straitjackets' put on women in the name of appropriate mothering and the dubious and gendered uses of psychology.[41] Her later comedy, *Roar Like a Dove* (April 1960), set in Dungavel Castle in the West Highlands, is in part a demystification of the fairy tale of the romantic Highlands, but also a stinging critique of the emotional and economic consequences of marriage, as Lord Dungavel's wife, the mother of six daughters, is tricked into a seventh pregnancy in order to provide a male heir.

Other plays raised further questions about the hypocrisy of the image of cosy and happy domesticity, including Emlyn Williams's *Accolade* (July 1950), which 'came close to blowing the cover off the sexual pretence which governed so many lives in the post-war theatrical, literary and political Establishment' and which certainly proved that the commercial theatre of the post-war era was not all 'fluff and frolic'.[42] Described by some critics as 'dirty' and 'vulgar', *Accolade* is the story of Will Trenting, a happily married, Nobel prize-winning author who is on the point of being knighted when he is revealed to have been regularly attending orgies in a Rotherhithe pub. He has been photographed having sex with a 14-year-old girl, although under the impression that she was older. The girl's father, a would-be writer whose work has been roundly condemned in the past by Trenting, attempts to blackmail him and then decides to report him to the police. The play ends with a mob threatening to storm the Trentings' house but with the family intact, as his wife and son both stand by him. As Trenting accepts that the price of being part of the Establishment is to play by their rules, his publisher sees things differently, telling him that

> we all have one thing we're ashamed of. All those out there have. Even the judge has, who'll be peering at you over his glasses making you feel like dirt. His secret may be the nastiest of the lot. Only you have committed the sin of being found out.[43]

The corruption and hypocrisy of the Establishment pointed to by Trenting's publisher also found echoes in Roysten Morley's *The Guilty Party* (October 1952). Here, an Attorney General is faced with a stark choice between telling the truth and loyalty to his family when a financial scandal breaks around him involving his father, his wife and a friend who is a junior minister. In this instance, it is truth that wins out and he finds himself presenting the Crown case against his own friends and family. Some thrillers also focused on the wrongs of Establishment figures, and

Emlyn Williams's *Someone Waiting* (September 1953) was about the revenge of the little man whose son has been framed and then hanged for a murder committed by a wealthy man.

Other plays dealt with social issues and changes. Sylvia Rayman's *Women of Twilight* (July 1953) is a tale of the lives of single mothers living on the margins of society, 'in the twilight zone'.[44] On first appearance, Helen Allistair, a widowed, middle-class woman, seems to be philanthropically providing shelter and child care for women who cannot find a home because they are single mothers, but in reality she is 'taking every penny they've got and lets them live in squalor and talks to them like the salvation army'.[45] Eventually, having caused the death of a child through neglect and imperilled the life of a woman about to give birth by pushing her down the stairs, Allistair's real thinking is revealed as she waits to be arrested:

> Sluts all of you with your rotten little bastards. I took you off the streets, when decent people wouldn't look at you. God when I think what I've done for you; slaved morning and night … I gave up my house to you and this is how you repay me. You've no gratitude, no loyalty … how dare you speak to me you sanctimonious bitch.[46]

Gale suggests that the play marked a new direction for the staging of motherhood, one in which women refuse to carry out their mothering role, just as Emma tries and fails to in *Roar Like a Dove*.[47]

Philip King's *Serious Charge* (September 1955) was one of a handful of plays that raised the issue of homosexuality, when an unmarried vicar is accused of a homosexual assault by the village 'spiv'. Joan Henry's *Look on Tempests* (February 1960), a 'dullish conventional drawing-room drama', chose not to include a homosexual character on stage, instead telling the story of the effect on a wife and mother of the arrest and imprisonment of a young publisher for homosexuality.[48] Racism was at the heart of Ted Willis's *Hot Summer Night* (November 1958), a play that caught the temper of the times, with the riots in Notting Hill having taken place two years previously. Set in Wapping, it focused on Jack Palmer, a trade union leader who hotly denounces racism when it rears its head in his workplace, but is less sanguine when his daughter announces that she wants to marry Sonny, a Jamaican. When the play arrived in London, *The Stage* reviewer asked,

> [i]s it a sign of the times that the West End can present a play about working-class people in the East End with a trade-union official talking about socialism, and without the caricature or patronising presentation so familiar in most plays still being written from the wealthy-class angle?[49]

However, at the Royal Court, in class terms, *Hot Summer Night* was very much the exception. Five years earlier, Charlotte Haldane's *Age of Consent* (August 1953) had been hailed as the first play since Joseph Colton's 1952 *The Gay Dog* to present a story about working-class people on the commercial touring circuit, but its depiction of the working-class characters was rather clichéd; the mother who brings accusations of under-aged sex against 'the likeable, hard-working' Ted was portrayed as common, pleasure-loving and brassy.[50] The same was true, unsurprisingly, of a 'holiday romp' starring George Formby, with Leslie Sands's *Beside the Seaside* offering the audience a chance to laugh at the capers of visitors to the Seaview Guest House being terrorised by the landlady, Mrs Austin. In terms of class, it would appear that the stage of the Royal Court catered for 'middle brow, middle class, middle aged' tastes.[51] Revues, with their pride in being up-to-date and satirical, also offered comment on the world from the Bomb to racial intolerance, with a particular eye on censorship in *The Lord Chamberlain Regrets* (June 1961), although much of their ammunition was aimed at artistic targets, with a special place reserved for amateur dramatic companies.

More than the specific issues focused on by some plays was an underlying sense of unease that runs through much of the work of these two decades. From John Whiting's *The Gates of Summer* (October 1956), with its group of eccentric exiles playing out their fantasies in Greece in a disintegrating world on the brink of war, to Willis Hall's adaptation from the French of *Chin-Chin* (October 1960), a story of tormented lovers in which Celia Johnson and Anthony Quayle use drink to cover the pain and disappointment of their lives, there is a sense that all is far from well in the world. It is a point underlined by Denis Cannan's satirical comedy *Misery Me!* (February 1955), a 'comedy of disillusionment' about a suicide pact that ends with hope and a toast to life and living happily ever after. By the mid-1950s happy-ever-afters were becoming something to satirise.

One play that illustrates this sense of insecurity is N. C. Hunter's *A Day by the Sea* (October 1953). It was a play that Tynan thought to be 'an evening of unexampled triviality' and that Sheridan Morley disparages as 'at best formulaic'.[52] The production was packed with stars, including John Gielgud, Ralph Richardson, Sybil Thorndyke and Lewis Casson, something that Binkie Beaumont, who produced the play, was known to cling to when he considered the dramatic content of a work to be thin. 'It was like watching a flight of eagles and macaws of magnificent plumage jammed for two hours into a suburban birdcage', concluded Tynan.[53] But there was more to the play than this. Set in a remote part of Dorset close to the sea (and the edge of the country), the play is peopled with discontented characters either trying to ignore the world outside, or trying, and failing, to change it. The matriarch, Laura

Anson, is mortified by her son, Julian, talking about the troubles of the outside world. 'I do get tired of these high-falutin' speeches, this everlasting talk of politics and war', she complains. 'Why must we have these wearisome world problems dragged into the garden, among the flowers?'[54] Julian, on a reluctant visit home from his job with the Foreign Office in Paris, is convinced that coming to this remote corner is like 'stepping out of the world into a kind of never-never land'. It is 'another civilisation' where people 'seem to inhabit a sort of vegetable world'.[55] He works at solving the problems facing Western civilisation, sometimes convinced at the end of a day that 'all of us, are like a lot of children absorbed in a game of marbles at the foot of a mountain, while overhead a great avalanche is beginning to rumble and slide…'[56] By working patiently, he hopes that things will get better. But his hopes are brought crashing down to earth by a visit from a senior civil servant who tells him he is to be recalled from Paris. He is unpopular, does not play the game, takes no leave and works too hard. Jolted, he comes to realise what he has missed out in life by throwing himself into his work. He ends the play convinced that what he used to be contemptuous about, living contentedly and with dignity, are not to be dismissed, and happily planning to clear away the undergrowth to make a 'great vista stretching away to the sea', bordered by azaleas.[57]

Hunter was also concerned with age and ageing and, by implication, with an old world. Uncle David, once a mountaineer who had travelled to places few Europeans had ever seen, is confined to being read to from geographic magazines, barely able to walk. Dr Gregson, supposedly in the house to look after David, drinks gin and offers a pessimistic view of a world he sees as cruel and murderous, as they go round and round 'day after day, like elderly goldfish in a bowl'.[58] For Laura, the old hang heavy around her. People 'of that age never seem to realise what a worry they are, what a responsibility', though there will be regrets when they die.[59] There are two children in the house, the offspring of Frances, who was adopted by the family when her parents died, and in the end they provide a flicker of hope, though that hope lies in some far distant future. For now, withdrawing to the garden is the only thing to do.

A Day by the Sea also brought with it a whiff of danger that might have ruffled the tidy feathers of Howard and Wyndham. It was due to open at the Royal Court on 26 October 1953, with Gielgud playing the role of the civil servant son. However, on the 21st he was arrested in a public toilet in Chelsea and charged with importuning. He appeared at the magistrates' court the following morning at a specially arranged early sitting in the hope of avoiding publicity, and fined £10. Unfortunately, he was overheard by a reporter who was on his way to another court, who, on hearing 'the most distinctive voice in British theatre', alerted his colleagues. By the evening the story was all over London and all over the papers.[60] Gielgud offered to step down, but with less than four days until the play's opening there was no time to find a replacement. The company travelled to Liverpool at the weekend and prepared for the opening night, with Beaumont taking the precaution of hiring extra security men 'to make sure that no enraged anti-homosexual Liverpudlians – and worse still, no journalists' could get past the stage door.[61] On the Monday, it was

> unlikely that there was ever a Tennent first night filled with such tension and gloomy foreboding. Gielgud's first entrance, as Julian Anson, the diplomat, was a quarter-hour into the first-act, probably the longest and most crucifying fifteen minutes of his life. When the moment came, he could not enter: he was paralysed and shaking with fear … it was Sybil Thorndyke who came to the rescue. She was on stage, just having completed a short scene with Irene Worth. When Gielgud failed to appear she could see him in the wings, knew what was the trouble and what had to be done. She walked off through the French windows, grabbed him and whispered fiercely, "Come on, John darling, they won't boo me," and led him firmly onto the stage. To everybody's astonishment, and indescribable relief, the audience gave him a standing ovation. They cheered, they applauded, they shouted. The message was quite clear. The English public had always been loyal to its favourites, and this was their chance to show that they did not care what he had done in his private life, he was still their adored leading actor, still a star … Sybil Thorndyke hugging him and smiling with unmistakeable defiance at the audience, as if to say "I don't think it matters, do you?" and Gielgud, the famous Terry tears visibly running down his cheeks, unable to speak. It was a long time before he could stammer out his first line, one of delicious triviality: "Oh dear, I'd forgotten we had all those azaleas," which, at a moment of such cosmic significance, was greeted by a roar of laughter and renewed applause.[62]

Overall, these two decades at the Royal Court present a more complicated picture than might at first be apparent from Howard and Wyndham's management bible with its advice on front of house manners and civility. On stage, it was not all cosy comedies or flimsy dramas. Farce offered a chance for the world to be less sensible. Plays asked questions about the world. Billington, writing about the 1940s but with comments equally applicable to the 1950s and 1960s, suggests that 'the tensions within the national psyche were being enacted on the nation's stage … you see a constant battle between nostalgia and progress'. Far from being a theatrical desert, the period was in fact one of 'turbulent activity'.[63] While the battles that happened on the Royal Court stage were perhaps a little muted, they did happen.

Notes

1 In 1972 the company also took on the New Theatre in Oxford. The Royal Court was the only theatre it held on leasehold.
2 Iles, 'Issues in Theatrical Management', 58.
3 G. Sandison, *Theatre Ownership in Britain* (London: Federation of Theatre Unions, 1953), 33.
4 Claire Cochrane, *Twentieth-Century British Theatre: Industry, Art and Empire* (Cambridge: Cambridge University Press, 2011), 55.
5 Quoted in Iles, 'Issues in Theatrical Management', 69–70.
6 Ibid., 70.
7 J. B. Priestley, *Theatre Outlook* (London: Nicholson and Watson, 1947), 20.
8 John Elsom, *Cold War Theatre* (London: Routledge, 1992), 29–30.
9 Dan Rebellato, *1956 and All That: The Making of Modern British Drama* (London: Routledge, 1999), 1.
10 Kenneth Tynan, *A View of the English Stage* (St Albans: Paladin, 1975), 148.
11 *The Stage*, 31 July 1952, 23; 2 August 1956, 10.
12 *Spectator*, 26 July 1957, 16.
13 *The Stage*, 29 August 1957, 11.
14 *The Times*, 14 December 1957, 8; 25 June 1964, 14; *The Stage*, 18 October 1956, 9; 24 December 1958, 8.
15 John Bull, *Stage Right: Crisis and Recovery in British Contemporary Mainstream Theatre* (Basingstoke: Macmillan, 1994), 53–4.
16 *The Stage*, 14 April 1961, 14.
17 *The Stage*, 24 October 1968, 27.
18 *The Times*, 30 November 1962, 16.
19 *The Stage*, 6 December 1962, 13.
20 Smith, *Modern British Farce*, 15.
21 Ray Cooney and Tony Hilton, *One for the Pot* (London: English Theatre Guild, 1963), 73.
22 *New Statesman*, 24 July 1964, 127.
23 *The Stage*, 11 May 1963, 13.
24 *The Stage*, 11 October 1967, 8.
25 Ibid., 8.
26 David Pattie, *Modern British Playwriting: The 1950s* (London: Methuen, 2012), 44.
27 Michael Billington, *State of the Nation: British Theatre Since 1945* (London: Faber and Faber, 2007), 73.
28 Andrew Marr, *A History of Modern Britain* (London: Pan Macmillan, 2009), 115.
29 Elsom, *Cold War Theatre*, 32.
30 *The Stage*, 24 February 1955, 8.
31 *The Stage*, 31 March 1955, 8.
32 *The Stage*, 13 August 1956, 19.
33 Ivor Brown in *The Observer*, quoted in Brian Rix, *My Farce from my Elbow* (London: Secker and Warburg, 1975), 93.
34 Rix, *My Farce from my Elbow*, 75.
35 The play returned as a musical in February 1963, renamed *Scapa!*
36 John Whiting, *Marching Song* (1957), in *New English Dramatists 5* (Harmondsworth: Penguin, 1962), 198.
37 *The Stage*, 22 April 1954, 9.
38 Charles Morgan, *The Burning Glass* (London: Macmillan, 1954), 12.
39 Ibid., 151–2.
40 Gale, *West End Women*, 128.
41 Susan Bennett, 'New Plays and Women's Voices in the 1950s', in Elaine Aston and Janelle Reinelt (eds), *The Cambridge Companion to Modern British Women Playwrights* (Cambridge: Cambridge University Press, 2000), 45.
42 Billington, *State of the Nation*, 41–2.
43 Emlyn Williams, *Accolade* (1950) (London: Samuel French, 2015), 93.
44 Gale, *West End Women*, 129.
45 Quoted in ibid., 129.
46 Quoted in ibid., 131.
47 Ibid., 131.
48 *The Stage*, 24 March 1960, 19.
49 *The Stage*, 4 December 1958, 11.
50 *The Stage*, 27 August 1953, 8; 18 June 1953, 10.
51 John Elsom, *Post War British Theatre* (London: Routledge, 1976), 75.

52 Sheridan Morley, *John Gielgud: The Authorized Biography* (New York: Applause, 2002), 259.
53 Huggett, *Binkie Beaumont*, 428; Morley, *John Gielgud*, 289.
54 N. C. Hunter, *A Day by the Sea* (London: English Theatre Guild, 1954), 33.
55 Ibid., 20.
56 Ibid., 16.
57 Ibid., 79.
58 Ibid., 28.
59 Ibid., 56.
60 Morley, *John Gielgud*, 269.
61 Ibid., 271.
62 Ibid., 272.
63 Billington, *State of the Nation*, 45.

1957

18 March	*Janus*	Carolyn Green	comedy with Googie Withers
26 March	*Peter Pan*	J. M. Barrie	with Janette Scott
1 April	*We Must Kill Toni*	Ian Stuart Black	comedy thriller
8 April	*White Horse Inn*		Birkenhead Amateur Operatic Society
15 April	*The Reluctant Debutante*	William Douglas Home	comedy with Anna Massey and Celia Johnson
22 April	*A Dead Secret*	Rodney Ackland	thriller with Paul Schofield
29 April	*The Man in Question*	Raymond Bowers	
6 May	Carl Rosa Opera		two weeks
20 May	*Silver Wedding*	Michael Clayton Hutton	comedy
27 May	*Dear Delinquent*	Jack Popplewell	comedy
3 June	*Meet Me By Moonlight*	Anthony Lesser	musical play
10 June	*Odd Man In*	Claude Magnier	comedy from the French with Donald Sinden
17 June	*The Importance of Being Earnest*	Oscar Wilde	with Margaret Rutherford
24 June	*The Pyjama Game*	George Abbott and Richard Bissell; music by Richard Adler and Jerry Ross	three weeks
15 July	*The Reluctant Debutante*	William Douglas Home	return of the comedy from April
22 July	*Towards Zero*	Agatha Christie	crime thriller
29 July	*Nest of Robins*	Robert Monro (Sonnie Hale)	comedy with Jessie Matthews and Sonnie Hale
5 August	*Doctor in the House*	Ted Willis	comedy

12 August	*Hotel Paradiso*	Georges Feydeau and Maurice Desvallieres	farce with Frankie Howerd
19 August	*Plaintiff in a Pretty Hat*	Hugh and Margaret Williams	comedy
26 August	Gilbert and Sullivan	D'Oyly Carte	two weeks
9 September	*Hamlet*	Shakespeare	Old Vic Company (in association with the Arts Council), with Judi Dench as Ophelia
16 September	*Man of Distinction*	Walter Hasenclever	burlesque comedy
23 September	Italian Opera Company		
30 September	*Love in Idleness*	Terence Rattigan	
7 October	The New York Negro Ballet		
21 October	*The Desert Song*		musical
28 October	*The Tunnel of Love*	Joseph Fields and Peter de Vries	Theatre Guild production with Ian Carmichael and Robert Morley
4 November	Urals Ensemble		celebrated Soviet choir and dance company of 70 artists
11 November	Inbal		Jewish National Dance and Ballet company from Israel; company of 80 dancers
18 November	*The Happy Man*	Hugh and Margaret Williams	comic domestic drama
25 November	*Dinner with the Family*	Jean Anouillh; translated by Edward Owen Marsh	comedy

Howard and Wyndham's circuit in the 1950s

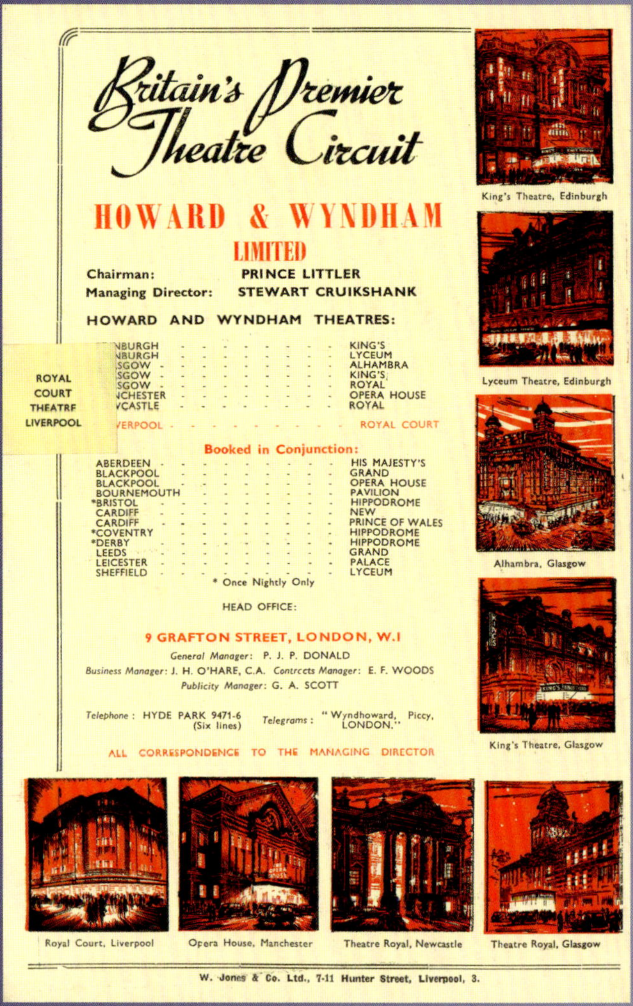

2 December	*The Rape of the Belt*	Benn W. Levy	comedy with Richard Attenborough
9 December	closed for pantomime rehearsals		
26 December	*Goldilocks and the Three Bears*	David Croft	

Christmas, 1950–1969

1950 *Goody Two Shoes*

> A tuneful production throughout, it has a mixture of modern melodies with older numbers, as, for instance, the 'Wish On The Moon' and ... and 'Me And My Shadow,' which Douglas Byng uses as his community song ... Douglas Byng, a stylish Dame with many hats of curious design – from a fish and a loofah to sweeping feathers, leads the comedy, in which there are many topical gags... (*The Stage*, 29 December 1950, 15)

1951 *Cinderella* by Peter Coke

> Devised and produced by Freddie Carpenter ... the book maintains faithfully the old fairy story, and the various specialities, of which there are several exceptionally well done, are made to fit in. Artistry and beauty are the keynote of the major scenes, rather than the spectacular ... Altogether the production is filled with good, clean humour, talented dancing and many well-sung numbers ... and a catchy community song, 'Sing After Me.'
>
> (*The Stage*, 3 January 1952, 20)

1952 *Queen of Hearts* by George Lacy

> A striking feature of the Howard and Wyndham pantomimes since the war has been their family appeal and this season's production is no exception. Almost from the outset, a direct appeal is made to the children through Jack Edge, and how well this whimsical Knave of Hearts succeeds, was quickly shown on the opening evening by the way the youngsters responded throughout. Of its ingredients, comedy is the strongest element with George Lacy making his Queen of Hearts a highly amusing figure who wears several sensational creations in gowns and millinery. (*The Stage*, 1 January 1953, 20)

1953 *Robinson Crusoe*

The Dame this year was again played by Douglas Byng. He had first appeared in pantomime at the Palladium in 1921 and played his first Dame in *Dick Whittington and his Cat* at the New Oxford in 1924.

> I did 26 in all, and was extremely snobbish about them. They were all ladies, you see, none of the usual charlady types. I used to arrive on a bicycle in a

yellow plaid frock, and my dames were always extremely well-educated and very gracious – none of your rubbish. (*The Times*, 17 March 1983, 15)

1954 *Puss in Boots* by Janet Green

Freddie Carpenter has devised and directed so many successful Christmas pantomimes here that his name has now become something of a hallmark. And this season's production in no way harms that reputation. He has again succeeded in staging an entertainment that will have a universal appeal to all ages … But more than anything else, the production is notable for the success of two artists new to the city – Margaret Miles and Freddie Sales. (*The Stage*, 31 December 1954, 27)

1955 *Babes in the Wood* by David Croft

[A]n entirely new and refreshing approach to the old pantomime story. There is a more modern touch about it, especially in the dance ensembles … George

Formby … is an ideal Simple Simon, whose droll humour contrasts vividly with the more vigorous brand from Tony Heaton, a buxom and lovable dame … Musically there is a great variety. There are the romantic numbers sung by Phyllis Holden … Completely different but no less enjoyable are the comic songs of George Formby and Tony Heaton, and then, of course, there are the former's own numbers sung to the accompaniment of his ukulele. He has three new numbers in 'When I Was a Boy,' 'Sitting on Blackpool Tower' and 'Hindu Yudo Man,' and an old favourite, 'Leaning on a Lamppost.' (*The Stage*, 5 January 1956, 14)

1956 *Aladdin* by David Croft

Presented with a splendour combined with artistry which one rarely finds in a pantomime, Stewart Cruikshank … scores a big success with *Aladdin* …The biggest surprise, perhaps, comes from Dickie Valentine, starring in the part of Wishee Washee. Unlike so many modern music hall, radio and television artists, Mr Valentine submerges his own strong personality into the part of the shy Wishee Washee. Apart from an interlude in which he gives a brilliant

impersonation of his contemporary fellow-crooners, he is Wishee Washee first and the 'fan-rave' Dickie Valentine after. (*The Stage*, 3 January 1957, 25)

1957 *Goldilocks and the Three Bears*

Tommy Steele has answered as effectively as is possible all those people who could not visualise him in pantomime … he proves that he is not only a 'pop' singer but a showman to his fingertips. Undoubtedly he will draw all the teenagers in Merseyside and surrounding districts, and doubtless he will have to appeal to them every evening, as he did within a few minutes of his initial appearance on the stage here, for quietness to allow the pantomime to be played, but he will also win over thousands of others by the enthusiastic way he moulds himself into the whole show and his ability as a comedian. His teenager fans will not be disappointed for they have their big moment when Tommy and his Steelmen give their speciality and cause the house to ring with squeals and shrieks. (*The Stage*, 21 January 1958, 20)

Mr Carpenter has set the old story in a Tyrolean circus, in which Mr Steele will be featured in a rock 'n' roll number with the three bears. (*The Stage*, 24 October 1957, 1)

1958 *Cinderella*

Devised and directed by Freddie Carpenter, probably the most lasting impressions the majority of those who see it will have, will be the exquisite costumes and settings, the delightful ballet scenes, the knockabout comedy and the excellent use made of the revolving stage … the pantomime is notable for its several novel scenes, among them one in the baron's library when Ronnie Ronalde, who as Buttons fits his versatile personality happily into the whole and sings, yodels and whistles his way into popularity, supported by the George Mitchell Singers, which introduces dancing visions of Switzerland, Italy and Scotland. (*The Stage*, 1 January 1959, 21)

1959 *Noddy in Toyland* (matinees)

> The best part of *Noddy in Toyland* by Enid Blyton … is the scenery which made a colourful spectacle of this show for young children. The sets include a room at the top of a great tree, inhabited by a character called Moonface, an enchanted wood, a goblin market, and a railway station complete with litter baskets telling patrons to keep Toyland tidy … Ooh's and aah's greeted a spectacular aerial ballet, which was probably enhanced for the children when two of the wire-suspended dancers bumped heavily in mid-air. (*The Stage*, 7 January 1960, 32)

1959 *Fun and Games* (revue; evenings)

> The age-long tradition of pantomime at Christmas has been broken at the Royal Court, Liverpool this year. Instead Howard and Wyndham are presenting a twice-nightly revue … devised and produced for them by Dick Hurran … From a spectacular point of view it seems a pity that this

production has been limited to a twice-nightly show for several of the scenes are worthy of a much bigger production. Outstanding among them are those depicting 'Evening in Venice,' 'Music Hall' and the 'Eve of Waterloo' ... Bill Maynard and Beryl Reid combine collectively and singly, to put across a lot of light-hearted fun in specialities and sketches, none of which are more amusing than that in which they appear as rock 'n' roll fans and as neighbours in the next flat... (*The Stage*, 7 January 1960, 32)

1960 *You'll Be Lucky*

Once again Howard and Wyndham have plumped for a twice-nightly revue instead of the traditional pantomime, but except in the matter of time no pantomime could give its audience more than does this show for which Dick Hurran is responsible. Several of the scenes are full of splendour ... there is an abundance of delightful singing, ranging from operatic arias from *Madame Butterfly* and *La Traviata*, sung by Sheila Paton, to many modern numbers ... But even stronger is the comedy provided by Al Read. (*The Stage*, 5 January 1961, 29)

1961 *The Black and White Minstrel Show*

If ever a show deserved to be tabbed with the rather over-worked phrase 'there's never a dull moment' it is ... *The Black and White Minstrel Show* ... It is a sheer impossibility to keep track of the numerous songs which the Minstrels ... sing in such excellent voice ... But there is also comedy in plenty ... The Les Mathurins provide some first class comedy acrobatics; there is a delightful and amusing little scene by Darly's Dogs; some broader fun from the Two Pirates and a touch of modern music from the Peter Crawford Trio. (*The Stage*, 4 January 1962, 28)

1962 *Yankee Doodle Comes to Town*

Yankee Doodle Comes to Town ... is a musical extravaganza rooted in tunes and melodies that were popular in America at the turn of the century and which are still in vogue today. There is no story as such; the score is the thing, and tunes such as 'Waiting for the Robert E. Lee' and 'Bill Bailey' flower in profusion as the two principal characters, Mary and Willie, make a musical journey across America, ending appropriately on Broadway. It is all pleasant and very nostalgic and if it adds up to little of importance in terms of theatrical entertainment, that is probably of small consequence. (*The Stage*, 22 November 1962, 15)

1963 *The Ken Dodd Show*

There can surely never have been a more zany comic – or a more generous one – than Ken Dodd judging by his contribution to the show that bears his name, certainly one of the brightest Christmas productions ever staged. His final contribution to the opening night's performance lasted 45 minutes as he gagged and clowned in his own irrepressible way, bringing howls of laughter from every part of the house. (*The Stage*, 2 January 1964)

1964 *The Ken Dodd Show*

Ken Dodd returned to his native city once more when his new show opened an extended season ... with a special gala performance. For many, with memories of last year's show still fairly fresh in their minds, there must have been a big question mark hanging over the opening night – could he and producer Dick Hurran do it again? And at the end of the performance there must equally have been one answer – a big 'Yes' – even when the production is cut down to twice-nightly size. With the show almost sold out before the first curtain went up, it is assured of full houses for its entire run. (*The Stage*, 7 January 1965, 27)

1965 *The Dora Bryan Show*

Beautifully dressed and staged ... *The Dora Bryan Show* is spectacular in the real meaning of the word. Colourful, full of divertingly comic material, the show opened ... with a bang ... Dora Bryan, spry, energetic, confidentially friendly puts over some old and new material in her own original manner, the old as welcome as she is herself and the new coming up to the same high standard.

She is extremely funny in the best traditional trooper fashion and reveals how good a really natural comedienne can be. David Nixon appears with her in some amusing sketches, and also contributes some of the pleasantest moments in the show with his easy manner of making things miraculously disappear. (*The Stage*, 6 January 1966, 27)

1966 *Tom Thumb*

It is some years since Jimmy Clitheroe appeared in pantomime in Liverpool. Then he was one of the lesser stars; now in *Tom Thumb* ... he appears as a star in his own right. And what a star! ... An artist to his fingertips. Mischievous, engaging and never slogging the stage to the detriment of his fellow artists (apart from when he was meant to do as in the case of Billy Winsor's 'cod' conjuring act when he 'blew the gaff' on all the tricks). (*The Stage*, 5 January 1967, 28)

1967 *The Bachelors Show*

The Bachelors, that engaging trio of young Irishmen, who have built for themselves such an excellent reputation in a very short time, never hog the bill, but fit in several times during the show with their own particular type of song, many of them great favourites with the audience who call for them in no uncertain manner.

Mike Yarwood in the supporting cast proves to be an excellent mimic, his impersonations of Harold Wilson, Edward Heath and others being so good that it seems unnecessary for him to resort to some of his patter. (*The Stage*, 4 January 1968, 27)

1968 *Cinderella*

Cinderella at the Royal Court is a very polished affair indeed. The first thing that strikes you is the freshness of the costumes and sets and the powerful singing and lively dancing soon confirm that impression. There are no big names in the cast list, but big names cost money and it looks as though the money saved has been put to good use in making this one of the most lavish and good looking pantomimes for many years. (*Liverpool Echo*, 27 December 1968, 2)

1969 *The Frankie Vaughan Spectacular*

With scintillating scenes which range from Elizabethan and Swiss Tyrolean to modern dress, Dick Hurran has ensured that the *Frankie Vaughan Spectacular* ... lives up to its name and charms the eye as well as the ear. It is virtually a show of two halves, the first being given over to supporting acts and Frankie Vaughan almost completely filling the second part.

Mike Yarwood sets the pace with a series of quickfire gags, and there are a lot more, also reeled off in double quick time ... a neat footjuggling act by Regina Baranton sets up the show's big moment, the appearance of Frankie Vaughan. In less than a minute he has the audience completely under his spell. All his well-known little tricks – the wiggle, the kick, the cane and the hat – are there as he reels off song after song... (*The Stage*, 8 January 1970, 23)

1966

25 February	*On the Level*	Ronald Millar; music by Ron Grainer	with Leslie Phillips
1 March	*Any Wednesday*	Muriel Resnick	West End comedy success
28 March	*The Dancing Years*	Ivor Novello	Birkenhead Amateur Operatic Society
4 April	*Present Laughter*	Noel Coward	from West End success; with Robert Fleyming
11 April	*Easter Parade: The Happy Holiday Show*		with The Bachelors, the Tiller Girls, the Kaye Sisters, for three weeks
4 May	*Oliver!*	Lionel Bart	with Marti Webb and Richard Easton
14 June	*The King's Mare: A Royal Comedy*	Jean Canolle; translated by Anita Loos	British premiere with Glynis Johns and Keith Michell
20 June	*The Bespoke Overcoat & The Dock Brief*	Wolf Mankowitz/ John Mortimer	
27 June	*Forever April*	Frank Barbara	comedy with Kenneth Connor
11 July	*Wait Until Dark*	Frederick Knott	thriller with Honor Blackman
18 July	*Adam's Apple*	Terence Feely	farcical comedy with Bill Simpson (TV's Dr Finlay)
29 August	*Who's Afraid of Virginia Woolf?*	Edward Albee	
5 September	*Dial Liverpool Royal 5063/4*	Peter Myers and Ronnie Cass	revue with Moira Lister, Leslie Crowther (cancelled)
12 September	*A Present for the Past*	John Hailstone	with Gwen Ffrangcon-Davies
19 September	English Opera Group		including Mozart's *The Impresario* and Benjamin Britten's version of *Beggar's Opera*

26 September	*Lady Windermere's Fan*	Oscar Wilde	with Corin Redgrave, Coral Browne and Wilfrid Hyde White
3 October	Royal Ballet		
10 October	*Forever April*	Frank Barbara	return of the comedy with Kenneth Connor
17 October	*Bang Bang Beirut*	Ray Cooney and Tony Hilton	farce
20 October	*Chase Me Comrade*	Ray Cooney and Tony Hilton	farce with Brian Rix
24 October	*Merrie England*		Birkenhead Amateur Dramatic Society
31 October	*On Approval*	Frederick Lonsdale	comedy with Michael Denison, Dulcie Gray and Robert Fleming
7 November	*The Cat and the Canary*	John Willard	comedy thriller
14 November	*An Ideal Husband*	Oscar Wilde	with Margaret Lockwood
28 November	*Kismet*		Wallasey Operatic Society
21 November	*Doctor at Sea*	Ted Willis	comedy with Alfie Bass and Bill Fraser
5 December	Olde Time Music Hall		presented by Don Ellis with Hetty King, Nat Gonella, Sandy Powell, Cavan O'Connor
23 December	*Tom Thumb*	Pauline Grant	with Jimmy Clitheroe

Dear Sir

An explanation is required of the disgusting appearance of a rat in the Grand Circle during the second act of *H.M.S. Pinafore* on 22nd November 1967. One does not expect to encounter vermin in a theatre and your assurance that steps will be taken to eradicate this menace before I come again, on Saturday, will be appreciated.

9 About to be Despatched with Dignity: The Decline and Fall of Howard and Wyndham and the Royal Court in the 1970s

Between 1920 and 1964 the number of regional theatres for touring productions declined steeply. *The Stage Yearbook* lists 255 in 1920, 106 in 1940 and only 24 regularly taking in touring productions in 1964.[1] Iles points out that the number of London theatres remained the same as in 1920, so 'the decline of theatre cannot be attributed to a general deterioration of interest', and he suggests instead that 'the mediocre quality of their productions reflected, and partly explained, that decline'. In essence, the touring theatres had become 'transit camps for a miscellaneous procession of speculative productions which ... had become scarcer and seedier and decreasingly profitable'.[2] Accompanying this downward trend, some regional theatregoing was being provided for by the growth in subsidised repertory theatres, which numbered close to fifty in the early 1960s. In Liverpool, the Playhouse was joined in 1964 by the Everyman, and while they could not provide the variety of productions enjoyed by touring houses, they could guarantee more consistent production values where an audience could be confident about the quality of the work they were to see and would get to know the actors over the course of a season.

The quality of touring productions had started to decline with the introduction of pre-London tours. These had begun towards the end of the war when London theatres were full and long runs meant that vacancies for new productions were rare. Rather than wait, producers took their shows on the road, sometimes in the hope that West End managers would come and see them and, eventually, offer them a London booking. After the war things began to change, and while there were still a number of good shows sent on the road prior to London, Iles notes that increasingly 'the plays labelled "prior-to-London production" all too obviously had little hope of reaching the West End' and even genuine West End productions 'on their way to "Town" were often below standard on their pre-London tour'.[3] Too often regarded as 'dress-rehearsals', actors did not always know their lines and plays had not been edited or rewritten prior to going on the road. The attitude of managers, suggests Iles, was one of leaving it how it was and seeing how it got on in the provinces before making any alterations.[4] Even better-quality plays that did have West End bookings, which were increasingly hard to find, were often not a great draw as they were unknown to audiences, and for a theatre that relied on proven successes to ensure advance sales, things started to get tough.

The 1970 Arts Council Report, *The Theatre Today,* also enumerated reasons for the decline in touring companies, which by then were 'a rarity'.[5] Alongside the 'disgraceful backstage conditions' and dilapidated interiors, the result of years of lack of investment by owners, television was blamed for capturing the audience and for the growing reluctance of actors to leave the capital for any length of time. Increasing costs in transport and labour were not helping either, and nor was the impact of the growing monopolisation of London-based theatre ownership, leaving local managers afflicted by 'a *malaise*', with no more status 'than a caretaker' and little scope or incentive.[6] Such was the state of affairs that Hugh Jenkins MP argued in 1967 that '[t]ouring theatre as such died years ago and will never come back again'.[7]

Despite such dire warnings, 1966 seemed to start out optimistically for Howard and Wyndham, despite the national picture. In February the *Illustrated Liverpool News* announced that the company was continuing with its policy that 'nothing is too good for our audiences', providing details of the annual Christmas spectacle (that year to feature Dora Bryan) which would introduce English audiences for the first time to a new Living Screen technique, which included live actors jumping out of the screen on to the stage and merging back into the film action.[8] However, behind the scenes, things were not quite so rosy. Howard and Wyndham was starting to consider getting out of the theatre business, having made a loss of over £10,000 the previous year, and was looking to sell the theatres it had interests in to local authorities.[9] Combined with the problem of finding good shows and 'star attractions', the company was also saddled with theatres that desperately needed investment in their infrastructure. Further problems were accruing, with growing numbers of once-commercial theatres being taken on by local councils as civic theatres to prevent their closure. In the process, these attracted funding from the Arts Council and became exempt from paying Selective Entertainment Tax, which cost Howard and Wyndham over £3,000 annually. In Liverpool, the corporation had taken out a 21-year lease on the Neptune in 1967, and then spent further money on refurbishing it.[10] In response to this state of affairs, Howard and Wyndham announced plans to seek permission to redevelop its six theatres, a proposal which *The Stage* thought might mean that the company was looking to sell these city-centre sites to developers or to rebuild smaller theatres on the sites, incorporated into office or shopping blocks.[11] In reality, Howard and Wyndham was developing other plans, although the threat of a sale to developers always lurked in the background. In June 1966 Peter Donald, the chairman of the company, announced a plan to save the Royal Court. The company offered to sell the lease to the council for £300,000. In

Curtain call for Margot Fonteyn on her last visit to the Royal Court, 23 February 1970 (Mirrorpix)

Nearly 1,000 children auditioned to be Ken Dodd Diddymen for the show that opened on 23 December 1970. (Mirrorpix)

return, it would rent the theatre back between September and April, running it as usual. In the summer months it suggested that the council rented it to amateurs and filled it with classical and experimental plays or music to be provided with help from subsidised companies. To support this, Donald argued that the Arts Council should provide extra money for all major cities and that companies such as the National Theatre should spend four to six weeks a year in each major city. In what could be seen as a gesture of goodwill, Howard and Wyndham spent £15,000 on extending the Court's scene dock to enable the theatre to take in larger touring productions, with the promise of more money to be spent on the infrastructure if the deal went ahead. However, Donald was also quick to note that this did not mean there were any guarantees for the future, and behind the offer was the veiled threat of closure and sale if the Arts Council and local authority did not help. 'All of our sites', Donald warned, 'are bang in the middle of big cities. I have quite a list of people keen to have details and to get on with the job of redevelopment.'[12] The council considered the plan and then turned it down flat. As the leader of the council said, the suggestion that the council should subsidise the theatre and that Howard and Wyndham would get the profits from the best months while the council stood the losses in the summer was not tempting.[13]

In 1967 Howard and Wyndham tried another approach to making a profit, applying for permission to organise bingo during the summer months at four of its theatres (including the Royal Court). Keeping the theatre closed during those months cost the company £10,000 and this was the only way it could see of keeping the building open. By 1968, despite a summer season of bingo, things still looked bleak. A letter to *The Stage* was furious about the appalling record of Howard and Wyndham in Liverpool, listing three months of variety, a recast version of a West End success, followed by 'more deplorable productions' as the best it could offer the city. This was alleviated a little by a pre-West End show, but things had rapidly gone downhill again with a week of amateur productions and South West Dance, to be followed by three months of bingo.[14] In an attempt to rectify the problem of programming, Howard and Wyndham appointed John Neville, the artistic director of Nottingham Playhouse, to help with play choices, but little seemed to change and the company was still intent on off-loading all of its regional theatres.[15] By this time it had sold the King's Theatre in Glasgow to the local council and negotiations were underway with Edinburgh City Council for the King's Theatre. Manchester Opera House was up for sale for £400,000 freehold. Newcastle Theatre Royal had a freehold price tag of £300,000. The company had also turned down an offer of £400,000 for the Glasgow Alhambra, determined to get half a million pounds for it.[16] The Royal Court, the only leasehold theatre in Howard and Wyndham's possession, now had a lower asking price of £250,000. By September the pressure was rising and the theatre faced its first real prospect of closure. Howard and Wyndham announced that *Cinderella*, to open on Boxing Day, was likely to be the last production. There had been no response from the council to its reduced price and it was angered that the council was ignoring it while 'helping tiny little theatres that did not mean anything'. As a result, the company was now looking at the options of either converting the theatre entirely into a bingo hall (the company that had run the summer bingo season made a profit of £4,000) or redevelopment, discussing the possibility that the theatre could become a restaurant-cum-cabaret.[17] The council did finally respond by not permitting the company to run the theatre as a year-round bingo operation, possibly encouraged in its decision by a petition against this signed by 30,000 people including Ken Dodd, Margot Fonteyn and Kenneth More. Somehow the theatre carried on into 1969 without closing, but increasingly with a sense of living on borrowed time.

By May 1970, with no movement from Liverpool City Council, the Royal Court again faced closure. Such was the lack of audience for the theatre that the appearance of Margot Fonteyn and the Royal Ballet in February was far from full even for their one-night appearance. When she had last performed at the Royal Court in 1968 the police had been called to clear the way for her after the performance.[18] Making a speech following her performance in *Lady Frederick*, Margaret Lockwood urged the audience that they needed to do more than sign a petition in order to save 'this lovely, lovely theatre'.[19] Howard and Wyndham estimated that it had lost £35,000 in the previous year and now offered two suggestions to save the theatre, both involving subsidy from the council.[20] The first was a repetition of its offer for the council to buy back the theatre and the second suggested that the council make a direct grant of £15,000 a year against losses. Alongside these proposals, a Save the Royal Court campaign had a third idea. Headed by Neil Tierney, it had been looking to businesses for donations to establish an endowment fund. But a threat to close on 16 May loomed large. Donald could no longer 'afford to keep the Royal Court open at [his own] expense', and he had told Tierney that if no help arrived by that date, he would rip out the seats and use it as a warehouse for scenery.[21] The deadline duly arrived, and with no solution in sight, following a week of *The King and I* performed by Wallasey Operatic Society, the doors closed. In July a Howard and Wyndham spokesperson said that he did not visualise the company reopening the theatre and rumours abounded that it had leased it to EMI.[22]

However, the doors did open again in October when Kenneth More, a patron of the Royal Court Theatre Club, appeared in a pre-West End tour of Rattigan's *The Winslow Boy*. This was followed by the New Shakespeare Company in *Othello*, D'Oyly Carte Opera and the musical *Hair*. The saving of the theatre at the time was attributed to Ken Dodd. This was a feat that was to recur a number of times over the coming years, as Dodd continued to come to the rescue, for example with his 1974 world-breaking 'marathon mirthquake', which gained him an entry in the *Guinness Book of Records* as the world's longest non-stop joke teller at three hours and six minutes. At Christmas 1970 the show to save the theatre was *The Ken Dodd Laughter Spectacular*, which ran until March 1971, a period of time that allowed all the parties involved to find an alternative to shutting the doors again.

The first 'solution' was found by Howard and Wyndham which, with help from the council and the Merseyside Arts Association (MAA), equipped the theatre with a projector so that it could offer a summer film season. More significantly, discussions with MAA and the Arts Council brought a solution to keep the theatre open for three years. This came in the form of the Dramatic and Lyric Theatre Association (DALTA), which offered Arts Council support for 'quality' touring productions.[23] It was guaranteeing a five-week spring and autumn season each year and the tours included high-profile companies such as Glyndebourne Touring

Actress Gail Grainger, who played Shirley Hughes in *The Man Most Likely To...* at the Royal Court, and co-star Leslie Phillips ran round the theatre clad only in a bikini and a dressing gown – for a bet, 8 November 1971. (Mirrorpix)

Opera, London Contemporary Dance and Scottish Opera (all performing at the Royal Court for the spring 1971 season), and the Oxford Playhouse Company, the Mermaid Theatre and the 69 Theatre Company (all at the Royal Court in the autumn of 1971). The companies would bring big names with them to attract audiences, which in 1971 included Michael Redgrave and Tom Courtenay, the latter playing in the Royal Court's perennial favourite, *Charley's Aunt*. Howard and Wyndham would then take on programming for the rest of the year, which would include the profitable Christmas show and films or bingo in the summer. It felt as though a solution had been found and, as *The Stage* noted, 'few theatres can have experienced so great a change of fortune in a few months'. In its eyes, the 'threat of closure which had hung over it for so long has virtually disappeared'.[24] Howard and Wyndham nationally could boast of a profit of £49,701 in 1971 (as opposed to a loss of over £52,000 the previous year) and plans were in development for new ventures at the Court, including Sunday evening events in order to make better use of the building.

However, the very plan to keep the theatre afloat through the DALTA tours was also inevitably going to undermine Howard and Wyndham's profits and its profile. The financial arrangements were less favourable to the theatre than commercial agreements and Iles argues that it also marginalised the theatres, with the Arts Council employing separate marketing managers in bigger cities, leaving the theatres as little more than 'passive garages' where productions were parked.[25] The arrangements also impacted on commercial touring companies which were still expected to provide the majority of weeks in the theatre. They not only faced competition from repertory companies but now also from subsidised, Arts Council-backed rivals on their own touring circuit. By aiding a minority of companies in any one year, the Arts Council kept down the general level of guarantees, thus making it increasingly hard for the commercial companies to keep going except on the routine level of low-cost comedies. *She Was Only an Admiral's Daughter* (October 1972), starring Leslie Crowther, attracted an audience of over 4,000 during the week but still made a loss.[26] Without wishing to hurt or damage the commercial producers and without trying to impair the circuit and its theatres, the Arts Council nevertheless succeeded in doing both.[27]

As the agreement with the Arts Council over DALTA tours limped on and with no movement from the council, by 1976 the Royal Court was facing what looked like a much more terminal situation. Howard and Wyndham was still trying to push the local authority into buying the lease back. The price for this was by now reduced to £150,000, but the council was still refusing. Howard and Wyndham was once again announcing diminishing audiences and growing losses. With no movement on local subsidy, it announced the closure of the theatre following a sell-out visit from Charles Laurence's comedy *My Fat Friend*, starring John Inman and Anne Stallybrass. It was really starting to look like the end of an era. Behind the scenes, however, people had not quite given up. A flurry of meetings between Howard and Wyndham, the Arts Council, local councils and the newly formed Theatre Trust raised small glimmers of hope. Locally, the Royal Court Theatre and Arts Trust was set up, headed by Sir Harry Livermore, who, among other things, was chair of the MAA. As in many theatres around the country, those involved sat with bated breath as Peter Plouviez, the General Secretary of Equity, appealed to the Prime Minister to intervene to save seven provincial theatres, including the Royal Court, that were in imminent danger of being sold, a feat he thought could be achieved with £5 million from the government.[28]

The Royal Court in the mid-1970s was unfortunate in being caught in the middle of both local and national problems. Faced with a rapid decline in commercial touring, the biggest push from everybody was for local authorities to take on the theatres, but in many cases, as with Liverpool, they were reluctant to do so, unwilling to take on new burdens at times of financial stringency. As the *Liverpool Echo* noted,

The Royal Court left in the middle of a building site during the rebuilding of St John's market, n.d. (Liverpool Record Office)

'ratepayers must be wondering, at a time when the belt has been tightened so much it hurts, what advantage to them buying the Royal Court will be'. As a prime city-centre site, it might be understandable if the council was buying it to develop it, but 'when a professional management cannot make the theatre pay, there is little hope of local government making a foray into the world of commercial show business and having box office success'.[29] By the mid-1970s there was little money to spare in a city that was 'ravaged by the fallout from severe global economic recession'.[30] The port had been affected by fundamental changes in international transportation and trading links. The profitable transatlantic passenger lines had inevitably suffered from the growth of air travel and were, in common with manufacturing and population, gradually moving south. The transportation of goods was changed

While appearing in *All for Mary*, Sally Thomsett chained herself to the theatre in protest against its threatened closure in May 1976. (Liverpool Record Office)

through the introduction of containerisation, reducing the need for dock labour, whose numbers fell from 11,500 in 1967 to 5,200 by 1979. At the same time, Liverpool discovered that it was now on the wrong side of the country, as the decline in trade with Commonwealth countries was replaced by the rise of the EEC. From handling 23 per cent of Britain's manufacturing exports at the end of the 1960s, by the end of the 1970s Liverpool dealt with only 9 per cent.[31] The decline of the port had been anticipated by planners and politicians in the 1960s who had worked to attract manufacturing industry, but manufacturing 'did not stick to the script it had been given' and restructuring and rationalisation took its toll.[32] Between 1971 and 1984 manufacturing employment in the city more than halved as 95,000 jobs disappeared, and male employment in the region fell by some 53 per cent. As the 1980 report *Merseyside in Crisis* noted,

> [u]nemployment levels have invariably been twice the national average ... but over the last few years the rate of unemployment in the Merseyside area has risen to such an extent that by 1978 it was 11.7 per cent, the highest in England. This year it is around 12.3 per cent – 100,000 people out of work. One-in-eight. A threefold increase over the last ten years...[33]

The report went on to suggest that if the government's own estimates of 40 per cent unemployment were anything to go by, Liverpool was looking set to become the Jarrow of the 1980s. Across the city, talk was of the closure of plants from Dunlop and Plessey to Courtaulds and Meccano. In 1978, as the Royal Court was asking the council for money, the closure of British Leyland's Speke factory was announced with the loss of 3,750 jobs. As jobs went, the people and the city suffered:

> Seemingly everywhere stood empty factories, boarded shop fronts and tracts of wilderness as some 15 per cent of property in Liverpool was either derelict or vacant by the end of the 1970s. From a peak census population of 855,000 in 1931, the numbers living in Liverpool had halved by the 1960s as people streamed out of a city that seemed to be in its death throes.[34]

In this context, one more empty city-centre building or its conversion into a bingo hall or a skateboarding park was not top of the council's priorities.

There was one more local problem facing the theatre, a product not of the 1970s downturn, but of the 'confident wave of urban renewal' of the 1960s.[35] Plans for the redevelopment of the city centre had been drawn up in 1942 and 1953, but provision of housing following the destruction of the Second World War had taken priority and it wasn't until 1959 that wholesale plans began to emerge. The developers Ravensheft proposed the total remodelling of St John's market into a much more modern precinct, and this was joined in 1962 by Graeme Shankland's proposals for inner-city motorways. By 1965 plans were afoot for 'an even better city in which to live, to work and to play', complete with futuristic-sounding high-level pedestrian walkways.[36] Much of this impacted directly on the Royal Court. The building of the new precinct left the theatre isolated next to a building site until the new St John's precinct was opened in 1971, which created its own problems, as this letter to the manager suggests:

> Dear Sir
>
> An explanation is required of the disgusting appearance of a rat in the Grand Circle during the second act of *H.M.S. Pinafore* on 22nd November 1967. One does not expect to encounter vermin in a theatre and your assurance that steps will be taken to eradicate this menace before I come again, on Saturday, will be appreciated.
>
> Yours faithfully
>
> G.W.[37]

As the manager explained in response, while the management was doing everything in its power to rectify the infestation of vermin, theirs was the only building left standing in a huge redevelopment centre which made it vulnerable to attacks.

To make matters worse, the new St John's led to the truncation of Great Charlotte Street, depriving the theatre of one of its frontages, which was now abutted by the shopping centre. At the same time, the city council took the opportunity to reshape the 'cobbled and lamplit' Queen Square and, in particular, to rid it of the fruit and vegetable market that had become increasingly neglected after the war, creating problems, in the eyes of the council, with litter and obstructions. The process of 'renovation' included the destruction of all the Georgian buildings surrounding the square, including the Stork Hotel, 'where white jacketed waiters and lace-capped waitresses served pre and post show cocktails and coffees', and which was a regular advertiser in the theatre's programmes from before the war.[38] It also saw the flattening of pubs, including the Magic Clock, the Roebuck and the Dart, which had been the focus of Liverpool's unofficial gay community since the 1940s.[39] The last stalls left the square in 1967 and Roe Street became the site of the new bus station. The proposed Civic Building which was to have been part of the Queen Square development was, like many of the proposals, never built and the site became a car park. Added together, these changes both removed facilities that the theatre's clientele had been using and left the theatre physically isolated and hard to access.

But the problems facing the theatre were far from being merely local. The Royal

The theatre converted for the summer bingo season

Court was at the heart of a national crisis for the theatre, a crisis noted at the start of this chapter – the death throes of commercial touring. By 1969 closures were making 'the country outside London a depressed and distressed area'.[40] The arguments were played out on the pages of the national press, arguments that outlined not just the bigger picture affecting the theatre but also the intransigent and sometimes aggressive approaches of the main parties involved in finding a solution, and in the mid-1970s the Royal Court found itself a player on the national stage. A leader in *The Times* on 7 July 1977, headed 'The Dark Theatres of the Provinces', outlined the wider picture, beginning by restating the already well-rehearsed story:

> No field of the arts has changed more in the last generation than the provincial theatre. The professional companies touring with plays aspiring to a West End success or riding on the glory of one have almost disappeared. So have many of the theatres whose worm-eaten boards they trod.

It continued by pointing to the spate of new theatre buildings and the growth of local repertory companies subsidised by the Arts Council, and then commented that those in danger were

> [o]f a different type. Dating mostly from the earlier period, they are large, imposing, expensive to run and difficult to fill. Usually, they do not have acting companies of their own and they often do not command the loyalty of a large body of regular theatre goers. They have survived on the diminishing returns from revues and pop concerts; even the pantomime season is not what it was. Their very size is often inimical to modern plays and modern styles of acting. To that extent they are anachronisms.

However, without the large old theatres, the scope for touring would be restricted. The key argument came at the end of the article:

> At this point the first priority must be to ensure that no theatre is demolished or irrevocably consigned to other uses unless alternative facilities for large-scale touring exist ... It is the buildings themselves that matter, even if they have to remain dark for a time. Nobody outside the capital cities is likely to put up a theatre with 2,000 seats and an orchestra pit ever again.[41]

Howard and Wyndham, named in the article as one of the owners who were keen to get rid of these buildings, responded angrily, arguing that the future of provincial touring was not endangered by 'rapacious property developers' but 'by a long-standing lack of any interest in or cohesive policy towards ensuring their future' from either the Arts Council or the local authorities. By this point, the company still owned three theatres (alongside the Royal Court, these were the Opera House in Manchester and the New Theatre in Oxford); all were at risk and none had been commercially viable for some time. At a recent meeting with the Arts Council, the company had been told by the chairman that the Council was 'uninterested and unwilling to participate in the future of the Royal Court', and it was convinced that if the local authorities in Manchester, Oxford and Liverpool had followed similar policies to the others it had been dealing with, the future of all three theatres would now be secure. The knives were out for Liverpool in particular, which had contributed substantial funds 'to new ventures catering to minority tastes such as the Playhouse, Everyman and the Neptune'. Having pointed the finger, the company ended by warning rather ominously that a 'closed theatre soon becomes an eyesore and even a danger'. If no one wanted to run them, then 'surely they should be despatched with dignity'.[42]

This bought a stinging response from Roy Shaw, secretary general of the Arts Council, who pointed out that it was in fact the Arts Council's *The Theatre Today* report of 1970 that had first drawn attention to the plight of touring theatres, arguing that if they were to stay open 'the only hope for nearly all of them is … to go municipal'. The report had also provided the foundation for the Council's subsequent policy of financing a national touring scheme in the shape of DALTA, and Shaw stated that the money supporting this had risen from £200,000 in 1970–71 to £3 million in 1977–78. The Council had also provided over £300,000 of capital funding for improvements in facilities, and he suggested that it had 'offered to make a substantial sum for this purpose' available to the Royal Court, but neither the local authority nor Howard and Wyndham 'could agree at the time on terms'. In his view, several councils, including Liverpool, had 'so far declined to assume' their responsibility for the theatres, but he had not 'lost hope' that they could be 'persuaded to play the leading role in acquiring and maintaining' the buildings. If they failed to do so, they would be responsible for depriving the public in those cities of the opportunity of seeing 'the productions of the national lyric and drama companies, not to speak of the pantomime seasons and light entertainment which are part of the tradition of theatregoing in this country'.[43] Sir Harry Livermore responded by leaping to the defence of the city council, which had been in discussion with Howard and Wyndham since the late 1960s. The issue for him was Howard and Wyndham; the 'price being asked was so high and the conditions attached so unfavourable that it was impossible for the city council to agree a satisfactory solution' and it had now withdrawn from negotiations.[44]

While this was all unfolding, another serious problem had arisen closer to home. The Empire Theatre was also in trouble and now arguments abounded about which of the two theatres should or could be saved. The Empire could host the largest touring shows. The Royal Court, however, was a more economic option for smaller touring shows. Most people agreed that 'Liverpool, like other cities, hasn't room for two theatres'.[45] In the end, following debates, discussions, arguments and reports, both the Arts Council and Merseyside County Council (MCC) came down in favour of the Empire, and in April 1978 a deal was struck. As the MCC moved towards acquisition of a 50-year lease for the theatre at a token rent, the Arts Council offered help to meet the £350,000 refurbishment costs. Things were now looking even more bleak for the Royal Court. With the county council now committed to the Empire

Ken Dodd was on hand to serve soup to those queueing up for tickets for his show that would reopen the once-doomed theatre, 20 October 1978. (Mirrorpix)

and the city council still struggling to make the Neptune pay, there was definitely no money left. The theatre had now been closed for over two years and despite the Theatre Club keeping an eye on the state of the building, things could not carry on as they were for much longer. Even Howard and Wyndham was desperately reducing the price to try and tempt a buyer; the Royal Court was now available for £90,000.

Into the breach stepped the Royal Court Theatre and Arts Trust, headed by Sir Harry Livermore and numbering Ken Dodd and Harold Wilson among its members. After brokering a deal to pay Howard and Wyndham just £70,000, the theatre was now owned by a charity 'on behalf of the people of Liverpool', and excitement grew as the theatre looked forward to reopening for the first time since May 1976 with *The Ken Dodd Laughter Show.*[46] With the help of money from Granada Television, an interest-free loan from the council and donations from local industry, commerce and individuals, things moved forward. When tickets went on sale in late October, queues formed from early morning. Ken Dodd was at the box office when it opened at 10 a.m. to sell the first ticket to Sir Harry Livermore and then to keep the crowds

Ken Dodd accepted a special Doddy flag, marking his residence in the theatre for the rest of the show to celebrate its record-breaking run in Liverpool, 16 February 1965. (Mirrorpix)

outside the theatre happy by cracking jokes, signing autographs and handing out hot soup to keep people warm as they waited. The performance on 21 December 1978 was ‘a rip-roaring, emotional, VIP-studded’ evening, and the theatre echoed again to Ken Dodd’s ‘inexhaustible supply of quips’. He was

> on home ground, knee-deep in chip buttys and scouse with the mention of such locals as Icky and the Fire-Bobby and Nellie Wetlegs to raise the roof … the gags crackle like lightning … it was pure delight to see the indefatigable Doddy working his audience with such joy.[47]

In Ken Dodd style, it seemed at one time as if the show was ‘in danger of becoming a two-day event’ and the curtain went down just before midnight.[48] The reopening looked promising and, with heavy bookings, the show was extended until March and was followed by a raft of what should have been popular successes, including Fiona Richmond in *Yes, We Have No Pyjamas*, Leslie Phillips in Frederick Lonsdale’s *Canaries Sometimes Sing* and Richard Harris and Leslie Darbon’s *Who Goes Bare*, billed as *Fawlty Towers* without the clothes.

However, as the *Liverpool Echo* had warned on the eve of Ken Dodd’s reopening, ‘it would be foolish to think that the going will be easy’, and despite all the fanfares, within six months the theatre was once again closed.[49] Repairs to the building had cost £50,000, eating away the Trust’s funds. Box office returns had not been high enough to meet the running costs and ‘attendance on many occasions had been lamentably poor’.[50] There had been criticism from the public and in the daily press about the state of the theatre and the quality of the product on show; *The Stage* reported that the *Liverpool Echo* had quoted audiences saying that the theatre ‘smelt like a dusty museum’ and was offering ‘entertainment on a shoe string’, with tatty supporting acts.[51] As Philip Richards wrote when reviewing *Blithe Spirit* (May 1979), the streets outside the theatre were deserted, the seats inside were generally empty, the theatre was cold and the audience that was there was quiet.[52] The doors were closed in early July 1979, almost exactly six months after the triumphal reopening, and the Trust made a plea to the council for £160,000 from the government’s fund for Inner Area Aid for refurbishment and to operate as a subsidy for running the theatre. It was all to no avail and it began to look as if this might be the end of the Royal Court.

However, in what seemed to have become a long-running Royal Court survival story, the 1970s ended on a brighter note. The theatre reopened briefly in November 1979 for three sell-out concerts by Wings. Paul McCartney had heard of its plight and started his tour there, handing over a cheque to the Trust for £5,000. And as the decade drew to a close rumours circulated about a mysterious new Irish buyer.

Notes

1 Iles, 'Issues in Theatrical Management', 89.
2 Ibid., 89.
3 Ibid., 90.
4 Ibid., 91.
5 Arts Council of Great Britain, *The Theatre Today: The Report of the Arts Council Theatre Enquiry 1970* (London: Arts Council, 1970), 13.
6 Ibid., 13.
7 *The Stage*, 14 December 1967, 1.
8 Undated cutting, *Illustrated Liverpool News*, February 1966, Liverpool Central Library.
9 Against this loss, Howard and Wyndham estimated that it held theatre property to the value of £2 million.
10 Ackroyd, *Liverpool Stage*, 96.
11 *The Stage*, 2 June 1966, 1; 21 January 1965, 5.
12 *Daily Post*, 23 June 1966.
13 *Liverpool Echo*, 10 December 1968.
14 *The Stage*, 9 May 1968, 10.
15 *Liverpool Echo*, 1 May 1968.
16 The Alhambra was closed in 1969 and with no purchaser found it was demolished in 1971.
17 *Daily Post*, 14 December 1968.
18 *Daily Post*, 21 February 1970.
19 *Daily Post*, 12 March 1970.
20 Nationally, it had lost £610,000 in the first eight months of the financial year, a loss compounded by a disastrous attempt to team up with the BBC to show lavishly mounted productions. The agreement was terminated with a total loss of £853,000. *Daily Post*, 7 April 1970; *The Stage*, 20 March 1969, 9.
21 *Daily Post*, 12 March 1970; 19 March 1970.
22 *Liverpool Echo*, 9 July 1970.
23 DALTA had been established by the Royal Opera House and Sadler's Wells to prevent clashes in their touring dates outside London and had later been joined by the National Theatre and the Royal Shakespeare Company. The Arts Council's report *The Theatre Today* suggested that an enlarged version of DALTA (incorporating more companies and more money) might help stem the closure of regional theatres (15–16).
24 *The Stage*, 30 December 1971, 14.
25 Iles, 'Issues in Theatrical Management', 94.
26 *Liverpool Echo*, 7 December 1972.
27 Elsom, *Post War British Theatre*, 139.
28 *The Times*, 7 July 1977, 4. These theatres were the Opera House and the Palace in Manchester, the New Oxford, and the Hippodromes in Bristol and Birmingham as well as the Liverpool Empire.
29 *Liverpool Echo*, 14 October 1976.
30 Jon Murden, '"City of Change and Challenge": Liverpool since 1945', in John Belchem (ed.), *Liverpool 800: Culture, Character and History* (Liverpool: Liverpool University Press, 2006), 428.
31 Ibid., 430.
32 Ibid., 431.
33 Merseyside Socialist Research Group, *Merseyside in Crisis* (Liverpool: Merseyside Socialist Research Group, 1980), 10.
34 Murden, 'City of Change and Challenge', 429.
35 Ibid., 399.
36 Ibid., 400.
37 Liverpool City Archives; unsorted correspondence.
38 *Liverpool Echo*, 13 October 2001, 14.
39 The Dart was located next to the Playhouse and its site became the theatre's 1960s extension.
40 *The Stage*, 18 September 1969, 1.
41 *The Times*, 7 July 1977, 17.
42 *The Times*, 14 July 1977, 15.
43 *The Times*, 18 July 1977, 13.
44 *The Times*, 21 July 1977, 3.
45 *Daily Post*, 5 July 1977.
46 *The Stage*, 4 January 1979, 4.
47 *The Stage*, 11 January 1979, 27.
48 *Liverpool Echo*, 22 December 1978, 3.
49 *Liverpool Echo*, 21 December 1978, 6.
50 *The Stage*, 11 October 1979, 1.
51 *The Stage*, 28 June 1979, 1.
52 *Liverpool Echo*, 8 May 1979, 5.

1972

25 January	*Peter Pan*	J. M. Barrie	with Dawn Addams
8 February	*The Beheading*	Thomas Muschamp	world premiere with Virginia McKenna
27 February	*Startime*		with Freddie Starr
6 March	*Those Were the Days*		variety
13 March	*The Marquise*	Noel Coward	with Glynis Johns
20 March	*The Vagabond King*		Walterloo and Crosby Amateur Operatic Society
DALTA Spring Season			
27 March	Royal Ballet		programme included *O.W.*, *Lady and the Fool* and *Les Patineurs*
4 April	Scottish Opera		programme included *The Barber of Seville*, *Cosi Fan Tutti* and *Die Walkure*
10–12 April	*Uncle Vanya*	Chekhov	Welsh Theatre Company
13–15 April	*A Pig in a Poke*	George Feydeau	Welsh Theatre Company; farce
17 April	*Forget-Me-Not-Lane*	Peter Nichols	
24 April	Kathakali		Indian dance
1 May	*The Boy Friend*		Wallasey Amateur Operatic Society
15 May	*Relative Values*	Noel Coward	with Margaret Lockwood and Patricia Hayes
23 May	*The Mating Game*	Robin Hawdon	premiere of comedy with Terry Scott and Julia Lockwood
26 May	Midnight Fantasia		charity evening with stars including Ken Dodd and Terry Scott

29 May	family film season, including *Fantasia*, *Thoroughly Modern Milly*, *Romeo and Juliet*		
14 June	*Romeo and Juliet*	Royal Ballet	with Margot Fonteyn and Rudoph Nureyev (one performance)
DALTA Autumn Season			
25 September	London Festival Ballet		productions included *Swan Lake*
2 October	*She Was only an Admiral's Daughter*	Harold Brooke and Kay Bannerman	with Leslie Crowther and Brian Rix
10 October	Glyndebourne Touring Opera		productions included *La Calisto*, *La Boheme* and *Die Entfurung*
15 October	Charity Gala Variety Evening		including Millicent Martin and David Nixon
16 October	*The Sound of Music* (film)		
22 October	The Pentangle		one night
24 October	*Stages*	London Contemporary Dance Theatre	
30 October	*Death on Demand*	William Fairchild	world premiere of suspense thriller
6 November	Gilbert and Sullivan	D'Oyly Carte	two weeks
12 November	*Strictly Motown*		return
20 November	Welsh National Opera		productions included *Rigoletto*, *Don Giovanni*, *Billy Budd* and *Nabucco*
26 November	Ralph McTell		
27 November	*Norman, Is That You?*	Ronald Clark and Sam Brobick	comedy with Alfred Marks

Howard & Wyndham's ROYAL COURT LIVERPOOL
Telephone: 051-709 5163/4
HOWARD & WYNDHAM LIMITED EST. 1895 H&W
ROBERT LUFF Holdings LTD.
(in assoc. with GEORGE MITCHELL)
Present
THE
NEW
£60,000 PRODUCTION
TV's FASTEST SPECTACULAR
BLACK & WHITE MINSTREL SHOW
OF 1973
BASED ON THE POPULAR B.B.C. T.V. SERIES
PROGRAMME: TEN PENCE

11 December	*Midsummer Night's Dream*	Shakespeare	Peter Brook's production with Patrick Stewart as Theseus/Oberon; special visit during world tour
18 December	Black and White Minstrels		ten-week season
23 December	*Toad of Toad Hall*	A. A. Milne	matinees

Christmas, 1970s

1970 *Ken Dodd Laughter Spectacular*

> Ken Dodd promised Liverpool a good show this Christmas and he has kept his word. On December 23 the *Ken Dodd Laughter Spectacular* opened at the Royal Court to a packed house of Doddy enthusiasts. The laughter is all his whether as Lord Mayor of Knotty Ash, circus ring master or stand-up comedian. His sustained clowning is a virtuoso performance … The children revel in the Diddy puppets, the miniature Diddy Men, the magic of Toreno and the fire eater in the magician's cave – one of the show's best scenes. (*The Stage*, 14 January 1971, 26)

1971 *Cinderella*

> It looks a safe bet that Liverpool's two major shows, which open next week, will have excellent seasons even if they don't break box-office records. Terry Jones, manager of the Empire, and Richard Gibson, of the Royal Court, which has a double-top billing with Vince Hill and Barbara Windsor in a £50,000 new production of Cinderella, both report above-average bookings … Vivacious little Barbara Windsor said, 'They've changed the old idea that Cinders had two ugly sisters and written the parts for Ann Emery and me as being a couple of naughty schemers instead.' (*Liverpool Echo*, 17 December 1971, 8)[1]

1972 *Toad of Toad Hall* (matinees)

> There's nothing particularly seasonal about Toad's eccentric exploits with his motor car, but it's an engaging enough tale and characters such as Badger, Water Rat and Mole have enough appeal to keep most youngsters spellbound for an afternoon of the school holidays. All the sadder to report then that the production at the Royal Court is not the best introduction to the magic of theatre. The costumes and settings are adequate but the whole production has a luck-lustre quality … Needless to say there's plenty to keep the kids amused in the way of a panto horse, a tree that walks and a whole wood full of assorted small furry animals. (*Liverpool Echo*, 27 December 1972, 5)

Singer Vince Hill as Buttons and Barbara Windsor as as one of Cinderella's 'wicked' sisters, 14 December 1971 (Mirrorpix)

1972 *The Black and White Minstrel Show* (evenings)

> There's little point in being critical about *The Black and White Minstrels*. Like Christmas pudding you can either take them or you can't. The main thing to be said about the present show at the Royal Court is that the ingredients seem to be right. And it's certainly served with a flourish. If there is something bizarre for instance about a band of blackfaced minstrels strutting about a Viennese ballroom in aristocratic splendour, the fans don't seem to be worried. (*Liverpool Echo*, 19 December 1972, 2)

1973 *Peter Pan*

> This year Peter returns to Liverpool lightly disguised as Anita Harris. And her only worry about playing the part is the thought of all the famous actresses who have worked in Never-never-land before her. At the Royal Court … the last Peter was Dawn Addams in January, 1972. The very first time Peter Pan flew in through the nursery window of the Darlings' house was in 1904 … In

Liverpool two years later Pauline Chase played the role, and the story goes that J.M. Barrie – the creator *of Peter Pan* – came here to see her. (*Liverpool Echo,* 17 December 1973, 8)[2]

1974 *The Ken Dodd Laughter Spectacular*

He has jokes for everyone delivered with consummate skill, superb sense of timing and the rapidity of gunfire. The Knotty Ash supremo tickles those chuckle muscles inside the ribcage and brings tidal waves of laughter rolling in … The fact that so many people can enjoy such an evening at the theatre makes laughter perhaps the most available (yet still the most precious) of human thermostats, It's a positive therapy. (*Liverpool Echo,* 21 December 1974, 9)

1975 *Aladdin*

After chuckling through three brilliant months of *Ken Dodd's Laughter Spectacular* last year, the Royal Court return to a pantomime format this Christmas. Millicent Martin, the talented lady best remembered for her song and dance routine in television's *That Was the Week That Was,* heads an obviously happy company who show the necessary zeal to cope with a theatre full of people. (*Liverpool Echo,* 24 December 1975, 12)

1976–77 closed

1978 ***Ken Dodd Laughter Show***

> The reopening night of Liverpool's Royal Court was a rip-roaring, emotional, VIP-studded success. Sir Harold Wilson was there, the Lord Mayor of Liverpool (Councillor Ruth Dean) was there and so were most of the City Council ... The show was opened by singer Mike Byrne who had augmented his own dance troupe, the Bare Essentials, by four more beauties to have an eight strong line-up ... Then on came the man himself – the Tycoon of the Treacle Wells, the King of the Diddymen, Ken Dodd. He struck up his usual and instantaneous rapport with the audience, and the mood was set for the rest of the show ... The second half introduced the Diddymen (and Ken Dodd is someone who can work with kids and come out in front!) ... Doddy was on stage for the majority of the show ... and on this opening night the show overran until just seconds before midnight, which was causing a few anxious looks from the MD ... The Ken Dodd magic has allowed the Royal Court Theatre to live again! (*Liverpool Echo*, 4 January 1979, 4)

1979 closed

Notes

1 The Empire pantomime was *Robinson Crusoe* with Marion Grimaldi.

2 The 1906 performance of *Peter Pan* in Liverpool was at the Shakespeare Theatre. Its first performance at the Royal Court was in 1916 when Eve Embury played the title role.

1979

22 March	*Dead on Nine*	Jack Popplewell	comedy thriller with Kenneth Farrington from *Coronation Street*
5 April	The Houghton Weavers		one night
7 April	David Essex		one night
12 April	Hinge and Bracket		one night
17 April	Scottish Ballet		10th Anniversary Spring Tour
23 April	*Yes, We Have No Pyjamas*	Andre Launey	'naughty' comedy with Fiona Richmond
24 and 25 April	*The Sooty Show*		matinees
30 April	*The Aspern Papers*	Henry James; adapted by Michael Redgrave	with Anne Stallybrass
7 May	*Blithe Spirit*	Noel Coward	
14 May	*The Wild Duck*	Henrik Ibsen	with T. P. Mckenna
21 May	*The Gingerbread Man*	book and music by David Wood	children's show from The Old Vic; matinees
21 May	*The Creeper*	Pauline Macauley	thriller with Bill Simpson from *Dr Finlay's Casebook*
28 May	*Who Goes Bare*	Richard Harris and Leslie Darbon	risqué comedy with *Confessions* star Robin Askwith
4 June	*Find the Lady*	Michael Pertwee	comedy murder mystery with Molly Sugden and Bill Pertwee
12 June	*Canaries Sometimes Sing*	Frederick Lonsdale	with Leslie Phillips
18 June	*The Duchess of Malfi*	John Webster	Triumph Theatre production with Janet Suzman and Ian McDiarmid
25 June	*Funny Peculiar*	Mike Stott	comedy
1 July	The Dooleys		one night
CLOSED			
25–27 November	Wings		

[m]any people carry such memories with them. Nights of jumping around in a dark, sweaty theatre, spilling drinks over each other and themselves, while some of the greatest bands we've ever seen (and some dreadful ones) lifted what was left at the time of the Royal Court's roof.

The rebuilt St John's Centre opened in 1971, depriving the theatre of its frontage on to Great Charlotte Street (Liverpool Record Office)

10 From Theatre to Music: The 1980s and 1990s

As it turned out, 1980 did dawn with a new owner for the Royal Court. An Isle of Man consortium, Douglas Entertainments Ltd, headed by Max Fine, purchased a 100-year lease for £110,000, to be paid in instalments. Fine was cagey about his plans, saying that while he would love to see the theatre alive, 'it has to be looked at from a business point of view'. They were hoping to have shows there but, being honest, 'the one-nighters and rock concerts pay the bills'.[1] Fine worked in property development and this was his first venture into the theatre business. He set up a subsidiary company, Douglas Entertainments (UK) Ltd, granting it a 37-year proportion of the lease, and set about looking for someone to run the theatre. Once again bingo looked as if it would be the likely winner. Mecca was interested, but after spending thousands of pounds on a feasibility study the company decided that Liverpool's city centre was too hostile an environment for its clients.[2] With no one else coming forward to run the theatre, Fine decided that he would have a go himself. He was in luck. The Empire, closed for redecoration, decided to use the Royal Court for an eight-week summer season, opening with *Brasil Tropicana* on

2 June 1980. The Rio de Janeiro carnival stage show, described as a 'Radio 2 disco version of *The Royal Hunt of the Sun*', heralded a successful summer which included sold-out performances of *Joseph and the Amazing Technicolor Dreamcoat* and Mary O'Malley's *Once a Catholic*.[3]

At the end of the season things were still looking bright for Fine, the Empire offering to work in collaboration with the Royal Court, using it as an overflow venue for shows it could not accommodate. Fine was being lauded as 'the only man in Britain to have re-opened a theatre single handedly and without subsidy at a time when even London's West End is experiencing its worst ever crisis'.[4] Richard Harris's *Outside Edge* (August 1980), a comedy about a suburban cricket team, found the theatre 'full to brimming', and 'the old theatre-going atmosphere of yesterday' seemed to have been reincarnated.[5] Success continued through the autumn and on to Christmas, with a mixture of theatre shows, including successful returns for O'Malley's play and *Joseph*, alongside concerts and films. Some outrage greeted *Oh Calcutta!* (November 1980), but overall the slightly eclectic mix of entertainments (which included Tangerine Dream, the Welsh comedian Max Boyce and Paddington Bear, and ended with a Christmas production of *Godspell*) seemed to be going well. So it was something of a shock when the start of 1981 brought news that the theatre had been bought by 'a Liverpool punk club'.[6]

In reality, Douglas Entertainment (UK) Ltd had been bought by Alan Knipe and Joe Beckett, who were at that time running Brady's, the renamed Eric's on Mathew Street, which had been closed during a drugs raid in April 1980. Like Fine, they had no theatre experience, having been taxi drivers before launching themselves into the music business, but they had organised a concert by Adam and the Ants at the Royal Court in November 1980 and thought it had real potential as a cabaret and rock venue. They took over in February 1981 and started out with the local comedian Tom O'Connor. He was to be followed through the year mostly by bands, and during 1980 they staged everyone from Sweet, Bow Wow Wow and the Selecter to Toyah, Whitesnake and the Clash. The Jam played a concert for the People's March for Jobs (April 1981) and the Court also catered for a different audience by programming acts such as Tommy Cooper, Freddie Starr and an Irish variety show. A surprise hit was the hypnotist Andrew Newton, who started out early in the year trying to break the record for the number of people hypnotised in the shortest time (his aim was for 17 people in 25 seconds), and who then settled into a highly popular series of Sunday performances throughout the year.

There were problems. The building was beset by costly glitches. Tudor Gates's play *Confession of a Murder* (February 1981) had to be cancelled after the heating failed. *The Faith Brown Variety Show* (March 1981) had to cancel two shows because of electrical failure. Steeleye Span (March 1981) found themselves and their equipment drowned when the sprinkler system went off without warning. The auditorium was flooded in August 1981 when vandals broke in and let off fire hydrants, causing the cancellation of a Siouxsie and the Banshees concert. Threatened cuts in evening and weekend train and bus services caused problems with audiences. And the Toxteth riots added to concerns for some that Liverpool city centre was a dangerous place to be. The road manager of Duran Duran phoned up to say that he did not want to risk his crew and half a million pounds' worth of equipment and had to be persuaded that it was all right, as did hundreds of people phoning up to see if the theatre was still open and if it was safe to come. The Court staged a charity concert in the wake of the riots for an injured taxi driver, but vetoed a performance later in the year by UB40, who were offering to pay the fines of some of the rioters.

The biggest problem was from competition in the city. On the opening night, the *Liverpool Echo* had noted that this marked the start of a 'fascinating behind the scenes battle in Liverpool's theatres, clubs and on the campus, to pull in the crowds in what looks like a "no-holds barred" contest'.[7] The biggest competitor for the Royal Court was the Empire, which since being taken on by the MCC had diversified, alongside opera and ballet, into concerts, hosting Echo and the Bunnymen, the Undertones, the Kinks and Barclay James Harvest in April and May 1981. However, all seemed to be going well for Knipe and Bennett, who announced a profit half way through the year despite receiving no help from the city council, which had not accepted their plea for a rates waiver or their request to set up a pavement café. By Christmas, however, everything started to unravel.

They had planned two Christmas shows. Mornings and afternoons were to be filled with the traditional pantomime *Snow White*. Evenings were given over to Ted Rogers from TV's quiz show *3-2-1* and his famous booby-prize partner, Dusty Bin, who was to be joined by local DJ Norman Thomas and ex-New Seeker Lyn Paul in what was promised as an all-round family show with competitions and prizes. Sales for both shows were good, but just days before Christmas Knipe and Bennett announced the immediate closure of the theatre. They had received a large VAT bill, they owed Fine money and they were in dispute with fuel suppliers, so there was no heating for the theatre. Hurriedly, a new home was found for *Snow White* at the Queen's Hall in Widnes. The cast of *Dusty Bin* packed up and left after just five shows. There was silence and much speculation over the Royal Court's future. Matters were made worse when the theatre was again flooded, along with many parts of the city, as a result of heavy snowfall followed by a quick thaw in January 1982. Throughout the first six months of 1982 the theatre remained closed amid rumours

The theatre's main façade, 1999

of liquidation and sale until, just as suddenly, in August Knipe announced that after several months of legal discussions, it was to reopen, which it did with the Associates on 18 September.

Within months, however, the future was once again uncertain. In April 1983 Knipe was citing ongoing problems with the lease and, with his partner Joe Beckett, the intention was to close in September of that year. This was prevented by the arrival of a new manager in the shape of Dave C.[8] At 24, he looked set to be the youngest theatre manager in the country, coming from a background in promoting gigs. He was promising a mix of big names and local acts and was particularly excited by the fact that the seats in the stalls had been taken out before the 1982 reopening, as it created 'the right kind of atmosphere'.[9] He was joined by Simon Geddes, who at 23 started out working in the box office but was over the next few years to become the theatre's driving force. Knipe maintained a backseat relationship with the Royal Court, still holding the lease from Douglas Entertainments. There were some bumps in the road ahead for him, including a spell in prison over Christmas 1996 for refusing to pay the rates, which he maintained were too high, but increasingly his interests lay elsewhere – promoting the hypnotist Andrew Newton and, later, taking on the management of Rafferty's Club. He was finally to part company with the Royal Court at the end of the decade, leaving Simon Geddes and his business partner Dave C. in charge.

Success as a Music Venue

For the next twenty years, under the guidance of Geddes, the Royal Court built on its reputation as the place to see bands, staging between 50 and 70 concerts a year. It was to become a leading venue in the music scene, playing host to an array of bands. One of its strengths was its eclecticism, offering everything from big names in decline, to local bands, to those who wanted to play Liverpool

Joe Strummer outside the Royal Court, 1982 (David Hynes)

PHIL McINTYRE PROMOTIONS
rtist
BEASTIE BOYS
enue
LIVERPOOL
CREW
LIVERPOOL
OPOLIS MUSIC PRESENT
HE CHRISTIANS
SUPPORT
rday, 7th November 1987
g 7.30
S STANDING
Retain This Portion
0473
ets Exchanged nor Money Refunded
eras or Recording Equipment
Programes sold only in the Theatre
ment reserve the right to refuse admission
Phil McIntyre by arrange
Outlaw Managem
Presents
JULIAN COP
Plus The Faith Bro
and Crazyhea
Thursday 30th Apr
7.30pm
STAL
00090
5.00 R.
RETAIN
Pogues + Gues
4th March 1988
TANDING
0325
ROYAL COURT THEATRE
LIVERPOOL
Doctor Feelgood
SUNDAY
JUNE 7
Evening 7.30
STALLS STANDING
£4.50 Advance £5.00 Door
№ 0005
Box Office Duplicate
McINT
ROMOTIO
ist
WET WET
enue
LIVERPO
CREW
oyal Court Theatre, Liverpool
A
verpool City Council Benefit
turday, 8th February, 1986
ening 7.30
LCONY
.00 (£1 Cost £5 Donation)
13
Ticket Exchanged nor Money Refu
Royal Court
LIVERPOOL
KSTAGE SECURITY
IGGY POP
18/6/87
ROYAL COURT THEATRE
LIVERPOOL
ZODIAC MINDWARP
SUNDAY
MARCH 13
Evening 7.30
STALLS STANDING
£5.00
№ 0113
To be given up
YAL COURT THEATRE
ERPOOL
E STRUMMER
IDAY
LY 15
ening 7.30
TALLS STANDING
.00
0609
be given up
MEAT LOAF
+ Special Guests SHOGUN
Thursday, 10th March 198
Evening 7.30
BALCONY
£8.00
L
23
No Tickets Exchanged nor Money Refund
No Cameras or Recording Equipment
ROYAL COURT THEATRE
LIVERPOOL
ROBERT PLANT
TUESDAY
MARCH 29
Evening 7.30
STALLS STANDING
£7.50
№ 1141
To be given up
ROYAL COU
LIVERPOO
THE BLOW
WEDNESD
APRIL 29
Evening 7.
STALLS ST
£5.00
№
To be given

but were put off by the all-seater Empire. Musically, the bands covered every contemporary musical genre, from punk to heavy metal by way of hip-hop, Goth and indie. A listing of those who played at the Court in those years is a roll call of all the big names across the decades – The Clash, The Jam, Echo and the Bunnymen, The Cure, REM, Gil Scott-Heron, Stereolab, The Smiths, Iggy Pop, David Bowie, the Charlatans, Killing Joke, Pete Wylie, The Specials, Blur, The Jesus and Mary Chain, Kraftwerk, The La's, Robbie Williams, Paul Young, the Cocteau Twins and Frankie Goes to Hollywood. To these should be added Ozzy Osbourne, Whitesnake, Showaddywaddy, Duran Duran, Def Leppard, Bauhaus and Tangerine Dream. Most famously, this period is remembered for the Beastie Boys riot in 1987 on the final date of their Licensed to Ill Tour, a night that ended after just 12 minutes with cans being thrown, the crowd being tear-gassed and the lead singer, Horowitz, being arrested. People blamed the band, the crowd and even the theatre's staff, and it has been seen both as a set-up by the band to build on their riotous, trouble-making reputation, and as an event provoked by the audience who turned the band's attitude back on them, happy in the aftermath to sing, 'We tamed the Beasties.'

However, while this has become a notorious incident, for everyone who went to the Court, who saw their first band there, or their favourite bands, or a band they had never heard of before, it became a mythic place and a place they felt at home. As Guy notes,

> [m]any people carry such memories with them. Nights of jumping around in a dark, sweaty theatre, spilling drinks over each other and themselves, while some of the greatest bands we've ever seen (and some dreadful ones) lifted what was left at the time of the Royal Court's roof.[10]

For many, the Court had a special, gritty atmosphere, as well as perfect acoustics. It was, as Dickie Felton remembered, 'like standing on the Kop for the very first time, it was a teenage discovery where I felt "this is where I belong" ... There was just something so special about the place from the Art Deco splendour to the spilt Stella.'[11] It had, according to the novelist (and at the time music writer involved in the setting up of Produce Records) Kevin Sampson, a 'tatty glamour and amphitheatre acoustics' that 'made for a wild and joyous atmosphere'.[12] It was variously described as 'a dirty, fantastic, old fashioned proper music venue' and as an 'ashtray of a venue, the smell of stale ale, stale bodies and cigarette smoke'.[13] On the right night, 'with the right band, it was a really special place. It was rough and ready like all the best venues' and on the best nights there was 'a really passionate crowd bouncing up and down on that huge sloping floor'.[14]

Interior, 2003

Perhaps inevitably, the venue seemed to 'come into its own when there was a local connection', as *NME* writer Kevin McManus recalled:

> The Coral and The Zutons had great nights, Elvis Costello loved playing there … Some of my favourite Bunnymen gigs ever were at the Royal Court. I loved the Bunnymen and saw them play all over the country. But the Bunnymen at the peak of their powers playing to an enthusiastic hometown crowd was always magical.
>
> But if I had to pick out one favourite memory it would probably have to be a gig that I actually reviewed for *NME* but would have been at anyway, and that was The Farm when they had a number one album and were one of the biggest acts in the UK. They came back to Liverpool and were on top form. Even if you weren't a Farm fan you would have been swept along by the sheer joy of the night and the celebration of their success.[15]

MRS. BROWN
RIDES AGAIN
ON SALE NOW!
FROM TUESDAY
20TH MAY 2003
F FOR FUN
Written, directed
and starring
Brendan O'Carroll
as Mrs Brown
royal court theatre
1 Roe Street Liverpool
contains strong language
Box Office: 0151 709 4321
Ticketmaster: 0161 385 1410 day or night!
Radio City Box Office: 0151 256 5555
www.royalcourttheatre.net

Many local bands started out in the World Downstairs, a smaller venue housed in the basement Queen Mary Lounge, a space that later morphed, as music tastes changed in the 1990s, into a club playing rave and Scouse House. But most importantly for the long-term future of the building, the music years built an audience who felt a real connection to the Royal Court.

The 1980s was still a time of protest and the theatre hosted numerous benefit shows. The first post-Hillsborough fundraiser on 29 April 1989 featured, among others, The La's, Pete Wylie and The Mission, and a couple of weeks later Elvis Costello played two nights, donating the proceedings to the Hillsborough campaign. One of the earliest benefits was The Jam's 1981 concert for the Right to Work March, which was starting out in Liverpool on 1 May. Drums Across the Mersey, in January 1985, was two nights of anti-drugs campaigning featuring Echo and the Bunnymen, China Crisis, Madness, The Mighty Wah!, Style Council and A Flock of Seagulls. In March 1986 the Red Wedge tour came, an initiative fronted by Billy Bragg in an attempt to get more young people to engage with the Labour Party, a night that ended with 'a rousing version of the reggae classic, "Many Rivers to Cross" by the full Red Wedge line-up'.[16] And, in the same year, 'the stuff of legend', a fundraiser for the 58 local councillors who were on the point of being sacked, Factory's Tony Wilson brought 'With Love From Manchester' to the Royal Court.[17] It was an evening that ended with members of New Order, the Fall and The Smiths being joined on stage by John Cooper Clarke, The Farm and The Redskins in a version of 'Maggie's Farm', and included Derek Hatton of Militant, telling the audience that the 'future of Liverpool depends on you having a go'.[18]

It Is Still Falling Down

Much was made by audiences and by bands of the state of the building throughout the 1980s and 1990s, commenting variously about the cold, the floors that your feet stuck to and the peeling walls. It was, claimed an *Echo* reporter there for a gig in February 1986, 'cold enough for us to have been outdoors'.[19] In reality, it was worse than that and Geddes claimed that if the roof and drainage were not dealt with urgently, there was a real danger that the theatre would have to close.[20] As the 1990s arrived attempts were made to rectify things. In 1990 the building received Grade II listed status, which offered it some long-term protection, and in 1994 a new Royal Court Theatre Trust was established, with Geddes as the chief executive and Neville Goldrein as the chairman. Goldrein was forthright about the dismal state of affairs: 'When I inherited the theatre it was a complete slum, the proscenium arch was in a state of collapse … there was no heating, the toilets were appalling – indeed nothing was right.'[21]

They set out to raise money, trading on their legacy of having kept the theatre open as a commercial venue through the dark days of the 1980s. They also appealed to all those who were 'misty-eyed' about the elegant nights at the Royal Court of old.[22] Some of their optimism was buoyed by suggestions that the National Theatre and the RSC were considering the Court as a northern base for touring productions, and the National did bring *Dealer's Choice* there in July 1996.[23] Virginia Bottomley, then Minister for the Arts, visited and made encouraging noises, but the 1997 election of Labour meant she could not deliver on her promises. Over the next three years, buoyed up by what they saw as a revival in touring theatre and the regeneration of Liverpool's city centre, the Trust raised over £1 million. Much of this came from private sources after the Trust was turned down for National Lottery funding in 1997. During that time there were also increasing, if sporadic, numbers of theatre performances mixed uneasily with the concerts. In March 1997 Birmingham Rep and Thelma Holt brought *The Merchant of Venice*. In June of the same year the National Theatre came with David Hare's *Skylight*, and in November Pete Postlethwaite performed in *Macbeth*, with pantomime returning in the form of Julie Goodyear in *Aladdin*. The refurbished building was officially relaunched in October 2001 with a charity evening and a new slogan – From Rock to Opera.[24] But apart from the return of the Birkenhead Operatic Society, which had decamped to the Empire for the previous thirty years, and the Wallasey Amateur Operatic Society, 2001 into 2002 continued much as before with bands and the occasional stand-up comedian. Once again, it looked like another false dawn for the Royal Court.

Notes

1 *The Stage*, 11 October 1979, 1.
2 *Liverpool Echo*, 18 August 1980, 6.
3 *Liverpool Echo*, 3 June 1980, 2.
4 *Liverpool Echo*, 18 August 1980, 6.
5 *Liverpool Echo*, 12 August 1980, 2.
6 *Liverpool Echo*, 7 January 1981, 1.
7 *Liverpool Echo*, 6 February 1981, 8.
8 His surname was Cadwallader, a name he said he couldn't stand. 'Surnames are such a drag, so I just call myself Dave C.' *Liverpool Echo*, 5 August 1983, 4.
9 *Liverpool Echo*, 5 August 1983, 4.
10 P. Guy, 'Lost Liverpool #9: The "Real" Court at The Royal Court', 2016, http://www.getintothis.co.uk/2016/06/lost-liverpool-9-real-court-royal-court/ (accessed 11 August 2018).
11 P. Guy, 'The Royal Court: Musical Magic Relived at Liverpool's Rock and Roll Theatre – Part One', *Get Into This*, 21 June 2012, http://www.getintothis.co.uk/2012/06/royal_court/ (accessed 28 November 2018).
12 P. Guy, 'The Royal Court: Musical Magic Relived at Liverpool's Rock and Roll Theatre – Part Two', *Get Into This*, 22 June 2012, http://www.getintothis.co.uk/2012/06/the_royal_court_musical_magic/ (accessed 28 November 2018).
13 Ibid.
14 Ibid.
15 Ibid.
16 *Liverpool Echo*, 24 March 1986, 18.
17 Guy, 'Lost Liverpool #9'.
18 *Liverpool Echo*, 10 February 1986, 18.
19 *Liverpool Echo*, 10 February 1986, 15.
20 *Liverpool Echo*, 31 March 1995, 55.
21 *Liverpool Echo*, 19 February 2009, 24.
22 *Liverpool Echo*, 28 January 1994, 27.
23 *The Stage*, 8 August 1996, 4.
24 *Liverpool Echo*, 5 October 2001, 6.

Christmas, 1980–1999

1980 *Godspell*

The flower power love and peace era of the late 1960s gave rise to a rash of religious rock musicals, of which *Godspell* has proved itself to be world champion. But Liverpool has a strange relationship with this particular outburst of evangelism; at the Royal Court, seven years ago, with Pip Miller in the role of Jesus, it did fairly well yet a later production, starring Stephen Pacey at the Playhouse, fell by the wayside.

It returns for a Christmas season with the immensely likeable David Easter as the hardworking top of the bill, but no one can deny that the show will sell by virtue of its reputation and its music, as in promotional terms it has a cast of unknowns. And that's going to be a monumental challenge in a city with four other Christmas shows, including Les Dawson at the Empire. (Joe Riley, *Liverpool Echo*, 22 December 1980, 9)

1981 *Snow White* (matinees)

If you enjoy end-of-the pier shows, you should warm to *Snow White and the Seven Dwarfs* ... The tradition embodied in these events lives on in this show. It is peppered with the characters you loved from those seaside entertainments. You have a camp drag act, a 'Welsh soprano', a conjurer with doves that appear before they should and 'dancers.' And best of all you have little kids who smile a lot but offer little in the way of talent. A fairy fills us in on the plot before we are 'treated' to a song-and-dance routine that is as organised as moths around a candle. (*Liverpool Echo*, 21 December 1981, 9)

1981 *Ted Rogers' Dusty Bin* (evenings)

These are hard times so one has to be prepared to forgo the tinsel and glitter that used to be the hallmark of festive entertainment. But even in a production built around four solo acts and a small but noisy band it should be possible to provide a more imaginatively presented package ... it gave the impression of having all been put together that morning. There is however, so much audience participation – and prizes included a portable television set and a bottle of whisky – that the comings and goings could mean few will be in their seats long enough to be too critical. (*Liverpool Echo*, 21 December 1981, 9)

Exterior, Christmas 1981

1982–96 no productions

1997 ***Aladdin*** (Neptune Theatre Production) by Ian Billings

> The Neptune at the refurbished Royal Court presents a gloriously opulent version of Aladdin … Danny McCall's scally Aladdin is hot on audience rapport, singing and clowning. He works exceptionally well with Julie Goodyear (Mrs Twankey), all personality and chutzpah in a plethora of preposterous outfits and wigs, flicking ad-libs left and right in her first ever panto… (*The Stage*, 8 January 1998, 17)

1998 ***Cinderella***

> Liverpool's Pantomime for Liverpool's People
>
> This year's cast once again has a firm local flavour and we are delighted to welcome back to the Royal Court panto, favourite Pete Price, a Liverpool Legend of many talents playing the comedy role of Buttons. Joining Pete are two of *Brookside's* most popular characters, Eithne Browne and Steven Pinder who play Chrissy Rodgers and Max Farnham. Eithne plays one half of the Ugly Sisters 'Paris Hardup' and Steven will delight the audience with his good looks and vocal talent as 'Prince Charming.' (Jane Brown, programme note)

1999 *The Adventures of Robin Hood and Babes in the Wood*

This production offers a double helping of entertainment with two classic pantomime stories rolled into one ... Comic duo Little and Large top the bill, and are very much in the music hall tradition with punchy one-liners and humorous repartee with the audience. The duo use their comic talents to the full with Eddie Large performing convincing impersonations and Syd Little a put upon stooge act ... This is genuine family fun – traditional pantomime as it ought to be. (*The Stage*, 20 January 2000, 15)

The other great star is the building itself, whose beautifully restored art deco auditorium now has a foyer to match. This summer, the Royal Court will receive its millionth customer since reopening in 2005 with a programme that does not receive a penny in public subsidy. If that sounds like a miracle in this day and age, it's a reminder that miracle is simply another term for extremely hard work.

– *Guardian*, 18 March 2016

11 Creating a Home for Scouse Comedy: The 2000s

At the beginning of the new century, things were again looking increasingly grim for the theatre. Alternative music venues were starting to take bands and audiences elsewhere and the dilapidated building was not helping to attract people. Caught on a series of short leases for over twenty years, Simon Geddes and the New Royal Court Ltd were finding it hard to keep going and, given the nature of the leases, were not in a position to attract the funding needed to refurbish the building. But by 2002 there were hints that the theatre was once more looking to reinvent itself, this time as a theatre rather than a music venue, and that once again the Royal Court would not give in without a fight. There had been signs of change during 2001 when Brendan O'Carroll's *Good Mourning Mrs Brown* had two sell-out runs at the theatre, totalling some six weeks of performance, and with O'Carroll's three nights of Christmas stand-up, *How's Your Snowballs?*[1] By 2002 the *Daily Post* was suggesting that the

Royal Court was gradually moving from a music venue to

> a theatre taking in classic theatre, drama, arts, events and occasional music acts ... The current season does at last look like a proper theatre season with Irish writer/actor Brendan O'Carroll's *The Course* completing a run at the theatre ... followed with a music concert featuring The Real Thing ... another ... run of local comedy about a taxi driver, *Night Collar,* Johnny Vegas headlines his own show ... and Donizetti's opera *Emilia di Liverpool* goes on stage July 24–27. Elvis impersonator Liberty Mounteen and his orchestra mark the 25th anniversary of Presley's death with a show ... and North West comic Peter Kay will make three appearances ... Queen tribute band are there ... and the Moscow Ballet perform *Swan Lake* ... Other shows in the season include a 1980s nostalgia night with Go West.[2]

While audiences from earlier times might have struggled to see this as a 'proper theatre season', this oddly mixed repertoire, where opera and ballet fought with comedy, music and comedy plays, did try to offer something for everyone. Key to future developments, alongside further successful shows in the Mrs Brown series, was *Night Collar* by Tony Furlong and Jimmy Power, which had first been produced as part of the Liverpool Comedy Festival, later moving to the Unity and then Liverpool's Everyman where, produced by Kevin Fearon, it became the fastest-selling show in that theatre's history. In essence a comedy sketch show, making it an easy move into theatre for audiences used to stand-up, *Night Collar* was built around a series of characters who hail a taxi on Christmas Eve, from an arguing couple and a naked man escaping a stag night party to a prostitute and an Elvis impersonator. In 2003 the Royal Court staged another Liverpool-based comedy produced by Fearon. With more of a through narrative than *Night Collar,* Len Pentin and Fred Lawless's *Slappers and Slapheads* was set in the madhouse that was the Palace nightclub on an over-25s Valentine's night, 'that special day of the year when the man in your life wakes you up in the morning with a single rose ... and then you bollock him cos the greedy get's eaten the rest of the box himself'.[3] In a show where soap opera met *Carry On,* everyone was frantic to have a few drinks and a laugh, but behind the jokes were sadder stories. Chris has only six months to live. Billy still lives with his mum and used to get beaten up by his dad. Elaine can feel her biological clock ticking and is desperate to get pregnant. Donna's husband sits at home hitting the bottle and then hitting her. But all ends happily with the birth of a baby in the basement 'Luv Bunker' and a rewritten version of a John Paul Young hit where:

> Love is in the air, at the Palace every night
> Love is in the air, even when you look like shite

Night Collar (Dave Evans)

But don't worry if she is a minger, don't worry if he is a meff
Just ignore the warts on her fingers
And ignore that he's got bad breath.[4]

The success of these two shows, alongside the obvious audience appeal of the Mrs Brown series, gave their producer Kevin Fearon and his partner Gillian Miller an idea.

Fearon had been the executive producer at Liverpool's Everyman Theatre between 1993 and 1998, seeing the theatre through some hard times and overseeing its move from a producing house to a mainly receiving theatre. While he was there, links had been made with the Royal Court through work that ran under the title of 'Playing Away', when shows that were too big for the Everyman played at the Court. These included Frank McGuinness's *Observe the Sons of Ulster* which reopened the Royal Court for theatre for the first time in fifteen years in 1996, Ibsen's *A Doll's House* with Janet McTeer, Slava Polunin's *Snow Show* and, in 1998, the Tiger Lilies *Shockhead Peter.* Fearon also had older connections with the Royal Court, remembering his first visit there in 1965 to see *Peter Pan*, and his father, a milkman in the mornings, had worked as a stage hand at the Royal Court in the evenings. By the late 1990s though, with theatre funding in the city having become precarious, 'all the fun had gone out of the game', and he left to concentrate on stand-up comedy.[5] Rawhide Comedy Club had started its life in 1995 in the Everyman foyer and now Fearon took it out into the city. For a number of years it moved around venues that included Baby Blue at the Albert Dock, the Lyceum Bar and Grill on Bold Street and finally Central Hall on Renshaw Street, becoming a key player in the Liverpool comedy scene and the heart of the Liverpool Comedy Festival, which was restarted in 2002 as part of the preparation for the Capital of Culture bid. But Central Hall was problematic as a venue, with acoustics unsuited to stand-up (and a hefty rent), and Fearon saw the chance to move the comedy club to the Royal Court where Geddes was struggling again.

By 2005 the momentary spark ignited by the move to a more mixed programme was flickering dimly and the theatre had only a handful of acts booked. Fearon asked Geddes if he would consider another operator taking over. Geddes agreed. The next chapter in the theatre's history began. Rawhide moved in in July 2005 with an understanding from Liverpool City Council that a lease would be forthcoming. From his experience of the previous few years, Fearon knew the city had an appetite for comedy. He also knew that audiences enjoyed a more relaxed atmosphere when watching performances, one where they could eat and drink and were not sitting in fixed rows, one where they could interact with each other as well as what they were seeing on the stage. So instead of reinstating the stalls seats, which had been removed for concerts (though were still in use when theatre shows were being staged), he terraced the sloping stalls area and installed cabaret-style chairs and tables. It reduced the seating capacity, although some of the lost revenue was made up for by food and drink sales, but it created a unique performance space where, with the removal of the orchestra pit, intimacy between stage and audience was paramount. This intimacy was further enhanced for Rawhide nights by the use of a giant Lycra ceiling which covered up the dress circle entirely. Plans for a more sociable, more welcoming theatre building were also in place with the idea of converting the basement bar into Downstairs, a cocktail bar that would be open six days a week, regardless of whether shows were on.

Fearon did not envisage that the Court would simply be the home of stand-up. He was also thinking about the success of Mrs Brown, of *Night Collar*, of *Slappers and Slapheads*, and promised they 'were committed to continuing the tradition of bringing the best in music and theatre to the Royal Court' alongside regular comedy dates.[6] The first season, however, did not deliver on this promise, and Rawhide's tenure kicked off with the fourth Liverpool Comedy Festival bringing acts such as Johnny Vegas, Paul

Merton and Dylan Moran alongside an evening called Best of Liverpool, hosted by Les Dennis, with Pauline Daniels and John Bishop. Other, eclectic comedy acts followed, including Joan Rivers, Ben Elton and Roy 'Chubby' Brown. Occasional shows were more challenging. *Puppetry of the Penis* invited the audience to watch as 'two strapping Australians' manipulated their manhood 'into various shapes, objects and landmarks', with a video camera projecting intimate details on to a large screen.[7] The Trachtenburg Family Slideshow Players, a surprise hit at the 2004 Edinburgh Festival, were an indie-vaudeville conceptual pop band who illustrated their set with vintage slide collections found in charity shops and car boot sales. Songs included 'Mountain Trip to Japan 1959' and a six-song mini-opera based on the contents of a 1977 McDonalds corporate slide show. Early 2006 saw more stand-up, from Tim Vine and the Mighty Boosh to The Liverpool 3, an irreverent look at the city's Capital of Culture status, which had been awarded in 2004.

In April 2006 disaster struck again. Rawhide was forced into liquidation by the city council which had not delivered on its promise of a lease. The bank got nervous and removed any credit facilities. Fearon had seen this coming and had taken steps to enable the business to continue, mortgaging his mother's house as well as using personal savings. The theatre was still open but its foundations were, once again, rocky, and it was, to make matters worse, on the point of producing its first show.

A Smash Hit: Brick Up the Mersey Tunnels (and the shows that followed)

Drawing on what they had learned from the recent successful comedy dramas at the Court, the theatre management had been working with writers Dave Kirby and Nicky Allt on *Brick Up the Mersey Tunnels*. For the theatre, this now *had* to be a success. Despite standing ovations at the first two previews, with a frozen bank account the company did not even have the money to pay the actors on the Friday and had to wait, hoping that the box office receipts that night would allow them to be paid on Saturday. Luckily they did. On Monday, word of mouth meant there was a queue at the box office by 10 a.m. and, as the day wore on, demand was so high they had to find extra laptops, plugging them in around the building wherever they had an internet connection, to keep up. The show sold out within days, becoming a surprise hit, the saviour of the theatre and a perennial favourite, with six runs between 2006 and 2016, selling over 175,000 tickets and attracting 'the sort of enthusiastic audiences not seen in the city for years'.[8] So all-pervasive did the show become that not only did it earn itself the nickname of 'The Scousetrap' in the local press, but by 2017 the *Liverpool Echo* could comment, '[u]nless you've been living hermit-like in a cave in Sefton Park, the chances are that over the past decade you have seen at least one performance of *Brick up the Mersey Tunnels*'.[9]

Based around the animosities between Liverpool and Wirral, the show focused on the Kingsway Three, who all had their own reasons for wanting to brick up the Mersey tunnels and leave the Wirral in splendid isolation. The Tunnel Man's wife has run off with a Wirral- based seafood millionaire. Dickie Lewis, the builder, is sacked by Anne Twacky, the Tory blue-rinse Wirral warrior, for being from Liverpool and not Wirral as he claimed when he got the job of building her a conservatory. She also puts in a complaint about ex-soldier turned GPO man Gerard Garner, for allowing a letter to be delivered to her with a Liverpool postcode when everyone knew that they'd had a much-prized Cheshire postcode since 1991. To add fuel to his fire, Maggie, the owner of the greasy spoon café, who Gerard has lost his heart to, goes off with Elliot Neston, the seafood millionaire's nephew and owner of a

Carl Chase as Nick Walton, Andrew Schofield as Dickie Lewis and Paul Duckworth as Gerard Gardiner in Dave Kirby and Nick Allt's *Brick Up the Mersey Tunnels* (Dave Evans)

Porsche, who seemed to promise her a way to escape the drudgery. But there is more to the decision to brick up the tunnels (and also, in the end, to blow up the Runcorn Bridge) than personal vendetta, as Dickie Lewis suggests in an argument with a Wirralean who works at Ford's who is trying to get through the tunnel before it is finally sealed. As well as trading arguments about which side can claim the most celebrities, the builder tells him they are fed up with people like him 'coming here every day earning a living and then going home and slagging us off'. In other words, they have had enough of people 'taking the piss'.[10] For their terrorist act, the three go down in folk history, names to be remembered alongside William Gladstone and the Beatles, and the show has the feeling of an urban myth, a tale to be told and retold, all but ending with Dickie Lewis's poetic conclusion:

But the question is – Was
Anything learned? For some, the
River is a big divide – that
separates Cheshire from Merseyside.
I mean – there'll always be those
who rant and rave – about how us
Scousers should behave. But when
they're coming here each week –
I think they've got a fuckin' cheek.
so if you know someone who feels
the need – to ever bite the hand
that feeds. Just give them a slap –
and send them to me. And I'll tell
them the tale – of the Kingsway three.[11]

The success of *Brick Up* led to a sequel. Following a solo attempt by Nicky Allt in 2010, staged at the Empire, Kirby and Allt reunited in 2017 in *Brick Up 2: The Wrath of Anne Twacky*. This time, in an attempt to prevent the reuniting of the two sides of the river with the reopening of the tunnels, Anne Twacky takes a 'Birkenexit' stance and comes up with her own plan to brick up the tunnels again (and build a Berlin Wall around Birkenhead), setting up WILLY (Wirral Ignores Lazy Liverpool Yobs). Inevitably, it all goes wrong and she ends with her own house being blown up.

Brick Up began the renaissance of theatre at the Royal Court and set a pattern for the shows that were to follow. They were all to contain well-known music. They were all comedies. And they were all 'so local that it almost hurts'.[12] The year after *Brick Up*, and following its second sold-out run, Dave Kirby wrote *Lost Soul* (August 2007), a play described by the *Liverpool Echo* as 'fun, nostalgic and poignant' and '100% Scouse' and by Kirby as a 'comedy about two couples getting older but not getting any wiser'.[13] The *Echo* continued, '[i]t is about loss. The lost soul music of their youth, of penny-round collars and flares, and the lost souls who believe that the only thing to look forward to is the past.' In a programme note, Kirby suggests that the idea for the show came from a Sunday night out when he went into a culture 'that I wasn't familiar with', a night that started at Coopers, the Liverpool, First National, and then involved taking a cab to the Beehive, Tess Riley's, the Big-house and the Yankee Bar. 'It was as though someone had transported me back in time to the 1960s & 70s. There was live retro music – retro discos and a retro audience mostly between the ages of 40 and 60.' And he ended up (as usual) in the Lobster Pot chippy. What surprised him most 'was the lack of young people on the streets – the whole centre was fossilised with over-forties'.

Andrew Schofield as Dee Estuary, Eithne Browne as Anne Twacky, Francis Tucker as Liz Card and Roy Brandon as Dennis Twacky in Dave Kirby and Nick Allt's *Brick Up the Mersey Tunnels* (Dave Evans)

In *Lost Soul*, two couples, sisters Donna and Pat and best friends Smigger and Terry, have been married for thirty years. Most Sundays they go out and dance to Tamla Motown, that is until Pat leaves Terry for 'the lion', a 29-year-old bouncer from the Yankee Bar. This is the catalyst for lives unravelling and questions being asked about growing old and growing up. For Smigger, they have earned the right to enjoy their Sunday nights in town. They have always worked. They have their own little house off Scottie Road and they have raised two good children. For him, 'there is nothing wrong with enjoying yourself before you're past it'.[14] But Donna thinks there must be more to life than going to town on Sundays. Struggling with an empty nest and the menopause, she complains that he doesn't treat her like he did in the seventies. He doesn't bring her presents 'like sweets, and records and ... knock off clothes'.[15] She sometimes stares 'at this wedding photograph and I can't recognise meself'. She wants romance. He suggests Coopers. She wants somewhere more romantic. He suggests the Wine Lodge. What she really wants is to go on holiday, maybe to the Lake District. He says that he isn't Heathcliff. He tries again. 'Come onnnn ... (*Coaxing*) a few dry martinis, a chicken omelette ... then when we get home (*Erotic*) y' can pretend I'm Brad Pitt in bed.'[16] Left at home alone, Donna asks, 'why can't things be like they used to be?'[17]

Pat has decided she has had enough of 'those nineteen sixties and seventies songs playing away ... reminding me what it was like to be young'. She wants to 'feel like that again. But in tomorrow's world – not yesterday's.'[18] However, leaving her husband for a younger man turns out not to be an answer, as he beats her up and she realises she 'loves the bones' of Terry.[19] In the end, it is Donna who comes to realise what is important. As she tells her sister,

> there comes a time in life when a girl's got to hang her friggin' stilettos up. This isn't a Disney film y' know. It's all about contentment. Look at Smigger. There's no one who's stuck in the past as much as he is. But he loves it there ... and d'you know why? Cos he's happy with his life.[20]

Dave Kirby's *Lost Soul* with Jake Abraham as Terry and Andrew Schofield as Smigger (Dave Evans)

Finding out she is going to become a grandmother, 'the answers start dropping like confetti. I know who I am … and I'm here because I met someone who loved Tamla Motown as much as I did. And if I'd have done something different with me life then I wouldn't have two lovely kids (*Beams*) and a grandson on the way.'[21] While it isn't 'easy looking in the mirror every day and seeing Vanessa Feltz staring back at yer', that is how it works. 'You have your day then you grow old – hopefully with someone you care about.'[22] The play ends with Terry and Pat reunited and the foursome all set for a nostalgic soul weekend at Pontins.

The year after *Lost Soul,* Dave Kirby wrote *Council Depot Blues,* a comedy about 'loyalty, layabouts and the lug at the end of the tunnel'.[23] At its heart were the men who worked for the Excrement Eradication Department in the council, drawing on Kirby's own experience of working for the 'corpy' for sixteen years. The only female character is the loud-mouthed, pyjama-wearing, beer-swigging Vera who lives next door and first appears accompanied by the Benny Hill theme tune. The discovery of a Gibson mandolin worth £150,000 in a house they are clearing is the dramatic driver for the plot, but it is also a story of men living lives of quiet desperation and, like *Lost Soul,* of lost dreams. From the outset, as Stan wakes up in a lonely room which is all he has to look forward to after his last day at work, this is a comedy tinged with a deep sadness. The play does make jokes and sing songs (tellingly blues-based in this instance) about hating work and skiving and counting down the seconds until you can leave, but when it comes to that point the realisation is that, for many people, however menial and grim and boring it might be, work and the friendship and the fun of workmates (here developed through the fact that they are all in a band and take the opportunity to rehearse in empty houses while at work) is all you have. Throughout, Stan counts down the hours, minutes and seconds to finishing work after forty years, but towards the end, left alone in the empty house, he wonders 'if everyone feels this way … unwanted … worthless'. Picking up his 'gob iron' (harmonica), a leaving present from the lads, he sings to himself:

> I never thought these empty places
> Would bear so heavy on my mind
> I hear the laughter – see the faces
> Lazy days – crazy times
> Now there's an emptiness inside me
> For the world I leave behind.[24]

After a party back at the depot, Stan is next seen sat on his bed covering his face with his hands and weeping. Next morning he is up, dressed and listening to Radio City's 7 a.m. news before he realises, dropping his bag to the floor and falling on to the bed.

Dreams of anything more, however narrow those dreams might be, seem destined to failure. The more Shorty, the young lad and wannabe drug baron, talks about wanting to go and open a bar in Ibiza, the more the audience knows it will never happen. And despite Stan asking Danny to promise him not to 'miss the boat' like he did, and to get out of there while he is still young enough, Danny's last lines, 'I'm definitely getting out of this place … definitely. (*Pause*) Some day', say it will never happen.[25] Kirby does not blame the men. They are not, as Shorty thinks, losers. They are trapped by children and mortgages but also by a wider world. Stan consistently blames Margaret Thatcher for everything that is wrong, and the song, 'Working Class Blues', adds a wider context:

> They stole the dream I cherished
> They came like thieves in the night
> They stole my education
> That's why I'm shovelling shite
>
> All around this God damn country
> The song is always the same
> We're all just part of the system
> We're all just playing the game.
>
> (*Chorus*) So we all count down the years
> Drown our sorrows in our beers
> Hearing voices in our ears
> Singing those old working class blues.[26]

All they can do is drink to escape (and they drink everything they can lay their hands on throughout the play) and skive and try to make things easier in between clocking on and clocking off by having a laugh. As the title song says: 'Lord knows I want so much more … but I don't get to choose.'[27] But when the Gibson is discovered and they start to realise what it might mean, rather than pulling together they all try and cheat on each other, planning to sneak away with their own fortune and live their own dreams. There is little real sense of community left here in the aftermath of Thatcher, but in the end no one gets the Gibson. It is destroyed by Harry, the violent and objectionable boss (who does get his come-uppance), who has been drugged at the leaving party and smashes it up in killing a rat.

Apart from the Christmas shows, all written especially for the Royal Court, to date the theatre has staged 16 new, home-grown shows. These have included two football plays – Nicky Allt's history of Liverpool FC *You'll Never Walk Alone* and a musical stage version of the film *Reds and Blues: The Ballad of Dixie and Kenny* by

Alan Bleasdale's *Down the Dock Road* with Michael Ledwich as Wonder Boy, Oliver Farnworth as Dobbo, Daniel Taylor as Mickey and Andrew Schofield as McKenna (A.B. Photography)

Dave Kirby, a play about two neighbours who ferociously support different teams, battling it out for supremacy. Workplaces have provided the setting for several plays. Fred Lawless's *A Fistful of Collars* (April 2010 and July 2016) is set in a dry cleaners that also doubles as a dress-hire business, as the owners battle to save their business from a grasping gangster landlord. *The Royal* by Lindzi Germain and Angela Simms (June 2016 and August 2017), one of only two plays to date written by women, is set in a Liverpool institution, the Royal Liverpool Hospital, in the days before the hospital is about to be demolished. In Mark Davis Markham's *Special Measures* (April 2014), the setting is a failing primary school, where a Northern Soul soundtrack is the background to 'a nation in a state'.[28]

Mam I'm 'Ere (June 2015 and July 2018), as the title suggests, is Stephen Fletcher's reworking of *Mamma Mia*, set, not on a Greek island, but in a down-at-heel and soon to be closed holiday centre that offers 70s disco holidays on an island somewhere near Rhyl. Dave has found a baby on the doorstep and brought her up by himself, not knowing who the mother is. Twenty-five years on, and unknown to him, his daughter, Sally, wants her mother at her wedding. She invites the three most likely candidates to the holiday centre, on the pretext that each is the winner of an all-inclusive, expenses-paid trip to a brand new spa – complete with expert staff, extensive facilities and a disco-trip down memory lane. Luckily, the failing holiday centre is saved by a big win on the lottery, an escape route that is popular in Royal Court shows. Other shows have taken in Laurel and Hardy via a music hall show (*Sons of the Desert*, adapted from the film by Ken Alexander, September 2013), the 1978 World Cup (Gerry Linford's *The Miracle on Great Homer Street*, June 2018) and a sex chat show (Claire Sweeney and Mandy Muden's *Sex and the Suburbs*, May 2014).

Alongside these there have been plays brought in from other venues, but always home-produced and localised. Mike Yeaman's plays were written for the Custom House in South Shields. *Lucky Numbers* (March 2010) is a story about a elderly woman losing control of her life and her independence, before she gets complete control back with a lottery win. *Canoeing for Beginners* (February 2015) was loosely based on the John and Anne Darwin case, in which a man faked his own suicide by canoeing out to sea to claim the life insurance and escape from a failing business. Another comedy that originated at the Custom House was *Dirty Dusting* by Ed Waugh and Trevor Wood (March 2009). When three cleaners are given their P45s, they decide to get their own back, and keep their heads above water, by setting up an adult chat-line in the office. As Alfred Hickling noted in the *Guardian*,

> [t]here's scope for a saucy Brit-com along the lines of Carry On Up the Blower, but if the characters bear the stamp of Victoria Wood, the dialogue could be courtesy of Roy 'Chubby' Brown. To give you a flavour, it comes in raspberry, lemon and sherbet surprise, like the condoms liberated from the gents' lavatory.[29]

Other plays have come from closer to home, and with styles very close to that of the Royal Court, including two plays by Bob Eaton, *Lennon* (October 2010 and August 2013) and *Good Golly Miss Molly* (October 2007). *The Salon* by Drew Quayle (October 2009) started life in the summer of 2009 at the Theatre Royal St Helens and told the stories of three women who work at the Curl Up and Dye hairdressing salon. The theatre has also drawn on 'classic' comedies for its repertoire, from Ray

Our Day Out by Willy Russell (Dave Evans)

Cooney's *Funny Money* (January 2010) and *Noises Off* (September 2014) to Amanda Whittington's *Ladies Day* (June 2013) and, a perennial favourite, John Godber's *Bouncers*, performed three times between 2013 and 2015 and in 2018 arriving in an all-black version produced by Boisterous and adapted by Maurice Bessman.[30] There has even been one attempt to stage Shakespeare with cut-down, localised versions of *Macbeth* and *A Midsummer Night's Dream* (September 2012) in productions with Max Rubin's Liverpool theatre company Lodestar, with *Macbeth* set in and around a high-rise housing estate and focusing on the rise and fall of an ambitious gang member. Very occasionally, shows have been brought in, including Anne Dalton's version of *Her Benny*, a musical take on Silas K. Hocking's classic Liverpool story of slum children fighting to better themselves.

The success of *Brick Up* and these subsequent plays was in latching on to a mood, catching a moment in the city's consciousness. While back in the 1960s Liverpool 'had seemed the focus of a revolution', that

> revolution was more apparent than real: just a minor shuffling of elites, as the exhausted old order made room for some energetic newcomers. It turned out that Liverpudlians were not in the vanguard of this movement after all, they were just its mascots. When grey day dawned and normality returned, Liverpool was back at the bottom of the heap. And national affection curdled into contempt. The Gods seemed of a mind to punish the place in jealousy of its brief dance in the sunlight.[31]

By the 1970s Liverpool had become the city with the worst reputation in the national consciousness. Images in the newspapers were less than exemplary. It was a city that could boast the dubious claim of being a 'destination for those seeking urban blight' or as a place 'always setting new benchmarks for urban barbarity'. It had, as the *Financial Times* stated as late as 2008, 'reputational issues'.[32] It has been associated with unemployment, riots, the Militant Tendency and economic meltdown, as well as gun crime, football violence and the murder of James Bulger by two ten-year-olds in 1993. Its television appearances included images of Toxteth on fire in 1981, Neil Kinnock condemning the 'grotesque chaos' of a Labour council hiring taxis to hand out redundancy notices to its own workers, and the death of 39 Juventus supporters at Heysel in 1985 as a wall collapsed. It filled the pages of newspapers, most notoriously the *Sun*, which accused Liverpool supporters of picking the pockets of victims and urinating on the police when 96 football fans died at Hillsborough. This was joined the following week by the *Sunday Times* weighing in with its own reflections, claiming that 'the futile erection of football into a cult is the city's only modern acquaintance with excellence, matches elsewhere being the one chance to swagger and intimidate'.[33]

Liverpool also gained a reputation as a city that paraded its victimhood. When Boris Johnson (name-checked in *Brick Up* for giving Liverpool grief even though he had never set foot in the city) wrote in the *Spectator* about the 2004 murder of Ken Bigley and criticised the city for its tribal sense of community, its excessive predilection for welfarism and its wallowing in victim status, he was greeted by howls of outrage and forced to make a penitent pilgrimage (which he termed 'Operation Scouse-grovel') to apologise.[34] So bad had matters become that the *Daily Mirror* famously pronounced in the 1980s that 'They should build a fence around and charge an admission fee. For sadly, it has become a show-case for everything that has gone wrong in Britain's major cities.'[35] Or, as Du Noyer writes, 'the 1980s saw Liverpool's old fame replaced by infamy. Suddenly this was Bad News

Town. Somebody dubbed it the Museum of Horrifying Example.'[36] Perceptions of Liverpool around the country were summed up by Margaret Thatcher's response to the Toxteth riots in her memoirs:

> 'I had been told that some of the young people got into trouble through boredom and not having enough to do', she wrote. 'But you had only to look at the grounds around those houses with the grass untended, some of it waist high, and the litter, to see that this was a false analysis. They had plenty of constructive things to do if they wanted. Instead, I asked myself how people could live in such circumstances without trying to clear up the mess.'[37]

Papers released in 2011 bear out the attitude of some of Thatcher's government towards the city, urging her to abandon it to managed decline. In the words of Du Noyer, '[t]he Beat City became the Beaten City'.[38]

Popular television drama also helped to enshrine these images. Tony Booth's Mike, in *Till Death Us Do Part* (1965–75), might have been a sharp-witted Scouser, but he was also a left-wing layabout. Carla Lane's *Bread* (1986–91) centred on a family abusing the welfare system (and drew mixed responses in the city for trading on stereotypical attitudes). Phil Redmond's *Brookside* (running for twenty-one years from 1982) might have had a more realistic air, but it painted the city's inhabitants as beset with troubles and happy to air their personal problems loudly and publicly in the close. Harry Enfield's 'Scousers', with curly perms and bad moustaches, were pugnacious and pugilistic, giving the country the all-pervasive and persistent 'calm down, calm down', and his Loadsamoney character was much imitated by London football fans, who taunted Liverpool supporters (alongside other northern fans) by waving money at them. Most iconic of all was Alan Bleasdale's *Boys from the Blackstuff* (1982), which came to speak for a nation under Thatcher. It too added catchphrases ('Gizza a job' and 'I can do that') to the national vocabulary and created a folk hero for the 1980s in the shape of Yozzer Hughes. Yet as an image of a city, Yozzer is an uncomfortable hero, suggesting a place that is destroying itself as it slides into insanity. He is grim and helpless and desperate, painfully descending into madness and desolation as he loses his job, his wife, his children, his dignity and his self-respect. He is reduced to head-butting lamp-posts, confessional boxes and policemen in an attempt to articulate his despair and take away the pain. Alongside him, the city slides into collective mania. In contrast to this, Bleasdale's hero is Chrissie; decent, honest and placid, the ordinary man living an ordinary life until his job is taken away from him and he is left shipwrecked with nothing left to do except cause carnage in his backyard as he slaughters the chickens, the geese for Sundays and the rabbit, becoming covered in blood and tears. As Chrissie leaves the pub at the end of the series, walking off into the sunset down a derelict back alley complete with a partly demolished warehouse bearing the sign 'Tate and Lyle 1922', his final plea of 'Beam me up Scotty. Beam me up' suggested that the only alternative to going mad was to get out.

In Liverpool itself, the theatre was all but turning a blind eye to the city. Throughout the 1980s, Glen Walford at the Everyman declared that 'if you live in a tower block you know how miserable it is – you don't want to see shows about it'. Instead, she insisted that 'people have dreams that they can't articulate' and you 'speak to them through theatre on the level of the imagination', offering magical Shakespeare productions with exotic settings, a version of *Tosca* and a new raunchy Everyman house style.[39] She was followed in 1989 by John Doyle who offered a season of Greek, Russian and Restoration plays. At the Playhouse, bailed out in those troubled times by Bill Kenwright, nostalgia reigned in a series of popular musical shows. Even with the arrival of Gemma Bodinetz and Deborah Aydon at the by then amalgamated Everyman and Playhouse in 2004, and their instigation of a series of plays under the umbrella 'Made in Liverpool', there was little on offer to celebrate the city and its people.

In all of this, something was missing and, in 2006, with the Capital of Culture looming and a sense of things getting better, people in Liverpool did want something to celebrate, something to laugh at, something positive and upbeat to be said about themselves and their city. It was this that the Royal Court picked up on.

Defining the Royal Court House Style

The 'secret ingredients' for a successful Royal Court show were neatly summed up by the *Daily Post* as being 'pop music, drama with a local touch and a healthy dollop of comedy'.[40] All the shows are comedies and much of the comedy is reliant on the laughter of recognition. The biggest responses from the audience are to the things they 'know', things that are local and things that are familiar. Widnes is smelly, Formby is posh, woollybacks are fond of sheep.[41] In one show, a radio report states that it's official that the capital of culture (or the England football team, depending on which year you saw the show) are 'shite'. Local references are everywhere. *Lost Soul* name-checks over ten pubs, from the Yankee Bar and Coopers to the Beehive and Chequers. Bleasdale's *Down the Dock Road* is littered with local places – Huyton, Prescot, Seaforth, Litherland, Kirkby, and Sefton and Newsham parks. The gangster landlord in *A Fistful of Collars* is Curtis, a nod to Toxteth-born drug trafficker Curtis Warren. The 66 designer dresses that mistakenly end up in the dry cleaners belong to Coleen Rooney, and the show constantly threatens (but never delivers) the arrival on stage of her husband Wayne to collect them. There are jokes about Derek Hatton, *Blood Brothers*, the Adelphi Hotel, the brass section of the Royal Liverpool Philharmonic Orchestra and Margaret Thatcher's dislike of the city. Most popular are mentions of nights out at the Grafton nightclub, which comes up in almost every play and is referred to as 'the sausage factory' or by reference to grab-a-granny nights. Taunting Everton and Everton supporters is also seen as fair game. In *Brick Up*, when Gerard is hiding after blowing up the bridge, he finds a perfect place that is dark and damp and has been empty for years – Everton's trophy room. In Eaton's 'Liverpoolised' *Bouncers*, there is a mindless day spent wood stacking and talking about the problems of getting Everton back into Europe. There is also a lot of laughter at Liverpudlian stereotypes, from the workshy men of the council who, in the words of the title song of *Council Depot Blues*, 'get to work then fuck off at noon' to Theresa the Tea in *The Royal* who sells knock-off perfume (among other things) from the bottom drawer of her tea trolley.

There are plenty of feisty female characters who know how to make a man laugh, keep him in his place and stand up to anyone who crosses them. The title character in *Good Golly Miss Molly* leads a gutsy fight against the proposed demolition of the street that she lives on, and Smigger in *Lost Soul* admits that Donna is the only woman who can wipe the floor with him, admitting that it was the fact she made him laugh 90 per cent of the time that first attracted him to her. Sometimes there is a sense that feisty women are being sent up, nowhere more so than with Anne Twacky in *Brick Up*, who keeps her line-dancing, John Wayne aspiring husband Dennis on a tight rein until he bites back, dons a Lacoste tracksuit and goes to join the other side. Anne is joined on Wirral by her two accomplices, Miss Dee Estuary and Miss Liz Card, played in drag and fond of jokes that can be read in a sexual way. But the fun had with Anne Twacky is based not on her feistiness but on her snobbery, her double standards (in reality she is from Marsh Lane in Bootle) and her championing of Mrs Thatcher. It is class that matters here, as it does in all of the Royal Court plays. Dave Kirby explained why all this localism led to the success of *Brick Up*: 'It's a bit cathartic for the audience because Liverpool people are naturally proud and parochial and they get sick and tired of seeing their city attacked by outsiders who don't really know anything about us.'[42] The play was 'a pop back at them on our behalf', a point that Joe Riley, the *Echo* arts critic, agreed with. 'This isn't the Royal Shakespeare Company and it isn't the West End', he argued. 'This is Liverpool and we have to offer audiences theatre that they can both relate to and enjoy.'[43]

Shows often have more than one airing. *Brick Up the Mersey Tunnels* tops the list at six outings, with others often being repeated, so that they are like old friends or a favourite DVD that you can watch again and again. Familiarity also leads to characters from one play reappearing in another; Father O'Flaherty, the intemperate priest who featured in the 2009 Christmas show *Merry Ding Dong*, reappeared in 2010 with his Sisters of Mersey in *Scouse Pacific*. By 2016 he had his own show, *Father O'Flaherty Saves Our Souls*. The language and accent is familiar; Lynne Walker advised *Independent* readers that they 'might need to brush up [their] Scouseology' if they were going to see *Council Depot Blues*, and *Scouse Pacific* makes great play of how the islanders were taught the fundamentals of the Scouse alphabet: R, A and U ('Arr-ey you'). The actors, too, are familiar and local. Andrew Schofield, Eithne Browne, Lindzi Germain, Paul Duckworth (among others) turn up in a variety of guises, and the theatre uses regular members from a pool of local actors. Many of the writers come from backgrounds that the audience can recognise; Fred Lawless was a local stallholder, Dave Kirby worked for the council. As Kevin Fearon pointed out in a programme note for *Special Measures*,

> As Liverpool's busiest producing theatre, we have Liverpool at the heart of what we do. All our shows are created here in the city at our Everton workshops. We rehearse all our shows here, we build our sets here and if there is a role for a Liverpool actor – they're in the show. Liverpool as a city needs the Royal Court. It needs a venue that is proudly Liverpool...

All this locality has come at something of a cost. National reviews have been thin on the ground and while the theatre stated in 2007 that it was interested in touring some of the work to other theatres, this has yet to happen.[44]

Familiarity also comes from things that are not specifically local. Many shows draw on popular culture references, from *Towering Inferno* in *The Royal* and Clint Eastwood films in Fred Lawless's *A Fistful of Collars* to *Mamma Mia* in *Mam I'm 'Ere*. The Christmas shows, in particular, pride themselves on punning popular references in their titles, from *Pharaoh 'Cross the Mersey* to *The Hitchhiker's Guide to Fazakerley* and *Scouse Pacific*. Music too has a familiar ring. In all the shows, the music is second-hand and well known; from the soul soundtrack of *Lost Soul* and the rock and roll of *Good Golly Miss Molly* to the disco hits of *Mam I'm 'Ere*, it is a musical memory lane.

Music also serves as a reminder of a youthful past, and running through all the plays is a deep sense of nostalgia, a sense of things lost. As Smigger tells Terry, the Liverpool they knew has disappeared: 'the clubs ... the characters ... the music'.[45] At the heart of *Lost Soul* is the clash between old and young, or at least middle-aged and young. Counterpointed to soul music, music with real harmonies that people sing together, music you can 'shag all night to', is rave, which 'sounds like a gang of navvies digging the road up'.[46] Smigger and Terry are out of place in a trendy Wood Street bar, turning up too early and not impressed by the idea of a DJ coming from

London, reminding the young bartender that the 'people with the talent are the ones who make the records … not the prick who puts them on'.[47] When Terry asks the barman, a student studying sociology, if he has ever heard of Motown, the response he gets is, 'Is it near Formby?'[48] He has never heard of Marvin Gaye. Smigger's son thinks the Stylistics is a hairdressing salon. Nor is it just music that has changed. The city has too. 'It wasn't always … properties – parties and pills', Smigger tells the barman. They had come through 'shitty times', had been 'skint – out of work, picket lines and all that lark', things that the sociology student has only read about in books.[49]

Nostalgia also comes from many of the cultural references used by the plays, which tend to draw on the 1970s and 1980s, from an extended *Blind Date* sequence and multiple references to *Father Ted* in *Father O'Flaherty Saves Our Souls* to a musical version of the 1970s sitcom *The Liver Birds* in Barb Jungr and Mike Lindup's *The Liver Birds Are Flying Home*, which counterposes the original setting with Sandra and Beryl meeting up again forty years later. In *Brick Up*, much is, comically, made of 'young scouser' talk. Phoning in the warning to the authorities, Dickie Lewis tells them 'Alright there kidda! I'm on one here lad … is right, is right … is right lid.'[50] In *Brick Up 2*, Dennis adopts the lingo as a mark of rebellion against his wife when he tells the GPO man to 'Smoke it lad' as they go to blow up the Thelwall Viaduct. And nostalgia is rife at the end of *The Royal*. Theresa is the last person left in the hospital, and she talks to the ashes of her husband, which she has kept on her trolley since he died four years ago:

> This is it then Charlie, time to get out of here. I won't lie, I'm bloody terrified. This is all we know Charlie, isn't it eh? Oh Charlie remember when this place opened … 1978 … We used to serve our tea in teapots with proper cups and saucers then, you'd get a doily and everything. How times have changed … I've been here for over twenty five years and I wouldn't change a thing … apart from that Costa moving in and stealing all my business … This place has seen tears of sadness and tears of happiness … We must have served billions of teas and walked thousands of miles up and down this hozzy … And finally we are going home, aren't we lad.[51]

As she continues, telling him how she has not gone home because this was the last place he was, the last place they had kissed, the nostalgia becomes tinged with another characteristic of Royal Court plays, sentiment:

> Who'd have believed it ey? A heart as big and full of love as yours could pack in. How could I go home? I haven't been home for over four years, you weren't there any more … This place has been my home, Charlie, the staff and the

> patients my family ... (*To the building*) Ey, are you listening to me? Thanks for everything old girl ... You're a city within yourself you are.[52]

Comedy at the Royal Court, however, relies on more than familiarity and sentiment and nostalgia. It often comes at the expense of authority and sometimes has a real sense of defiance. Bosses and authority are generally absent from the stage, but when they appear, they are there to be sent up or ridiculed. In *Special Measures*, the minister who visits a failing school is not only a 'patronising potty-mouthed politician' but also 'such a hiss-and-boo figure he almost warrants a puff of green smoke'.[53] He is held hostage by the teachers, who threaten to take him down to the Cabbage pub and tell everyone who he is, selling him to the highest bidder. In *Dirty Dusting*, the owner of the business who sacks the women is Dave, described as a

> bully: obnoxious, bitter and ageist. A despicable no-hoper, who gets irate over the lack of respect he commands. Still under the thumb of his mother (with whom he still lives), he takes his frustrations out on the women. Eventually exposed as someone having sex with a vacuum cleaner and, despite the evidence, still denies it.[54]

The theatre employs a 'Can I Bring My Gran-o-meter' in its publicity, marking each show for swearing, nudity and general rudeness; sex, ribaldry, bawdiness and double entendres are rampant, satisfying a taste for revelry, plain speaking and hearty laughter, as Barrett argues (via Bourdieu).[55] Barrett goes on to suggest that the double entendres also

> depend on a shared reference point, further breaking down the barrier between audience and performers, and trade on the 'cleverness' of 'getting it,' of decoding the double entendre. In this way they bring audience members together with the performer and moreover invite them to collude in something they know to be tasteless, but are guilty of enjoying despite themselves.[56]

Although ribaldry runs through almost every show, the key play is Claire Sweeney and Mandy Muden's *Sex and the Suburbs* (May 2014). Set up as a live radio phone-in about sex with agony aunt Penny Crowe and guest presenter, the Baby Doll member Willow Wallace, the show is introduced directly to the audience by its producer, Rory Reynolds. He reminds the audience that the show is live so the use of video and photographic equipment is strictly prohibited, as is the use of 'blenders, pneumatic drills and rampant rabbits. (*To the woman in the front row*) So turn it off, madam.'[57] A moment later he is reminding them to turn off their phones, and he does mean turn them off, not 'put them on vibrate and shove them down your knickers'.

Later in the show, following a series of calls in which situations are played out for the audience, giving plenty of scope for bawdy comedy (these involve a knickerbocker glory, a tin of fruit and a chocolate fountain among other suggestive household items), super sexpert Annie, with her constant assurance that everything is 100 per cent wipe clean, demonstrates sex toys from her catalogue. This enables her to get the audience involved as well as producing a lively response from them, as Barrett describes:

> It's a raucous performance. People are crying laughing. There are 'whoops' when she mentions 'fully working tools' ... She asks for a drum roll. She gets one. Louder. Louder. And then ... she unleashes a huge black dildo. 'Here it is. The Rampant Roadster. Fashioned on TV's Jeremy Clarkson. Not that he's got a big cock. He just is one.' There is huge laughter. 'Shop in Iceland. Buy one, get one FREE! You buy one, you get one FREE!' A woman in the audience is shouting 'No! No!' as if she can't take it anymore. Annie takes the top off another vibrator. Applause when she switches it on and great laughter when she says, 'They both come together.'[58]

There is a sense of liberating laughter here as the audience enjoys indulging in the freedom to be risqué. Significantly, the enjoyment of sex is not the preserve of young women but stretches to those who are older. Gladys, Elsie and Olive in *Dirty Dusting* are described as being in their late 60s or early 70s, but discover there is 'life in the old dogs yet'.[59] But there is also a strong sense of morality that runs through the plays, as Smigger, in *Lost Soul*, explains to his wife. While everyone gets tempted, 'that's where it ends. You don't do the dirty on someone you're supposed to love.'[60] When Pat wants to stay with them, he won't let her. To him, she is a 'slapper' who has broken the rules.

There is nothing new about this style of theatre in the city, and reviewers have often been quick to draw parallels with the Everyman in the 1970s and 1980s. Joe Riley described the first performance of *Brick Up* as '80's Everyman at its rip-roaring best reincarnated at the Royal Court', and Dave Kirby suggested that the first run of *Brick Up* recreated 'the verve of the Everyman of the 70s and 80s when there was so much local talent being used'.[61] The Everyman, under Alan Dossor in the 1970s, developed the local musical with shows such as *Love and Kisses from Kirkby* and *Under New Management*. More directly political in tone than most of the Royal Court shows (*Under New Management* was a verbatim show about the Fisher Bendix factory occupation), they all drew on a house style picked up by Bob Eaton, who was artistic director there between 1981 and 1983, and defined by him as including a firm local commitment to the city both past and present, an abundant use of music, the use of local writers and actors and an informal and lively style of presentation. Eaton has also become a key player at the Royal Court, directing many shows (including *Brick Up*) and writing shows (including *Maggie May*, the final show before the pantomime in 2018), providing, with Fearon, a link to the old Everyman. Key here is *Lennon*, which had its premiere at the Everyman in 1980, just a month after John Lennon had been shot, and has run three times at the Royal Court, the only Beatles play to appear so far. While the revivals have lost some of the raw emotional immediacy the show had at the Everyman, the 2010 show, marking what would have been Lennon's 70th birthday, had a poignancy for the city. The style reflects that of the Royal Court, with a multi-role, fast-moving biography of Lennon and over forty songs that comment on the action.

Eaton is also keen to define the Royal Court style as 'Fish and Chips' theatre, an idea drawn from Stephen Joseph, the champion of theatre-in-the round, and much of the ethos Joseph described, late in his life, is embodied there. He had envisaged a theatre where all sections of the auditorium were organically connected 'to encourage the free flow of the audience from one place to another, even during the performance'. He thought seats should be generously spaced, and that all around the theatre there should be a viewing bar 'arranged so you can stand for a drink and snack and watch the play at the same time', with the kitchens serving food and drink, including fish and chips.[62] The specifics might be different in the Court, which has a proscenium arch stage and where the bar at the back of the stalls stays firmly closed during the show (meals are served before the show starts, with desserts arriving in the interval) but, as Paul Elsam points out, Joseph's design for a 'socially inclusive theatre' was suited to 'madcap … comedies' and high-energy performances, and the essence of the Royal Court reflects Joseph's dreams.[63]

Also reflecting Joseph's ethos, at the heart of the Royal Court is the audience. They are constantly thanked, praised and encouraged in Fearon's programme notes. They are always acknowledged and invited to share from the stage, be it by direct address (from actor or character) or sideways nods or the sharing of the laughter with the actors over corpsing when things go wrong. The finales of shows are often an invitation to dance or join in. Sometimes the audience is portrayed as being a little wild, the *Daily Post* reporting cheering, dancing on tables and generally going a little mad, and Eithne Browne describing how on some nights, 'it is like the pit in Shakespeare's Globe Theatre with people shouting out'.[64] Such accounts suggest an 'unruly' audience not bound or bowed by 'acceptable' theatre behaviour. Unquestionably, the theatre has attracted an audience, many of whom do not go to any other theatre, and a 2011 survey suggested that 29 per cent of the audience had never been to a theatre before. The top six postcodes represented by the audience include areas in the city such as West Derby, Croxteth, Kirkdale, Everton, Aintree and Huyton, which are far from being the affluent suburbs generally associated with theatre attendance. Many come to the Royal Court through visits to the pantomime or stand-up or concerts, and the demands from all of these for joining in and taking part. It is something that Paul Du Noyer (by way of Geoff Brown in *Melody Maker*) identifies as key to the city as a whole:

> Liverpool is an entertainment city … To entertain or be entertained is the one aim of life, once a living has been earned, and there seems damned little difference between the watcher and the watched. The enjoyment of entertainment isn't the desperate and often self-conscious style of the Southerner nor the dour, determined style of the Midlands but an exuberant, robust celebration of the laugh-today-for-tomorrow-we-die sort.[65]

It is the sort of response celebrated in the popular epithets of the fifth Beatle or the twelfth man at the Kop. All of this helps to add to a real sense of the theatre having become a People's Theatre. As Gillian Miller comments,

> at the heart of the success of the Royal Court over the last twelve years is our audience, most of whom come from Liverpool and the surrounding area. They've played a big part in driving the renovation of the building coming back time and time again often when the theatre was a building site![66]

2008: Capital of Culture

Digs at the Capital of Culture appeared on the Royal Court stage long before 2008, and reviewing *Council Depot Blues*, in Capital of Culture year, Lynne Walker was moved to remark that 'in a kind of "Carry On Liverpool" style, it sends up so-called high culture in a way that has the audience cheering to the rafters'.[67] The digs and the divisions were to continue long after 2008 was over; as Elliot Neston, seafood salesman, tries to convince Maggie, greasy caff owner, in the 2009 version of *Brick Up*, to place an order for 'Lescargot' which he claims has become quite popular in the city since the Capital of Culture, Dickie Lewis is dismissive. 'Ah it was a load of shite that capital of culture', he proclaims. 'It was just for students and arty people. (*Pause*) And them tit-heads who go to the theatre. (*All the cast slowly turn and look at the audience*).'[68] Luckily Maggie comes to the rescue. She loves theatre and has seen all the classics – *Mrs Brown, Mrs Brown's Boys, Mrs Brown Rides Again.*

A large part of the disaffection stemmed from the sense that Liverpool had won the bid because of, as John Bennett puts it (for want of a better term), its 'Liverpoolness'.[69] The Department of Culture, Media and Sport website at the time made this point clearly, stating that 'Liverpool won the 2008 race because people – the city's greatest asset – were at the heart of the bid.' In the run-up to 2008, however, it started to feel to people as if they, the greatest asset, were being sidelined and were not to be seen as a part of the 'World in One City', the strapline chosen by the city to define its bid. This was epitomised in a disastrous production, billed as one of the highlights of Liverpool's 2006 cultural programme.[70] *Super Vision* by the Builders Association and dmax, a show about surveillance, was programmed at the Royal Court in May by Robyn Archer, artistic director of the Capital of Culture. She was keen to bring new and unusual productions to the city as part of the build-up to 2008, not wanting to replicate what was already on offer and instead wanting to create new audiences. The show sold less than 600 tickets for its three-day run (many of which were cut-price offers to partners) and in the wake of this, Archer resigned.[71] In contrast, reviewing *Brick Up*, which premiered (and sold out) in August of that year, Joe Riley commented, 'It may not be what Ms Archer and her ilk would have ordered for Capital of Culture, but it's clearly what their paymaster Scousers relish.'[72]

The Capital of Culture bid had also made much of the importance of local talent, asking 'who could overlook the Beatles' contribution to popular music or that of writers such as Alan Bleasdale and Willy Russell to theatre?'[73] In reality, the official programme ignored both Bleasdale and Russell, but the Royal Court was not quite so forgetful. The programme for the year did champion newer local work; it marked the premiere of Kirby's *Council Depot Blues* and there was also space for Andrew Sherlock's *The Shankly Show*, a multimedia celebration of Liverpool FC's most famous manager, which had secured funding from the Capital of Culture and which offered the audience a 'local' hero to boost local pride. There was also, almost inevitably, a third revival of *Brick Up the Mersey Tunnels*. But significantly, there was also space for work by both Bleasdale and Russell.

The year, almost as a statement of intent, kicked off with Willy Russell's 30th anniversary production of *Stags and Hens*. Originally performed at the Everyman in 1978, Russell had originally been sceptical of the Royal Court, because the last time he had been there 'it was in a terrible state' and he had heard 'that they did not have proper seating in the stalls'. Worried that the audience would be a 'baying mob' who did not watch the show, he had been to see *Lost Soul* and discovered instead a 'great buzz from the theatre' and an audience who, far from behaving badly, were 'having a great time and a good night out'. He also thought it refreshing to 'find a theatre operated by a tiny group of people who were all so fantastically committed' and which did not have 'four marketing managers' and was not 'stifled by administration'.[74] In reality, however, this was not a 30th birthday production of *Stags and Hens*. It was in essence a new show, the third version of the play (the second being the 1990 film version *Dancin' Thru the Dark*). This was what Russell called a remix. It kept to the original period but was 'told at a much faster twenty-first century pace'. Thirty years ago, 'one told stories at a different pace and moments that held audiences back then now seem like longeurs'.[75] Described as 'unexpectedly good' in a very short review by Dominic Cavendish in the *Daily Telegraph* – Cavendish was one of only a handful of reviewers from national papers to notice the Royal Court throughout the whole of 2008 – *Stags and Hens* still told the same story it had told thirty years before, a story of tribes and trying to escape.[76] For Russell, the success of the show was encouraging and the following year saw a 'remix' version of *Our Day Out*, a show the theatre had wanted to stage for 2008 but, receiving no subsidy and no money from the Capital of Culture pot, had not been able to afford at that time. As with *Stags and Hens*, the new version told the same story, but this time the 'remix' added songs and dance to its twenty-first-century language.

Bleasdale's 1993 play, *On the Ledge* (April 2008), originally written for Nottingham Playhouse and the National Theatre, was a very different proposition to *Stags and Hens*. Set high above Liverpool, it is a play that sets before the city problems that still confronted it in 2008. The opening image of two disenfranchised boys spitting angrily about how London hates us, as one holds the other upside down over the roof to write the misspelled graffiti 'ANACHRY RULES', sums up the mood of the play. It is a howl of uncontrollable rage, a dark look at the despair and self-hatred behind the easy phrase 'inner-city dereliction', in which a motley collection of misfits and criminals, the dispossessed and the displaced, cower on the outside ledges of a block of flats as those below set fire to the city and their own homes. The characters cling to the ledges as the only place of safety, both physically and emotionally, in what Alfred Hickling described as an almost Beckettian metaphor for characters with nowhere to go.[77] Below, the world has gone truly mad and, in the words of the fireman sent to their rescue, 'the fuckin' community doesn't exist any more'. As Shaun, the villainous property developer who has returned to his home town having made a dubious fortune out of rebuilding the city after earlier riots, shouts across the rooftops at the end of the play: 'Let them eat stale cakes, give them false dawns and broken dreams, shoddy goods and shitty lives, cheap gin and hard drugs. Let despair and squalor and disease be theirs…'[78] Hickling commented that if in 1993 the play felt nihilistic, 'now it seems prophetic'.[79] As a comment on the perils and pitfalls of regeneration, the return of Bleasdale's play suggested that the Royal Court was willing to offer its audience more than celebration and stereotypes, comedy and nostalgia.

This is also true of Bleasdale's subsequent play staged at the Court. *Down the*

Dock Road (March 2016), originally written for Liverpool Playhouse in 1976, carries echoes of *Council Depot Blues*. Set on Grandad's last day at work, the all-male workforce drink their way through the day, do as little work as they can and dream of escaping, but there is a much bleaker heart. Instead of ending with the band performing alongside Stan, here Grandad has a heart attack. Amid the camaraderie and banter of the dockers, there are also tensions and rivalries in a cut-throat world where everyone is on the rob and some are prepared to stitch each other up. At its heart is McKenna, shop steward, fighter and bully, who takes on the world through his fists having learned from the early death of his docker father not to do things for others or to dream of something better. As he tells Grandad, when his father died,

> I knew then it was a shitty world, an' we were nothin' but the worms I'd used f'bait, dug up an' held wrigglin' in me hands ... lobbed out an' left danglin' at the end of a line, an' I said it wasn't goin' t'happen t'me, they weren't goin' t'get me – not the bosses – oh no, not them, they'll never get me – but our own kind ... Sure I'm a shop steward, 'course I do all that, but I don't do it f'you or f'him or t'carry a banner f'a better world. I do it f'me ... Oh sure, I've got beliefs, I've got ... sort of sacred things if y'want, but they don't get in the way, an' none of you bastards're ever goin' t'get near enough t'me t'turn those beliefs into dreams, passions, bloody causes. Anythin' t'die for.[80]

He is pitted against Marley, the security boss, 'the only villain in the play', an ex-policeman, 'and a bad one', who is determined to fit McKenna up and get rid of him.[81] The rivalry is played out against a fast-disappearing world. Grandad represents the old world of McKenna's father where there is nothing wrong with dreaming, but has come to realise that whatever they do, however much they strike and fight, nothing has changed, 'everythin's still the stinkin' same' except they kow-tow t'different bosses'. It is just 'suicide instead of murder'.[82] Around them the city is going to rack and ruin, it is 'The Arsehole of the Empire an' the docks are six miles up it' and there are no easy answers.[83] McKenna is glad that Grandad's last memory of the docks 'was the sight of shite flyn' cos that's what it's like. No heroes, in the hold.'[84]

Capital of Culture year also saw a production of Jim Cartwright's *Eight Miles High*, originally performed at the Bolton Octagon in 1991, but a show that incorporated many of the stylistic characteristics of home-grown Royal Court shows. From the start, audience members were invited to sit on the grassy knoll that formed part of the set, and to add to the festival atmosphere those who had booked meals with the show were offered a picnic basket to take with them. 'Welcome, plenty of grass for everyone. Just settle yourselves in some place, here, there, wherever the mood takes ya', urged the MC, as they entered. 'Keep on the grass. Not "Keep off the grass" but keep on the grass, eh?'[85] They found themselves not just watching the show but also becoming embedded in it, encouraged to chant away the rain and join in the singing. Set at a festival being held in a field outside Liverpool (Cartwright encouraged the relocation of the show to the city where it was being performed), *Eight Miles High* invoked the spirit of the sixties and was an excuse for a concert. The band, in Royal Court style, was made up of the actors who played in the intervening scenes, and the show was full of songs the audience knew, from 'Purple Haze' and 'California Dreamin' to 'Black Magic Woman'. Between the songs, a variety of characters, from a Hell's Angel and a traveller to a housewife who has been seduced away from her washing line and apron by discovering that talking to the hippies was like breathing cool, fresh air, played out their stories. For all the sense that Cartwright wanted his work 'to be life affirming', the ending allowed a hint of cynicism to creep in. Tod, who has arrived with the neighbouring landowner who is determined to get hold of the land for development, has little time for the festivalgoers but has his eyes opened to possibilities after eating doped cake. He tells the landowner,

> look at the harvest before your eyes, old man. Just aching to be cropped. It's a push over. Let's get them all back into the market. Give them their counter culture over the counter. Package it and sell it back to them. Ha! We'll give them revolution alright and grow fat in the fucking process ... Let's join with them, win them over and exploit them. And before you know it there will be nothing left of this time, just tunes. Young people clamouring, clamouring not for world peace, love and freedom but for cash cash cash, if anyone drops out no one will notice as they are crushed to death under foot. Love and peace will go back between the thick covers of the bible, only let out come the Christmas sermon. They won't know what hit them cause we will have approached so silently, flutter on you pretty wings, the nets are being drawn, your age of Aquarius is almost over. 'Oh so soon'. Yes.[86]

As the cast arrive on stage singing 'The Times They Are a Changing' and petals fall from the sky, they encourage the audience to join in. Inevitably they do and they keep singing and dancing through a finale of Joe Cocker's 'Little Help From My Friends', one big happy family with the actors, playing out Tod's scornful prediction.

Making it Better: Redevelopment

In the run-up to the Capital of Culture, the city council was still reluctant to grant Kevin Fearon and his partner Gillian Miller, who had been involved from the outset, a lease. The theatre's extensive artistic programme throughout 2008 was not recognised by the council as part of Liverpool Capital of Culture. In fact the then council leader, Warren Bradley, tried to evict Fearon in 2007, saying, in a leaked email, that they should be made to leave so that the venue could be used for the official Capital of Culture programme. But two arguments (and some pressure) prevailed. With Capital of Culture looming in 2008, who wanted an empty theatre in the city centre, visible as soon as you stepped out of Lime Street station? And how could Liverpool, a city that prided itself on its wit, host the Capital of Culture without a home for comedy? To add to the pressure, and to try and get the council onside with the renovation of one of its own assets, Miller formed a charitable Trust with three trustees as custodians of the building. Jonathan Falkingham CBE and Mark Featherstone-Witty OBE, led by Her Honour Elizabeth Steel DL, made a formidable team, working relentlessly to persuade the council that the theatre could be fully renovated if given the chance. Still the council was reluctant to grant a lease, before eventually bowing to the pressure and giving the theatre first a temporary lease until 31 January 2009 at a cost of £3,000 a month, and the promise of exploring funding possibilities for a much-needed £10 million revamp of the building, and

Architect's impression of the exterior, 2018

then, in 2008, extending the lease to three years. However, the theatre management needed longer if they were to persuade people to invest the significant amounts needed to save the city's landmark theatre. As Kevin Fearon pointed out, they were not really asking for very much:

> We are not asking the council to fund the works. We are not even asking for any of the £2.5 million in annual funding that goes to other venues in the city. We are simply looking to refurbish this great building.[87]

In fact, the Trust was offering the council something they had been looking for since the dark days of the 1970s – a way to restore the building at no cost to the city.

Despite these constraints, plans moved ahead for a multi-million pound grant application to upgrade, conserve and improve the building. A competition was launched to choose the architects, and in 2009 Allford Hall Monaghan Morris were awarded the contract. In 2010 the council awarded the Trust a 30-year lease (with a rent-free period of the same length if the building was completely renovated) and things could really start to happen. Money started to come in from the Heritage Lottery Fund, the European Regional Development Fund and a long loan from the building's owners, Liverpool City Council. Importantly, the audience were also connected to the rebuilding work, with £1 from each ticket going towards the renovation. In 2012 the first of what was framed as three acts of improvement started, the first substantial renovation work for nearly seventy-five years. Act 1, with money from the Heritage Lottery Fund, left the theatre dark for four months as work focused on the auditorium to make maximum impact on audiences who were desperate for new seats, better bar facilities and improved access. Act 2, supported through a partnership between Liverpool City Council and the European Regional Development Fund, took place three years later, concentrating on the Welcome Project, an extension of the building to fill the space covered by the canopy, creating a new entrance. The box office was moved to the front of the building, a new foyer and 'welcome' area for the audience were created, and a first-floor terrace was constructed above the new extension, all adding to a sociable and hospitable atmosphere, now complete with a view. Act 3, with support from Arts Council England, was completed in January 2018 and added a new, 150-seat basement venue to operate independently of the main theatre and to be a home for comedy, music and small-scale theatre. Act 3 remodelled the balcony seating to create a new entrance with better access for all, as well as focusing on bringing backstage up-to-date and restoring the original revolving stage, one of the largest outside London. The ethos of the conservation focused on a raw, distressed aesthetic, exposing the original 1938 brickwork. It looked to create, in the words of the Royal Institute of

Exterior, 2018 (Tim Soar)

British Architects, which awarded the building three prizes, a building that was 'open, welcoming and sufficiently grand but without pretension or extravagance'.[88]

In 2016 the theatre purchased the Penny Farthing, the pub next door, having persuaded St John's shopping centre to sell it and Liverpool City Council to increase its loan to the theatre to enable the sale to be completed. In the future there are plans to create an extension linking the pub to the theatre and in 2017 it reopened as the Courtyard Bar and Kitchen, adding to the theatre's social spaces, with the Welcome Centre now also boasting Café 38. With views of St George's Hall and the newly refurbished Lime Street plateau, the theatre was placing itself at the heart of the regeneration of the St George's Quarter, an area that includes St George's Hall, the Empire and many of the city's museums and galleries. As well as marking the 80th birthday of the building, 2018 also brought more good news. For the first

Interior, 2018, showing the exposed original brickwork (Tim Soar)

time in its history the theatre was awarded a revenue grant, becoming a National Portfolio Organisation at Arts Council England. This significant addition to the Arts Council's national portfolio demonstrates its commitment to reaching audiences who come from lower socio-economic backgrounds and are less engaged with the arts in general. As well as helping the theatre to be more resilient and sustainable going forward, the award brings the Royal Court to the attention of people across the UK and gives it the opportunity to be part of the creative conversation. It might also allow, in the city, for a little more joined-up thinking, as Kevin Fearon explained to *The Stage*:

> Here you've got the Unity, Everyman and Playhouse, Epstein and us, and the Empire, and there's no forum for sitting down. Everyman and Playhouse and Unity are part of LARC (Liverpool Arts Regeneration Consortium), but

> we've never been allowed to be a member of that. When theatres co-produce, they share the costs of marketing, as well as set-building and costumes ... We could be doing that here in Liverpool. We could be doing a joint brochure. We could be building sets together.[89]

Money for the building also enabled and encouraged additional work to happen within the theatre. 2011 saw the setting up of a free-to-access Youth Theatre for 11–19 year olds. The theatre also started to produce the already successful play *Terriers* by Maurice Bessman, a partnership project with Merseyside Police about the dangers of gun crime and gang culture, which is still being successfully performed in schools as well as prisons. Heritage Tours opened up the newly refurbished theatre for wider inspection and the theatre also hosted open forum events as well as instigating a volunteer programme and offering work experience. The Variety Lunch Club events for the over-60s began, offering an afternoon of entertainment, socialising and a bowl of scouse. Alongside the new Welcome areas and the Courtyard, these activities were opening up the theatre for more and more new people. The theatre has also started to build partnerships in the city, including the establishment of the Liverpool Hope Playwriting Prize in 2015, which offers £10,000 for a new comedy script with the chance to have the play performed at the theatre. *Omnibus* by Katie Mulgrew was the first winner of the Hope Prize and the play was produced by the Royal Court and shown at the Unity Theatre in 2017. *The Miracle on Great Homer Street* by Gerry Linford, produced at the Royal Court in 2018, was a runner-up in the second year of the competition. In 2014 the theatre became one of Liverpool John Moores University's Principal Partners, giving students and university staff access to a range of cultural activities.

2018 and Beyond

As with 2008, the theatre's 80th birthday programme was a mix of old favourites and new work, although this time the old favourites were drawn from its own repertoire and not the works of Bleasdale and Russell. A revival of *Council Depot Blues* kicked off the year and was followed in July by *Mam I'm 'Ere*. But it was the two new works that suggested most about where the Royal Court found itself in 2018. Gerry Linford's *The Miracle on Great Homer Street* caught the eye of Les Dennis, one of the judges in the Hope Playwriting competition. It had certain qualities that suggested it as a Royal Court play. It was a comedy and, being set in 1978, it was also nostalgic, or, as the *Liverpool Echo* proclaimed, 'too content', at times, 'to ride on the nostalgia train'.[90] It was also timely, being about the World Cup. But the story was darker, more

View from the Courtyard bar and restaurant, 2018

moral and less musical than many Royal Court shows. Father Aherne has discovered that he has a direct line to St Cajetan, the patron saint of Argentina (where the 1978 World Cup was held), of gamblers and of the unemployed, which offers him some useful winning tips. As a priest he cannot be seen to gamble, so he finds himself lodgings with Terry and Marion. Terry, a lapsed Catholic, and Father Aherne bond over the 'bookie busting fortune' they start to amass.[91] The moral quandary arises when the question comes up as to how the fortune is to be spent. Originally, the priest had suggested that he would follow the lead of St Cajetan, who had set up a bank to help the poor as an alternative to the high interest rates of the moneylenders. But when the crunch comes, there is a sting in the tale as the play turns 'on a knife-edge and stuns its guffawing audience into silence'.[92]

The final new play in 2018 was Bob Eaton's *Maggie May*. Based on a legendary character, a prostitute from a folk song who was renowned for preying on sailors, Eaton turned the story into one of a woman regaining control of her own destiny. His Maggie is a feisty Irish girl who falls victim to a bag snatcher as she arrives in Liverpool on her way to New York and a new world, 'a land of dreams that lies awaiting'.[93] With no money for her fare, she is forced to stay and find a job, thinking she has landed on her feet when she becomes a housemaid to Campbell, a wealthy young sugar importer, who claims that he really wants to be an artist. Campbell seduces her, leaving her pregnant and in the workhouse. With a baby who dies at three weeks old, she looks to regain control of her life, deciding that

> I don't intend to be
> Anybody's property
> It's a business deal
> That is all that's real
> And a businessman should understand
> The way I feel.[94]

She turns to prostitution, later becoming Campbell's mistress, set up in a grand house in a prosperous neighbourhood. In revenge, and to help her old friends, she runs the house as a high-class brothel, eventually escaping to New York with Charlie, her true love.

Behind Maggie's story is the city, from the docks and St George's plateau to the First World War and the 1919 police strike. The battle is between classes and the fight is between capitalism and socialism. The men of Martins Bank, hosting a soirée to mark the end of the First World War, sing of capital being the future of the nation:

> Capital will be the world's salvation
> Capital needs no explanation
> It just means you know who is boss
> Capital! That's what we believe in
> Capital! That's why we're not grievin'
> Capital! Some might call it thievin'
> But frankly we don't give a toss.[95]

On the other side is Maggie, who devours books while cleaning – including *Das Kapital*, George Bernard Shaw, Engels, Emma Goldman and Sylvia Pankhurst – and the poor and the strikers of the city. But they are not righteous either. On her arrival, Maggie is met at the dockside by Charlie, greeted with a song about the ills of Liverpool, 'a terrible place' where 'poverty is awful cruel' and she will learn things she never learned in school. It might be 'the richest city in the world' but she will never see poverty like it and will always be 'yards from a living hell'. And it is all fuelled by alcohol, as Charlie (joined by the drinking chorus) explains:

> Drunk for a penny and blind for two
> Sober as a Judge means nothin' at all
> They're rolling round St George's Hall
>
> Tip that bottle and raise that glass
> Work is the curse of the drinking class
> Sweet Australian white's the fuel
> Driving Liverpool.[96]

Towards the end of the play, as rioters gather in front of St George's Hall, prepared to fight for 'a new world/ Where dreams aren't bought and sold', they decide that they need a drink before the revolution.[97] As the magistrate steps up to read the Riot Act, he is prevented by a man who snatches away the paper and offers him a bottle, asking, 'D'yer wanna bevvy?' as the rioters break out in song:

> The time for revolution's near
> Break out the wine, whisky and beer
> We're gonna smash the capitalists
> But first of all we're gonna get pissed
> It's free for all to do as you please
> Loot the pubs and distilleries
> Break the windows, break the rules
> Drink up Liverpool.

The song continues as shop windows are smashed and a piano is dragged out on to the streets:

> You can send your gunboats and your troops
> We'll be ready when we've had a few scoops
> We're always willing to stand and fight
> When we've had enough Australian white
> Once we've had sufficient gin
> The revolution can begin
> I might be falling off a bar room stool
> But I'll fight for Liverpool.[98]

It is the individual, or rather the couple finally reunited, who board the ship for New York where they 'hold the future in our hands'. The crowd stops its celebrations and

The new basement studio, 2018

watches them 'looking into the future', suggesting, maybe, that they should be more like Maggie.[99]

The show has resonances of old Everyman shows and new Royal Court shows. It is full of music and much of the story is told through song. It is fast-moving, with short scenes drawing on popular images set against a broad sweep of Liverpool history. The city and its people are at its heart, but it isn't the people and the city who win. It is the feisty, independent Irish woman who sails away to the 'land our dreams can all come true', and the show is critical of the city, for all its sense of celebration.[100] Here the question is who will things be different for – the individual who takes control and leaves or the collective city that stays and drinks? And, like the *The*

Miracle on Great Homer Street, it leaves its audience with something to think about.

In 2007, in the theatre's first season brochure since 1970, Kevin Fearon wrote that when they took over the theatre, 'our plan was always to re-establish the Royal Court as the home of popular theatre. A theatre for the people of Liverpool and Merseyside presenting plays by Liverpool's great writers, performed by Liverpool's great actors.' In 2018 his brochure note was celebrating the last eighty years and confidently looking forward to the next eighty. In thirteen years, Kevin Fearon and Gillian Miller turned around the fortunes of a theatre that had been written off by everyone since the late 1960s, not only keeping it open but also restoring it physically. As the 1938 reopening brochure had stated, it was 'a brave venture in the times through which we are passing', and for the first time in its history, since becoming the Royal Court, the theatre has become a full-time producing house. It is not without its detractors, who see its reinvention as the home of Scouse comedy as parochial and inward looking, especially at a time when Liverpool wanted to reinvent itself as the 'World in One City'. But it is in choosing to speak to and about the people in the city who are often forgotten that the Royal Court has found its twenty-first-century place. Fearon has 'never been so excited as I am now about the Royal Court ... With the Penny Farthing redevelopment, the basement, and the confidence we have with the work on the stage, we're in a good place.'[101] Both Fearon and Miller see the audience as being at the heart of their success:

> They have been amazing and are the reason that we now have support from the Arts Council of England who recognise our audience as being unique, special and deserving of their funding, most of which is collected through the purchase of lottery tickets. It's a privilege to have been able to make the theatre a better place to visit and to expand the offer to include all those things that make a building come alive: our free to access youth theatre, community choir, gardening and drama groups and the hugely popular Variety Lunch Clubs and *Terriers* Project. And we've not quite finished so the journey continues to make Liverpool's Royal Court and the surrounding area even better![102]

Notes

1 *Mrs Brown's Boys* had started life in 1992 on Irish radio and had then been developed into a series of books prior to the stage shows, described by O'Carroll as a trilogy even though there were five of them. *Mrs Brown* wasn't to make it to the BBC until 2009.
2 Quoted in Barrett, 'Fish out of Water', 106.
3 Len Pentin and Fred Lawless, *Slappers and Slapheads* (unpublished), 2.
4 Ibid., 123.
5 *Liverpool Echo*, 13 July 2007, 3.
6 *Liverpool Echo*, 10 May 2005, 3.
7 September–December 2005 season brochure.
8 *Daily Post*, 18 August 2007, 7.
9 *Liverpool Echo*, 3 February 2017, 16.
10 Dave Kirby and Nicky Allt, *Brick Up the Mersey Tunnels* (2009, unpublished), 79.
11 Ibid., 87.
12 *Daily Post*, 17 August 2007, 3.
13 *Liverpool Echo*, 10 September 2008, 25; *Daily Post*, 18 August 2007, 7.
14 Dave Kirby, *Lost Soul* (version 6, unpublished),1.
15 Ibid., 4.
16 Ibid., 7.
17 Ibid., 18.
18 Ibid., 55.
19 Ibid., 83.
20 Ibid., 55.
21 Ibid., 42.
22 Ibid., 55.
23 Programme note.
24 Dave Kirby, *Council Depot Blues* (unpublished), 69–70.
25 Ibid., 79, 87.
26 Ibid., 15.
27 Ibid., 88.
28 Programme note.
29 *Guardian*, 19 March 2009, 36.
30 Boisterous is a new Liverpool theatre company, established in 2018 with the support of the Royal Court, that aims to nurture talent within the city's black and ethnic minority arts community. The company is run by Miriam Mussa and Maurice Bessman.
31 Paul Du Noyer, *Liverpool – Wondrous Place: Music from the Cavern to the Coral* (London: Virgin Books, 2004), 174.
32 Quoted in Ros Merkin, 'Liverpool', in David Wiles and Christine Dymkowski (eds), *The Cambridge Companion to Theatre History* (Cambridge: Cambridge University Press, 2013), 96.
33 Quoted in Du Noyer, *Liverpool – Wondrous Place*, 181.
34 *Spectator*, 16 October 2004; 23 October 2004.
35 Philip Boland, 'The Construction of Images of People and Place: Labelling Liverpool and Stereotyping Scousers', *Cities* 25.6 (2008), 363.
36 Du Noyer, *Liverpool – Wondrous Place*, 174.
37 Quoted in Marr, *History of Modern Britain*, 390.
38 Du Noyer, *Liverpool – Wondrous Place*, 175.
39 *Arts Alive*, October 1984, n.p.
40 *Daily Post*, 29 October 2007, 9.
41 Woollybacks (or Wools) originally referred to those who travelled into Liverpool to work at the docks, and is now used to refer to anyone who lives in the towns around the city.
42 *Liverpool Echo*, 27 August 2007, 10.
43 Ibid., 10.
44 *Liverpool Echo*, 13 July 207, 3.
45 Kirby, *Lost Soul*, 81.
46 Ibid., 25–6.
47 Ibid., 25.
48 Ibid., 25.
49 Ibid., 27–8.
50 Kirby and Allt, *Brick Up the Mersey Tunnels*, 65.
51 Lindzi Germain and Angela Simms, *The Royal* (unpublished), 71.
52 Ibid., 72.
53 *Guardian*, 11 April 2014.
54 Ed Waugh and Trevor Wood, *Dirty Dusting* (2006, unpublished), 2.

55 Barrett, 'Fish out of Water', 210.
56 Ibid., 211.
57 Claire Sweeney and Mandy Muden, *Sex and the Suburbs* (2014, unpublished), 1.
58 Barrett, 'Fish out of Water', 212.
59 Waugh and Wood, *Dirty Dusting*, 18.
60 Kirby, *Lost Soul*, 6.
61 *Liverpool Echo*, 9 August 2006, 23.
62 Stephen Joseph, *Theatre in the Round* (New York: Taplinger Publishing, 1968), 117.
63 Paul Elsam, *Stephen Joseph: Theatre Pioneer and Provocateur* (London: Bloomsbury Methuen, 2014), 166.
64 *Daily Post*, 17 August 2007, 3; *Liverpool Echo*, 16 November 2007, 1.
65 Du Noyer, *Liverpool – Wondrous Place*, 2.
66 Email to author from Gina Miller, September 2018.
67 *Independent*, 5 November 2008, 14.
68 Kirby and Allt, *Brick Up the Mersey Tunnels*, 20.
69 John Bennett, 'Answering to the Audience: Opportunities and Tensions in Popular Theatre Programming with Particular Reference to the Royal Court Liverpool and the 2008 European Capital of Culture', in Wim Coudenys (ed.), *Whose Culture(s)?* (2008), 102, https://www.academia.edu/506573/_Minoritics_margins_peripheries_and_the_discourse_of_Cultural_Capital_ (accessed 28 November 2018).
70 In the run-up to 2008, the city ran a number of themed years.
71 Other Capital of Culture shows were also staged at the Royal Court in that year, including *Scrap Arts Music*, a Canadian percussion ensemble, Bang on a Can's multimedia *The Carbon Copy Building* and *The End of Cinematics*.
72 *Liverpool Echo*, 9 August 2006, 23.
73 Quoted in Bennett, 'Answering to the Audience', 102.
74 *Daily Post*, 18 January 2008, 2.
75 Ibid., 2.
76 *Daily Telegraph*, 11 February 2008, 26.
77 *Guardian*, 3 May 2008.
78 Alan Bleasdale, *On the Ledge* (London: Faber & Faber, 1993), 49, 63.
79 *Guardian*, 3 May 2008.
80 Alan Bleasdale, *Down the Dock Road* (2016, unpublished), 113–14.
81 Ibid., 2.
82 Ibid., 80–1.
83 Ibid., 44.
84 Ibid., 98.
85 Jim Cartwright, *Eight Miles High* (2008, unpublished), 3.
86 *Liverpool Echo*, 11 July 2008, 1; Cartwright, *Eight Miles High*, 59.
87 *Liverpool Echo*, 7 May 2008, 11.
88 RIBA website. The building won a number of awards including RIBA Northwest 2018, RIBA North West Conservation 2018, RIBA National Award 2018 and *Architects Journal* Retrofit of the Year 2016.
89 *The Stage*, 26 January 2018.
90 *Liverpool Echo*, 7 June 2018.
91 Ibid.
92 *The Stage*, 7 June 2018.
93 Bob Eaton, *Maggie May*, with lyrics by Bob Eaton and Sayan Kent and music by Sayan Kent (June 2018, unpublished), 7.
94 Ibid., 89.
95 Ibid., 72.
96 Ibid., 10–12.
97 Ibid., 110.
98 Ibid., 120.
99 Ibid., 121.
100 Ibid., 121.
101 *The Stage*, 26 January 2018.
102 Email to author from Gina Miller, September 2018.

2008

1 February–1 March	*Stags and Hens*	Willy Russell	30th anniversary remix
7 March	*Russell Howard Adventures*		
14 March–12 April	*Brick Up the Mersey Tunnels*	Nicky Allt and Dave Kirby	
25 April–24 May	*On the Ledge*	Alan Bleasdale	
Festival of Comedy including			
29 May	Nina Conti		
30 May	Paul Merton: *Impro Chums*		
5 June	John Bishop: *Stick Your Job up Your A**e*		
7 June	Frankie Boyle		
14 June–5 July	*Misery*	Stephen King	with Andrew Schofield and Joan Kempson
18 July–16 August	*Eight Miles High*	Jim Cartwright	
5–27 September	*Lost Soul*	Dave Kirby	
3–18 October	*The Shankly Show*	Andrew Sherlock	
31 October–29 November	*Council Depot Blues*	Dave Kirby	
11 December–24 January 2009	*Night Collar*	Tony Furlong and Jimmy Power	

Alan Bleasdale's *On the Ledge* (Clare Bennett)

Willy Russell's *Stags and Hens* (Dave Evans)

Christmas, 2000–2018

2000 ***Aladdin***

2001 ***Dick Whittington and his Amazing Cat***

> Most of the human ingredients are tried and tested. Michael Starke starring in the enhanced role of Idle Jack; comic Mickey Finn (as shipmate) contributing a stand-up routine; Herbert the hairdresser donning frocks more Technicolor than Joseph's dreamcoat; Roger Phillips' sea captain sounding much more like a drill sergeant major than Popeye's cousin; and the ever-reliable and smiling Danny McCall shoulder-bundling the title role. But somewhere, there must be story trying to get out? ... Where things fail is in the mixing, not the matching of individual strengths. It proves that pantomime is a much more difficult recipe to get right than the public imagine, and time-served artists assume. (*Liverpool Echo*, 28 December 2001, 12)

2002 ***Cinderella***

> Fairy Good in a Wishy-Washy Way Soap: The Empire scrapped pantomime 15 years ago, saying there were fewer big name variety stars available. The Royal Court revived panto six years ago, determined to prove that sufficient talent could be mustered locally. The stage debut of Craig Phillips, TV's New Age handyman and first *Big Brother* winner, continues that belief ... surprisingly low key, and virtually absent after an initial burst of mischief is superdog Schnorbitz. Maybe there's something in the small print of the Canine Union Handbook preventing longer bouts of animal magic, but Schnorbitz even pretending to help pull Cinders' coach would have been preferable to four stuffed reindeer. (*Liverpool Echo*, 30 December 2002, 16–17)

2003 ***Snow White***

> If it ain't broke, don't fix it appears to be the motto of the team behind this year's offering at the Royal Court ... The main comedy comes from Roy Brandon as Dame Academy (TEN costume changes) and Radio City's Pete Price as her idiotic son Muddles. They are at their most successful when they ditch the wordy gags for simple slapstick humour. A decorating scene is pure Laurel and Hardy, while a version of the Twelve Days of Christmas degenerates into chaos with Muddles rugby tackling a giggling Fairy Liquid

(Leanne Campbell) to the ground ... The kids love it and that's showbiz folks.
(*Liverpool Echo*, 31 December 2003, 11)

2004 *Jack and the Beanstalk*

Time to help kill the wicked giant. No really big names, but producer Jane Joseph is hoping a strong cast of mainly local favourites – plus a dog – will pull in the crowds for Liverpool's main panto. (*Liverpool Echo*, 3 December 2004, 18)

2006 *Snow White*

Liverpool's family panto this year is led by young Merseyside TV talent. Grange Hill star Chris Perry Metcalfe and former *Hollyoaks* actress Christina Baily appear in *Snow White and the Seven Dwarfs* ... They are joined in the all-local cast by hairdresser Herbert Howe as dame, and *Echo* comedian of the year Chris Cairns as Muddles. There is also a special role for the *Echo* mascot, Lily the Liverbird ... Pantomime is being revived at the Court ... *Snow White* ... will be Liverpool's only large-scale traditional panto. (*Liverpool Echo*, 20 September 2006, 12)

2007 *Cinderella*

As so often in panto, the nominal leads have little to do but stand back and let the 'characters' do their stuff. In this case it is Eithne Browne and Crissy Rock as the ghastly pouting and flouncing ugly Hardup sisters Paris and Nicole. Browne in particular has a ball working the audience threatening the crown of Pete Price, whose Buttons acts as the panto's compere ... And two hours into the show he still manages to persuade excitable children and interval drink-fuelled adults to dance and sing about Wiggly Woo the worm. (*Liverpool Echo*, 21 December 2007, 13)

2008 *Night Collar* by Tony Furlong and Jimmy Power

[T]he play ... has undergone constant up-dating, which makes it far better than a TV soap (where the outside world never intrudes), and readily explains why the current run has gags about tax cuts, Barack Obama and (inevitably!) Capital of Culture ... 'The object is to keep things bang up to date', says Tony. 'We want the audience to think that we must have written it the night before.' (*Liverpool Echo*, 12 December 2008, 37)

2009 *Merry Ding Dong* by Fred Lawless

It wasn't until after the Capital of Culture that the Royal Court found its stride with its Christmas shows. With the arrival of Fred Lawless, the theatre hit on a formula that came to define Christmas at the Court and establish a new Royal Court tradition. Aimed at an older audience, these were shows that took stories an audience knew and went one step further.

> Cue much squaring up on the pair's front gardens in Speke's Western Avenue (described as 'the only Western John Wayne was too scared to set foot in'), shouting from windows and one-up-manship over a Christmas lights competition ... This latest show ... is billed as 'a combination of Scouse comedy and rock'n'roll panto.' And indeed the action is woven together with a never ending supply of well-sung festive favourites whose lyrics have been given a rude Royal Court twist... (*Liverpool Echo*, 17 December 2009, 27)

> 'O Welcome to our Little Show' (sung by the cast as a choir to the tune of 'O Little Town of Bethlehem')

> O welcome to our little show
> We're pleased to see you all
> Sit back, relax and have a drink
> We're going to have a ball
> This show's a story of two families
> You'll know them all we're sure
> But if you don't like swearing
> Then there's the fucking door...

> In this little town of Liverpool
> True Scousers are born and bred
> Our story is of two such men
> A blue nose and a red
> They live in Speke near the Boulevard
> By the airport and the Hall
> There's Morrisons there and a car factory
> But apart from that sod all.[1]

2010 *Scouse Pacific* by Fred Lawless

> Fred Lawless has a knack for spinning Merseyside variants of old sitcom formats. Last year's *Merry Ding Dong* was a fractious update of *Love Thy*

Merry Ding Dong by Fred Lawless with Eithne Browne as Holly and Lindzi Germain as Ivy (Dave Evans)

Neighbour ... Now he has created a version of *Gilligan's Island* set in a South Sea paradise colonised by a lost race of Liverpudlians.

Father O'Flaherty, the intemperate Irish priest who featured in last year's show, has been hauled before the bishop and ordered to adopt the missionary position (pardon the innuendo, but it's that kind of show). So he and a nubile team of 'Sisters of Mersey' are despatched to the island of Secosu, inhabited by the descendants of a shipwrecked Scouser named Billy Riley.

And are they happy there? Not remotely: 'Nothing to do, no footie on a Saturday and nothing to eat but friggin' bananas.' Yet there is trouble in paradise as a team of rapacious developers comes tunnelling through with plans to develop the island into a luxury resort... (Alfred Hickling, *Guardian,* 3 December 2010, 56)

2011 *Little Scouse on the Prairie* by Fred Lawless

We are continuing to create our very own Royal Court Christmas tradition. (Kevin Fearon, programme note)

First there was *Merry Ding-Dong*. Then Father O'Flaherty and Co. decamped to an island paradise in *Scouse Pacific*. Now the good Father and his flock are back, this time transported to the wild, Wild West ... Estate agent Mr Baddington (Paul Duckworth) turns up at the St Nick's club Wild West-themed karaoke night demanding money with menaces, while Donna Marie (Rachel Rae) believes husband Dick (Stephen Fletcher) has forgotten their wedding anniversary and after a strop drifts off to sleep on a Superlambanana, waking up in a saloon bar in the Arizona town of Halewood.

(Toto) I don't think we're in Speke any more.

Never mind *The Wizard of Oz*. In Fred Lawless's lawless land no cultural reference is safe, no one is immune from a good skitting, from *High Noon* to *Calamity Jane*, from the Three Amigos to *Back to the Future*. (*Liverpool Echo*, 30 November 2011, 31)

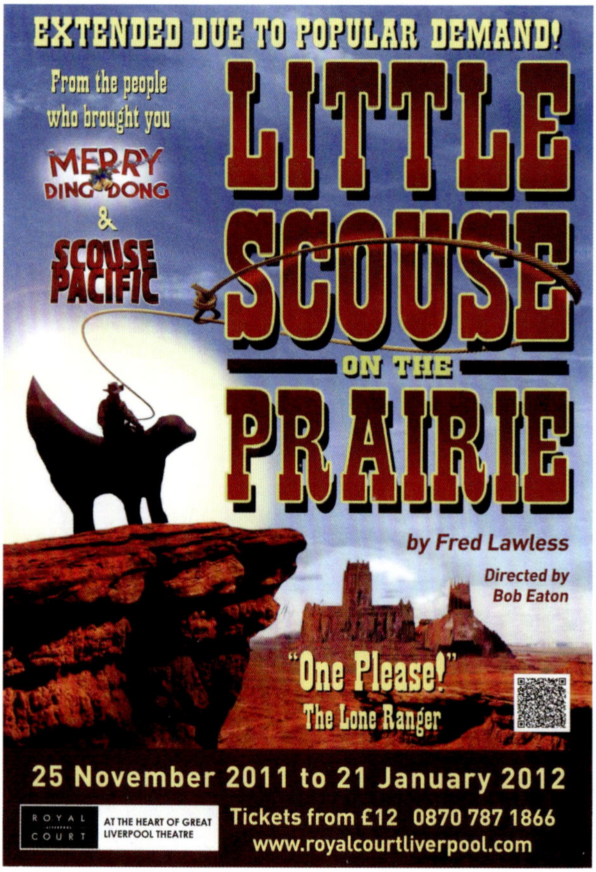

2011 *Snow White and the Seven Dwarves* (matinees)

The Royal Court is going for broke this season with not one but two festive shows, meaning the return – after several years – of its traditional panto … even the kids get the *Desperate Scousewives* gags which have crept into every Merseyside panto this season. (*Liverpool Echo*, 14 December 2011, 27)

2012 *A Nightmare On Lime Street* by Fred Lawless

I've always been a fan of horror movies, in particular the early black and white Frankenstein and Dracula movies … However the genre I enjoyed even more was comedy horror … My earliest memory of this type of movie was the 'Abbot and Costello meets…' series of movies which brought the hapless duo up against the likes of Frankenstein and Dr Jekyll/Mr Hyde … but for me, the best of the bunch was Mel Brooks' 1974 classic, *Young Frankenstein* … What I particularly liked about *Young Frankenstein* was that it was written as a sort of sequel of Mary Shelley's original story, and posed the question 'What if Frankenstein had had a grandson?' In writing *A Nightmare on Lime Street* I also started with a 'What if?' question, but the question I asked myself was 'What if Frankenstein had moved to Liverpool after it all went wrong for him in Bavaria?' (Fred Lawless, programme note)

2013 *The Hitchhiker's Guide to Fazakerley* by Fred Lawless

Boldly go where no Christmas show has gone before.

Our story today begins in a town called Fazakerley. A strange place where the girls have weird orange skin and wear pyjamas all day long. A place where the people have endured tremendous hardships over the years, like living next door to Kirkby. But today, something strange is about to happen in Fazakerley. So make sure you've got a stiff drink in front of you, strap yourself in and get ready for … *The Hitchhiker's Guide to Fazakerley*! (*lots of echo on last word*)

Bleed through gauze to reveal THING, THONG and the SPACE GIRLS. The gauze lifts after the bleed through to reveal the girls surrounded by stars, there are various space type props on stage.[2]

2014 *Scouse of the Antarctic* by Fred Lawless

Going where snowman has gone before

So to this year, and to the Antarctic! Well, actually that isn't strictly true, the show is set in the North Pole ... The 'error' will be explained during the course of the play. (Fred Lawless, programme note)

The overture plays, it then merges into the opening song ... The stage is set as the North Pole, icebergs, an igloo, an ice hole, a SNOWMAN *etc.* NB *the* SNOWMAN *will be static but will be voiced with a recorded dialogue (Scouse accent).* JIMMY *enters from the igloo. He's carrying a washing basket full of clothes.*

JIMMY (*sings*): I've got no worries, I've got no cares
All my mates are polar bears
It's a great place to relax
And I pay no bills and no Poll tax
Jimmy walks over to the ice hole
I fish for breakfast in this hole
Cos now I'm living up the Pole

Various polar animals enter and sing the chorus (played by the cast). The animals include two POLAR BEARS *(the female* KYLIE *wears pyjama bottoms and has her hair in rollers), penguins etc. Some will be puppets. The animals and* JIMMY *occasionally acknowledge each other with waves and the occasional 'alright' ... Underscore.*

JIMMY (*to the* SNOWMAN): Isn't it great here eh Frosty?

SNOWMAN: No it's shite!

JIMMY: What d'yer mean?

SNOWMAN: It's fuckin' freezing!

JIMMY: Course it's freezin', it's the North Pole! Anyway you're made of snow, that shouldn't bother you.

SNOWMAN: Yeah, well it does!

JIMMY: You're always moaning you. Two years I've lived here now and I've loved every minute of it!

SNOWMAN: God knows why you'd want to move here?

JIMMY: Well it wasn't intentional, but I'm glad this is where I've ended up. (*Sings*)

Back in Liverpool things were bad
Cos when you're skint it makes you sad
Seven summons and a date in court
Getting' out of town was my last resort

So I packed my bags, signed off the dole
And somehow ended up the Pole…

SNOWMAN: I'd like to live somewhere warm, like the Bahamas.[3]

2015 *Pharaoh 'Cross the Mersey* by Fred Lawless

The playwright is about to launch his seventh successive seasonal smash-hit show at the Roe Street theatre … [the cast] will be hot footing it across the desert to an assortment of original songs and sing-a-long hits. And there might well be some walking like an Egyptian, and a sand dance or two. Well, with Wilson of Wilson, Keppel and Betty being a Scouser, surely that's a given? Fred explains: 'We've actually brought two characters forward from *Scouse of the Antarctic* last year … Boris and Daisy fell in love last year, so now he's proposed to her and they're on holiday celebrating their engagement …' The pair start in the modern day before being transported back to Ancient Egypt where they meet King Tut and Queen Nefertiti and, in the grand traditions of Royal Court 'pantos', get into all sorts of scrapes. (*Liverpool Echo*, 20 November 2015, 5)

2016 *Scouse of the Rising Sun* by Kevin Fearon

It's a well-known fact that, wherever you are in the world, you're bound to bump into a Scouser. So, with that in mind, surely the plot of the Royal Court's festive offering, *Scouse of the Rising Sun*, isn't really as outlandish as all that? Actually, it IS pretty outlandish, but then devotees of the Court's traditional Christmas show expect nothing less … For the first time in seven years, the show hasn't been penned by Fred Lawless. Instead, writing duties have been taken on by Royal Court producer Kevin Fearon, with the entire cast having a hand in bringing the final product to the stage. Be assured, though – all the components that Royal Court audiences expect are still present and correct. A band of plucky Scousers find themselves in peril – but, despite some mishaps, contrive to save the day.

There's a comedy animal (in this case, two – an early appearance for a drum playing panda, and the return from last year's *Pharaoh 'Cross the Mersey* of one of the Bernie Clifton-style camels) … you've got to doff your hat to a show that manages to include not just a *Full Monty* skit and a send-up of *Blood Brothers*, but a heartfelt version of a Smiths song, to boot. (*Liverpool Echo*, 5 December 2016, 16)

Scouse Pacific by Fred Lawless with Rachel Rae as Donna Marie, Andrew Schofield as Terry and Lindzi Germain as Mary (Dave Evans)

2017 *The Scouse Nativity* by Kevin Fearon

> What better theme for a Christmas show than the greatest ever told? And lo, the Nativity came to Liverpool. But this being the Royal Court, it's a Scouse Nativity, told in grandiose fashion, the story unfolding to the strains of Orff's O Fortuna and against the backdrop of Mark Walters' inspired pop-up storybook set … Like *Life of Brian*, the big laughs come from the peripheral characters – a brilliant Wilson, Keppel and Betty trio of hapless shepherds, a pantomime baddie Herod (Paul Duckworth channelling Abanazar as played by Rik Mayall), and a raucous, good-hearted angel earning her wings … festive treats to win over even the most curmudgeonly this Christmas. (*The Stage*, 1 December 2017 online)

2018 *The Scouse Cinderella* by Kevin Fearon

> Baron Joe Hardupson is skint and the Council want to turn his mansion into student accommodation. Then his daughter goes to a party, pretends to be something she isn't and gets so drunk she loses a shoe ... We've got a biff called Buttons, a Prince with a foot fetish and a pumpkin that turns into a Delta. There will be minging sisters, a lairy fairy and probably some dwarves who've got lost. (Royal Court website)

Notes

1 Fred Lawless, *Merry Ding Dong* (draft 2, 2009, unpublished), 1.

2 Fred Lawless, *Hitchhiker's Guide to Fazakerley* (2013, unpublished), 1.

3 Fred Lawless, *Scouse of the Antarctic* (2014, unpublished), 2–5.

Bibliography

Published playtexts

Ambient, Mark, A. M. Thompson and Robert Courtneidge, *The Arcadians* (London: Samuel French, 1909; repr. 1945)

Beckwith, Reginald, *A Soldier for Christmas* (London: Samuel French, 1946)

Bleasdale, Alan, *On the Ledge* (London: Faber & Faber, 1993)

Boucicault, Dion, *The Poor of New York* (New York: Samuel French, 1857)

Constanduros, Mabel, and Denis Constanduros, *Acacia Avenue* (London: Samuel French, 1944)

Cooney, Ray, *Chase Me Comrade* (London: English Theatre Guild, 1966)

Cooney, Ray, and Tony Hilton, *One for the Pot* (London: English Theatre Guild, 1963)

Coward, Noel, *This Happy Breed* (1943), in *Coward. Plays: Four* (London: Methuen Drama, 1979)

Draper, Ruth, *The Art of Ruth Draper: Her Dramas and Her Characters* (Oxford: Oxford University Press, 1960)

du Maurier, Daphne, *The Years Between* (1945), in Fidelis Morgan (ed.), *The Years Between: Plays by Women on the London Stage 1900–1950* (London: Virago, 1994)

Hamilton, Patrick, *Rope* (1929) (London: Constable, 1985)

Hellman, Lillian, *Watch on the Rhine* (1941), in *Six Plays by Lillian Hellman* (New York: Vintage Books, 1979)

Home, William Douglas, *The Reluctant Debutante* (1956) (London: Samuel French, 2015)

Hunter, N. C., *A Day by the Sea* (London: English Theatre Guild, 1954)

Hutton, Michael Clayton, *Silver Wedding* (London: Samuel French, 1958)

Kerr, Geoffrey, *Cottage to Let* (London: Samuel French, 1941)

McCracken, Esther, *No Medals* (London: Samuel French, 1947)

McCracken, Esther, *Quiet Week-End* (London: Samuel French, 1945)

Morgan, Charles, *The Burning Glass* (London: Macmillan, 1954)

Novello, Ivor, *The Dancing Years* (London: Samuel French, 1939; repr. 1953)

Priestley, J. B., *Three Plays* (London: William Heinemann, 1943)

Rattigan, Terence, *Flare Path* (1944) (London: Nick Hern, 2011)

Sherriff, R. C., *The White Carnation* (1953) (London: Oberon Books, 2013)

Sherwood, Robert, *There Shall Be No Night* (New York: Charles Scribner's Sons, 1945)

Smith, Dodie, *Dear Octopus*, in *Plays of the Thirties. Volume 1* (London: Pan, 1966)

Smith, Dodie, *Service*, in *Three Plays* (London: Samuel French, 1939)

Terry, J. E. Harold, and Lechmere Worrall, *The Man Who Stayed at Home* (London: Samuel French, 1916)

Travers, Ben, *Five Plays* (London: W. H. Allen, 1977)

Wallace, Edgar, *The Ringer* (London: Samuel French, 1926)
Whiting, John, *Marching Song* (1957), in *New English Dramatists 5* (Harmondsworth: Penguin, 1962)
Williams, Emlyn, *Accolade* (1950) (London: Samuel French, 2015)
Williams, Emlyn, *The Collected Plays of Emlyn Williams, Volume 1* (London: Heinemann, 1961)
Williams, Emlyn, *The Morning Star* (London: Heinemann, 1942)
Williams, Hugh, and Margaret Williams, *The Grass is Greener* (London: Evans Brothers, 1960)
Williams, Hugh, and Margaret Williams, *The Irregular Verb to Love* (London: Evans Plays, 1962)
Winsloe, Christa, *Children in Uniform*, in *Famous Plays of 1932–33* (London: Victor Gollancz, 1933)

Unpublished plays

None of the plays written for the Royal Court since 2005 have been published, and many have been through a number of versions, and changed even more in rehearsal. Not all manuscripts are dated, so it is not always possible to tell which version from which year has been used.

Bleasdale, Alan, *Down the Dock Road* (2016)
Cartwright, Jim, *Eight Miles High* (2008)
Davies Markham, Mark, *Special Measures* (second draft) (2014)
Eaton, Bob, *Maggie May*, with lyrics by Bob Eaton and Sayan Kent and music by Sayan Kent (June 2018)
Germain, Lindzi and Angela Simms, *The Royal* (n.d.)
Kirby, Dave, *Council Depot Blues* (n.d.)
Kirby, Dave, *Lost Soul* (version 6) (n.d.)
Kirby, Dave, and Nicky Allt, *Brick Up the Mersey Tunnels* (2009)
Lawless, Fred, *Hitchhiker's Guide to Fazakerley* (2013)
Lawless, Fred, *Merry Ding Dong* (draft 2) (2009)
Lawless, Fred, *Scouse of the Antarctic* (2014)
Pentin, Len, and Fred Lawless, *Slappers and Slapheads* (n.d.)
Sweeney, Claire, and Mandy Muden, *Sex and the Suburbs* (2014)
Waugh, Ed, and Trevor Wood, *Dirty Dusting* (2006)

Secondary works

Ackroyd, Harold, *The Liverpool Stage* (Erdington: Amber Valley, 1996)
Appleton, Alexandra, 'In Search of an Identity: The Changing Fortunes of Liverpool's Theatre Royal, 1772–1855', PhD thesis, Royal Holloway, University of London, 2015

Arts Council of Great Britain, *The Theatre Today: The Report of the Arts Council Theatre Enquiry 1970* (London: Arts Council, 1970)

Barker, Clive, 'Theatre and Society: The Edwardian Legacy, the First World War and the Inter-war Years', in Clive Barker and Maggie B. Gale (eds), *British Theatre between the Wars, 1918–1939* (Cambridge: Cambridge University Press, 2000), 4–37

Barker, Clive, and Maggie B. Gale (eds), *British Theatre between the Wars, 1918–1939* (Cambridge: Cambridge University Press, 2000)

Barrett, Maria, 'Fish out of Water: Habitus, Cultural Capital and the Working Class Experience of Theatre', PhD thesis, University of Warwick, 2017

Belchem, John, 'Celebrating Liverpool', in John Belchem (ed.), *Liverpool 800: Culture, Character and History* (Liverpool: Liverpool University Press, 2006), 9–57

Belchem, John, *Merseypride: Essays in Liverpool Exceptionalism* (Liverpool: Liverpool University Press, 2000)

Belchem, John, 'The New Livercool: History, Culture and Identity of Merseyside', in Christoph Ehlnd (ed.), *Thinking Northern: Textures of Identity in the North of England* (Amsterdam: Rodopi, 2007), 217–38

Belchem, John (ed.), *Liverpool 800: Culture, Character and History* (Liverpool: Liverpool University Press, 2006)

Bennett, John, 'Answering to the Audience: Opportunities and Tensions in Popular Theatre Programming with Particular Reference to the Royal Court Liverpool and the 2008 European Capital of Culture', in Wim Coudenys (ed.), *Whose Culture(s)?* (2008), https://www.academia.edu/506573/_Minorities_margins_peripheries_and_the_discourse_of_Cultural_Capital_ (accessed 28 November 2018)

Bennett, Susan, 'New Plays and Women's Voices in the 1950s', in Elaine Aston and Janelle Reinelt (eds), *The Cambridge Companion to Modern British Women Playwrights* (Cambridge: Cambridge University Press, 2000), 53–68

Berry, Ralph, 'Benson's Shakespeare', in Richard Foulkes (ed.), *British Theatre in the 1890s: Essays on Drama and the Stage* (Cambridge: Cambridge University Press, 1992), 184–91

Billington, Michael, *State of the Nation. British Theatre Since 1945* (London: Faber and Faber, 2007)

Black, Kitty, *Upper Circle: A Theatrical Chronicle* (London: Methuen, 1984)

Boland, Philip, 'The Construction of Images of People and Place: Labelling Liverpool and Stereotyping Scousers', *Cities* 25.6 (2008), 355–69

Booth, Michael R., *Prefaces to English Nineteenth Century Theatre* (Manchester: Manchester University Press, 1980)

Booth, Michael R., and Joel H. Kaplan (eds), *The Edwardian Theatre: Essays on Performance and the Stage* (Cambridge: Cambridge University Press, 1996)

Bratton, Jacky, 'What is a Play? Drama and the Victorian Circus', in Tracy C. Davis and Peter Holland (eds), *The Performing Century: Nineteenth-Century Theatre's History* (Basingstoke: Palgrave Macmillan, 2007), 250–62

Broadbent, R. J., *Annals of the Liverpool Stage* (Liverpool: Edward Howell, 1908)

Bull, John, *Stage Right: Crisis and Recovery in British Contemporary Mainstream Theatre* (Basingstoke: Macmillan, 1994)

Butler, Nicholas, *John Martin-Harvey: The Biography of an Actor-Manager* (Colchester: Nicholas Butler, 1997)

Calder, Angus, *The People's War: Britain 1939–1945* (London: Pimlico, 1992 [1969])

Campton, David, 'Stephen Joseph and After', Scarborough in the Round, http://theatre-in-the-round.co.uk/styled-49/page-7/styled-146/index.html (accessed 10 July 2018)

Cannadine, David, 'Gilbert and Sullivan: The Making and Un-Making of a British "Tradition"', in Roy Porter (ed.), *Myths of the English* (Oxford: Polity Press, 1993), 12–32

Cochrane, Claire, *Twentieth-Century British Theatre: Industry, Art and Empire* (Cambridge: Cambridge University Press, 2011)

Collins, L. J., *Theatre at War, 1914–1918* (Basingstoke: Macmillan, 1998)

Conan Doyle, Sir Arthur, *The History of Spiritualism*, vol. 1 (London: Cassell, 1926)

Courtneidge, Cicely, *Cicely* (London: Hutchinson, 1953)

Crowley, Tony, *Scouse: A Social and Cultural History* (Liverpool: Liverpool University Press, 2012)

Darlington, W. A., *The Actor and His Audience* (London: Phoenix House, 1949)

Davies, Andrew, 'The War Years', in Michael Balfour (ed.), *Theatre and War 1933–1945* (Oxford: Berghahn Books, 2001), 54–64

Davies, Jim, '*The Only Way* and the Other Way: A Dickens Adaptation for the 1890s', in Richard Foulkes (ed.), *British Theatre in the 1890s: Essays on Drama and the Stage* (Cambridge: Cambridge University Press, 1992), 59–70

Davies, Sam, et al., *Genuinely Seeking Work: Mass Unemployment on Merseyside in the 1930s* (Birkenhead: Liver Press, 1992)

Disher, Maurice Wilson, *The Last Romantic: The Authorised Biography of Sir John Martin-Harvey* (London: Hutchinson, 1948)

D'Monté, Rebecca, *British Theatre and Performance 1900–1950* (London: Bloomsbury, 2015)

Donaldson, Frances, *The Actor Managers* (London: Weidenfeld and Nicolson, 1970)

Duggan, Sally, *Baroness Orczy's The Scarlet Pimpernel* (Farnham: Ashgate, 2012)

Du Noyer, Paul, *Liverpool – Wondrous Place: Music from the Cavern to the Coral* (London: Virgin Books, 2004)

Elsam, Paul, *Stephen Joseph: Theatre Pioneer and Provocateur* (London: Bloomsbury Methuen, 2014)

Elsom, John, *Cold War Theatre* (London: Routledge, 1992)

Elsom, John, *Post War British Theatre* (London: Routledge, 1976)

Fawkes, Richard, *Fighting for a Laugh* (London: Macdonald and Jane's, 1978)

Finn, Michael, 'Local Heroes: War News and the Construction of "Community" in Britain, 1914–1918', *Historical Research* 83.221 (2010), 520–38

Forrester, Helen, *By the Waters of Liverpool and Lime Street at Two* (London: Harper, 2010)

Foulkes, Richard (ed.), *British Theatre in the 1890s: Essays on Drama and the Stage* (Cambridge: Cambridge University Press, 1992)

Frost, Thomas, *Circus Life and Circus Celebrities* (London: Chatto and Windus, 1881)

Gale, Maggie B., *J. B. Priestley* (London: Routledge, 2008)

Gale, Maggie B., *West End Women: Women and the London Stage 1918–1962* (London: Routledge, 1996)

Ganzl, Kurt, *The British Musical Theatre: Volume 1, 1865–1914* (Basingstoke: Macmillan, 1986)

Ganzl, Kurt, *The British Musical Theatre: Volume 2, 1915–1984* (Basingstoke: Macmillan, 1986)

Gardner, Viv, 'Provincial Stages, 1900–1934: Touring and Early Repertory Theatre', in Baz Kershaw (ed.), *The Cambridge History of British Theatre. Volume 3: Since 1895* (Cambridge: Cambridge University Press, 2004), 60–85

Gardiner, Juliet, *The Blitz* (London: Harper Press, 2011)

Gardiner, Juliet, *Wartime: Britain 1939–1945* (London: Headline Review, 2005)

Green, Julius, *Curtain Up: Agatha Christie – A Life in Theatre* (London: Harper Collins, 2015)

Griffin, Stephen, *Ken Dodd: The Biography* (Reading: Michael O'Mara, 2005)

Grove, Valerie, *Dear Dodie: The Life of Dodie Smith* (London: Chatto and Windus, 1996)

Guy, P., 'Lost Liverpool #9: The "Real" Court at the Royal Court' (2016), http://www.getintothis.co.uk/2016/06/lost-liverpool-9-real-court-royal-court/ (accessed 11 August 2018)

Guy, P., 'The Royal Court: Musical Magic Relived at Liverpool's Rock and Roll Theatre – Part One', *Get Into This*, 21 June 2012, http://www.getintothis.co.uk/2012/06/royal_court/ (accessed 28 November 2018)

Guy, P., 'The Royal Court: Musical Magic Relived at Liverpool's Rock and Roll Theatre – Part Two', *Get Into This*, 22 June 2012, http://www.getintothis.co.uk/2012/06/the_royal_court_musical_magic/ (accessed 28 November 2018)

Harwood, Ronald, *Sir Donald Wolfit: His Life and Work in the Unfashionable Theatre* (Oxford: Amber Lane Press, 1971)

Hoare, Philip, *Noel Coward: A Biography* (London: Mandarin, 1995)

Hogan, Robert, *Dion Boucicault* (New York: Twayne, 1969)

Horton, Steven, 'Horseplay at the Royal Court' (2014), Liverpool Hidden History, http://liverpoolhiddenhistory.co.uk/horseplay-at-the-royal-court/ (accessed 19 October 2017)

Huggett, Richard, *Binkie Beaumont: Eminence Grise of the West End Theatre 1933–1973* (London: Hodder and Stoughton, 1989)

Iles, Paul, 'Issues in Theatrical Management: Howard and Wyndham and the Evolution of the British Touring Circuit', MPhil thesis, University of Glasgow, 1997

Joseph, Stephen, *Theatre in the Round* (New York: Taplinger Publishing, 1968)

Kendal, Madge, *Dame Madge Kendal by Herself* (London: John Murray, 1933)

Kennedy, Dennis, 'British Theatre, 1895–1946: Arts, Entertainment, Audiences – an Introduction', in Baz Kershaw (ed.), *The Cambridge History of British Theatre. Volume 3: Since 1895* (Cambridge: Cambridge University Press, 2004), 3–33

Krivanec, Eva, 'Staging War. Theatre 1914–1918', in *1914–1918 online: International Encyclopaedia of the First World War* (2014), https://encyclopedia.1914-1918-online.net/article/staging_war_theatre_1914-1918 (accessed 28 November 2018)

Kwint, Marius, 'The Circus and Nature in Late Georgian England', in Peta Tait and Katie Lavers (eds), *The Routledge Circus Studies Reader* (Abingdon: Routledge, 2016), 331–48

Kwint, Marius, 'The Legitimization of the Circus in Late Georgian England', *Past and Present* 174 (2002), 72–115

Light, Alison, *Forever England: Femininity, Literature and Conservatism between the Wars* (London: Routledge, 1991)

Liverpool City Library, *Liverpool Women at War* (Liverpool: Picton Press, 1991)

Lloyd, Matthew, Arthur Lloyd: The Music Hall and Theatre History Site, http://www.arthurlloyd.co.uk/index.html (accessed 28 November 2018)

McGreal, Stephen, *Liverpool in the Great War* (Barnsley: Pen and Sword Military, 2014)

MacQueen-Pope, Walter, *Carriages at Eleven: The Story of Edwardian Theatre* (London: Robert Hale, 1947)

Marr, Andrew, *A History of Modern Britain* (London: Pan Macmillan, 2009)

Merkin, Ros, *Liverpool Playhouse: A Theatre and Its City* (Liverpool: Liverpool University Press, 2011)

Merkin, Ros, 'Liverpool', in David Wiles and Christine Dymkowski (eds), *The Cambridge Companion to Theatre History* (Cambridge: Cambridge University Press, 2013), 91–103

Merseyside Socialist Research Group, *Merseyside in Crisis* (Liverpool: Merseyside Socialist Research Group, 1980)

Moody, Jane, 'The Theatrical Revolution, 1776–1843', in Joseph Donohue (ed.), *The Cambridge History of British Theatre. Volume 2: 1660–1895* (Cambridge: Cambridge University Press, 2004), 199–215

Morley, Sheridan, *John Gielgud: The Authorized Biography* (New York: Applause, 2002)

Muir, Ramsay, *A History of Liverpool* (Liverpool: Liverpool University Press, 1907)

Murden, Jon, '"City of Change and Challenge": Liverpool since 1945', in John Belchem (ed.), *Liverpool 800: Culture, Character and History* (Liverpool: Liverpool University Press, 2006), 393–485

Neilson, Julia, *This for Remembrance* (London: Hurst and Blackett, 1940)

Pattie, David, *Modern British Playwriting: The 1950s* (London: Methuen, 2012)

Pearson, Hesketh, *The Last Actor Managers* (London: White Lion, 1950)

Perrett, Bryan, *Liverpool: A City at War* (Burscough: Hugo Press, 1990)

Picton, James, *Memorials of Liverpool. Volume II: Topographical* (Liverpool: Edward Howell, 1907)

Platt, Len, *Musical Comedy on the West End Stage, 1890–1939* (Basingstoke: Palgrave Macmillan, 2004)

Postlewait, Thomas, 'George Edwardes and Musical Comedy: The Transformation of London Theatre and Society, 1878–1914', in Tracy C. Davis and Peter Holland (eds), *The Performing Century: Nineteenth Century Theatre's History* (Basingstoke: Palgrave Macmillan, 2007), 80–102

Priestley, J. B., *Theatre Outlook* (London: Nicholson and Watson, 1947)

Ralph, Edgar, 'Are War Plays Wanted?', *The Stage*, 6 June 1946, 1

Rebellato, Dan, *1956 and All That: The Making of Modern British Drama* (London: Routledge, 1999)

Rix, Brian, *My Farce from my Elbow* (London: Secker and Warburg, 1975)

Rix, Brian, *Tour de Farce: A Tale of Touring Theatres and Strolling Players* (London: Hodder and Stoughton, 1992)

Rodmell, Paul, *Opera in the British Isles 1875–1918* (Farnham: Ashgate, 2013)

Rowell, George, *Theatre in the Age of Irving* (New Jersey: Rowman and Littlefield, 1981)

Ruddin, Lee P., 'The "Firsts" World War: A History of the Morale of Liverpudlians as Told through Letters to Liverpool Editors, 1915–1918', *International Journal of Regional and Local History* 9.2 (2014), 79–93

Sandison, G., *Theatre Ownership in Britain* (London: Federation of Theatre Unions, 1953)

Saxon, A. H., *Enter Foot and Horse: A History of Hippodrama in England and France* (New Haven, CT: Yale University Press, 1968)

Saxon, A. H., *The Life and Art of Andrew Ducrow and the Romantic Age of the English Circus* (Hamden, CT: Archon Books, 1978)

Smith, Leslie, *Modern British Farce: A Selective Study of British Farce from Pinero to the Present Day* (Basingstoke: Macmillan, 1989)

Stein, Marguerite, *A Pride of Terrys* (Harlow: Longman, 1962)

Stephens, Russell, *Emlyn Williams: The Making of a Dramatist* (Bridgend: Seren, 2000)

Stokes, John, 'Body Parts: The Success of the Thriller in the Inter-war Years', in Clive Barker and Maggie B. Gale (eds), *British Theatre between the Wars, 1918–1939* (Cambridge: Cambridge University Press, 2000), 38–62

The Stranger in Liverpool, 10th edn (Liverpool: Thomas Kaye, 1833)

Sullivan, Jill A., *The Politics of Pantomime: Regional Identity in the Theatre 1860–1900* (Hatfield: University of Hertfordshire Press & Society for Theatre Research, 2011)

Travers, Ben, *A-sitting on a Gate: Autobiography* (London: W. H. Allen, 1978)

Trewin, J. C., *Robert Donat: A Biography* (London: Heinemann, 1968)

Trewin, J. C., *The Turbulent Thirties: A Further Decade of the Theatre* (London: Macdonald, 1960)

Tynan, Kenneth, *A View of the English Stage* (St Albans: Paladin, 1975)

Ward, Steve, *Beneath the Big Top: A Social History of Circus in Britain* (Barnsley: Pen and Sword, 2014)

Warren, Dorothy, *The World of Ruth Draper: A Portrait of an Actress* (Carbondale, IL: Southern Illinois University Press, 1999)

Warwick, Lou, *The Mackenzies Called Compton* (Northampton: Lou Warwick, 1977)

Whittington-Egan, Richard, *Liverpool Roundabout* (Manchester: E. J. Morten, 1976)
Williams, Emlyn, *Emlyn: An Early Autobiography 1927–1935* (London: Bodley Head, 1973)
Williams, Gordon, *British Theatre in the Great War: A Revaluation* (London: Continuum, 2003)
Wilmut, Roger, *Kindly Leave the Stage: The Story of Variety 1919–1960* (London: Methuen, 1985)
Wilson, A. E., *Edwardian Theatre* (London: Arthur Barker, 1951)
Wolfit, Donald, *First Interval: The Autobiography of Donald Wolfit* (London: Odhams Press, 1954)

Index

Numbers in italics refer to illustrations